THE PURPLE AND GOLD

Colonel J. W. CLARK, D.S.O., V.D.

THE PURPLE AND GOLD

A HISTORY OF THE 30th BATTALION

Compiled by
LIEUT.-COLONEL H. SLOAN

They shall grow not old, as we that are left grow old:
Age shall not weary them, nor the years condemn.
At the going down of the sun and in the morning
We shall remember them.
—LAURENCE BINYON.

The Naval & Military Press Ltd

Published by
The Naval & Military Press Ltd
5 Riverside, Brambleside, Bellbrook
Industrial Estate, Uckfield, East Sussex,
TN22 1QQ England
Tel: +44 (0) 1825 749494
Fax: +44 (0) 1825 765701
www.naval-military-press.com
www.military-genealogy.com
www.militarymaproom.com

In reprinting in facsimile from the original, any imperfections are inevitably reproduced and the quality may fall short of modern type and cartographic standards.

TO THE
OFFICERS, NON-COMMISSIONED OFFICERS, AND MEN
OF THE 30TH BATTALION, A.I.F.
WHO GAVE THEIR LIVES IN THE GREAT WAR
THIS BOOK IS REVERENTLY
DEDICATED

FOREWORD.

By Major-General E. TIVEY, C.B., C.M.G., D.S.O.

I WOULD like to pay a tribute to the 30th Battalion which, during the Great War, I had the honour to command in the 8th Infantry Brigade, A.I.F.

When I first inspected the battalion in Sydney, I was impressed with the appearance and bearing of all ranks, and through all the years of active service in Egypt, France and Belgium, I had no reason to alter the high opinion I had formed of the battalion. Officers, Non-commissioned Officers and men were imbued with the same spirit of service, and from first to last the battalion was always ready to do its duty. From the Battle of Fromelles, when our troops showed superb gallantry in face of one of the greatest ordeals of the war, until the breaking of the Hindenburg Line, the 8th Brigade took part in most of the great battles on the Western Front, and the 30th Battalion has every reason to be proud of its fine record of service.

EDWIN TIVEY,
Major-General.

AN APPRECIATION.

By Colonel J. W. CLARK, D.S.O., V.D.

I HAVE been requested by the Secretary of the 30th Battalion A.I.F. Association to write an appreciation of the unit which I had the honour to command from its infancy until the final three months of the war, and, if a fond parent may be pardoned for evincing pride in his child, I trust that I too may be pardoned when I wax enthusiastic over the 30th's record in the Great War.

I would like first to pay a tribute to our beloved Brigadier-General Edwin Tivey for the fine example of gentlemanly and soldierly bearing he set us at all times, and for his quiet but firm, tactful, and just administration, which quickly secured for him the unswerving loyalty and co-operation of all ranks in the 8th Brigade. From the outset I tried to emulate the standard set by our brigadier and in this I was ably seconded by as a fine a lot of officers, N.C.O's., and men as anyone could wish for, who did their job so well that we quickly became a happy family and a very efficient fighting unit. Our achievements are graphically outlined in the pages of this book and will, I hope, be a source of inspiration to those who follow us.

I have more than once referred with feelings of pride to the fact that the 30th never permanently lost a position or a single yard of trench on the Western Front, but prouder still am I in recalling the discipline and bearing of the men at all times. The wonderful spirit of camaraderie engendered is still carried on in our happy reunions.

In conclusion, I want to pay a tribute and register my thanks to our first adjutant, Lieutenant-Colonel Sloan, for

AN APPRECIATION

his years of hard work and interest, not only in the compiling of this book, but also as President of our Association. His long service in the Permanent Forces made him an ideal officer in the moulding of young soldiers, and I am eternally grateful to him for his loyalty and the wonderful work he has done for the battalion.

J. W. CLARK.

PREFACE.

THE following account of the activities of the 30th Battalion A.I.F. makes no pretence whatever to literary merit. It merely records the unit's movements, and refers briefly to the various engagements in which it took part, describes the French and Egyptian countryside and inhabitants, incidents grave and gay in the life of the battalion, and mentions the names of as many individuals as is practicable.

The points of view put forward are those of the man in the ranks, and any criticism of divisional and higher formations are merely those which the writer has heard expressed on many occasions and with which he is heartily in accord. Being of Scottish descent, he may perhaps be pardoned when he asserts that his personal attitude is summarised in the following lines from the "Flowers of the Forest":—

> "Nae mair your smiles can cheer me,
> Nae mair your frowns can fear me."

The story is, of course, written primarily for the members of our old unit, of which the writer was the original adjutant and with whose survivors he is proud to be still associated. While the narrative will probably recall many sad incidents, it may also revive many pleasant memories which he hopes will predominate.

It is quite impracticable here to give due and adequate recognition to all who sent along their diaries and other records for perusal, but it is hoped they will individually accept this expression of appreciation of their assistance.

The thanks of the Association are also due to those who by their generous donations have made it possible to include

PREFACE

the many photographs with which the book is interspersed, and also to ensure that all externals, such as paper, printing, blocks, etc., are of the best. These include C. E. Alcorn, Ray A. M. Allen, C. A. Backhouse, R. H. Beardsmore, B. A. Bragg, S. C. Butler, Geo. Cann, Don. Chalmers, John A. Chapman, James A. Chapman, R. C. Chapple, P. Charlton, W. J. R. Cheeseman, J. W. Clark, H. K. Cook, F. J. Daly, F. H. Deffell, Fred Duncan, F. C. Florance, J. J. Witton Flynn, T. C. Fricker, I. G. Fullarton, H. D. Gooding, Geo. Gibson, M. Griffin, C. L. Gunning, C. E. Harrold, N. W. S. Hamilton, W. M. Herriott, R. C. Hogan, C. J. Holford, T. S. C. Horgan, N. B. Jehan, A. Langan, Alan Lett, A. J. McCallum, T. W. Milgate, C. H. Morrison, Wes. Oakes, E. F. O'Sullivan, G. W. Paterson, M. Purser, S. A. Railton, D. M. Reuben, E. C. Robertson, E. D. Robinson, Grahame Sands, C. D. Savage, Vic. Smith, M. F. Sinclair, H. H. Stevenson, H. L. G. Stinson, T. A. Storey, Fred. Street, L. A. Stuckey, A. H. Treloar, E. J. Tysoe, C. G. Westbrook, L. C. Wellings, H. J. Wells, A. C. White, F. C. Winn, and J. C. Yeomans.

In conclusion, the writer's special thanks are due to Major J. L. Treloar, Director of the Australian War Memorial, Canberra, for giving access to the official records; to Mr. J. Robinson, the Officer in charge of the Base Records, Melbourne, for the nominal roll; to Dr. C. E. W. Bean and Mr. A. W. Bazley, for their advice and assistance; and, lastly to Mr. R. C. Hogan, the Honorary Secretary of our Association, whose fertile brain is responsible for the title of the book—"The Purple and Gold."

H. SLOAN.

"Achray,"
   Hampden Road,
      Artarmon, N.S.W.
12th October, 1938.

BATTLE HONOURS

FROMELLES	BAPAUME
POLYGON WOOD	PASSCHENDAELE
AMIENS	WYTSCHAETE
MORLANCOURT	BELLICOURT

CONTENTS

PART I

Chapter		Page
I.	FORMATION OF THE BATTALION	3
II.	ARRIVAL IN EGYPT	15
III.	TEL EL KEBIR	26
IV.	THE SINAI DESERT	32
V.	ARRIVAL IN FRANCE	47
VI.	THE MOVE TO BOIS GRENIER	56
VII.	THE BATTLE OF FROMELLES	68
VIII.	FLEURBAIX AND ARMENTIERES	88
IX.	WINTERING ON THE SOMME	106
X.	BAPAUME AND BEAUMETZ	125
XI.	SENLIS AND LE CROQUET	142
XII.	POLYGON WOOD AND PASSCHENDAELE	148
XIII.	THE WINTER OF 1917-18	156
XIV.	THE GERMAN OFFENSIVE, 1918	169
XV.	MORLANCOURT	177
XVI.	THE BATTLE OF AMIENS	189
XVII.	FOUCACOURT AND PERONNE	201
XVIII.	THROUGH THE HINDENBURG LINE	209
XIX.	ARMISTICE AND REPATRIATION	219
EPILOGUE		232

PART II

CONTRIBUTIONS FROM MEMBERS OF BATTALION	235
THE COMFORTS COMMITTEES	237
"LITTLE WILLIE"	240
A VERY OLD SOLDIER	241
FRUIT	242
GENESIS OF 30th BATTALION TRANSPORT	243
A SAND BLAST IN AN OUTPOST	244
A RECONNAISSANCE IN EGYPT	246
A PLACE FOR EVERYTHING	248
IT HAPPENED AT FERRY POST	248

CONTENTS

ALL'S WELL ON THE LEFT OF THE LINE	252
AN INCONVENIENCE	254
AN UNOFFICIAL MEDICAL INSPECTION	256
THE LANGUAGE UNINVITING	257
AN OUTSTANDING "CHARACTER"	257
TURNING OVER A NEW LEAF	258
THE HEADQUARTERS LEWIS GUN SECTION	259
THE 30TH's FIRST RAID IN FRANCE	263
HOW THE 30TH WAS PUT TO ROUT	264
INTIMATE PICTURES OF NO-MAN'S-LAND	266
PERCY AND HIS "PIPPINS"	269
MEMORIES OF FROMELLES	270
STEAK AND ONIONS FOR SIX	272
COMPANY RUNNERS	272
"PADDY" OF THE LEWIS GUN SECTION	274
THE PILGRIMS OF THE SOMME	275
A PRISONER OF WAR	277
HOODWINKING THE MINNIE KINGS	279
THE 30TH MEETS THE BLACK WATCH	282
LONGPRES TO BUSSUS	284
THE TEST	285
MUCH ADO ABOUT NOTHING	286
"NO COMPREE"	287
AN ANGELIC VISIT	288
NOT MENTIONED IN DESPATCHES	288
BAPTISM AT BOIS-GRENIER	290
THE BAPAUME "SPECIAL"	295
THE QUARTER-BLOKE	297
THE LE TRANSLOY GHOST	298
A DUD JOKE	300
ONE WAY OF GETTING A RUM RATION	302
OEUF DANS LE CHAPEAU	303
A PRESENTIMENT	303
MUSIK	304
THE WRONG SIDE OF THE PILL-BOX	305
"SCOTS WHA HAE"	307
THE BOX OF TRICKS	309
"BAD NEWS" FROM THE DIVISIONAL COMMANDER	311
THE INTENTION WAS GOOD	313
MORLANCOURT—AND AN UNOFFICIAL ARMISTICE	314
A VISIT TO GERMANY	318

CONTENTS xvii

VIN ROUGE 320
WAR IN RETROSPECT 321
A PICKWICKIAN RIDE 322
THE BATTLE OF AMIENS 324
A SOMME SIDELIGHT 327
A MEAL FOR THE MAJOR 328
SIGNALLERS LEADING 330
WAT IT *JAMES* OR WAS IT *JOHN*? 333
A CUP THAT CHEERED 334
CHRISTMAS IN BEUGNIES 336
TREASURE TROVE 339
THE 8TH TRAINING BATTALION 340
FORWARD TO THE HINDENBURG LINE 343
HOMEWARD BOUND 352

PART III
NOMINAL ROLL 355

ILLUSTRATIONS

COLONEL J. W. CLARK, D.S.O., V.D.	*Frontispiece*
LIEUT.-COLONEL F. STREET, D.S.O.	16
LIEUT.-COLONEL JOHN A. CHAPMAN, D.S.O.; COLONEL R. H. BEARDSMORE, D.S.O., M.B.E., V.D.; LIEUT.-COLONEL H. SLOAN; LIEUT.-COLONEL W. J. R. CHEESEMAN, D.S.O., M.C., CHEVALIER LEGION D'HONNEUR	17
LIEUT.-COLONEL M. PURSER, D.S.O., V.D.; CAPT. T. C. BARBOUR	32
CPL. G. E. WEILEY, M.M. AND BAR; PTE. R. MATHER, M.M.; SGT. W. G. SMITH, M.M.; COY. SGT.-MAJ. T. ECCLES, D.C.M., M.M.	33
CAPT. S. A. RAILTON, M.C.; LIEUT. J. C. YEOMANS, D.S.O.; MAJOR P. CHARLTON, M.C.; CAPT. A. C. WHITE, M.C.	36
LIEUT. W. T. HANLON, M.C.; MAJOR I. G. FULLARTON, M.C.; LIEUT. F. A. BUTTERWORTH, M.M.	44
SGT. A. E. FORBES, M.M.; SGT. E. C. E. AMPS, D.C.M., M.M.; COY. SGT.-MAJ. D. M. RUEBEN, D.C.M., M.M., AND BAR; SGT. D. SMITH, M.M.	48
COLONEL C. J. HOLFORD, V.D.; CAPT. RAY A. M. ALLEN, M.C.	64
SKETCH SHOWING DISPOSITION OF 5TH AUSTRALIAN DIVISION AT FROMELLES BATTLE	68
SGT. T. M. MASSEY, M.M.; PTE. G. W. PITTAWAY, M.M.; SGT. W. F. MUNDAY, M.M.; SGT. J. W. LAING, M.M.; PTE. W. A. McDERMOTT, M.M.; SGT. A. D. BURNS, M.M.; PTE. P. H. MOTBEY, M.M.; SGNLR. F. M. HESLEWOOD, M.M.	76
LIEUT. H. J. WELLS, M.C.; CAPT. R. D. MULVEY, M.C.; LIEUT. B. A. BRAGG, M.C.; LIEUT. J. WITTON FLYNN, M.C.	80
LIEUT. S. C. BUTLER, M.C.; MAJOR JAMES A. CHAPMAN, O.B.E.; LIEUT. V. W. BIDDLE, M.C.	81
CPL. R. E. LORDING; SGT. R. C. HOGAN; CPL. C. S. SMITH, M.M.; PTE. P. J. NANKIVELL, M.M.	96
"C" COMPANY SOMEWHERE IN FRANCE	112
STRETCHER BEARERS, BAPAUME	128

ILLUSTRATIONS

STREET SCENE, BAPAUME	129
COY. SGT.-MAJ. GEOFFREY COWEN, BAPAUME	132
AT BAPAUME	133
"B" COMPANY GROUP, BAPAUME	140
BATTALION OFFICERS, DESVRES	164
N.C.O's AT DESVRES, 1917	172
LIEUT. D. T. BREWSTER WITH SIGNALLERS AND RUNNERS, BLARINGHEM	173
AT ZONNEBEKE	176
IN THE TRENCHES AT ZONNEBEKE	177
LIEUT. W. C. ABBOTT, M.M.; LIEUT. B. O. DAVIES, D.C.M.; LIEUT. C. E. ALCORN, BELGIAN CROIX DE GUERRE	192
"A" COMPANY, WESTHOEK RIDGE	196
"B" COMPANY GROUP, BAPAUME	204
THE FIFTH DIVISION'S SECOND SOMME CAMPAIGN	212
BATTALION OFFICERS, FOUCACOURT, NOVEMBER 1918	224
C.S.M. GEOFF. COWEN, D.C.M.; SGT. F. McGILLICUDDY, M.M.; PTE. P. MILLGATE, M.M.; CPL. F. C. NORTH, M.M.	240
PTE. E. L. BAKER, M.M.; PTE. H. E. WILLIAMSON, M.M.; SGT. J. REGAN, M.M.; SGT. D. WOODBINE, M.M.; SGT. J. C. FORD, D.C.M.; PTE. GEO. GOTT, M.M.	256
SGT. C. H. McCLOSKEY, D.C.M.; BANDMASTER L. C. WELLINGS, M.S.M.; SGT. R. J. ESTELL, M.M.	272
30TH BATTALION, A.I.F. ASSOCIATION'S TREE OF REMEMBRANCE	288
MAKING AND PACKING COMFORTS FOR MEN OF THE BATTALION	304

PART I

CHAPTER I.

FORMATION OF THE BATTALION

By the middle of 1915 the war had assumed serious proportions and the outlook was indeed grave, The predictions of financial experts and others that no great European conflict could last more than three months had long since been dispelled, it now being fully realised that the warring nations were committed to a long and bitter struggle. The fighting on Gallipoli had been indecisive, the Russian "steam roller," of which so much had been heard, had been held up by the Austro-German Armies, and the position in France had developed into a more or less static system of trench-warfare.

The necessity for raising more troops was apparent, and in Australia the Commonwealth Government authorised the formation of yet another infantry brigade—the 8th. The personnel for its battalions—29th, 30th, 31st, and 32nd—was to be drawn from all the States, and Colonel Edwin Tivey, the citizen soldier then commanding the officers' school at Broadmeadows in Victoria, was entrusted with the task of fusing them into a brigade.

The 30th Battalion was born at Liverpool (N.S. Wales) on the 5th of August, 1915, about one-fourth of its members consisting of ex-naval ratings of whom the majority came from Victoria. From the outset it was exceptionally fortunate in the officers allotted to it. The command of the battalion was given to Lieutenant-Colonel J. W. Clark (of Newcastle), and when it was completely organised the other officers were as follows:—

Second-in-command, Major C. J. Holford; *Adjutant*,

Captain H. Sloan; *Medical Officer,* Captain G. E. Marolli, *Quartermaster,* Lieutenant W. E. Hartnett; *Machine Gun Officer,* Lieutenant T. R. Marsden; *Signalling Officer,* Lieutenant S. W. Evers; *Transport Officer,* Lieutenant R. Barnett.

"A" Company: Major R. H. Beardsmore, Lieutenants W. W. Wilkinson, C. Webber, A. P. Hext, R. H. Orpen, C. J. Walker.

"B" Company: Major H. K. Denham, Captain F. Street, Lieutenants W. J. R. Cheeseman, P. Charlton, John A. Chapman, R. Cudden.

"C" Company: Major M. Purser, Captain F. S. McClean, Lieutenants B. A. Wark, R. A. M. Allen, I. G. Fullarton, J. J. L. McCall.

"D" Company: Captain H. L. Morrison, Lieutenants F. M. Couchman, James A. Chapman, A. Mitchell, F. Krinks, T. C. Barbour.

1st Reinforcement: Lieutenant E. A. C. Macfarlane.

Attached: Chaplains F. G. Ward and T. J. King.

All of the foregoing achieved higher rank and most of them were decorated for gallantry in France, while eight, then holding subordinate rank, were themselves destined to command battalions before the war was over.

Lieutenant-Colonel Clark, who was to command the 30th for the next three strenuous years, was born at Newcastle (N.S.W.) in 1877. He had received his first commission in 1897, in "E" (Wallsend) Company of the old 4th Infantry Regiment; and, with the discontinuance of the practice of appointing British Army officers as adjutants of Australian militia regiments, he had become adjutant of the 4th, whose territory extended from Newcastle to Armidale. When the Universal Training scheme came into being, Clark received a captaincy in the 16th (Newcastle) Infantry, to the command of which he succeeded on July 1st, 1914. Two days after the outbreak of war he was made responsible for the Newcastle defences, and was also given command of the 4th (Northern) Infantry Brigade

FORMATION OF THE BATTALION

in place of Colonel J. Paton, who had gone to German New Guinea with the A.N. & M.E.F. These appointments Colonel Clark retained until posted to the 30th Battalion, A.I.F. Several times in France he was called upon to take charge of the 8th Brigade during the temporary absence of General Tivey; and in August, 1918, he was sent across to England to command the Overseas Training Brigade. He remained in England after the Armistice to assist in the repatriation of the A.I.F. and it was December, 1919, ere he returned to Australia.

Major Holford, who was 46 at the time of his appointment to the A.I.F., had been soldiering since 1880, when he joined the N.S. Wales cadet corps. He received his commission in 1896, and on the Commonwealth's taking over the N.S. Wales Defence Forces he was given command of "G" Company 2nd A.I.R. at Goulburn. This regiment which later became the 43rd Infantry, he commanded from July, 1912, until the time of his joining the A.I.F. Though something of a rough diamond, he was a popular officer and spared no effort in the interests of the rank and file. After the battle of Fromelles he was appointed to the command of the 54th Battalion.

The senior company commander, Major Beardsmore, had also a long period of service to his credit in the militia, and from 1912 to 1914 was Area Officer at Homebush. A crack shot, he had for many years been associated with the National Rifle Association of N.S. Wales. At the outbreak of war he joined the Naval and Military Expeditionary Force, which captured and occupied German New Guinea, and for a time he was in charge of the garrison at Rabaul. Of a genial disposition, Beardsmore will long be remembered by members of the 30th Battalion for his willingness to oblige with a song on festive occasions—his favourite ditty being "Cock Robin" of many verses. After the Fromelles battle, in which he was wounded, he went to the 32nd Battalion, which he commanded at Armentieres and on the Somme until May, 1917, when he was transferred to the 5th Divisional Base Depot.

Major Denham, who prior to 1910 practised as a barrister, subsequently qualifying for the medical profession, had served with the Sydney University Scouts. He left us at Tel el Kebir in March, 1916, to become second-in-command of the 46th Battalion, and succeeded to the command of it in the following December, on the Somme.

Major Purser, who was born in 1887, was a keen soldier and one of the youngest officers of field rank to join the A.I.F. After nearly four years in the N.S. Wales Public Schools Cadet Force, at the age of 16 he had joined the St. George's Rifles, in which he received his commission in 1906. Looked upon as an officer of sound judgment and quick action, he distinguished himself in the Battle of Fromelles, after which he was transferred to the 32nd Battalion as second-in-command. From December, 1916, to March, 1918, he commanded the 29th Battalion.

Captain Morrison, though of quiet disposition, was a man of strong and determined character. Prior to the war he had held commissioned rank in the 2nd and 24th (East Sydney) Regiments, and, like Major Beardsmore, had commanded a company of the A.N. & M.E.F. in New Guinea in 1914-15. During the reorganisation of the A.I.F. in Egypt early in 1916 he transferred to the 5th Pioneer Battalion, and in October, 1917, was given command of the 4th Pioneers. He died in 1935.

Of the other officers, six came from the Australian Instructional Staff, and four—Lieutenants James and John Chapman, McCall and Fullarton—were graduates of the Royal Military College, Duntroon. The writer, who was then adjutant of the battalion, had seen long service in the N.S. Wales Garrison Artillery and on the Australian Instructional Staff. He subsequently commanded "C" Company in France, and in February, 1917, became C.O. of the 8th Training Battalion in England. The Quartermaster, Lieutenant Hartnett, had also been a member of the

FORMATION OF THE BATTALION

permanent forces. Born in India in 1860, he typified the old school of the British Army, clean as a button stick, and as upright in character as physique. To all and sundry he was known as "Soldier Bill."

Warrant Officer W. Jackson was appointed R.S.M., Warrant Officer T. Fricker R.Q.M.S., and Sergeant L. C. Wellings bandmaster. James McDuff was the battalion's first sergeant-cook. Other senior N.C.O.'s and sergeants were: T. Tillbrook, F. Colman, D. Dunworth, J. Smythe, E. Coady, D. T. Brewster, A. W. Wedd, E. F. Walker, H. M. Croudace, V. Levitt, A. K. Flack, F. G. Butterworth, J. W. Axtens, A. R. Paine, W. E. Oakes, A. H. Treloar, E. Menzies, F. Field, H. F. Pennefather, T. C. Fricker, R. L. Cadden, J. G. Langmaid, J. Willis, A. H. E. Whipp, W. H. Zander, R. Bartlett, D. Barty, E. Ridley, G. E. Gray, C. C. Hart, F. W. Taylor, J. A. Guy, L. S. Allen, R. Gaskell, E. J. Tysoe, W. E. Rees, R. H. Herps, N. B. Jehan, L. F. Mason, D. Chalmers, H. H. Stevenson, N. J. Sutherland, J. Hudson, N. R. McCoy, R. M. Milwain, B. A. Bragg, R. Watterson, F. Steed, R. M. Taylor, J. S. Lees, J. Parker, S. D. Dickson, H. Palmer, E. J. Dunkley, J. T. Bentley, D. Vincent, O. Vincent, W. H. Hanlon, H. Doust, W. Barrett and E. E. Haviland.

The rank and file of the 30th were of as fine a material as has ever been welded into a battalion. Many of the recruits coming forward at this period of the war had been deterred from enlisting earlier because of family responsibilities, but, with the realisation that the Empire was faced with the certainty of a long drawn-out struggle, they hastily arranged their private affairs and offered their services. Thus a large proportion of the 30th Battalion were married men. Among its N.C.O.'s were a number of eager youngsters who had held commissions in the militia, and they soon took advantage of the opportunities of active service to gain further promotion.

"B" and "C" Companies consisted largely of men from the Newcastle district, which was also well represented in the drafts of reinforcements that joined the battalion from time to time. The majority of "D" Company came from country districts, while "A" included in its ranks the Victorian ex-naval men previously referred to. One of them, Private H. Rogers, writes:

"We were sent to Seymour camp in May, 1915, and on arrival the mustered volunteers were lined up on the parade ground and all ex-naval men asked to take two paces forward. All complying were drafted into what was known as the Victorian Naval Unit, and we were told that we were to proceed overseas as seamen to man minesweepers.

"After some weeks at Seymour we were sent to Broadmeadows and were still wearing naval rig and also still called the naval unit. The troops were paraded each day and the practice of the Camp Commandant was to place the naval unit at the rear of the parade, which according to etiquette was quite incorrect. We stood this for a few mornings, but 'Tosh' Ridley eventually approached the Camp Commandant and requested that he should march the naval unit from the rear of the parade to the front, which he did. After some weeks at Broadmeadows we entrained for Sydney, and although we arrived at Liverpool 100% strong, we probably gave the Lieutenant in charge a rather strenuous time."

The arrival of this detachment (some 130 strong), on August 28th, was an event unique in the annals of the 30th Battalion. Clad in their blue uniforms and marching with that peculiar rolling gait which marks the seaman, they made a picturesque entry into the camp between long lines of cheering onlookers, the band meanwhile playing "Sons of the Sea." Long after they had shed their navy blue for khaki they remained a separate entity in the battalion, never completely submerged, and always expressing their own breezy, but nevertheless strong, personality.

Among the bandsmen of the 30th were a number who, like their leader—Sergeant Wellings—had belonged to the

FORMATION OF THE BATTALION

Manly Municipal Band. On the long voyage to Suez the band was a great factor in relieving the monotony of shipboard life, and the men never tired of listening to its programmes. The favourite piece was undoubtedly the regimental march, "Association." Later on the band's stirring strains gave a fillip to many a jaded spirit and encouragement to countless pairs of weary feet ploughing through the sands of Egypt and Sinai or tramping the cobbled roads of France. In 1917 its music was heard in the still-smoking ruins of Bapaume; and with the war won, tired backs straightened and packs felt lighter as it led the long khaki column over the many-kilometred road to Charleroi. Sergeant Wellings still treasures a tie pin which he received at the hands of the Prince of Wales at Ismailia in 1916.

When the battalion had been completely organised some elementary training was carried out. Interest naturally centred on the men of "A" Company, whose quaint naval expressions gave rise to much amusement. An incident that is worthy of note was the manner in which Orderly Sergeant "Tosh" Ridley one morning reported the state of his company to Major Beardsmore, his remarks being to this effect: "220 men aboard, Sir, 5 ashore, 4 adrift, and 2 in the bay"—translated into military parlance, this meant, 220 present, 5 on leave, 4 absent, and 2 sick. A story concerning "A" Company's cook, "Pansy" McBride, may also be quoted here. The C.O., accompanied by Sergeant McDuff, was making his daily inspection of the cooks' lines when he noticed a pot boiling violently. On his asking what the vessel contained, Mac., who was never at a loss for an answer, replied: "Plum duff for 'A' Company, Sir." The C.O. passed on, pleased to know that "A" Company was being so well looked after; and probably to this day he does not know that the pot contained nothing more than "Pansy's" dungarees, having the grease boiled out of them.

Colonel Tivey visited the battalion at the Showground.

Born in 1866, he had served as a captain with the Victorian Imperial Regiment in the South African War, and had gained the D.S.O. and a double mention in despatches. When we got to know him in Egypt and during the campaign in France and Flanders, we found that he was a most tolerant, kindly, and sincere man, but none the less capable of sharp decisive action. His consideration for his men was most marked. More than once, by taking a firm stand with higher authority, he was able to secure a decided improvement in their conditions. It sometimes happened that a battalion commander found it necessary to parade a recalcitrant soul to the brigadier. Usually the offender would return to his unit, by no means uncensured if the case merited it, but nevertheless completely satisfied with the treatment he had received at General Tivey's hands. Very often he would be sent on his way with a kindly word of encouragement as proof that the hand of every man was not against him. General Tivey commanded the 8th Brigade throughout the whole of its fighting days. He was mentioned six times in despatches and was awarded the C.B. and C.M.G. and on 28th November 1918, on assuming command of the 5th Australian Division, he was promoted major-general.

On September 2nd the battalion moved to the Royal Agricultural Showgrounds at Moore Park, where further equipment was issued and training continued. The change was greatly appreciated by everyone. Liverpool camp in those days was either dusty or muddy, whereas Moore Park provided an excellent training ground, and, furthermore, the new quarters were within easy reach of Sydney.

Two very successful tattoos were staged at Moore Park, in which light horse and other units besides the 30th took part. Strange to relate, the "Balaclava *melee*" was won by our infantrymen. These entertainments, for the successful organisation of which Captain McClean was largely responsible, were exceptionally well patronised by the public, and they resulted in the raising of some hundreds

FORMATION OF THE BATTALION

of pounds, which became the nucleus of our comforts fund.

On October 27th the battalion was inspected at Moore Park by the Governor-General, Sir Ronald Munro-Ferguson, and the District Commandant, Colonel E. T. Wallack, both of whom expressed themselves as pleased with the appearance and turnout of the men. The left-hand man of the "C" Company that day was the giant Private Florance McGillycuddy, some 6ft. 3in. in height, who had seen service in the Royal Irish Constabulary. As they approached him, Colonel Wallack remarked to Sir Ronald: "Here's a fine sample of a Cornstalk," upon which the Governor-General said to Mac.: "And what part of Australia did you come from?" "From County Kerry, Sorr!" was the reply. Mac., who as a stretcher-bearer, did some excellent work at Fromelles, was subsequently awarded the Military Medal for this and other actions, later becoming battalion bombing sergeant. After the war he was for some years a member of the N.S. Wales Water Police, in which he also distinguished himself by diving off a wharf in the darkness and rescuing a man who had fallen into Sydney Harbour. He died in 1929.

The battalion embarked for Egypt in the *Beltana* (transport A.72) on November 9th. The scene at the showground on the previous night was a memorable one, some thousands of relatives and friends assembling to bid farewell to their loved ones. Other well-wishers also turned up in force. Embarkations were generally a nightmare to the authorities, but ours turned out to be a model one. This was possibly due to the fact that the battalion left camp at 4.30 a.m. and was safely aboard before the hotels opened. In accordance with the usual practice, a party of 25, fully equipped, had been sent from Liverpool, so that any vacancies that might be caused by men "falling by the wayside" en route to the wharf could be filled immediately; but in our case the complete party was able to return to camp, since we did not lose a single man.

The strength of the battalion on embarkation was 31

officers and 971 other ranks. In addition, 100 men under Lieutenant Macfarlane, comprising the 30th's first reinforcements, also sailed in the *Beltana*. The transport section—40 other ranks and 71 horses, under Lieutenant Barnett—had left four days previously in the *Katuna* (A.13). Major Denham was placed in charge of all troops in that ship, and with him was the Rev. Father King, our Roman Catholic chaplain.

Before the *Beltana* pulled out from Woolloomooloo wharf the battalion was visited by the Archbishop of Sydney (Dr. Wright), who moved from deck to deck, conversing with small groups of officers and men, and finally shaking hands with as many men as possible. While the vessel was anchored in the stream the Governor-General came aboard and in a short address complimented all ranks upon the orderly embarkation and their appearance generally. He referred to the importance of our mission, but said that he was confident of the eventual outcome. His remarks were well received, and on moving down the gangway he was loudly cheered.

The *Beltana* carried other A.I.F. details as well as the 30th Battalion. Colonel Clark was given command of all troops on board for the period of the voyage, and Captain Sloan was appointed ship's adjutant. In consequence, Major Holford temporarily assumed command of the 30th, with Lieutenant Couchman as his adjutant.

The sea being calm, officers and men soon settled down to shipboard routine. "Reveille" was blown at 6 a.m. Breakfast was taken by the troops at 7.30, dinner at noon, and tea at 5 p.m. The "Last Post" was sounded at 9 o'clock, and "Lights Out" at 9.15. The times of all parades, "smokos," recreational periods, etc., were clearly defined in the ship's "Standing Orders," and were cheerfully observed by all ranks. Unfortunately, the food provided for the troops, though according to the scale prescribed by the Australian Victualling Authorities, was most unsatisfactory, as it was found to be contaminated by weevils and other

FORMATION OF THE BATTALION

vermin. The ship's staff appeared to do their best with the material available, but little improvement resulted, despite numerous complaints.

The weather remained fine throughout the voyage, with the exception of a little roughness in the Great Australian Bight. No port was called at and only two vessels were sighted during the 28 days' non-stop run to Suez. No use was made of the *Beltana's* wireless, either to receive or send messages, and much speculation was indulged in as to the progress of the war.

Each officer was called upon to prepare and deliver a lecture on some military subject, thus enabling the C.O. to form an opinion as to the capacity of his subordinates in the matter of imparting instruction. The men were exercised daily in physical and musketry training, and the N.C.O.'s were assisted in the art of controlling their sections. The machine-gun and signal sections, less affected by lack of room than were the riflemen, made rapid progress.

A favourite sport was the firing at cases and casks thrown overboard, by means of which machine-gunners and riflemen got in some useful practice. For defence against submarines, a squad of expert shots was chosen, among them the international marksman, Armourer-Sergeant Fred. Harrison. The vessel also carried aft a 4.7-inch gun, which was fired occasionally in practice. A surprising feature was the rapidity with which the target dropped astern, thus showing the speed of the vessel.

Concerts, boxing tournaments and various competitions were arranged throughout the voyage, and these brought out some excellent talent.

The time-honoured ceremony of "crossing the line" was successfully carried out, much to the amusement of everyone on board. Among the many charged and dealt with by King Neptune and his court were Lieutenant John Chapman and bandmaster Les. Wellings, the former for having left his mother without her permission, the latter for making discordant noises.

The great majority having never previously crossed the equator, were much impressed by the tropical sunsets and beautifully clear nights, most of which they spent on the open decks. There were also those who felt a tinge of sadness as the Southern Cross gradually disappeared over the horizon, never again to be seen by many on board.

Cape Guardafui, though barren and forbidding, was a welcome sight after so long a sojourn at sea, as were the many lighthouses at the entrance to, and throughout the Red Sea. A glimpse was obtained of the tip of Mount Sinai, which, no doubt, reminded the more thoughtful of the tablets which originated there some thousands of years ago.

CHAPTER II.

ARRIVAL IN EGYPT

THE *Beltana* anchored off Suez at 8 a.m. on December 8th, after a pleasant voyage, during which, to quote from the official records, "there were no deaths, no serious sickness, discipline was good, with an absence of crime of a serious nature."

As the ship lay about a mile and a half from the wharf, the adjutant was sent ashore in a boat manned by a crew of ex-naval men from "A" Company—under an officer of the *Beltana*—to interview the disembarkation authorities, as well as to despatch cables, mails, etc., and to ascertain as far as possible, how the war had progressed during the previous four weeks. The crew, now in their element, excelled themselves in handling the boat in the most approved naval style, evoking not only the plaudits and admiration of the ship's company, but also of a siege battery, nurses, passengers and crew of an Orient liner which had arrived from Australia about half an hour ahead of the *Beltana*.

After the adjutant had completed formalities with the port authorities—who, not expecting the *Beltana* so soon, were to some extent unprepared—the boat's crew, stimulated no doubt by the short period of shore leave they had enjoyed, and the fact that eleven hundred of their comrades were anxiously awaiting their return, again gave of their best, the boat being propelled through the water in perhaps record time. Many were the questions fired at them as they climbed up the gangway, "Is the war over?" "Who is keeping the pub in Suez now?" "What did it taste like?" etc. The only news of importance was that fighting was still proceeding on Gallipoli, and that an attack on the Canal was expected.

Arrangements were made to land the troops the following day, and all necessary preparation was made, but, for some unexplained reason, the order was cancelled and the men, much to their disgust, remained on board for another three days. However, the best was made of the situation, and, among other sports, miniature regattas in the ship's collapsible boats were held, in which most of the events were won, naturally, by members of "A" Company.

Dressed in quaint costumes, itinerant vendors of fruit and other Eastern produce, surrounded the ship in their queerly fashioned boats, and for the first two days they did a roaring trade. By means of baskets, attached to stout string, the articles were hoisted aboard after the necessary cash had been lowered. Portion of the produce thus received, such as orange and banana skins, potatoes, wrappings, and deck refuse of various kinds, was subsequently returned to the vendors by the force of gravity, much to the discomfort of the said vendors, but greatly to the amusement of the purchasers. Even the eagerly-awaited pilot, arriving to take the *Beltana* to the landing stage, did not escape these little pleasantries, and the more he and his boat's crew shouted and gesticulated, the more intense became the barrage. When, however, he was recognised as an Egyptian official, hostilities ceased and he was permitted to climb the rope ladder to the deck without further molestation. His remarks to the Captain concerning us have not been recorded. A shout went up as we started to move, and at 2 p.m., December 11th, we commenced to disembark.

Three trains were provided to convey the troops to Helmieh railway station, en route to Aerodrome Camp, Heliopolis, on the outskirts of Cairo. The first train, in charge of the senior major, left at 4 p.m. and arrived at its destination without incident. The second train (in

LIEUT.-COLONEL F. STREET, D.S.O.

Lieut.-Colonel JOHN A. CHAPMAN, D.S.O.

Colonel R. H. BEARDSMORE, D.S.O., M.B.E., V.D.

Lieut.-Colonel H. SLOAN
President, 30th Bn. A.I.F. Assn.

Lieut.-Colonel W. J. R. CHEESEMAN, D.S.O., M.C., Chevalier Legion d'Honneur

ARRIVAL IN EGYPT

charge of the adjutant) was, however, not so fortunate. On its being held up for half an hour at a wayside station near Ismailia, the troops, who were travelling in goods trucks, took advantage of the halt to stretch their legs on the sand and, incidentally, to buy or otherwise procure oranges and cooked eggs from a nearby stall. The purchasers were so eager to do business that pressure from behind upset the structure, with the result that oranges and eggs rolled in every direction. While none of the fruit was wasted, the irate stallholder, plus an apparently more irate station-master, made extortionate demands on the unfortunate adjutant, who, new to Egyptian ways and wiles, and unwilling further to delay the train, settled matters with the exploiters by handing over three Australian sovereigns.

The second train arrived at Helmieh about 2 a.m., but the guide whose duty it was to lead the party to its camping place evidently took the wrong turning as, after following him for more than an hour through soft sand and over stony ridges, the company found itself back at the railway station from which it had started. The guide, naturally, was subjected to remarks more forcible than polite from the men, who, carrying full packs, were very tired. After a short rest another start was made, and this time the camp was reached without further incident. In the meantime, the C.O. (Colonel Clark) had arrived in the third train with his contingent and was somewhat perturbed when informed that portion of his command was missing. Fortunately, our tents had been erected by the 31st Battalion, which arrived there before us, and all ranks settled down to a few hours' sleep.

The C.O. was liberal in the matter of leave and during the next three days facilities for sightseeing were accorded to as many men as possible. A lecture given by Major Purser during the voyage, based on the following extract from Field Service Regulations, namely, "Time spent on reconnaissance is rarely wasted," had apparently been absorbed by the troops, as they lost no time in exploring Cairo and its environs. Large numbers journeyed by tram to the site of the old Mena Camp, Mena House, the Sphinx, and the great pyramid, Cheops. Some scaled the latter to obtain greater visibility of the Nile valley, and also to obtain a birdseye view of the city, some seven miles away. A few (miners, perhaps) preferred exploring the tortuous underground passages of the great limestone pile. Another spot of great military importance to our men was the Citadel, manned then by a British garrison. This dominates the entire city and is doubly interesting by reason of the fact that about the year 1798 it was held by Napoleon, and evidence of his occupation is seen by a number of cannon balls which are still embedded in the masonry of a mosque some 500 yards away. A suggestion by one of our number, who possibly had a premonition of the formation of the Salvage Corps which later materialised in France, that these relics might be recovered, was not favoured, firstly, by reason of their inaccessibility, and, secondly, the probable hostility of the local populace. Other and less pretentious portions of the city were also reconnoitered, and commented upon, but all this came to a sudden end when at 7 p.m. on December 15th, we were ordered to be ready to entrain at 3 o'clock next morning. Sleep was out of the question, for arms had to be issued, and the obsolete leather equipment brought from Australia replaced by that of an up-to-date pattern. However, the long night came to an end and daylight saw our trains speeding in the direction of Ismailia.

The battalion arrived at Moascar about noon on 16th, and bivouacked for the night at a spot south of the railway station. The men, very tired after their Cairo experiences and the sleepless night at the Aerodrome Camp, made themselves comfortable on the soft sand, but a heavy morning dew drenched them almost to the skin.

At 8 a.m. on December 17th, we marched through Ismailia to Ferry Post, an entrenched position on the

ARRIVAL IN EGYPT

eastern bank of the Canal, at the northern end of Lake Timsah. The crossing was made over a pontoon bridge, which was controlled by a party from the Royal Australian Naval Bridging Train. It was here that we first learnt the necessity of breaking step when crossing a stream on a temporary structure.

As our first line transport had not yet joined us—a mishap which overtook it will be referred to later—our stores and baggage, including the cumbrous gear of the officers' and sergeants' messes, were conveyed by Indian mule transport, small two-wheel carts each carrying about 600 lbs. and drawn by a single animal.

Colonel Clark took over the command of the post from the C.O. of a Punjabi regiment, which moved out at 12.30 p.m. Other units of the command consisted of one squadron of Hyderabad Lancers, a unit of the Bikaner Camel Corps, a Battery of the Ayrshire Royal Horse Artillery, and "C" Section of the 8th Field Ambulance.

After quarters were allotted, the defence scheme for the post was explained to the officers, and night outposts were placed in position. The 8th Brigade was the first Australian formation to take up defensive positions on the eastern bank of the Canal, being reinforced later by practically the whole of the troops withdrawn from Gallipoli.

The first defences had been situated on the Canal banks only, but at this period, as another attack by the Turks was anticipated, a line of outposts was constructed between seven and nine miles out in the Sinai Desert, parallel to the waterway. The decision to do this is credited to Lord Kitchener, who, when inspecting the Egyptian front, is said to have remarked to the G.O.C.: "You are not protecting the Canal, the Canal is protecting you." But whatever the cause, the fact remains that roads running east from various points on the Canal were commenced, as was the new line of defence.

The battalion remained at Ferry Post until 6th February, 1916. A certain amount of section, company, and battalion training was carried out, night marches on compass bearings were practised with varying success, and a proportion of the men fired a musketry course. The provision of night outposts also occupied the time of a considerable number of men, and the manning of the pontoon bridge and two punts, which were among the fatigues incidental to the garrisoning of the post, absorbed others. The bridge had frequently to be swung parallel to the stream, to permit ships to pass along, while the punts—heavy and cumbersome affairs to work—were in use for about twelve hours each day, conveying stores and road and trench material for the front line defences.

On December 21st, the C.O. received orders to establish a post at Hill 353, a barren eminence in the desert about nine miles distant, having a bearing of 80° from Ferry Post. Major Purser (of "C" Company) was directed to make a reconnaissance, escorted by a detachment of the Bikaner Camel Corps, and on his return was detailed to occupy the position with his unit. Of this operation and its purpose Purser long afterwards wrote:—

"In accordance with orders, I left Ferry Post on 29th December, 1915, with 'C' Company and 2 machine guns of 30th Battalion, some A.A.M.C. details and a detachment of Bikaner Camel Corps to establish a post at Hill 353 (later renamed 'Australia Hill'), which was to serve as a base from which Royal Engineer survey officers would operate, and where a dump of engineering material was to be built up for subsequent use in the line of entrenchments to be constructed in connection with the Canal defences.

"My orders were to arrive at the hill before dark, but the late arrival of the Egyptian Camel Transport Corps, which was to carry our camp equipment, etc., delayed our start until after lunch. The band played us out. Immediately outside the bastions I formed line of platoons in fours, so as to minimise the amount of broken sand to be marched over by those in the rear. On front and flanks

ARRIVAL IN EGYPT

rode Bikaners, and in rear were the transport camels under the charge of C.Q.M.S. Menzies.

"The heat, our 'softness' after the voyage from Sydney, and our inexperience of marching on sand made the march a very trying one, and as it progressed, frequent halts became necessary. The 9 or 10 miles we had to cover seemed interminable, and at each halt the hill, the peak of which we could see, seemed as far off as ever; but we reached it just as darkness set in, and, after posting sentries, bivouacked for the night. The next day we commenced putting the hill into a state of defence, and about a week later my command was augmented by a field company of Australian Engineers and a further detachment of Bikaners.

"Hill 353 (so named from its height) was just sand, and as far as the eye could see, was sand. Of vegetation, there was little—widely scattered clumps of 'camel grass' and a small grey shrub which when in flower was covered with white convolvulus-like bells about the size of a florin. Without preliminary drying, these shrubs burned readily and were a welcome acquisition to our fuel supply. How anything grew in that sandy waste is hard to understand, for although we dug deeply in places indicated by R.E. officers as likely to yield water, we found no trace of moisture.

"Rations, water, firewood, and engineering material were brought to us daily by camel trains from Ferry Post, with which we were in field telephonic communication. We could also communicate by helio and lamp with H.M.Ss. *Jupiter* and *Minerva* lying in Lake Timsah. The latter's searchlights swept the desert around us every night.

"Life at the Hill was hard, but except for one case of appendicitis, our health was excellent. Various generals and staff officers visited the hill to study the surrounding country, and we also received visits from Colonel Clark, Captain Marolli (R.M.O.), Chaplain F. G. Ward, "A" Company, of the 30th Battalion (which made the Hill its destination on a route march), and a patrol of Mysore Lancers from a similar post situated to the north of us. Other incidents were a man's accidental shooting of himself during a test alarm, the capture of a wandering Arab, and a false alarm by the Bikaners of the proximity of a party of Turks.

"An amusing episode which took place was when Private Charlie Westbrook volunteered to go back with the camel train as a special messenger to battalion headquarters. It was extremely funny to see him perched between two water fantasses on a camel. For every stride the beast took downhill, Westbrook bounced a foot off its back. How he stayed on the animal is a mystery, but on arrival at his destination he was probably a sorer but wiser man.

"After the hill was entrenched a bayonet fighting range was constructed, and while two platoons were engaged in unloading camels, etc., the others practised bayonet fighting or went for short route marches to accustom themselves to marching on the sand, and when we rejoined the battalion we were all very fit.

"Having been relieved by the 5th Brigade, A.I.F., on the previous day, we left Hill 353 on January 30th, 1916, the band of the 20th Battalion playing us out. By this time several miles of road had been constructed across the desert from Ferry Post. We were met on this road by our own band, and covered the distance back to the Canal in a much shorter time than we took on the outward journey."

Although the duties at Ferry Post were fairly strenuous, a number of incidents occurred to relieve the monotony which may be worth recording.

It will be remembered that a large force of Turks had invaded Egypt in this neighbourhood during the earlier months of 1915, apparently with the view to seizing the important railway junction of Ismailia, visible evidence of which was forthcoming in the shape of shot perforated steel boats which were left stranded on the shores of Lake

Timsah. Some of our enterprising signallers, who, with a platoon of infantry, were stationed at Ridge Post and Benchmark (small posts a few miles to the north), salvaged one of these which was partially embedded in the sand, and, after plugging the holes with various substances and making it reasonably watertight, enjoyed a great deal of fun when off duty, journeying between their station, and Ferry Post. The usual procedure was to use a horse to tow the pontoon south and utilise the slow current, usually flowing north, on the homeward trip. The real function of the horse was to draw an ordinary railway sleeper horizontally along the sandy shore of the Canal each evening, thus forming a smooth surface, the object of which was to indicate if efforts to place mines or other obstacles in the waterway had been made during the previous night.

Fish were fairly plentiful in Lake Timsah on our arrival, due to the fact that for some time previously the local fishermen had, for military reasons, been prohibited from following their calling. This safety measure, however, was overcome by our unit providing a fully armed man to take charge of each boat, in return for which we were to receive half of the fish caught. Our sergeant-cook, the versatile McDuff, was appointed to take delivery of each catch, and his interpretation of half the fish was as follows: If a boat, for example, landed 40 fish, Mac took 20 of them, but these 20 would invariably be the largest ones. The unfortunate Gyppos always violently raged and gesticulated in protest but to no purpose. Mac was adamant, 20 was half of 40—in Australia, anyhow.

The matter partially righted itself after a time, as the smaller fish netted were returned to their element, thus to some extent preserving the industry.

The fuel issued was on a very meagre scale, but our cooks did not suffer much inconvenience on this account. A large dump of sleepers, about a mile away on the opposite side of the Canal, was occasionally raided by Mac and his staff, much to the consternation of the caretakers, who never succeeded in catching them red-handed.

One night a thatched hut, occupied by the subalterns of "C" Company, was completely destroyed by fire, and among the gear lost was a rifle on issue to an officer (officers at this period carried rifles). A board of enquiry, presided over by Major Denham, reported on the cause of the outbreak and assessed the damage. Incidentally, the loss of a rifle was but a bagatelle to the O.C., "C" Company, whose "well-trained" Q.M.S. ensured that his company (which was encamped close to an Indian Unit) marched out a few hours later with its complement of arms complete.

An incident that worried the regimental staff was the shooting of a wandering camel some 500 yards in front of our sentry posts. No one, of course, admitted to having fired the shot, but it was afterwards understood that the owner of the animal was, after a fruitless inquiry, compensated for his loss.

On Christmas Eve we experienced a heavy rainstorm. The water poured into our thatched huts and gave us all a thorough drenching. This was a most unusual occurrence in this part of Egypt. However, no real damage was done.

Christmas Day was enjoyed by all ranks, due, in a great measure, to the distribution of a large parcel of "comforts" which arrived from Australia the previous day. Among the gifts was a highly-spiced pudding sent by a Chinaman from Wollongong (N.S.W.). It was not known whether the Oriental was personally responsible for the confection, but the recipient, after sharing it with his mates, remarked that it was "welly good".

Visits to the warship *Minerva* and impromptu concerts ended an enjoyable day for those off duty.

The battalion's first casualty occurred when a man who took French leave to Ismailia was overtaken by Nemesis, in the shape of an army motor waggon. The unfortunate

ARRIVAL IN EGYPT

soldier was taken to hospital with a broken thigh, which ended the war as far as he was concerned.

Another regrettable incident was the drowning of two horses which, attached to a G.S. waggon, became alarmed by the swaying of the narrow pontoon bridge as they were crossing the canal, and jibbed. Fortunately, the driver was able to jump clear in time.

On January 28th, the 5th Brigade passed through our Post on its way to the front line defences. The men looked fit and well, but they were noticeably weather-beaten and ragged, thus giving evidence of the hardships they had endured on Gallipoli. A comic element was provided by the beards worn by certain individuals. Quite a number had written in indelible pencil on their hatbands the name of their home town, thus indicating that they hailed from Bega, Orange, Lismore, Tamworth, Albury, Bathurst, Bourke, etc.

As each battalion crossed the canal it was met by our band, which played "Boys of the Dardanelles" and other appropriate tunes. This little compliment was much appreciated by the war-worn veterans, and has been favourably commented upon many times since.

Reviewing our seven weeks' stay at Ferry Post from December 16th, 1915, to February 6th, 1916, it can be asserted that all ranks spent a reasonably comfortable time. The ocean liners passing through the canal were a constant source of delight, especially when lit up from stem to stern at night time. Incidentally, many a parcel of cigarettes, newspapers, books, etc., thrown overboard, was retrieved from the water by the troops.

Cameras were much in evidence and some thousands of photographs were taken of the picturesque natives, their camels, and surroundings generally. Swimming in the lake was permitted in the morning and evenings and was very popular.

CHAPTER III.

(TEL EL KEBIR).

OUR next move was to the historic battlefield of Tel el Kebir, where we arrived by train from Moascar at 12.30 p.m., February 6th, 1916, and on being allotted our camping ground proceeded to pitch the tents which our personnel was to occupy during the ensuing seven weeks. The site was of a hard gravelly nature, devoid of vegetation of any kind, and extremely hard to lie upon. The choice of this spot for a huge concentration of men—apart from its historic association—was stated to be its strategic position, being practically midway between Cairo and Suez; another reason, not universally approved by the troops, was its distance from the capital city. South-East from the camp could be seen the valley known as the Wadi Tumilat. When the inundations of the Nile attained their greatest height in years gone by, the flood waters coursed from the river near Cairo through this depression into Lake Timsah (the "Crocodile Lake"). Over 2,500 years ago a canal followed this route, providing a connection between the Nile and the Red Sea. This work, begun by Necho, was completed by Darius (doubtless the famous Eastern potentate whose "suavity and dignity" is commemorated in an anecdote well known to members of the A.I.F.). The whole of the wadi used to be a very fertile area, but the desert has gradually encroached upon it and drifting sand now covers stretches of the depression which was at one time under intense cultivation. In place of the canal of Necho, the Sweet-Water Canal now runs between Cairo and Suez, with the railway closely parallel to it.

All ranks were interested in this neighbourhood, realising that they were occupying the ground over which Sir Garnet Wolseley's troops marched when they made their famous night attack, which culminated in the defeat of the rebellious Arabi and the restoration of Egypt to its rightful ruler, the Khedive. Some no doubt were aware that they were resting on the very ground over which the Highland Brigade —guided by the gallant Rawson—walked barefooted in order to lessen the chance of their approach being detected by the enemy.

Standing on the high grand—something in the nature of a plateau which rises from the valley of the Sweet Water Canal—and viewing the remains of the line of trenches and redoubts, originally some four miles in length, it was easy to visualise the troops advancing in the early morning, the consternation that must have arisen in the breasts of many when an unexpected comet made its appearance in the east and was mistaken for dawn, the short, sharp, decisive fight, the enemy scattering in all directions, the Cavalry Brigade under Drury Lowe almost racing the 65 miles to the Citadel, while the Indian contingent—held as a reserve on the south side of the Sweet Water Canal—hastened on to Zag-a-Zig. Those of us approaching the sere and yellow will remember the greeting "All Sir Garnet", which for some years signified "All correct."

Our men soon settled down to the new conditions, but they lost no time in scouring the country-side for mementoes of the battle. These were easily found, the shifting sands unearthing articles which had perhaps been deeply buried for many years. Souvenir hunting did not stop at buttons, badges, or pieces of equipment—skeletons were unearthed and more than one tent was embellished with skull and crossbones. This sacrilege was naturally objectionable to the Egyptian population, who protested to the army authorities, whereupon the practice was stopped and the bones were reinterred.

It was at Tel el Kebir that General Tivey's command

assembled for the first time as a unit, prior to its becoming part of the newly formed 5th Division. The men of the 8th Infantry Brigade came from all parts of Australia—the 29th Battalion from Victoria, the 30th principally from N.S. Wales, the 31st from Queensland and Victoria, and the 32nd from South and West Australia. As each of the battalions contained a number of officers who were either graduates of Duntroon College or members of the Australian Instructional Corps, an exchange of visits and other social activities brought about an *esprit de corps,* which was manifested many times during the ensuing years of the war. Incidentally, an officer of the 32nd Battalion, Captain Jack Paul, from the Australian Instructional Staff, had participated in the battle of Tel el Kebir, and was able to give us first-hand information of that historic event.

Various phases of infantry training were now carried out and a number of officers and N.C.O's. sent to schools of instruction at Zietoun, near Cairo—among the former was Lieutenant John A. Chapman, who did well at a grenade school, and on being subsequently appointed battalion bombing officer, initiated the training in bomb fighting so highly developed at a later stage in France and Belgium. In the signalling school Corporal R. E. Lording carried off the honours of his class by obtaining 99.7 per cent. of marks in the final examination, and would probably have achieved further distinction but for the disaster which befell him some months later.

Men who were indifferent rifle shots were exercised on an improvised range on the fringe of the desert south of the camp, the march to which lay across the Sweet Water Canal, spanned by the bridge on the parapet of which Wolseley wrote the despatch announcing his victory. Adjacent to this spot is the native village of mud huts shown on the map as Tel el Kebir, and from which the battlefield derived its name.

The transport section joined us here under Lieutenant R. Barnett, one of our most popular officers, who was known to all and sundry as "Barney". An incident, which happened shortly after his disembarkation, and which kept him busy for several weeks was the rounding up of his horses, which one night broke from their lines at Serapeum and scattered in every conceivable direction. "Barney's" experiences in crossing deserts, scouring native villages, and interviewing various sheiks, would take up too much space to be recounted here, but it suffices to say that he eventually succeeded in recapturing every one of his renegade animals plus a few more.

The main camp fronting the Ismailia-Cairo railway line was over a mile long and probably contained the largest concentration of Australian troops that had yet occurred. The lines were kept scrupulously clean, and every effort was made to avoid the spread of disease; inoculations were made to combat various scourges, and a yard of mosquito netting was issued to each man, which also served to ward off flies during the daytime.

During one of the regular medical inspections the irrepressible Sergeant McDuff came into conflict with the R.M.O. regarding the efficacy of grease traps. After much argument the "Doc" sought to bring the discussion to a finish by remarking, "You should have been a politician." Quick as a flash came Mac's retort: "I was, Sir, before I joined the army."

Such a large encampment naturally attracted a host of followers, and shops of every conceivable kind sprang up in which Eastern wares of various descriptions were on sale. Two Spaniards did particularly well in selling silks, a large number of which were sent to relatives and friends in Australia. Major Holford, as President of our brigade committee, levied rentals from the establishments situated in our lines, which augmented battalion funds considerably, but it was suspected that the wily tradesmen probably got even by increasing their charges.

The reorganisation of the A.I.F. was now proceeding rapidly, and each battalion was called upon to provide a large number of men for the new formations. The 30th supplied several officers and about 140 other ranks, most of whom were absorbed by the 5th Divisional Artillery, the 5th Pioneer Battalion and Camel Corps. Among those so transferred were: Major H. K. Denham, to the 46th Battalion; Captain H. L. Morrison, Lieutenants W. T. Wilkinson and C. J. Walker and Sergeants D. Barty and G. S. Gray, to the 5th Pioneer Battalion; Captain F. S. McClean, Lieutenant R. Barnett and C. Webber, to the 5th Divisional Artillery; Lieutenant R. Cudden, to the 48th Battalion; Lieutenant T. R. Marsden and Sergeants A. K. Flack and J. W. Axtens, to 8th Machine Gun Company. About this time, too, our second reinforcements arrived from Australia but, much to their disappointment, they were drafted to other units of the division.

One immediate result of these transfers was the promotion of Lieutenants W. J. R. Cheeseman, P. Charlton, R. A. Allen, B. A. Wark and F. Krinks to rank of Captain, and the appointment of the following N.C.O's. to commissioned rank:—R.S.M., E. B. Jackson; C.S.M's., J. Parker, J. S. Lees, W. H. Hind and R. Cadden, and Sergeant A. H. Treloar. All the newly appointed officers became platoon commanders, with the exception of Lieutenant Treloar, who was selected to command the recently raised Lewis Gun section.

During this period distinctive colour patches to be worn on both sleeves of the tunic just below the shoulder, were issued to the various units of the 8th Brigade. For a time they were worn horizontally, but at a later date, for purposes of uniformity in the division they were changed to the perpendicular.

To control the battalion's canteen and comforts fund a committee was appointed, consisting of Major Purser (President), Captain Street and Lieutenant John Chapman.

A large consignment of comforts from Sydney and Newcastle, including a number of highly prized Canterbury cakes, reached us at Tel el Kebir. Colonel Clark, who personally supervised the distribution of these confections, accused the Q.M.S. of "C" Company (Eric Menzies) of having taken more than his share. Menzies pretended to make a recount and handed one back with profuse apologies, though still retaining two more than his quota. If Eric had survived, he would have made the perfect Quarter Master.

A successful sports meeting was held on March 2nd, at which the sum of £10 was disbursed from battalion funds for prizes. Brigadier-General Tivey officiated as one of the judges, and his decisions gave general satisfaction. On the 22nd the camp was inspected by H.R.H. the Prince of Wales, who was accompanied by General Birdwood and a host of staff officers. He received a wonderful welcome from the assembled troops, who vied with each other in showing their appreciation of the heir to the throne.

CHAPTER IV.

(THE SINAI DESERT).

ON completion of its formation the 5th Division was ordered to move to the new defensive line east of the Canal. The 8th Brigade went by train to Moascar, while the 14th and 15th Brigades marched on parallel routes some days later. The story of the hardships endured by the latter Brigades does not directly concern this narrative, but it gave rise to some good natured comment as to the reason for one brigade being carried by train and the remainder having to move per boot. What the real reason was is now a matter of indifference. It may have been military expediency, such as the necessity for one portion of the division to reach the front quickly, or more likely, congestion on the railway line precluded the whole division moving by train. Be this as it may, the 8th Brigade shortly afterwards became the target for many personal remarks (both complimentary and otherwise) from the other brigades, and for a time we were referred to as "The Gentlemen of the Desert," "Tivey's Pets," and "Tivey's Chocolate Soldiers." In the course of time this was abbreviated to "Tivey's Chocs," a nickname that will stick to the 8th Brigade as long as A.I.F. history lasts. None of us objected to it and there was probably no man prouder of the appellation than General Tivey himself, who, during the following years, spared no effort in contributing to the health, welfare and efficiency of his men, while they, in turn, never failed him in emergency.

On detraining from the cattle trucks at Moascar we marched through Ismailia to Ferry Post, crossed the canal

Lieut-Colonel M. PURSER, D.S.O., V.D.

Capt. T. C. BARBOUR

Cpl. G. E. WEILEY, M.M. and Bar.

Pte. R. MATHER, M.M.

Sgt. W. G. SMITH, M.M.

Coy. Sgt.-Maj. T. ECCLES, D.C.M., M.M.

there, and pitched our tents at Ferry Post East, the staging camp which became the base of the 5th Division during practically the remainder of its sojourn in Egypt.

During our absence at Tel el Kebir, a line of defences parallel to and from seven to nine miles distant from the canal, had been partially constructed, and was connected to a narrow but good road along which was laid a pipeline for the conveyance of water.

On March 31st the battalion moved out to the road-head, and on a gentle slope which someone with a sense of humour had named "Brighton Beach," we prepared our main camp. Facing us was a huge sandhill which from its shape was dubbed the "Hogsback," and about a mile beyond it were the trenches and wire-entanglements designed to stop the Turk should he make another attempt to invade Egypt. On April 1st the 30th was allotted a section of these defences, from "Katoomba Hill" on the left to "Gazelle Heights" on the right, which had previously been held by the New Zealand Mounted Rifles.

The normal procedure was to employ two companies supported by half the 8th Machine Gun Company in the front line, while the remainder of the battalion either rested or was exercised in the main camp.

Mounted patrols from the 10th Light Horse Regiment and the Bikaner Camel Corps patrolled in front of the position. Incidentally, most of the landmarks in this neighbourhood were given Australian names, such as "Duntroon Plateau," "Lithgow," "Round Hill," "Mount Kembla," "Albury," "Gundagai," "Mount Macedon," "Lightning Ridge."

Hill 353, referred to in the previous chapter, was renamed "Australia Hill."

In addition to digging trenches and revetting their sides with matting and stakes, and erecting wire-entanglements, each company was exercised in the "trained soldiers" course of musketry. Field firing was also carried out from the occupied trenches, thus obtaining the exact range of points

D

which the enemy would have to pass in the event of his making an attack. This, however, did not eventuate.

One of the main discomforts to which we were subjected was a great storm, known as the "khamseen," which lasted for two days and nights. In a few hours the trenches were filled with sand and the entanglements buried, thus destroying months of work. Quite a number of men had narrow escapes from being engulfed by sand-slides, and Sergeant Cody, of "A" Company, in charge of the delivery of rations, became isolated and spent a couple of days in the desert with the Arabs and their camels. The storm almost changed the entire face of the landscape; what were formerly hillocks became depressions, and *vice versa.*

Fuel was scarce and the water-supply scanty. At times we were rationed down to one quart per man daily for both washing and drinking purposes. This, however, had its amusing side, as the sight of a person washing his face in his mess-tin lid could not fail to raise a laugh. One of the most economical methods was for a man to pour a few drops into his mate's cupped hands and thus reduce waste to a minimum.

Flies were a source of great annoyance and quite a number of men suffered from an internal complaint known locally as "Gippo stomach."

A slight diversion was the forced landing, near "Gazelle Heights," of an R.F.C. aeroplane, which, after reconnoitring enemy country, had run short of petrol while flying "blind" through a sand-storm. Although the machine had been struck by several bullets the occupants were unhurt. A party from "A" Company dragged it over the sand to the road-head, whence it was conveyed by truck to Moascar.

Apart from the foregoing disabilities, which were trifling as compared with those experienced later in France and Belgium, our stay in the Sinai Desert had its compensations. Though the days were hot, the nights were invariably cool, with beautifully clear skies. The desert has an attraction peculiarly its own, especially in the small hours of the morning, when all is hushed and the stillness is perhaps broken only by the winging of migratory birds high overhead. Nor is the country absolutely devoid of animal and vegetable life. Gazelles were occasionally seen by our patrols and wild dogs were known to exist there. Quite a number of shrubs and flowers spring up almost in a night and the landscape is, in places, a blaze of colour. The shrubs survive for a considerable time and are much appreciated by the camels, but the flowers, some of which are surprisingly beautiful, fade away almost as rapidly as they appear, which reminds one of Gray's expressive lines:

"Full many a gem, of purest ray serene,
The dark unfathomed caves of ocean bear;
Full many a flower is born to blush unseen
And waste its sweetness on the desert air."

On April 15th we were relieved by the 58th Battalion and returned to the staging camp. The rush to bathe in the cool waters of the canal immediately after dismissal can be better imagined than described.

While all ranks were glad to escape from the disabilities of the front line, and to enjoy again the comparative comfort which proximity to the canal afforded, there was a growing desire to move to a more definite field of action. The 1st and 2nd Divisions, having crossed to France some weeks previously, the remaining units were naturally eager to follow them. The feelings of our men in this respect were to some extent expressed in a song composed by Private R. Court, of "B" Company, which was frequently sung by the troops to the tune of "Boys of the Dardanelles."

The 5th Division, however, was destined to remain in the land of the Pharaohs until the 15th of June. In the meantime, intensive brigade and divisional training was carried out; in view of the intensive heat, this was usually performed between 2 a.m. and 9 a.m., and again in the evenings between 5 and 7 o'clock.

The training, which no doubt hardened all ranks and was

valuable to the leaders, was extremely monotonous to the men. An opinion has been expressed that portion of the time allotted to open warfare training and route marches might more profitably have been devoted to trench attack and consolidation. The stalemate on Gallipoli supported this contention, as did the fact that the fighting in France had long since developed into trench warfare. However, it is very easy to be wise after the event; possibly to the authorities the wish was father to the thought that the trench warfare would not be of long duration.

Church parades, which were held each Sunday at 9.30 a.m., were not always popular. It was not that the troops objected on principle, but largely because at such parades, which of necessity were held in the open, they had to sit in a semi-circle on the sand and contend with the rays of the sun, the myriads of flies, and the dust. In such circumstances it was sometimes difficult for them to appreciate fully the efforts of the padre. One notable exception, however, was a service conducted by the Rev. S. A. Beveridge, who vividly described the battle between the Israelites (led by Gideon) and the Midianites, as recorded in the seventh chapter of the Book of Judges. While space will not permit of completely traversing the sermon, to which the troops listened with rapt attention, the fact that the encounter took place in the adjoining country of Palestine added much to its interest.

Although not stressing the fight from the military point of view, the speaker brought out two points which are as supremely important to-day as they were in Gideon's time, namely, the element of surprise, and the fact that a small, thoroughly efficient army, well equipped and amenable to discipline, is much superior to a large ill-organised force. Readers are invited to peruse the chapter of the good book referred to and extract for themselves the lessons contained therein.

The battalion remained at the staging camp from April 15th to 23rd, after which it renewed its acquaintance with

Capt. S. A. RAILTON, M.C.
Major P. CHARLTON, M.C.
Lieut. J. C. YEOMANS, D.S.O.
Capt. A. C. WHITE, M.C.

THE SINAI DESERT

Ferry Post, taking over from the 54th Battalion. We had pleasant recollections of this spot, as it was here that we spent the previous Christmas and New Year, and obtained our first experience of soldiering in a foreign country. Our sojourn this time was of seven days' duration only, but during that period Anzac Day was celebrated by a holiday and a sports programme, which included swimming events and polo matches, the contestants in the latter event being mounted on donkeys. A sight long to be remembered was the spectacle of some 4,000 men, mother naked, bathing in the canal; incidentally, our colonel was believed to be the only man in the A.I.F. who availed himself of a bathing suit. Weaklings had been eliminated during the months spent on the desert, and it was indeed thrilling to see so many perfect specimens of young manhood disporting themselves in the cool waters.

On May 1st we were relieved of garrison duty by the 53rd Battalion and resumed our normal training at the staging camp. Three weeks later we again took over Ferry Post, this time from the 29th Battalion, remaining here until May 28th when, on being relieved by The Queen's (Royal West Surrey Regiment), we crossed the canal for the last time and made our way to Moascar.

Among the more or less important happenings during the previous two months were the unfortunate drowning of two men, one of them a member of the 30th, who were struck by the propeller of a passing steamer; Colonel Clark being under fire during an air raid on Port Said; Russian transports going north laden with troops, whose destination could only be guessed at; the transfer to the 32nd Battalion of Padre Ward, who had acted as our postmaster, censor, etc., and to whom the troops were much attached; an issue of khaki uniforms and helmets to counteract the rays of the sun; an instruction to use both sides of paper in official and private correspondence; the withdrawal of old rifles and an issue of weapons sighted for the use of the new Mark VII. ammunition;

an instruction that in future the place of payment was not to be shown in the pay books; the arrival of the new and interesting Lewis gun; a campaign to destroy all dogs in the vicinity of the camps, due to the prevalence of rabies; lastly, and not necessarily associated with the dog hunt, a prohibition on the importation of whisky to Egypt.

An incident which somewhat compensated for the long weary wait that seems to be inseparable from all reviews, happened prior to the inspection of the 5th Division by the Commander-in-Chief, General Sir Archibald Murray, on April 18th. Our newly appointed Lewis gun officer, Lieutenant Treloar, had selected Private "Paddy" Ryan— a migrant from Erin some months previously—as his groom and batman. Whether Paddy had experienced difficulty in saddling his officer's charger and was late in consequence is not known, but after the whole parade had been called to attention — the reviewing host was in the offing — he arrived on the centre of the parade ground at full gallop. In pulling the horse up suddenly, the luckless Paddy was thrown over its head into the sand. The C.O. looked round in disgust and, if he could have cancelled Treloar's commission at that moment would probably have done so. This trivial incident highly amused the men and probably contributed to the success of the parade. Another incident, in which Paddy was the central figure, occurred when Lieutenant Treloar noticed that his horse was growing thin and, on investigating the cause, found that his well-intentioned groom had been feeding the horse in the next stall and neglecting his own. When the mistake was discovered Paddy made sure of recognising his horse in future by tying a handkerchief around one of its fetlocks.

During this period a number of promotions occurred in the battalion. Sergeants D. Chalmers, E. E. Haviland, W. H. Zander, and F. C. Winn received their commissions, Winn being seconded for duty with the 8th Machine Gun Company. Sergeants W. E. Rees, W. E. Oakes, F. Hamilton, and S. C. Butler were advanced to the rank of Company Sergeant-Major, Corporals J. C. Yeomans, F. W. Keen, and W. Lambourne to sergeant, and Privates H. D. Gooding, Gordon Begg, and T. Eccles to corporal. Transfers out included that of Lieutenant Couchman—a former member of the Australian Instructional Staff—to the 46th Battalion, in which he reached the rank of major and was awarded the D.S.O. Lieutenant Evers went over to the 53rd Battalion, where he also gained promotion. His place in the signals section was filled by Lieutenant J. H. Facey. Sergeant H. J. Wells, who hailed from Newcastle and was well known to many of the unit, came to us from the 13th Battalion.

The 3rd reinforcements, under Lieutenant A. C. White, had the misfortune to join us at "Australia Hill." Marching through the sand almost direct from the troopship, they had a very trying time.

The line of defences east of the canal, on which so much time, energy and material had been expended, was now practically abandoned, the mounted troops pushing forward to Katia and other positions well in advance of them.

On May 30th we received our first definite orders that we were to proceed to France, and preliminary arrangements for departure were at once put in hand. Rumour had been rife for months past as to our probable destination; some asserted that the reason for our being kept so long in Egypt was that we were destined to reinforce the troops in Mesopotamia, while others asserted, with equal force, that our next move would be to Salonica. The news that we were bound for France was very welcome, as the novelty of the Near East had worn off and all ranks were eager to move to a new field of action. The weather was extremely hot, the temperature never less than 120 degrees for days on end. Our tents were pitched on loose fine sand, and the slightest movement brought up a cloud of dust which, with the assistance of myriads of flies, impregnated the food and made living conditions very uncomfortable. An offset to these disabilities was the proximity of Ismailia, a town of some importance, at the junction of the Suez-Cairo and Suez-Port Said railway. Prettily situated on the western shore of Lake Timsah, it supposedly occupies the site of the ancient city of Succoth. Its principal attractions, apart from a picture theatre and other amenities, were its well ordered parks and gardens, kept alive by the fresh water which, in common with the whole of Lower Egypt, comes from the Nile. The principal buildings in the town are occupied by the Canal Commission, which is almost entirely a French administration, despite the fact that Britain holds many shares in the company.

It will be remembered that in 1875, Disraeli, afterwards Lord Beaconsfield, taking advantage of the impecuniosity of the reigning Khedive, made a deal that has proved more profitable to his country than perhaps any other transaction of modern times.

On account of the excessive heat, training, everlasting training, was reduced to a minimum, and consisted principally of route marches in the mornings and evenings. Marching order was temporarily discarded, the dress being khaki drill with only rifle, bayonet, waterbottle, and haversack. One day was pleasantly spent with a battalion of the Rifle Brigade, which occupied a semi-permanent camp in a park adjoining the lake. Our English hosts placed their canteens, sporting materials, and other amenities at our disposal, and as the sum of £15 was disbursed in prizes from our comforts funds, all ranks thoroughly enjoyed themselves.

"C" Company, by reason of the fact that it won most of the events, was given the honour of leading the battalion back to our lines, but tragedy nearly overtook its O.C., Major Purser, when his horse, unable to retain its footing on the slippery surface of the convex road, fell and prac-

THE SINAI DESERT

tically rolled over him. His particular deity, however, stuck to him and he escaped with only a severe shaking.

Another incident on the march that will be remembered, occurred during a halt in the vicinity of a market garden containing ripe water melons and tomatoes. Fortunately or unfortunately (it depends entirely upon the point of view), the head of the column had just rounded a bend in the road, so that the C.O. and his senior officers were unable to see the raid which was soon in progress. Prior to the resumption of the march the pioneer squad had quite a busy time burying the tangible evidence of the repast.

It was at Moascar that we heard of the sad fate of Kitchener. For once the Gyppo paper boys' "very good news," the phrase with which the wags had taught them to precede their announcements, whether good or bad, was not appreciated, and more than one news-vendor left camp hurriedly that morning. A memorial service that was subsequently held was listened to attentively.

Brigade and divisional sports meetings, at which the 30th won its share of prizes, helped to fill in the tedious period of waiting. Each day we expected to get our entraining orders, but for various reasons, including submarine activity in the Mediterranean, our embarkation was postponed time and again. At last, when Lieutenant James Chapman and a small advance party left for Marseilles, we knew that the hour of departure was not far away.

During our six months' stay in Egypt we had accumulated collectively and individually considerably more stores, clothing and personal effects than was allowed by army regulations, and when the order was issued enumerating the articles to be carried on the soldier and in his kit bag, consternation reigned for a time. Eventually tons of clothing, boots, shirts, socks, vests, and innumerable articles which comforts committees, fond mothers, wives, sisters and sweethearts had laboured to provide their loved ones, were dumped in a heap on the sand and abandoned to the mercy of anyone who cared to carry them away. Cameras were anathema to the authorities, and, although there were facilities for the sending of these and other valuable articles to "Cooks" in Cairo, for transhipment to England, such had to be done at the expense of the individual. Despite the vigilance of the officers in the matter of inspection, a few cameras found their way to France disguised as the field dressing which was sewn on the inside of each man's jacket.

A pathetic incident, due to our being over strength, was the selection of ten men to remain at Tel el Kebir, with the details which were subsequently sent to England to form the nucleus of the training battalions. At last on June 15th, 1017 strong, the battalion entrained in cattle trucks for Alexandria, which was reached at 2.15 a.m. the following day, after an uneventful moonlight journey. Detraining at the wharf, we immediately embarked on the good ship *Hororata* (Drooping Vine), of the New Zealand Shipping Company's fleet. She had been specially built for transporting migrants from Britain to the dominions and by reason of her large cabin accommodation, was a particularly comfortable ship. On this voyage she also carried the 31st Battalion and other details, the total approximating 2200 all ranks. Our first line transport and horses were shipped on the *Rhesus*.

Apropos of a dog hunt previously recorded, it is of interest to quote here another dog story which Les Wellings describes as follows:—

"Prior to embarking at Sydney a presentation was made to the band of a two or three weeks' old Australian terrier, which was designated with the honoured name of 'Bobs'. The problem, however, was how to smuggle the presentation aboard the troopship. The difficulty was solved by Bandsman Knight, who stowed away the pup in his large brass band instrument. 'Bobs' shared the sleeping accommodation and meals of the bandsmen and duly landed in Egypt, where he became the regimental pet and a great favourite with all, particularly the Gyppo kids, wherever the battalion was quartered.

"The regimental pet participated with the troops in the hardships and vicissitudes of Egypt, one of his chief delights being to bathe in the cooling waters of the Suez Canal whenever the opportunity occurred. When the battalion was ordered to France the problem again presented itself of devising means of smuggling 'Bobs' on to the troopship, but the strict eye of officialdom defeated the strategy of the bandsmen and the regimental pet was handed over with pangs of sadness to an English regiment stationed in Egypt."

At 4 p.m. on June 16th the *Hororata* moved out into the stream for the usual settling down period. Officers and men were in good heart and apparently without a thought as to what the future might hold in store for them. All were thoroughly glad to leave Egypt with its squalor, heat, sand, flies, and (from their point of view) its poverty-stricken people. The reason for the development of this carefree attitude was perhaps due to the fact that the average man had now reached the point of realising that he was only a cog in an immense machine, and to this fact, accentuated by a further three years of dependence on higher authority, may in part be attributed the long period taken by many members to accustom themselves to the competition inherent in civil life on their demobilisation. Viewing the lights of Alexandria from the decks was a tantalising one, as few on board by reason of the distance of the various camps, had been privileged to visit this historic place. However, much as a few hours' shore leave would have been enjoyed, military expediency prevailed, and it was with a sense of relief that at 7 o'clock the following morning we heard the anchor being raised, and felt the movement of the ship as she headed for the open sea.

A few, no doubt, cast their eyes eastward in the direction of Aboukir Bay and tried to visualise the great defeat which Nelson in 1798 inflicted on the very nation which we were now hastening to aid. It would be difficult to describe the feelings of the Scotsmen as the *Hororata* passed the shoal on which the unlucky *Culloden* grounded. Pride of Empire would probably conflict with pride of race. However, this was no time to indulge in memories of Bonnie Prince Charlie or the happenings of bygone days. The immediate concern of all on board was to prepare against the possibility of submarine attack, the first precaution being to don lifebelts, which all ranks were instructed to wear continually.

Few of us had any idea in which direction we were travelling; sometimes the sun would be seen on our right, and an hour later it would appear on our left, thus showing the zigzagging nature of our course. The fact that we did not sight a single vessel throughout the voyage indicates the unusual route which the ship must have taken.

Although we carried a 4.7-inch gun and practised with it occasionally, our main protection was provided by fast sloops which relieved each other at intervals. These vessels were of a surprising speed, doing up to 28 knots; at times they appeared ahead, then on each flank, and then astern; literally running rings around us. On one occasion the escort disappeared for a couple of hours, quite disconcerting our captain, who was much perturbed at being left so unceremoniously.

In order to meet emergencies and to ward off possible attack, a fully armed party of one officer and fifty other ranks was maintained day and night on the saloon deck, and a party of similar strength in a reserve position just aft the main saloon, where signals could be seen from the bridge on which two officers were stationed. The voyage, however, was uneventful and all ranks were thankful at having avoided the submarine menace, which was taking such deadly toll of our nation's shipping.

While the *Hororata* was the third vessel of our flight to leave Alexandria, she was the first to arrive at Marseilles at about 7 o'clock on a beautiful midsummer evening. As

Lieut. F. A. Butterworth, M.M.

Major I. G. Fullarton, M.C.

Lieut. W. T. Hanlon, M.C.

she threaded her way up the steel-netted harbour we had a magnificent view of the city.

Unfortunately, this was all that the majority, at least of the 30th, were destined to see of it, as some hours later the battalion less "A" Company marched direct to the railway station. On the wharf to greet us was Lieutenant James Chapman, wearing an imposing R.T.O. (Railway Transport Officer) arm-band. Besieged with questions, he gave us some information of recent happenings. Of his stay in the city he writes as follows:—

"As the 30th Battalion representative of the Divisional Advance Party, I arrived at Marseilles some ten days ahead of the first flight of the 5th Division. On the surface the job appeared to be smooth enough, but to carry it out properly proved to be quite a worrying one. We were billeted in various hotels and were later required to make a detailed reconnaissance of all camping and bivouacking areas, routes thereto, and times taken to reach same. Timetables had to be studied and conferences with port and railway authorities were of frequent occurrence. We had to be ready for all emergencies, as sometimes three or four boats came in about the same time. However, there was no hitch and after we had despatched the last of the 33 trains (at the rate of about three per day), which were required to convey the whole of the division, our party followed on. We enjoyed about three-fourths of a day in Paris, and later rejoined our respective units in the neighbourhood at Hazebrouck. Incidentally, after this experience I always seemed to be detailed for the job of battalion entraining and embussing officer, and when later I joined the divisional staff the same task was often allotted me."

Offsetting Jim's implied protest, it would appear that the zeal which he displayed at Marseilles, and which is emphasised in the following letter, must be held responsible for his frequent employment as entraining and embussing officer in the years that followed:—

"Major King,
  5th Division,
  I have the honour to bring to your notice the very smart and disciplined way in which the officers named below have done their duties as Divisional R.T.O's. They are the best that have gone through my hands of all the Divisions, so much so that on one or two occasions, when Base R.T.O's. were ill, I gave them trains to work alone, with very satisfactory results.

  I would ask that their names be brought to the notice of the Headquarters of the Division, in order of merit as written. I would also express to you my formed opinion that the 5th Australian Division has given us, the R.T.. the least trouble of all in all matters. This is due in great measure to your and your assistants' great help and work.

  1. Lieutenant Chapman, 30th Bttn., A.I.F., 8th Brigade.
  2. Lieutenant Stuchberry, 55th Bttn., A.I.F., 14th Brigade.
  3. Captain Harris, 57th Bttn., A.I.F., 15th Brigade.

                                Lieutenant-Colonel A. POPE,
                                                      D.A.D.R.T.
Marseilles.
  2nd July, 1916."

CHAPTER V.

(ARRIVAL IN FRANCE).

"The scene was changed, it was the land of France,
The chosen home of chivalry, the garden of romance."

MUCH as all ranks would have revelled in exploring the cafes, gardens, and promenades of Marseilles and the localities made familiar to those who had read *The Count of Monte Cristo*, this privilege had to be denied to all except "A" Company, which was left behind on guard and other duties. But the cheering crowds, consisting largely of women and children, that lined the streets as we marched behind our band to the railway station, and whose colour, dress, and characteristics generally reminded us of our homes in far-away Australia, compensated to some extent for our inability to remain and avail ourselves of their obvious hospitality.

While few of the officers or men understood the language, there was no mistaking the fervour of the "Vive L'Australies" and other expressions of goodwill towards the A.I.F. It will be realised how welcome these greetings were when it is remembered that we had spent the previous six months in a country of deserts, amid a coloured population alien to us in every respect, whose ideals, mode of living, attire, and thinly veiled hostility we had been glad to leave behind.

The train provided for the 30th consisted of 31 carriages. After what seemed an interminable wait, it moved slowly out of the station, through a tunnel into the darkness, and we commenced our long journey through the heart of France. All hands made themselves as comfortable as possible but, naturally, few were able to sleep. As day dawned (about 4 a.m.) we found ourselves in the neighbourhood of Avignon, bowling along the beautiful Rhone Valley, and were dumbfounded at the glorious panoramas that were continually unfolding themselves before us. "This is a country worth fighting for," "No wonder the French are patriotic," and other appreciative remarks were freely indulged in. As the sun rose the exclamations of delight increased; window seats were much in demand in order to view the countryside, every foot of which appeared to be carrying its wealth of wheat, peas, beans, vines, etc. The red-roofed cottages were models of neatness and each seemed to be surrounded by vegetable and flower patches, the former a mass of greenery, and the latter a blaze of colour. To the right were the terraced, vine-clad hills, to the left the gently flowing river known symbolically as one of the four horses of France.

Travelling almost due north we reached Lyons early in the afternoon. Then, crossing the Rhone, we entered the beautiful valley of the Saone—and so on through Macon, Dijon, Fontainebleau, past the outskirts of Paris, where we obtained a glimpse of the Eiffel Tower and the park lands surrounding the Palace of Versailles, down the valley of the Seine, thence north to Amiens, across the Somme, through the country in which the famous English victories of Crecy and Agincourt were obtained, on to Boulogne, Calais, and finally to our destination in the neighbourhood of Hazebrouck, an important railway junction a few miles from the Belgian border and from the English Channel. Although a cold rain greeted us on detraining, we were glad to exercise our cramped limbs after the continuous journey of three nights and two days.

As previously stated, "A" Company was left at the great seaport on divisional duties, Colonel R. H. Beardsmore, who commanded it at the time, afterwards penned the following account of its experiences.

"As the *Hororata* was approaching the wharf at Mar-

Sgt. A. E. FORBES, M.M.

Sgt. E. C. E. AMPS, D.C.M., M.M.

Coy. Sgt.-Maj. D. M. RUEBEN, D.C.M., M.M., AND BAR

Sgt. D. SMITH, M.M.

ARRIVAL IN FRANCE

seilles the C.O. (Colonel Clark) happened to mention to me that the O.C., 31st Battalion, was rather perturbed at having been asked to leave one of his companies at Marseilles to see the whole division through. I at once remarked that I only wished I could have the refusal of the job. He asked me how long it would take me to get my company ready. I replied, 'Ten minutes at the outside,' with the result that 'A' Company was detailed for the duty.

"Within a few minutes the company disembarked, sentries were posted on the wharf, and the remainder marched to a camp on the environs of the city, within a short distance of the shipping centre.

"The duties of the company were mainly to provide guards at the wharves and the camp, and to regularly patrol the city with the view of picking up any stragglers of the 5th Division. With the able assistance of my second in command (Captain Ray Allen) and the subalterns and N.C.O's., the work was well carried out and the 5th Division safely piloted through Marseilles. Indeed, the whole of the company laid themselves out to show the local authorities what Australians could do, and a day or two before our departure from Marseilles we were inspected by the officer commanding the Base troops and publicly thanked for our services. He paid us the compliment at this inspection of inquiring whether we were picked men from the whole of the division, so well had we behaved and so competently had we carried out our duties.

"One fortunate result of the detail of 'A' Company for this duty was that their O.C. was given a few days' leave to visit Nice. I understand he was the first Australian soldier to dine at the Hotel de Paris at Monte Carlo, where he was royally entertained by a number of English and American visitors. The gaming tables, however, were taboo. The O.C. was by no means the only one of the company who had quite a good time at Marseilles.

"The journey from Marseilles to join the battalion was full of interest, and the local inhabitants at each town most hospitable. The train was hardly an 'express' and the halts along the road were frequent and long. One new experience was the billeting arrangements at the various towns along the route. As a rule, sleeping accommodation consisted of a straw shakedown in the stable of some hotel or *chateau*. Eventually, after four or five days on the train, the company joined the battalion at Jesus Farm, near Sailly."

So pleased was the British Commandant at Marseilles with the work of "A" Company and the behaviour of the 5th Division generally that he wrote the following letter to our G.O.C.:—

Dear General McCay,
    The last details of your Division are gone, and I trust all will reach you safely.

    It gives me very genuine pleasure to be able to tell you that the conduct of the Division during its passage through this place has been exemplary. Notwithstanding the many and varied attractions and temptations of this huge seaport, I am glad to say that not a single case of misbehaviour or lack of discipline has been brought to my notice. It is a record, and one that the Division may be proud of. The officers and men of the Divisional Guard, commanded by Major Beardsmore, performed their duties in a soldier like, firm and tactful manner, and their smartness was very noticeable.

    I am personally indebted to Major King, of your staff, for the very valuable assistance which he in many ways afforded me, and it is a pleasure to tell you so. The good work of the Divisional A.M.L.O's. and R.T.O's. deserves mention also.

    The best of good luck to you and your fine Division.

                    From yours very sincerely,
                        G. F. N. TINLEY, Colonel,
             Commandant, British Base, Marseilles.

Marseilles, 1st July, 1916.

These econiums do not occasion surprise when it is remembered that among the personnel were such sterling characters as Sid Coleman, Bill Claydon, Harry Cann, Bob Case, Fred Eltis, Stan Evans, Geoff. Evans, Wally Godwin, George Gillingham, Bob Goldie, Bill Hyden,

ARRIVAL IN FRANCE

Freddy Hale, Frank Hanley, Eric Johanssen, Syd. Jordan, Billy Lethbridge, Tom McCann, Mal. McGraw, Herb. McCoy, Ted Muggeridge, Roy Norris, Frank Orth, Fred. Pleass, Bill Perry, Harry Rogers, Tosh Ridley, Vic. Smith, Dave Story, Jim Storey, Ted Woods, Jim Massey, Jack Spencer, Bob Dunbar, Tom Slaughter, Artie Burns, Charrie Barnfield, Fred Millwood, Jack Allan, Alex. Brien, Fred. Batten, George Goode, Jack Christian, Dick Hall, Dave Kemp, Snowy Lawson, Dave Lynch, Ted Mitchell, Pansy McBride, Bill Parker, Frank Ramus, Dave Scott, Jack Urquart, Dug. Vincent, Oscar Vincent and Fred. Harris.

But to return to the main part of the battalion, which on detraining at Steenbecque, marched to the neighbourhood of Morbecque, a prosperous farming district on rising ground, some two miles from Hazebrouck. Here commenced our long experience of what is described as "billeting" in one of the military manuals, a study of which gives one the impression that small groups of men are accommodated in the homes of the inhabitants with whom they share the amenities and comforts of an ordinary household.

When nearing the end of our stay in Egypt we had been surfeited with lectures on the necessity for observing correct deportment and behaviour while in billets, thus giving to the unsophisticated a vision of sheets, pillows, and other homely surroundings. These pleasant contemplations were rudely shattered when it was found that the accommodation provided usually consisted of either a barn, loft, shed, outhouse, or abandoned building. However, as this part of the country had not up to this period suffered from the effects of artillery bombardment, the battalion was soon comfortably distributed by half-companies or smaller groups in the substantial outbuildings of some eighteen farms. Straw was plentiful, rations were good, *vin blanc, vin rouge,* rum, milk, and other creature comforts were available—so what more could an Australian soldier need? Furthermore, the facilities for free expression which a barn afforded were much preferable to the circumscribed conditions of the most comfortable household. For a few hours after settling down all hands appeared to be busy writing home and, in consequence, the censor had a hectic time reading the various impressions which had formed during the long journey from the south. It was not permitted to give the address of our location, but letters could be headed "Somewhere in France." One wily individual—clearly a naval man—endeavoured to get over this difficulty by adding an inconspicuous postscript in which he gave his position as 50.44 N., 2.31 E., but the obliterating pencil came down heavily upon it and ruined an effort which deserved a better fate.

Northern France, being very fertile, the landscape in every direction is dotted with intensely cultivated farms, set amid a network of hedged lanes. Along these the troops loved to ramble during the long evenings, oblivious and perhaps careless as to what the future held in store for them. Twenty miles away across the plain, beyond Armentieres, could be seen the reflection of flares, rockets, incendiary shells, etc., while the sound of the guns belching out their evening "hate" was heard distinctly.

The farm buildings of France and Flanders are usually erected on the sides and ends of an oblong, and consist of the living rooms, floored with brick or tiles, an attic, roofed with straw thatch from 9 to 12 inches thick, stables, cow sheds, calf pens, pig sties, fowl roosts, dairy, hay and corn sheds, and accommodation for agricultural implements, etc. In the centre of the oblong is a pit, perhaps 70 feet long by 30 feet wide and 3 feet deep, into which every conceivable particle of animal and house refuse is thrown and left to "mature" until the early spring, when the unsavoury mess is carted to the fields and becomes valuable fertiliser. These apparently insanitary surroundings surprised us, but evidently the climate is such that no ill-effects are felt by the inhabitants. "Waste not, want not," appears to be their slogan. At one billet "madame" even objected to the troops walking on the grass, which she said was wanted for the cows—a request that was more honoured in the breach than in its observance.

Judged by Australian standards, the food of the French country folk was of an extremely simple and meagre nature, and their only recreation appeared to be attendance at church on Sundays. Newspapers, books, musical instruments, and other home amenities were almost non-existent. Their deeply rooted religious convictions were exemplified by the numerous wayside shrines and crucifixes situated in the acute angles of converging lanes and roads.

As all the eligible men were serving with the colours, the farms were being worked by old men, women and boys, who laboured almost continuously in the fields from daylight to dark—a matter of from 12 to 16 hours. After parades, therefore, and during the long evenings khaki clad figures were to be seen hoeing, carrying hay for the animals, milking cows, drawing water from the wells, and in various ways assisting the womenfolk of the farms. Wine and other liquors were, legally or otherwise, on sale at most of the billets, but surprisingly little drunkenness occurred. It is a noteworthy fact that up to this time, and for a few months later, a large proportion of the men in the battalion were abstainers, while most of the others were moderate drinkers. In this respect Colonel Clark set an example which was largely followed by all ranks until the awful conditions of the ensuing winter on the Somme necessitated a more general acceptance of the rum issue.

In their spare time also many of the troops devoted themselves to the rather pleasant task of substituting the smattering of Arabic which they had acquired in Egypt (and with which they amused and puzzled the farm children) for a working knowledge of colloquial French. Miles had to be reduced to kilometres, the relative values of the franc and English money overcome, as also the intricacies of note issues, which while current in one district would be valueless in others.

Training was principally confined to route marches along hard and, in places, cobbled roads, which differed widely from the soft sand of Egypt. One of these excursions was made to the outskirts of historic Cassel, the most elevated town in Flanders, and at that time the headquarters of the Second British Army, which was commanded by the veteran General Plumer. Subsequent events were to prove that a longer period should have been devoted to route marching, in order to harden both officers and men.

Lectures and demonstrations were also given in the use of the P.H. gas helmet, and all ranks were practised in the use of goggles to combat tear gas, while a course of musketry was carried out on a miniature range which had been erected near Morbecque. It was here that we made our first acquaintance with the steel helmet, which at first caused so many headaches but subsequently saved so many lives. The variety of other purposes for which the old "tin hat" was used, such as food receptacle, frying pan, etc., will be remembered by all who served in France.

To ensure that all ranks were completely equipped, a kit inspection was held at which the principal deficiencies were found to consist of badges, buttons, colour patches, etc., but as the inspecting officers had themselves experienced the wiles and blandishments of souvenir-hunting mademoiselles, the reason for these "losses" was not absolutely insisted upon.

One morning the transport officer received a shock when, on waking, he discovered that some horses which he had permitted to be turned loose in a small paddock, had completely stripped between twenty to thirty valuable young trees of their bark from the ground up to as high as they could reach. Whether the trees survived or what compensation was paid to the owner is not known, but the "ringbarkers" were not again privileged to leave their lines.

Our stay in this neighbourhood, from June 29th to July 8th, came to an end all too soon, for all ranks were thoroughly enjoying their association with the French peasants. However, as we had now served for almost twelve months without striking a blow at the enemy, very few regretted that the time had arrived for us to justify our existence as a unit of the A.I.F., although we had no inkling of the disaster which was to overtake all three brigades of the 5th Division before the end of the next fortnight.

CHAPTER VI.

(THE MOVE TO BOIS GRENIER).

ON the morning of July 8th billets were vacated and inspected—the latter a very necessary precaution in order to combat extortionate claims for compensation—and we began our move towards the front area. Each unit of the brigade proceeded independently to the starting point, in the long straggling main street of Morbecque. Although the four battalions had camped as a single formation on the Egyptian desert and had co-operated in brigade manoeuvres, this was the first occasion on which the whole brigade participated in a route march under service conditions.

As the troops had been billeted over a widely scattered area, much delay occurred in starting, the earlier arrivals having to wait on the uneven *pave* for upwards of half-an-hour. The weather was hot, the humidity high, and the men overloaded. The official historian of the A.I.F. records that in one battalion (the 29th) each man carried a weight of 70 lbs., and that the length of its march was nineteen miles.

Portions of the route traversed were paved with stone cubes, which in shape and size resemble a baker's tinned loaf and present a very uneven surface. Other parts consisted of partially rounded water-worn stones, cemented together, which are even worse than the *pave* to walk upon.

General Tivey and his staff did their best to nurse the brigade along, but the weight of the packs, the heat, and the unfamiliar roads proved too much for a large number of men, who commenced to fall out, first singly, and later

THE MOVE TO BOIS GRENIER

in larger groups up to whole sections. The men of the 30th hung on determinedly, but eventually quite a number had to give in. The second-in-command, Major Holford, who brought up the rear, had a busy time issuing fall-out permits to those affected, but his supply of them, and also his temper, eventually gave out, and the stragglers were left to plod along as best they could. Transport waggons relieved the situation to some extent by carrying the packs and blankets of the most distressful cases, but others, left to their own devices, completed the journey without assistance. The brigade was thus considerably disorganised before reaching its destination, having quite lost the cohesion indispensable to a fighting unit. This, however, was a common experience of all new formations unused to the cobble-roads.

A diversion, which caused a little excitement and amusement to those not immediately affected, was the bolting of a mare ("Calamity Kate") attached to a mess cart, and the elbowing of a number of men into a slimy ditch about three feet deep.

Among those whose memories of this march are still vivid is Pay-Sergeant E. J. Tysoe, who has in his possession the document (Army Form LL.456) charging him with "falling out of the ranks without permission," a most heinous offence for an N.C.O., and for which he was "severely reprimanded" the following day by the C.O.

On arrival at Estaires, the battalion was billeted in a group of old school buildings near the centre of the town, and, although the brick and concrete floors were broken and uneven, the men, after a wash and a hot meal from the "cookers", which had been simmering during the journey, soon settled down and made themselves as comfortable as possible. Such is the recuperative power of youth, that after a rest most of the troops forgot the hardships of the march, and were soon busily engaged in exploring the avenues of amusement which the little town afforded;

naturally, the *estaminet* keepers came in for quite a lot of attention.

Estaires had not up to this time been heavily shelled, and the inhabitants were following their ordinary avocations as though nothing of an extraordinary nature was happening a few miles away.

A feature of the place was the market-square, which contained a covered well from which the people—mostly housewives—drew their daily supplies of water. Although the use of the pump handle was on the principle of "first come, first served," many of the women willingly gave up their places in the queue to the troops who, not to be outdone, were often heard gallantly remarking, *"Apres vous,* Madame," much to the amusement and satisfaction of all concerned.

On the morning of July 9th the brigade resumed its march to Erquinghem. Little could be seen of the effects of the previous day's march. The brigadier, occupying a point of vantage along the road, eyed his whole command as it swung past him. The 30th reached its billets, at Jesus Farm, in good order about 3 p.m.

Our billets, which consisted of a number of huts that gave evidence of having sheltered many bodies of troops, were situated on the northern bank of the River Lys, a considerable stream, more in the nature of a canal, which flows in a north-easterly direction into Belgium and eventually *viâ* the Scheldt, reaches the sea at Antwerp. As the railway lines converging on Armentières had long ceased to function, this canal was used by large numbers of barges conveying army stores, road-making material, and the requirements of the civilian population generally. On the opposite side of the river were the villages of Sailly, Bac St. Maur, and Erquinghem, all of them still largely occupied by civilians who were apparently unconcerned at the proximity of the enemy. Almost every one of their buildings showed signs of damage from hostile shelling, while doors and windows facing the east were barricaded with sand-

THE MOVE TO BOIS GRENIER

bags. As the area was under observation from enemy balloons, which could be seen hovering between Armentières and Lille, movement in daylight had to be reduced to a minimum, and in consequence our men, who usually wandered round in search of novelty, were obliged to spend the daylight hours under cover. The time, however, passed quickly, as all ranks, if not resting after the march, were busily engaged in overhauling gas helmets, cleaning arms and equipment, and removing, cleaning, and replacing in chargers the 120 rounds of ammunition which each man carried. Especially busy were the Lewis gun sections and signallers.

Some days before the battalion left Morbecque the commanders of "B" "C" and "D" Companies—Captain Street, Major Purser, and Captain Cheeseman—were sent up to the front line to become acquainted with local conditions. Purser, writing of their experiences, says:—

"As I was leaving, Major Holford came from his bedroom to wish me 'good-bye' and said, 'We may never meet again, so we will have a stirrup cup before you go.' I replied, 'Well, you are a Job's comforter,' but helped him to dispose of the contents of the bottle of champagne he produced.

"At Brigade H.Q. we boarded an ex-London omnibus along with the company commanders of 29th Battalion, and travelled through country quite different to any we had seen before. We had an excellent lunch in one of the towns *en route*. A couple of hours later the 'bus stopped, and Captain Tracy (29th Bn.), who was riding alongside the driver, asked me to come down from the upper deck. He had ascertained from the driver that our destination was a couple of miles distant, but that we would not be able to go right there by 'bus, as the driver's instructions were that he was not to leave the main road. The driver, however, said he would depart from those instructions if I, as senior officer present, would order him to do so. I promptly gave the necessary order, for I did not relish the idea of carrying my valise for a couple of miles (we had no batmen with us), and, besides, why walk when we had a perfectly good 'bus to ride in?

"Because the members of a nearby working party of 'Diggers' had found it convenient to hang their jackets on a notice board, thereby hiding its wording, we passed the point beyond which vehicular traffic was not supposed to proceed. We were wondering just how much further we had to go when I noticed a rope of telephone wires across the road and, thinking they would just about catch the heads of those of us on the upper deck, shouted 'Look out for the wires!' and ducked my head. Unfortunately, I had misjudged their height; they were two or three inches too low to clear the 'bus, which tore them down. We had arrived at 4th Brigade H.Q.

"The brigade major came and asked whether we had not seen the beforementioned notice, pointing out that we had severed telephone communication between Brigade H.Q. and its battalions, and that the arrival of our 'bus might result in Brigade H.Q. receiving the attention of the enemy's artillery. He was really very nice about it, and I told him why we had not seen what the notice board indicated. He agreed with me that, as it was rather foggy and visibility very poor, it was improbable that our arrival had been noticed on the other side of No-Man's Land. Meantime, Captain Cheeseman (who had been a signal officer in the C.M.F.) had quickly repaired the telephone wires. So that was that.

"Guides took us to the front-line battalions, and by the evening we of the 30th Battalion found ourselves attached to different companies of the 14th Battalion in the rat-infested front line, which consisted not of trenches, but of sandbag breastworks.

"A week later we went back to our battalion, which was then at Jesus Farm, told our companies what it was necessary for them to know, and the same evening returned to the line with our C.Q.M.S's., signallers, and others. The next

THE MOVE TO BOIS GRENIER

night the 14th Battalion was partially relieved by two platoons from each of our companies, and on the following night, July 11th, we relieved the remainder of that battalion and command of the sector passed to Colonel Clark."

The reason for spreading the relief over two nights was to give the first half of the incoming troops an opportunity of mingling in the line for twenty-four hours with parts of the outgoing battalion. This enabled the newcomers to obtain a thorough knowledge of the sector, to ascertain (among other things) the position of the flanking troops, the width of No-Man's Land, particulars of the opposing Germans, and spots made dangerous by snipers, and also to take over unhurriedly the necessary trench-stores, maps, standing orders, etc.

The first night of the relief was beautifully fine, and much subdued excitement was noticeable as the selected platoons fell in for their final inspection. Those who were to remain behind for another day lounged about on the outskirts of the parade ground, freely indulging in caustic remarks at the expense of those in the ranks. Eventually all was ready and the column, led by the C.O., with the regulation distance between companies, marched off in the direction of the bridge over the Lys at Erquinghem.

Moving up to the line at night may on first sight appear to be a simple enough matter, but with every road and lane crowded with men and vehicles, hold-ups and jams occur which upset the most carefully prepared plans. Our first compulsory halt occurred immediately on reaching the main road leading to Armentiers, where our way was barred, first by a long supply column going east and, as soon as it had passed, by another moving in the opposite direction. The next delay took place some twenty minutes later when a brigade officer met us and advised Colonel Clark to observe a distance of fifty yards between platoons with a view to minimising possible casualties.

Soon we stumbled over a long-disused railway line almost entirely hidden in long grass and weeds, then crossed a small canal (misnamed the "River" Laies), and went on past the eastern edge of the ruined village of Bois Grenier. After several twists and turns we eventually reached what appeared to be a hole in a hedge, but was actually the beginning of a long, winding, duckboarded communication trench known as "Safety Alley" by which, after many halts and stoppages, we were led to the front line.

As the company commanders had already acquainted themselves with the details of the position and of the various support and reserve lines, no time was lost in effecting the relief. The outgoing half of the 14th Battalion was naturally anxious to get away, while our men were intensely interested in the new phase of service opening before them. The following day—during which the position was occupied by half of each unit—the men of the 14th readily passed on to our people the result of their experiences in the sector. Needless to say, much friendly banter was indulged in. That night Major Holford brought in the remainder of the 30th, and, after our Colonel Clark had taken over the defence scheme, maps, etc., from the C.O. of the 14th (Lieutenant-Colonel Dare) the relief was completed and we were at long last facing the enemy, in the famous "nursery" of the British front.

One reason for the quietude of the Bois Grenier sector (according to the Official History, Vol. III., p. 93) was the desire of the British to refrain as far as possible from damaging the great city of Lille or causing harm to its civil inhabitants. "Moreover, the nature of the country, intersected with ditches and hedges, was unfavourable for active operations. The line had consequently become very quiet, the Germans, by a sort of tacit agreement, seldom shelling the main part of Armentières—although it lay within a mile and a half of the trenches—so long as the British spared the city and environs of Lille." All hands consequently derived a certain amount of satisfaction from the knowledge that they were not likely to meet their

THE MOVE TO BOIS GRENIER

opponents hand to hand before familiarising themselves with front-line conditions.

We held about 1,000 yards of the 400 mile line which stretched from the North Sea to Switzerland. The frontage was divided equally between "B", "C", and "D" Companies, each having three platoons in the front line and one in support. "A" Company—which had arrived from Marseilles the previous day—garrisoned the reserve trench 300 yards in rear. On our right flank was the 29th Battalion, on our left the 2nd Battalion of the New Zealand Rifle Brigade.

On the morning after the relief, great was the temptation by those who were not on sentry duty to take a peep over the sandbagged parapet and it was not long before a man was shot in the forehead and the cry went up for stretcher bearers. Fortunately the damage was not serious, as the bullet, having been deflected, emerged somewhere behind his right ear, and as he was being carried away to the aid post he shouted, "Are we downhearted?" The hearty response from his mates can well be imagined. The wag of his section could not, of course, help referring to Nature's habit of compensating lack of brains by a thick skull.

Such a practical demonstration of the enemy's watchfulness and the efficiency of his snipers, however, had a salutary effect and did much to ensure the carrying out of instructions, and from this time onwards no one was ashamed to bend his back or quicken his pace when passing dangerous spots.

While the sector was a comparatively quiet one, machine-gun fire went on almost continuously, particularly on the communication trenches during the hours of darkness when rations and stores were being sent forward. Shrapnel had also to be contended with, and occasionally 5.9-inch shells played havoc with our parapets. The "heavies", however, were directed chiefly against artillery positions and dumps in the back areas, and as they passed overhead their whine could be distinctly heard, as could sometimes the sound of their explosion. Incidentally, most of the cooking was done in the front line and, as the enemy was apparently doing the same, the resultant smoke appeared to go unnoticed.

No-Man's Land was about 300 yards wide on our front, a desolate wilderness of rank grass, barbed-wire, and splintered trees. At night it became a "fairyland" by reason of the sheaves of flares which each side sent up with a view to detecting raids or the activities of patrolling parties. We were obliged to admit that the enemy fireworks were superior to ours. One disagreeable feature was the presence of thousands of large grey rats, which played havoc with equipment, clothing, and food. They were extremely bold, and for a time the troops derived a certain amount of pleasure in bayoneting them, but their numbers were so great that the sport soon became nauseating and was discontinued.

On the night of July 16th we handed over the sector to the 3rd Battalion, N.Z. Rifle Brigade, and moved out without incident to the village of Fleurbaix.

During our four-day stay in the "nursery" we had two men killed and fifteen wounded, among the latter being Lieutenant Hext.

In view of the fact that we had previously transferred Captain Roy Mulvey and a number of our best men to the newly formed 8th Light Trench Mortar Battery, it may be appropriate here to refer to their first experience of front-line warfare, which occurred in the Bois Grenier sector at this period. The following account from Captain A. D. Ellis's history of the 5th Division applies equally to all three batteries of the division:—

"The first shoot of the newly-formed L.T.M.B.," he says, "deserves to be chronicled. The front line infantry watched their enthusiastic preparations with a good deal of dubious curiosity. The instructions to the gun crews were to get off their ten rounds as quickly as they could and to make back to the support line with all possible haste. They

Colonel C. J. HOLFORD, V.D.

Capt. RAY A. M. ALLEN, M.C.

carried out their programme to perfection. 'They issued Fritz his ration,' said an infantryman who watched Lieut. Scurry's first operation on the 15th Brigade front. 'Ten in the air and they were half-way down Pinney's Avenue before the first one burst. Then Fritz issued his ration and we got it.' On the Battery's next arrival in the front line the infantry were not slow to remind them of their last performance. They were dubbed 'The Shoot and Scatter Mob', 'The Imshi Artillery', 'The Stovepipe Howitzers', 'The Crab Drawers', and 'The Duckboard Harriers'. Despite this friendly banter, the infantry was quick to recognise both the extraordinary value of the L.T.M. as an offensive weapon, and the gallantry of the officers and men of the various batteries. The Stokes mortar soon grew to be one of the most valued arms of the division, as well as one most cordially hated by the enemy, and before long this arm of the service took rank and precedence as one of the most elite of the several 'Suicide Clubs' of the army."

The battalion spent the night of July 16th-17th at Fleurbaix, but as the village for some weeks had been continuously shelled by the enemy, the billets were in a precarious condition. Most of the troops sheltered in what had once been a large school, the remainder occupying adjacent buildings. Numbers of men, however, although light rain was falling, preferred to camp in the open spaces, away from the danger of falling bricks and masonry. Enemy shelling caused a few casualties, and it was with a feeling of relief that the battalion was next day ordered to move to a reserve position in the Rue-de-Quesne, a country road some miles in rear, bordering farms still being cultivated by their owners. Here we were comfortably billeted for the next three days, during which the companies were employed in carrying large quantities of ammunition, wire, Mills' bombs, duckboards, sandbags, picks, shovels, and various other articles to large dumps that were being specially formed behind the front line.

During these early days in Flanders much excitement was caused by the alleged activities of spies. Farmers were continually being suspected of signalling to the enemy, and their every movement was interpreted as having some baneful significance. For example, when one of them drove a black horse in the morning and a brown one in the afternoon, the change was supposed to convey some mysterious message to our opponents.

The moving from one field to another of peculiarly coloured cows was also construed as a message-bearing agency. The gunners of one battery, whose position was shelled, observed that a farmer working in a nearby field had a white horse in his plough-team. That night the gunners visited the farmers' stable and stained the horse with permanganate of potash. Clothes lines, too, were scrutinised with more than usual interest, the number of articles suspended in the breeze supposedly corresponding with various codes of which the good housewife and the enemy alone held the keys.

The real truth, of course, was that the enemy, occupying the higher ground of Aubers Ridge and with observers in the towers of the village churches and in stationary balloons, could easily see every movement. Our men, so prone to wander round rather carelessly at first, and to assemble in groups in full view of these observers, thus largely contributed to the locating of crowded billets and their subsequent shelling.

An amusing incident was the scattering of a "two-up" school, which at first had assembled in the shelter of some trees. The lower branches, however, interfered with the free action of the tossed pennies, so the operators and the increasing circle of spectators moved by degrees into the open. Here they were spotted by the enemy who, with a well-directed shot, sent all hands scurrying for shelter.

It was here that our Pioneer Sergeant came into conflict with an economical housewife, who could not understand why men of his sanitary squad buried matter which, in her

THE MOVE TO BOIS GRENIER

opinion, should have been conserved for the enrichment of the land, instead of being deposited in a pit some two or more feet deep. The sergeant tried to explain the Army point of view on these matters, but the lady was unconvinced and ended the discussion by shouting the French equivalent of "Waste, waste, waste!"

CHAPTER VII.

THE BATTLE OF FROMELLES.

THE first definite information as to what lay ahead of us —a full dress attack on the German line—was the receipt, on July 16th, of 8th Brigade Order, No 23. It is unnecessary here to quote the order in full, since the following extracts give the vital details:

"(1) With the object of preventing the enemy drawing troops from his Front, offensive preparations are to be carried out by the troops of 11th Corps and 2nd Anzac Corps, under the command of G.O.C. 11th Corps (General Sir Richard Haking)."

"(2) The 61st Division (British) and 5th Australian Division will capture and hold the German Front Line and support trenches along the front opposite our trenches from the Fauquissat-Tilleloy Road to south of Cordonnerie Farm."

"(3) Each brigade will attack with two assaulting battalions and two battalions in reserve. The two reserve battalions in each brigade will be at the disposal of the divisional commander and will assemble within the brigade sector as follows:—30th Battalion on the line Rue de Quesne; 29th Battalion on line Rue de Quesnoy."

"(4) The brigade will move into position as follows:—31st and 32nd Battalions, each one company less one platoon, in the front line. One platoon from each of above companies in 70 yards (support) line. Remainder of 31st and 32nd in 300 yards (reserve) line."

"(5) The method of attack will be: Each battalion of the assaulting battalions will have two companies in the

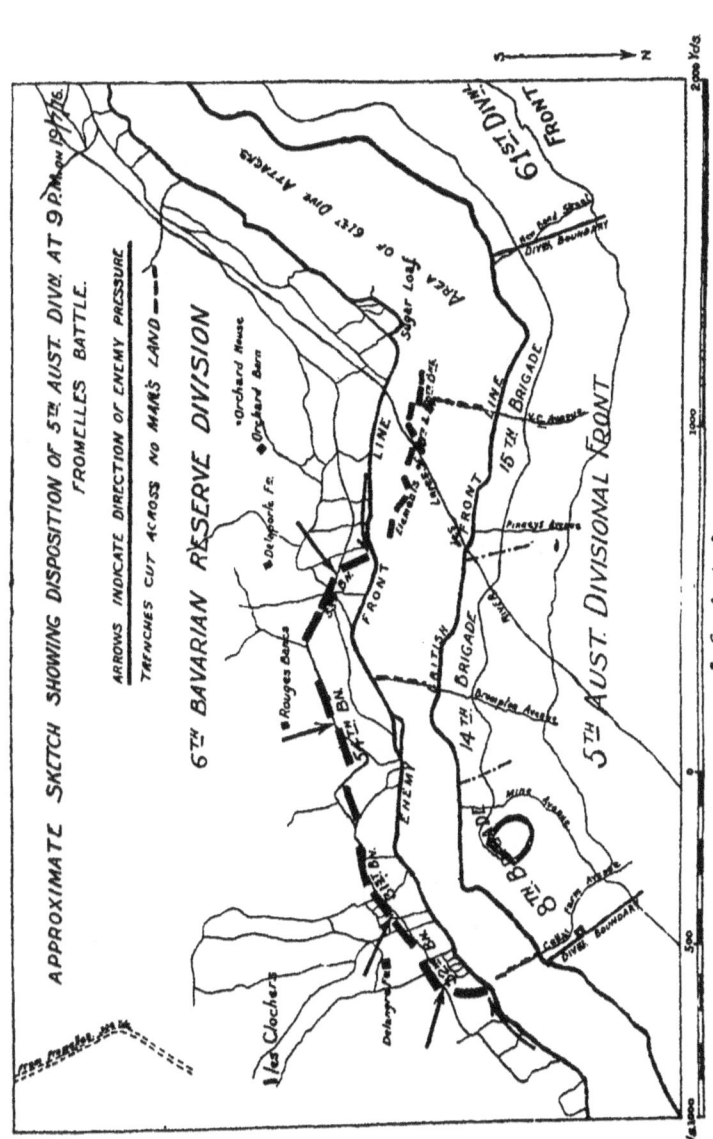

SKETCH SHOWING DISPOSITION OF 5TH AUSTRALIAN DIVISION AT FROMELLES BATTLE.
(Reproduced from "The Story of the Fifth Australian Division" by permission of Captain A. D. Ellis, M.C.)

THE BATTLE OF FROMELLES 69

first and second waves, and two companies in the 3rd and 4th waves. Companies distributed in depth—that is, two platoons in front and two platoons of same company in rear."

"(6) A little before the bombardment of enemy parapet finally lifts, (remember, it will lift to support trenches and return to parapet several times), the 1st and 2nd waves will cross our parapet and take up a position in No-Man's Land, as near as possible to enemy wire with an interval between sections. One wave to go through enemy wire before next wave reaches it, unless front wave breaks up."

"(7) One company of the 30th Battalion, assisted by 8th Field Company Engineers, will carry out the special duty which has been allotted to them after the 4th wave has cleared our parapet."

"(8) During the last phase of intense bombardment, the infantry of 1st and 2nd waves will deploy into No-Man's Land, as near as possible to the enemy, and will assault immediately the artillery fire lifts, which will be at 7 p.m."

"(9) The infantry will indicate their positions to the Flying Corps at 8 and 9 p.m. by mirrors, flares and ground sheets. Every work in the enemy first line system is to be taken, but no troops are on any account whatever to go beyond that line. See that the communication trenches leading from the enemy first line are not mistaken for portion of his front line."

"(10) C.O.'s will detail special parties to construct covered communications back from the captured trenches, which must be done as quickly as possible."

"(11) Each man is to carry 150 rounds of ammunition, 2 bombs, and 2 sandbags. A pick and shovel, one each per three men, will also be carried."

Such were our orders for the "feint" which afterwards became known as the Battle of Fromelles, the first major engagement of the A.I.F. in France, and the most ill conceived in its annals. At the time we were blissfully ignorant of the tragedies which had befallen British troops at this spot on May 9th and September 25th, 1915, and it is more than likely that our divisional and brigade commanders were equally unaware of the facts concerning those reverses.

The London *Times* in a leading article dated May 14th, 1915, referring to the disaster which overwhelmed the 8th Division five days previously, stated "British soldiers died in vain on Aubers Ridge on Sunday because more shells were needed." Naturally The *Times* did not add that the losses on this occasion were 192 officers and 4,490 men. The British Official Historian records this failure as being due to three causes—

(1) Strength of German defences and clever concealment of machine guns.

(2) British lack of sufficient shells of large calibre to deal with such defences.

(3) Bad gun ammunition.

It may be noted here that the 8th Division, which made the assault, was covered by 192 guns on a 1400-yard front. On 19th July, 1916, the 5th Australian Division attacking on a 2000 yards frontage had the support of 176 guns and 20 trench mortars. The calibres of the artillery on each occasion were much the same.

In the second attack, on September 25th, the 8th Division attacked south-east of Bois Grenier, penetrating the German line about Le Bridoux. A similar feint was made south of the Sugar-loaf salient by an Indian Division and the 60th (British) Infantry Brigade. In both cases the attackers, after holding for a time a sector of the enemy's line, were partly surrounded and lost a number of men killed or captured. The casualties of the 60th Brigade (which was to protect the left flank of the ill-fated attack) were 11 officers and 391 men.

The Australian Official Historian (Dr. Bean) says: "By the time when the Australians entered the line, the story of these operations had been almost completely forgotten; it remained only in the vague rumour that, quiet as the sector

THE BATTLE OF FROMELLES

now was, certain famous English regiments spoke of it with dreadful memories of some futile and tragic attack."

The foregoing serves to indicate the precarious nature of the enterprise thus allotted to the 61st and 5th Divisions, and to induce one to speculate on the reasons actuating the higher authorities in undertaking it. The chief reason put forward was that it would pin down some enemy units which might otherwise be moved to the Somme battlefield. In that case surely an artillery demonstration would have sufficed, and some thousands of British and Australian lives been saved.

It was only after twelve days of procrastination on the part of the higher commanders that the attack had been definitely ordered. Commenting on this, Dr. Bean scathingly remarks (Vol. III., p. 350):

"Suggested first by Haking as a feint attack; then by Plumer (the commander of the Second British Army) as part of a victorious advance; rejected by Monro (First Army) in favour of attack elsewhere; put forward again by G.H.Q. as a 'purely artillery' demonstration; ordered as a demonstration but with an infantry operation added, according to Haking's plan and through his emphatic advocacy; almost cancelled—through weather and the doubts of G.H.Q.—and finally reinstated by Haig, apparently as an urgent demonstration — such were the changes of form through which the plans of this ill-fated operation had successively passed."

The artillery finally allotted to the 5th Division, began registering on the enemy parapets and wire-entanglements two days beforehand, but—due to foggy weather, the inadequate number of guns, and lack of experience on the part of the majority of the Australian gunners—the result was far from satisfactory. The divisional trench mortar batteries had been in existence for no more than two weeks, while a large portion of the artillery personnel had been but recently transferred from the infantry. There is therefore little cause for wonderment at the erratic shooting of some of the guns, and it is easy to realise that numbers of our men dreaded the effects of our own artillery-fire to a greater extent than that of the enemy. Quite a number of casualties thus occurred, the most notable perhaps being the destruction of a party of the 8th Field Company, Engineers, who were engaged in cutting a sally-port through our own parapet. The losses of the 8th Brigade in this respect were greater than those in the other units by reason of the fact that its line was only 130 yards distant from the German parapet, whereas to the right No-Man's Land gradually widened until, opposite the Sugar-loaf salient, the opposing lines were as much as 420 yards apart.

The morning of July 19th gave promise of a clear midsummer's day. The main artillery bombardment commenced at 11 a.m. and continued with varying intensity for seven hours, which was considered sufficient to smash the enemy parapets and flatten out his wire. Our artillery certainly did much damage to the former, and our men were much elated at seeing the sandbags being ripped to pieces and the fragments thrown into the air, but they little knew of the deep concrete dug-outs and electrically-lit galleries which sheltered the enemy while his surface works were being shattered. Moreover, large areas of wire entanglement remained intact, particularly in front of the Sugar-loaf. At four definite periods—3.25, 4.4, 4.29, and 5.20 p.m.—the guns lengthened their range for periods varying from four to eleven minutes, during which the infantry officers in the front line sounded their whistles, and the men waved their fixed bayonets above the parapets and thrust forth dummy figures. The object was to give the enemy the impression that an attack was about to be made, and thus cause him to reoccupy his fire-steps, our artillery suddenly dropping back to its former range in the hope of catching him unawares and thus inflicting heavy casualties. It is now generally accepted that these ruses were of too transparent a nature to have much effect, and probably caused the Germans more amusement than anxiety.

THE BATTLE OF FROMELLES

In the meantime, the 30th Battalion, after two days of much needed rest in billets in the Rue de Quesne, had come forward, eager and anxious to give of its best. The quartermaster had been more liberal than usual in the matter of breakfast, and the familiar army legend, "The unconsumed portion of the day's rations will be carried in the haversack," was on this occasion a reality. For once at least, the orderly officer had received no complaints.

The movement to the front through the various saps and communication trenches, and in some cases over the open ground, was a slow process, and was much hampered by stretcher-parties bearing wounded men to the rear, casualties becoming heavy from the time when the intensification of the bombardment commenced at 11 a.m. The enemy had already guessed that we were massing for an attack, and in consequence concentrated the fire of his guns on our front line systems. As our artillery were doing precisely the same to his line, little or no counter-battery work was being undertaken by either side, hence the trivial losses sustained by our gunners during the battle.

In accordance with the orders issued, the attacking battalions of our brigade were formed into four waves, each consisting of approximately 400 men. Some units moved out into No-Man's Land through specially cut sally-ports, but most of them over the parapet. Each wave suffered severely at the moment of deployment; in the case of the 31st Battalion the initial loss was so great that the last two waves had to be amalgamated.

The attack commenced at 5.45 p.m. Each brigade had two battalions in the front line, another to carry stores across No-Man's Land, and the fourth in reserve. The 8th Brigade was on the left of the 5th Division's front, the 15th Brigade on the right and the 14th Brigade in the centre, each occupying about 650 yards. The 61st Division attacked on the right of the 15th Brigade.

While the part played by the British troops was much criticised at the time (the survivors were back in their original front lines by 9 p.m.), it must be remembered that their physique was, generally speaking, much poorer than ours, drafts of their best men having been sent to reinforce other units on the Somme; moreover, the strength of their battalions was only about 600, the frontage of their attack was slightly wider than that of the 5th Division, and their losses were considerable.

The retirement of the British Brigade (the 184th) naturally had a fatal influence on General Elliott's 15th Brigade. When subjected to unrestrained fire from the deadly sugar-loaf salient, this fine unit, containing many Gallipoli veterans, simply melted away, the remnants being withdrawn from No-Man's Land about midnight.

The 14th Brigade (Colonel Pope) succeeded in breaking the enemy front, and subsequently reached the whereabouts of its objective, which, according to divisional orders, was the supporting trenches of the enemy front-line system. It was soon found that these defences did not exist and the leaders were confronted with a series of water-logged ditches partially concealed by rank grass, and apparently running in all directions. The losses were heavy, but, after almost superhuman efforts, the men of the 14th Brigade managed to build up something in the nature of a breastwork. Here they remained, fighting hard, until 7 o'clock the following morning, when, due to the withdrawal of the troops on their flanks, they were compelled to retire. The covering of their retirement by a gallant band of the 55th Battalion under Captain Gibbins is one of the epics of the whole war.

The 8th Brigade, like the 15th, suffered very much from flanking fire throughout the operation. The Oxford and Bucks Light Infantry (60th Brigade), holding the trench system on the left of the 8th Brigade, occupied their firesteps all night and kept up a practically continuous fire in their endeavour to keep down the heads of the enemy. Their efforts, however, were of little avail, and did not

THE BATTLE OF FROMELLES

prevent the Germans from moving laterally along their deep concrete trenches and attacking our flank.

The first wave crossed our parapet at 5.58 p.m., followed at intervals by the second and succeeding waves, and after many casualties in No-Man's Land, finally reached and occupied the German front line. It is true that the surface works gave evidence of the devastating effect of our artillery fire, but a superficial inspection of his line revealed the existence of numerous concrete-lined galleries and shelters which had not been damaged to any extent. All were fitted with electric light and the various compartments had been kept dry by electrically driven pumps. The contrast with our exposed and comparatively flimsy earthworks was most marked, but it has to be remembered that, while the idea of the German was to hold all he had won, ours was to drive him back eventually to his own country.

Beyond the front line, however, the 8th Brigade's attacking troops, like those of the 14th Brigade, to their consternation could find no rear defences. What was shown on their maps as a supporting system of trenches some 150 yards away was found to be merely a series of open ditches partially concealed by long grass and containing from one to two feet of water. It soon became apparent that the air-photographs had not been properly studied by the higher staffs, with the result that the hastily prepared maps were incorrect and misleading.

Lieut.-Colonel Toll (31st), accompanied by his adjutant, a signaller, and a runner, at great risk of being caught in our covering barrage, explored the country about 300 yards farther out but found no trace of a supporting system. During this period of delay, casualties increased considerably, and by now most of the officers and N.C.O's. of the 31st and 32nd had been killed or wounded, for in addition to the enemy fire, numbers of our own shells were falling short. On Colonel Toll's return, heroic efforts were made to connect up shell-holes and construct some form of breastwork along the edge of some of the existing ditches. It was impossible to see what was happening on the immediate flanks, and therefore little or no progress was made by way of co-ordination in the construction of a continuous line. The work was much hampered by the slime of the ditches and the sticky nature of the soil. One member of the 30th, Private Tom Donnellan, said that it clung to the shovel like an oyster, necessitating removal by hand, and that when filled into sandbags and placed on the parapet it became as slippery as an eel and could not be kept in position. Colonel Toll hung on grimly until 5.30 o'clock the following morning, when, fired at from the front and flanks, he reluctantly ordered the remnants of his own unit and those of the 29th and 30th to make the best of their way back, he being the last of his battalion to leave the enemy trench.

The experiences of Colonel Coghill, who commanded the 32nd Battalion, were somewhat similar to those of the other attacking units. His men, despite great initial losses, gained the enemy front line and, after clearing same, went on in a vain endeavour to find the non-existent support system. The same disabilities in the matter of lack of men and material were encountered, and in addition the very difficult job of holding the left flank was borne by this battalion, thus accounting for its losing more heavily than other brigade units.

As soon as our front line was vacated by the attacking troops, the 30th moved in and commenced its allotted tasks. To "A" Company (Major Beardsmore), assisted by the 8th Field Company, Engineers, was entrusted the task of cutting a trench across No-Man's Land, and if the division had been able to hold its temporary gains, this would not only have formed portion of the new front line, but would have secured the whole position from a left-flank attack. The official historian has given unstinted praise to the officers and men who, in the face of continuous fire, succeeded in practically completing the trench from our front line to within a few yards of the German wire-entangle-

ABOVE: *Left to right*: Sgt. T. M. Massey, M.M., Pte. G. W. Pittaway, M.M., Sgt. W. F. Murday, M.M., Sgt. J. W. Laing, M.M.
BELOW: *Left to right*: Pte. W. A. McDermott, M.M., Sgt. A. D. Burns, M.M., Pte. P. H. Motley, M.M., Sgnlr. F. M. Heslewood, M.M.

THE BATTLE OF FROMELLES

ment. It was 175 yards long, 6 feet in depth at the Australian end, and 3 feet 6 inches near the German wire.

"When the assault was launched (writes Dr. Bean), the allotted troops began to emerge at this point, but found that the barbed wire in front of the Australian line had not been sufficiently cut. An opening was, however, presently found, and the first section of the working party passed through it and began to cross No-Man's Land. To ensure the trench being dug in the right direction, there went with this section Sergeant Garland, carrying a sign-post which he was to plant on the German parapet at the easternmost point captured by the brigade, and Lieutenant Lees with tape and pegs to work across No-Man's Land a 'traversed' line for the trench. As the enemy was still in possession of his front fifty yards beyond the point towards which these men were making, and towards which the men would be strung out for digging, the task obviously involved extreme danger. Garland had almost reached the far side of No-Man's Land when he was shot dead; but Sergeant Harrison, who was in charge of the first party, and a few men crossed No-Man's Land unhurt. The survivors were lined out near the old German trench, and, taking advantage of such partial cover as was afforded by shell-holes, began to dig a series of potholes, the intention being, as the excavations extended, to send out more men to connect them into a continuous trench. Lieutenant Lees, however, was very soon killed, and, of the handful of men working on the farther side of No-Man's Land, Privates Rich and Tisbury, while digging, were shot dead by snipers in the German line.

"On the side of No-Man's Land nearer to the Australian trench, the work had met with even greater difficulty. The two digging parties which were to follow the first wave were met, as they passed through the gap in the entanglement, by the fire of a German machine-gun which was evidently laid on to that point, but which the first party, emerging unexpectedly, had escaped. The second and third parties were thus practically annihilated. It was noted, however, that the gun caught the men about the knees, it being apparently fixed, or possibly so screened that it could not fire lower. Thus Captain Allen, second-in-command to Major Beardsmore, whose company was making the attempt, and a sergeant of engineers, keeping low and protected in a measure by the bodies of the fallen men, were able to push forward sandbags, gradually screening part of the deadly passage way; and so, in spite of almost overwhelming difficulties, the work on this trench proceeded. The taping of its course had proved out of the question, but the officers concerned—Lieutenants Farr, of the 8th Field Company, and Lees and Cadden of the 30th—dispensed with this proceeding as unnecessary, since an irregular trace would give sufficient protection against enfilade fire.

"During the night, on account of the heavy German shellfire and the deadly enfilade of machine-guns on the old No-Man's Land, the carrying parties were directed to use this trench even while it was being steadily excavated. Again referring to this work at a later stage of the battle, Dr. Bean writes: "Captain Allen, who, though wounded before the attack commenced, was still in charge, had discovered, at some distance to the right in the Australian entanglement, an opening upon which the German machine-gun was not playing. Through this he passed another working party, with orders to make contact with the men digging on the far side, and thence to construct a sandbag barrier to meet the one which he and the engineers were pushing forward through the Australian wire. A corporal and some men whom he sent to the old German front line with orders to suppress the machine-gun were not successful, but, in spite of this, the separate sections of the trench, though shallow, were gradually linked up except near the old German line, where, most of the Diggers having been shot, it remained merely a series of pot-holes. The enemy was shelling it constantly from the north-east, breaking in some portions of the trench. The casualties among parties attempting to cross were severe, and, although quantities of sandbags and grenades were sent forward into the trench, only part of them got through, and the men of the 30th Battalion and 8th Field Company attempting to dig it were hampered almost past endurance by the slow congested passage of men with burdens. The Germans at one stage appeared to be moving to counter-attack in No-Man's Land, and the digging party was bombed and driven in; yet towards morning Major Beardsmore was able to report that the trench almost reached across No-Man's Land, though still shallow and unfinished at the farther end. But much of the ammunition intended to be forwarded through it remained, clogging the sap."

Captain Allen, who continued to carry on until nearly the end of the action, received the Military Cross for his splendid efforts. Sergeant "Tosh" Ridley was reported as being killed, but he had in fact been badly wounded and was later dragged in by the Germans, to spend the remaining years of the war in captivity. His many attempts to escape and the trouble that he caused his guards are recounted in Part II. of this volume.

It is difficult to set out in detail the work of the other companies—"B" (Captain Street), "C" (Major Purser) and "D" (Captain Cheeseman)—as all were from the outset engaged in carrying stores to the assaulting battalions, thus giving their commanders no opportunity of tactically directing them. The platoons and sections that set out on the heels of the attacking waves with the boxes of ammunition, bombs, shovels, barbed-wire, sandbags, and many other articles, less than half returned for a second load, and eventually, after some parties had made several trips, their survivors all became absorbed by the battalions in the German line. Although the instructions to officers and N.C.O's. in charge of carrying parties were definitely to the effect that they must strictly adhere to the work allotted them, and to leave their "iron rations" with the front-line troops, it did not take much persuasion to cause them to throw in their lot with some party or other of the 31st or 32nd Battalion. As Sergeant H. H. Stevenson ("B" Coy) afterwards remarked: "We did not mind going forward with our load, and thus face the enemy fire, but the thought of being hit in the back on the return journey was too much for most of us, hence our inclination to remain with the fighting troops."

Colonel Clark established his headquarters at a sally-port in our old front line behind a particularly thick portion of the parapet, which, though shaken many times by shellfire, gave sufficient cover in which to receive and issue orders, and generally to control his unit. For the first few hours he had the satisfaction of seeing his men cheerfully carry out their allotted work, but, as the night wore on he realised that the task of supplying two battalions with sufficient stores to build up a new front line and at the same time to supply bombs and ammunition for machine-guns and rifles, was beyond the resources at his disposal. A report from the front line to the effect that a number of the bombs being sent forward were without detonators caused additional anxiety, but fortunately Lieutenant John Chapman—who had qualified at a grenade school in Egypt—was available, and with the remnants of his platoon, at considerable risk in the darkness, ensured that subsequent supplies were properly primed.

As time went on Colonel Clark's worries increased. By reason of casualties and their absorption in the front line, his carrying parties gradually disappeared, with the result that the frantic and futile appeals for bombs, shovels, ammunition, etc., could not be fully satisfied. His application to brigade headquarters for men from the 29th Battalion were at first refused, due partly to ignorance of the real situation, partly to adherence to training-manual maxims regarding the maintenance of reserves. When eventually permission was given to employ a portion of the reserve, a company of the 29th under Captain Mor-

Lieut. H. J. WELLS, M.C.

Capt. R. D. MULVEY, M.C.

Lieut. B. A. BRAGG, M.C.

Lieut. J. WITTON FLYNN, M.C.

Lieut. S. C. BUTLER, M.C.   Major JAMES A. CHAPMAN, O.B.E.   Lieut. V. W. FIDDLE, M.C.

THE BATTLE OF FROMELLES

timer went forward with stores and to act as a reinforcement. Both he and his second-in-command were killed, and few, if any, of his men returned.

While it is not possible to record in detail the activities of each unit of the 30th Battalion, the part played by No. 14 Platoon under Lieutenant T. C. Barbour calls for more than passing mention. This platoon started off with its load of ammunition, sandbags, and tools, and, after suffering casualties in crossing No Man's Land, reached the enemy front line, and on to the supposed support system, but, finding nothing in the shape of organized defences, Barbour came to the same conclusion as other leaders, namely, that nothing of the kind existed. The platoon occupied portion of the large gap which existed between the advanced posts of the 31st and 32nd Battalions, and here Barbour started to build up an independent cover for his command. Sentries were posted in forward shell holes, and the men working with a will, some of them waist-deep in mud and water, contrived to raise a parapet which gave them protection from rifle and machine-gun fire. A rough sketch of the position was taken back by Private P. J. Nankivell, who, though dreadfully wounded on the journey, managed to crawl into battalion headquarters and hand it over. For his bravery he was awarded the Military Medal. Private J. J. Anderson, who though twice wounded, refused to leave his comrades, was also awarded the Military Medal. An unusual casualty was that of Private J. Ross, who, instinctively raising an arm to ward off a blinding flash, had his hand cut clean away by a piece of shell. The measure of protection afforded to the head by the severed limb no doubt saved Ross' life. After completing their trench, Barbour employed his men in collecting ammunition from the dead and wounded. Some of this was eventually used by two Vickers guns, under Lieutenant F. C. Winn of the 8th Brigade Machine Gun Company, in helping to repel the German counter-attacks, and a portion was sent to posts on the left. With the approach of dawn, Barbour, realising the hopelessness of hanging on any longer, made his way back to his own lines with the remnant of his platoon, he had lost more than half of his strength. Lieutenant A. C. White, who had only joined the battalion the previous evening, was placed in charge of No. 15 Platoon, and, to use his own words, was "not too sure of what the fuss was all about." The platoon (48 strong) was detailed to carry stores, but after reaching the front with its load, threw in its lot with the men of the 31st Battalion and hung on with them until the end of the fight, its casualties totalling 23.

On the left flank of the 8th Brigade was a solidly built communication trench, known to the Germans as the *Kastenweg*, which ran back at a right angle from the enemy front line and linked up with a strongly defended fort at Delangre Farm. It had been taken by the 32nd Battalion almost to the farm but from its uncaptured section an insistent fire was enfilading the advanced line of the 31st and 32nd, and causing heavy casualties. Captain Krinks, arriving at the front with a carrying party, found the situation on the left highly critical, and at once took some of his men to the extreme flank to reinforce the post in the *Kastenweg*, which was being bombed by the enemy. On entering that trench they strengthened the barricade in it by pulling down some of the earth-filled ammunition boxes of which the trench walls were made. The Germans, however, were bombing so fiercely from the other side of the block that Krinks ordered his men to take cover in shell-holes on slightly rising ground some twenty yards to the left of the trench, and from here they sniped at any German who showed himself. After a while Krinks made his way back to the Australian line, got two Lewis guns, and returned with them to his post, and for the remainder of the night it was able to assist in preventing the Germans from moving up the *Kastenweg*.

As daylight approached, however, the advanced line of the 31st Battalion was driven back on to the old German

THE BATTLE OF FROMELLES

front trench, a number of its men being killed or captured. This allowed the enemy to surround the main body of the 32nd, with whom were scattered remnants of the 29th and 30th Battalions. At 3.45 with machine-guns firing at them from front, flank, and rear, some 150 men attempted to charge back to the Australian lines. A considerable number cut their way through the Germans, but many were shot down as they streamed across No-Man's Land. Some of the posts near the *Kastenweg* did not receive the order to retire, and were quickly overwhelmed, but Captain Krinks and his men—eleven in all—being on the other side of that trench, were missed by the Germans. Realising that they were cut off, they decided after consultation to make a dash for their lives, but they would keep together and assist any of their number who met with trouble. Half of them succeeded in crossing two enemy trenches, each containing Germans. In the second trench two of the party were captured; the remainder at once turned round and released them, and all escaped into No-Man's Land, but in the wire entanglement Lance-Corporal S. B. Wells was shot down and Private E. C. E. Amps injured.

Krinks and three others—Corporal A. H. Forbes and Privates J. H. Wishart and T. L. Watts—eventually reached the front line of the 60th (British) Brigade. That night all four went out into No-Man's Land with a stretcher to find their comrades. They succeeded in doing this, and were bringing in Wells when a sentry from our line fired at them, killing Wishart and Watts with a single shot.

Lieutenants James and John Chapman and Ian Fullarton, the three Duntroon graduates in the battalion, worthily upheld the traditions of their college. Fullarton, who was wounded by a piece of shell, was awarded the Military Cross for his work as Intelligence Officer during the battle. Lieutenant James Chapman's platoon was detailed by headquarters to escort prisoners to the rear. Jim's instructions being rather sketchy, in trying to carry them out he and his command saw the battle from many vantage points extending from the reserve line to enemy territory. Normally the platoon was not expected to go beyond our own front line, but "dearth of material" caused it to go farther afield, with the result that both Chapman and his men found themselves absorbed by the troops consolidating the ditches in the German lines.

The runners deserve special mention for their efforts to keep up communication. Unfortunately few of them survived. The signal section under Lieutenant Horgan did its best to keep their telephone service going, but the continuous shelling made it impossible to maintain communication by that means for any length of time. It was on this work that Corporal "Rowley" Lording—who with Privates Gerald Brocklehurst and Frank Raysmith, shared the honour of being the youngest members of the 30th Battalion—received the wounds that 53 operations have failed completely to heal. As an example of human suffering, coupled with a determination to live, Lording's case is probably unique in the annals of the A.I.F.

Shortly after the troops had withdrawn to the Australian line, the German artillery opened a heavy bombardment along the divisional front, and enemy infantry were seen to be crowding their trenches. Anticipating a counter-attack, Colonel Clark made provision to man our parapet; but the enemy, probably as tired as we were, did not venture across No-Man's Land. Our artillery laid a counter-bombardment on the German front line until midday, when the guns of both sides ceased firing. In the meantime the 29th Battalion took over the 8th Brigade frontage and the disheartened remnants of the 30th, 31st and 32nd Battalions were withdrawn to positions in the rear. The 30th was temporarily halted at Croix Blanche, near Fleurbaix, to act as reserve to the 29th.

The most pressing question now was the rescue of the hundreds of wounded who lay helpless in No-Man's Land in the sweltering rays of the sun. Their agonising cries

THE BATTLE OF FROMELLES

were responded to by a number of men, who, despite the risk, went out to try and succour them. Among such rescuers was a Private W. Miles, of the 29th Battalion, who (according to the Official History) was hailed by a Bavarian Officer and told, in perfect English, to go back to his lines and ask one of his officers to come across and see if some arrangement could not be made about collecting the wounded. Miles returned to his battalion and spoke to Major A. W. Murdoch, who decided that the idea was worth trying, and accompanied by Miles, he made his way across to the German parapet and asked if an informal truce could be arranged. The Bavarian officer, after holding a telephone conversation with his headquarters, said that his instructions were that the proposal would be agreed to on condition that the Australian stretcher-bearers should work only in their own half of No-Man's Land, the wounded in the German half being cleared by German stretcher-bearers. As a bond of good faith Murdoch, after consulting his own division, was to come back blindfolded to the German trenches, to be held there as hostage until the collection was finished. Murdoch at once carried back this proposal, which was telephoned to the headquarters of the 5th Division, but the divisional commander, acting on definite orders from corps headquarters that no negotiations of any kind were to be had with the enemy, could not accede to it.

Despite the ban, individual men and small parties continued to go out by day into No-Man's Land and bring in their stricken comrades, while at night large parties of volunteers from all units were organised for the purpose. This magnificent work went on for three days and three nights, it being discontinued only after no one was found on the fourth night.

Too much praise cannot be given to the stretcher-bearers, who were largely reinforced from the battalion band. From the morning of the 19th until days after the battle they persevered in their noble work, and also assisted the burial parties in their gruesome tasks. Most of them suffered with strained backs and skinned knuckles for weeks afterwards.

The musical instruments had been returned to store some weeks before the battle and the bandsmen distributed among the four companies. Losses among them commenced on July 17th when "Billy" Eyles and Frank ("Lofty") Brennan were wounded by shrapnel; later H. H. Williamson was stricken with rheumatism, C. S Cryer and H. Sharp were shell-shocked, W. June and F. V. Pearce fell ill, W. C. Upton suffered from concussion, and C. S. May received a collar-bone wound. The R.M.O., Captain Langan, and his principal assistant, Sergeant Lambourne, worked in their regimental aid-post without respite throughout the night of July 19th-20th and well into the following afternoon, and were often showered with dust and clods of earth from bursting shells. Ken Lewis, who strove particularly hard, fully earned the congratulations he subsequently received from Colonel Clark.

The roll call of the battalion at Croix Blanche was a sad affair, for each man present had lost some good mates. In all, our casualties amounted to 9 officers and 343 other ranks. Of the Officers, Lieutenants J. Parker and A. Mitchell were killed at the head of their platoons near the *Kastenweg*, and Lieutenant J. S. Lees, as previously mentioned, while supervising the digging of the communication across No-Man's Land. Captain B. A. Wark—who in 1918 was to win the Victoria Cross while commanding the 32nd Battalion—was hit in both legs, and was carried back across No-Man's Land by Private C. Grogan, who received the Military Medal for this splendid action. The other officers wounded were Major R. H. Beardsmore, Captain Ray. A. M. Allen, and Lieutenants I. G. Fullarton, H. R. Orpen, and E. E. Haviland.

The total loss of the 5th Division was 5,533 (including 54 officers and 1,846 other ranks in the 8th Brigade), and

THE BATTLE OF FROMELLES 87

that of the 61st (British) Division, 1,547. The German casualties were apparently under 1,500.

The fatuous messages of congratulation received by the 5th Division from the army and corps commanders will not be repeated here. The British official communiqué issued to the press, however, which makes interesting reading because of its remarkable concealment of the truth of the disaster, ran as follows:

"Yesterday evening, south of Armentières, we carried out some important raids on a front of two miles in which Australian troops took part. About 140 German prisoners were captured."

The German official accounts, on the other hand, were fairly accurate—"as usual," remarks Dr. Bean, "when German troops were successful, but not otherwise." They read:

"20th July. Considerable British forces attacked our positions north and west of Fromelles. They were repulsed and wherever they succeeded in penetrating our trenches they were ejected by counter-attacks, in which we captured over 300 prisoners, among them being some officers."

"21st July. The English attack in the region of Fromelles on Wednesday was carried out, as we have ascertained, by two strong Divisions. The brave Bavarian Division, against whose front the attack was made, counted on the ground in front of them more than 2,000 enemy corpses. We have brought in so far 481 prisoners, including ten officers, together with sixteen machine guns."

CHAPTER VIII.

(FLEURBAIX AND ARMENTIERES).

On July 22nd, having rested in the open fields around Croix Blanche for two days, we relieved the 6th Shropshire Battalion (60th Brigade) in the front line. On our immediate right the 29th Battalion held the battered breastworks from which three days previously the futile attack had been made. Our frontage extended roughly from Devon to York Avenues, and included the site of a "convent" famous in pre-war days for the manufacture of a special liqueur. Only the outer walls remained, the buildings themselves having been destroyed early in the war. The remains of the western wall screened our support line from enemy view, and also gave protection from machine-gun's fire. The front and support lines consisted of practically parallel lines of traversed sandbag walls some nine feet high and of about the same thickness, which, complete with bays, fire-steps, loop-holes, shelters, alcoves, stores, and emplacements, constituted our main defence. Communication between the front and support lines was maintained by means of strongly constructed zig-zagged alleys, through which passed out of view of the enemy, the reliefs, food, ammunition, stores, etc. The mild weather of late summer and early autumn suited the troops and, despite the presence of rats, parasites of smaller dimensions, inability to bathe, or completely undress, the position was reasonably comfortable. Although the front and support troops relieved each other frequently during the seven weeks spent in this sector, the life was strenuous, for all ranks had to be on the alert, particularly at night, in case of a sudden raid by the enemy. During the hours of darkness each side maintained machine-gun and rifle fire with more or less intensity, and rarely was it permitted completely to die down. On the German side, the artilleryman appeared to be more methodical than his infantry brother, and usually sent over his 5.9 inch shells in the evening, with a good-deed-for-the-day or task-faithfully-completed sort of attitude, which we quite appreciated. We were, in fact, often able to forecast with reasonable accuracy the hour at which he would commence operations and the number of shells he would liberate. The most tranquil part of the day was that between the hours of about 5 a.m. and noon, during which each side obtained its beauty sleep and rest. Battalion headquarters, situated in the remains of an orchard which still contained a few apple-bearing trees, consisted of a partially sunken dugout of three compartments, occupied respectively by the C.O., the senior major, and the adjutant. On the evening of August 20th the C.O.'s compartment was struck by a 5.9 shell—had the range been increased six feet there would have been a vacancy for a new commander. Fortunately no damage was done, the incident merely causing Colonel Clark to smooth down his hair several times—a characteristic attitude of his when solving some knotty problem.

About this time several of our senior officers were transferred to other battalions of the 5th Division, which had suffered heavily in the Battle of Fromelles. Majors Holford and Beardsmore were given command of the 54th and 32nd Battalions respectively, each being promoted to the rank of lieutenant-colonel. Major Purser went to the 32nd Battalion as senior major, and was subsequently appointed to the command of the 29th Battalion. These transfers, and our own casualties in the Fromelles battle, resulted in a number of promotions in the 30th. Captain Street obtained his majority and was appointed second-in-command. Lieutenants John Chapman, I. G. Fullarton, and A. P. Hext became captains, Lieutenant James

Chapman a temporary captain, and Regimental Sergeant-Major R. Gaskell, Company Sergeant-Majors S. C. Butler, W. E. Oakes, and F. Hamilton, Company Quartermaster-Sergeant V. Levitt, and Sergeants J. H. Facey, H. J. Wells and L. F. Mason second-lieutenants. Sergeants A. H. E. Whipp and W. A. Sutherland, Corporals A. W. Chivers, A. J. McCallum, J. C. Yeomans, T. S. C. Horgan, and T. Massey, and Privates F. C. Sharman, N. A. Elliott, C. G. Westbrook, and W. E. Shipp also received promotion.

The honours and awards lists subsequently published in connection with the battle of Fromelles contained the names of the following members of the 30th Battalion: Major R. H. Beardsmore, D.S.O.; Captain R. A. M. Allen and Lieutenant I. G. Fullarton, Military Cross; Privates W. Barrett and J. C. Hunter, D.C.M.; Sergeant F. A. Butterworth and Privates J. J. Anderson, T. H. Davies, T. C. Grogan, P. J. Nankinell and H. G. Wilson, Military Medal.

Raiding the opposing trenches was a form of warfare indulged in by both sides, but more frequently by the Australians, this adding to the tension of front line work. The Germans were decidedly "nervy" at this time and expended much energy in flare-lighting, possibly anticipating another large-scale attack. The principal object of these incursions was to secure prisoners, in order to identify the regiments facing us and, by interrogating them, to obtain information about the enemy's food and ammunition supplies, the position of his supports and reserves, the state of his morale, etc. The strength of our raiding parties varied from 20 to 200 men, and necessitated much preliminary training. The normal procedure was to study an aerial photograph of the area and, after selecting a length of the enemy line, to construct a replica of it in the back area, where every man became thoroughly acquainted with the part he had to play. These preparations often took weeks to complete, as every probable contingency had to be anticipated and provided for.

Beforehand the artillery and trench-mortars would

FLEURBAIX AND ARMENTIERES

bombard the enemy position and wire entanglement, and during the operations they would enclose the raided area with a "box-barrage," and afterwards cover the retirement of the raiders.

Our first attempt at a raid was made on August 27th, by a party of 3 officers and 70 other ranks of "D" Company. In the first instance, volunteers were called for, but as these largely exceeded the number required, Captain Cheeseman, the company commander, was able to select a very fine team. The officers were Captains F. L. Krinks (in charge), and Lieutenants E. A. C. Macfarlane and E. Adams. The names of all the N.C.O's. and men cannot now be remembered, but among them were "Sandy" Bragg, Archie Forbes, Jack Corlett, Athol Cooper, "Snowy" Low, Frank Curran, Bob Mather, Jack Westaway, Bill Hanlon, Norm Sutherland, "Rube" Herps, Jimmy Ford, Ted Hales, Jack Turnbull, Eric Robinson, Harry Staples, Bill Ward, Billy Player, Ernie Pockett, Ted Larkin, and Oliver Edmunds. While the system of calling for volunteers was not universally approved—the contention being that all men should be detailed in turn for these dangerous duties—a factor that induced many to volunteer was the prospect of several weeks' sojourn in a back area away from the monotony of front-line duty. The comparative immunity from enemy fire, a minimum of night work, and the proximity of baths, *estaminets,* and other amenities outweighed (as one man said) "the risks involved during the wild and woolly hour that would be devoted to the operation." Nevertheless, the spirit of adventure that animated most Australians unquestionably played a decisive part in inducing the majority of them to hand in their names.

The training was carried out at the 5th Divisional School near Sailly, an important village on the south bank of the River Lys. Captain R. A. Geddes, of the 32nd Battalion was in charge of the school, the instructors being British sergeant-majors, most of whom had served with the "Old Contemptibles," and were in consequence able to impart solid instruction based on experiences they had undergone both in peace and war. They were a fine type of soldier, reminiscent of those referred to in Kipling's *Pharoah and the Sergeant*, and not unknown to Australians in the early days of the Commonwealth Military Forces.

The first days of training took toll of our men, particularly the early morning runs through leafy lanes and along hedge-bordered roads, followed by "physical jerks." But the tired feeling soon wore off and they became a team of trained athletes ready and fit for any emergency. In addition to daylight training, excursions into No-Man's Land were carried out by small parties when conditions were suitable, each man thus gradually becoming acquainted with the terrain over which he and his comrades would eventually operate. Lectures were given by the chief instructor on the part to be played by the supporting artillery and trench-mortar batteries, and all individuals and groups frequently catechised as to their various duties. A matter of paramount importance was the maintenance of secrecy, and many warnings were given of the danger that might arise from a carelessly dropped word in an *estaminet*, or a conversation with an apparently loyal villager. Following these admonitions, Private Athol Cooper developed a flair for observation, and was dubbed "Sherlock" by his mates—a name which stuck to him throughout his service —for his activity in interpreting signs which might possibly convey information to the enemy. Thus on one occasion when a low-flying enemy 'plane neared a house where "madame" had just spread some newly-washed linen on the grass to bleach, he concluded that the layout of the articles conveyed some sinister meaning, and promptly kicked the whole into an unrecognisable heap with his muddy boots. Madame became frantic and ran from the house shrieking, "Brigand! brigand!" much to the amusement of the onlookers.

The raiders were divided into right, left, and covering parties, which included scouts, bomb carriers, bomb throwers, bayonet men, stretcher-bearers, telephonists, runners, prisoners' escorts, intelligence details and other specialists. The training was very thorough, the parties being exercised by day and night over and through the dummy trench-system, and as far as was humanly possible all contingencies were provided for. The school was visited frequently by divisional and brigade officers, who freely expressed themselves as being satisfied at the preparations made and the ability of the personnel successfully to carry out the operation.

At last—unknown to the men—the eventful day arrived. General Tivey came on the scene about 10 a.m. and, after seeing a rehearsal of the raid, closely questioned most of the men as to their particular duties. The brigadier gave no indication as to what he thought of the rehearsal, but said: "Bring back one man who can speak, and the raid will have been successful; come back without a prisoner and you will have failed." Before the dismissal of the parade Captain Krinks bluntly informed the men that the brigadier was not quite satisfied with their showing, and that he would see them again in the dusk of the evening, when all ranks were to be dressed, equipped, and armed in complete raiding order. At the appointed time the raiders assembled in discarded British uniforms from which all distinguishing marks had been removed. Their faces and hands were blackened with charred cork to lessen the chances of their being seen in the light of the flares and rockets—and possibly also with the idea of causing consternation in the ranks of the enemy; bayonets, buckles, and other bright articles had been treated in a similar manner, and the dials of watches were screened. Electric torches were fitted to the rifles of the bayonet men. A supply of Mills grenades was carried, and each man supplied with an entrenching tool handle to the head of which had been fitted a metal attachment for added weight. A playing card drawn from a pack constituted the only means of identification of each officer and man.

The party had been subjected to a searching inspection by its three officers, and apparently the next development would be the arrival of the brigadier. In the meantime two motor lorries arrived, their drivers apparently waiting for orders. The habitual grin on the face of Captain Krinks was more pronounced than usual, and when it deepened to a broad smile the truth gradually dawned on the men that the brigadier had taken no risk in regard to the leakage of information. "Now was the day, and now was the hour". The pious trick that General Tivey had played on the men was at first slightly resented, but a little thought convinced them that he had done the right thing and that his action was really in their own interest. Soon all hands were scrambling aboard the lorries and no band of nigger minstrels en route to a concert could have been in gayer mood than were our raiders as they headed for the front.

As they approached our defensive lines, their conversation and hilarity became more subdued and eventually ceased. The dangerous nature of the enterprise was probably dawning on each individual and he was content to commune with his own thoughts. The party dismounted from the lorries at the entrance to the long communication trench, and quickly made its way to our front line. As the men passed through a sallyport into No-Man's Land, they received many words of encouragement from our sentries, and reached the starting point some twenty minutes before "zero" hour. The German position which was to be attacked was known as "The Tadpole", about 300 yards from our parapet. Half-way across was a disused trench (named "XY" for the purpose of the operation) which made an excellent jumping-off spot, and from which a drain, lined on each side with the stumps of willow trees, ran straight towards the enemy line, thus precluding loss of direction in the darkness.

It was now that the co-operation of the other arms came in. The artillery was to bombard the enemy front line for three minutes, then lift its fire to the support line for ten minutes, after which it would return to the front line. The raiders thus had but ten minutes in which to carry out their attack. The role of the trench-mortars was to cut the enemy wire, which they effectively did, despite the fact that some of their "plum pudding" bombs fell short.

"Zero" hour was fixed for 10.30 p.m. and to the men waiting in No-Man's Land the time seemed to drag on interminably. The crash which eventually heralded the opening of the barrage came as a distinct relief to their overstrung nerves, and all were anxious to traverse the 150 yards which separated them from the German parapet. As the barrage lifted they moved rapidly forward in perfect order, but to their utter dismay, found on reaching the supposed enemy trench that it was filled with iron spikes and barbed wire, and unoccupied. Actually it was a deep ditch about twelve feet wide, in front of the German front line.

Although Sergeant Bragg and Private Corlett sprang into the "trench" in an endeavour to push through, it was soon realised that the task was hopeless. Apparently, as in the case of Fromelles, aeroplane photographs had again proved unreliable. As our artillery barrage was due to return to the trench in a few minutes, no time was available in which to search for a suitable crossing place, and Lieutenant Macfarlane took the only course open to him, namely, to call out "tallyhena", the prearranged word for retirement.

The rush back to the shelter of "XY" trench was not such an orderly affair as the advance had been. The enemy opened fire on the retreating party, one man being wounded. Naturally all ranks were bitterly disappointed at the failure of the enterprise, but they had the satisfaction of knowing that their unsuccessful efforts were due to causes over which they had no control, some perhaps, consoled themselves by remembering a poetical assertion concerning "Mice and Men."

Our first experience of a happening that armies the

world over have to contend with occurred on August 20th, when a "self-inflicted" wound case came up for investigation. One of our men, while attending to his rifle, shot himself in the left foot, and although the C.O., on the evidence of half-a-dozen witnesses, was quite satisfied that the wound was caused accidentally, army regulations prevented him from dealing with the matter. The unfortunate man therefore had to face the ordeal of a court-martial, a practical illustration of "adding insult to injury". He was acquitted, the President of the Court (Major Purser) being a man who never wasted time on non-essential details.

An incident that caused considerable excitement during this period, was the arrival of one of our 'planes, which had been hit by an enemy anti-aircraft shell while operating in the neighbourhood of Lille. The disabled machine volplaned to the ground about 700 yards behind our lines, its pilot and observer being practically unhurt. During the passage of the 'plane over the enemy front-line area it was subjected to heavy rifle and machine-gun fire—so excited, indeed, were the Germans that they exposed themselves on their fire-steps, thus providing targets of which our men did not fail to take advantage. Within one minute of the 'plane's reaching earth, some scores of shells of various size were fired at it, ploughing up the ground for a radius of 100 yards or more. Incidentally one of our senior officers, subsequently exploring the wreckage, took charge of a time-piece which he still retains as a souvenir of the occasion.

Another incident worthy of record is that while Lieutenant Jim Chapman's platoon was repairing an exposed portion of our breastworks, it suffered a few casualties from enemy "pigeons" (trench-mortars bombs). The discharge of the mortar was accompanied by a peculiar noise, and as the projectile was highly pitched and travelled comparatively slowly it was possible to dive for cover before it arrived. It was Private "Scotty" Mather who made this discovery, and as a reward he was immediately

CPL. R. E. LORDING,
Founder 30th Battalion, A.I.F. Assn.

SGT. R. C. HOGAN,
Secretary, 30th Battalion, A.I.F. Assn.

CPL. C. S. SMITH, M.M.

PTE. P. J. NANKIVELL, M.M.

struck off duty and appointed watchman, Chapman handing him his whistle. For a time he unerringly gave the alarm and earned the plaudits of his comrades.

His success, however, was short-lived as, to quote his own words "I started not only to taunt my mates on my newly acquired ganger's job, but also to sound the whistle with unnecessary vigour, with the result that the Germans became alive to our little ruse and promptly fired a machine gun at the same time as the mortar, thus screening the noise of explosion. I thus had to give up the whistle and return to the shovel, also to submit to ribald remarks for the remainder of the day." Whether Bob is a descendant of Jessie of Lucknow is not known. Probably he retains the keen sense of hearing so necessarily developed by his ancestors in the clan collisions of his native highlands.

Mining operations, under the direction of Professor Edgeworth David, were being carried out in the Bois Grenier sector, and such officers as could be spared were privileged to listen to a lecture on the local geology by this gifted man, whose every word was to the point and thoroughly understandable.

On September 6th we were relieved by the 32nd Battalion, and moved back to the brigade reserve position in the Rue Biache where we remainded for fourteen days. Our casualties during the six weeks' tenure of the front line were comparatively slight, 8 men being killed 43 wounded and 66 evacuated sick. Private C. Dykes, who was among the killed, was shot in the forehead in the presence of his brother. During the same period 81 men who had been sent away with slight wounds, returned from hospital, and 134 of our 4th and 5th reinforcements arrived and were taken on strength.

Although the farmhouses in the Rue Biache in which we were billeted were well within the range of the German guns and had been much damaged by shell-fire, straw was plentiful, *estaminets* were within walking distance, vegetables and fruit were obtainable by purchase, or more direct means, and we were able to make frequent visits to the divisional baths at Sailly. One company was kept in readiness to move to the front line at a moment's notice in case of emergency, the remainder being employed from about 4 a.m. to noon each day in deepening dug-outs, burying cable, improving drainage systems, and generally preparing the sector for the ensuing winter. The news that Colonel Clark was relieving General Tivey during the latter's absence on leave was received with much satisfaction, as it opened up a vista to which all had been looking forward, namely, a trip to the land of our forbears, the heart of the Empire, the hub of the world, Merrie England, Bonnie Scotland, the land of the leek, and the home of the shamrock.

On the night of September 16th "D" Company made another attempt to raid the German line, and on this occasion met with success. Captain Cheeseman commanded the party, which consisted of himself and two other officers, Lieutenants Macfarlane and Adams, and sixty other ranks, practically the same force as attacked on August 27th. Training had been continued at the divisional bomb and raiding school, and the men, in view of their previous experience, were fitter than ever for the operation. Errors in range by the artillery and trench mortars on the former occasion were rectified; and a foot-bridge, on which the raiders would cross the large ditch or moat which had caused the failure of the first attempt, was carried by a special party.

"XY" trench was reached without incident, though on this occasion it was found to be full of water. Immediately the barrage opened the bridge carrying party pressed forward with all haste, but was much hampered by tangled barbed-wire and undergrowth through which it had to force its way. Closely followed by the raiding parties, it experienced a breathless moment as the bridge was upended preparatory to its falling across the ditch. At first it seemed that the contrivance would fall short of the opposite bank,

FLEURBAIX AND ARMENTIERES

but fortunately this was not the case. The raiders sped across and were soon in the enemy trench.

Bombing parties pushed out to right and left from the point of entry and held the enemy at bay until the signal was given for the retirement. Twelve German dead were counted and two prisoners of the 20th Bavarian Reserve Regiment captured. The raiders also brought back eight rifles, three gas helmets, and a quantity of personal equipment and papers. Our losses amounted to one man killed and one officer and two other ranks wounded. The co-operation of the artillery and trench-mortar batteries in wire-cutting and maintaining the "box-barrage" was very effective, and contributed largely to the success of the operation. The divisional and brigade commanders were highly pleased and the following comments appeared in 8th Brigade Orders:—

"Captain W. J. Cheeseman commended for the training, organization and co-operation of the whole party.

"Lieutenant E. A. C. Macfarlane acted with coolness and judgment throughout, and was the last to leave the enemy trench. He had previously reconnoitred the locality, taking in turn the whole of the raiding party over the ground.

"Lieutenant E. Adams, in charge of the covering party, was wounded in the right foot as he entered the enemy trench. He directed the operation of the bombing parties and, although wounded, showed high courage and cheerfulness; he deserves very great praise for the work performed. He also had reconnoitred No-Man's Land nightly.

"Corporal A. H. Forbes and Private E. W. Hales, of the right bombing party, entered the enemy trench in the face of heavy opposition, driving the enemy bombers back, and taking a prisoner. Corporal Forbes was wounded in three places and partially stunned by bombs, but would not leave his post until ordered to do so.

"Private R. H. Herps and Private E. D. Robinson, in the face of heavy artillery and machine-gun fire, offered to go out from the assembly trench after the raid, and bring back an identity disc from a dead German lying close to the enemy parapet. This they succeeded in doing, and also secured papers containing valuable information. Private Herps also did good work inside the enemy trenches, examining and combing dug-outs. Both men also assisted in bringing back our wounded from No-Man's Land.

"Corporal H. E. Staples, in charge of the scouts, went into No-Man's Land night after night, often getting behind the enemy wire and closely approaching his parapet. On the night of the raid he went out before our artillery bombardment and cleared wire from the line of approach.

"Private W. A. Ward, of the right bombing party, by giving timely warning to Lieutenant Adams of the approach of enemy bombers, probably saved the lives of several of his comrades. He was severely wounded and did excellent work throughout the operation."

Further changes in the personnel about this time included the promotion of Temporary Captain James Chapman to substantive rank, Sergeant F. W. Harrison to 2nd Lieutenant, Sergeant Norman Jehan to Company Sergeant-Major, and Corporals Gordon Begg, C. S. Johnson, G. McClosky, C. Watts, F. T. Bickley, J. A. Hogg, E. J. Tysoe, A. H. Forbes, E. R. McBride and T. J. Schmitzer to Sergeant; and Lance-Corporals W. Barrett, J. B. McGowan, A. Thompson, H. Cox, E. King, A. A. Low, R. C. Mitchell, H. Craven, B. Smith, V. Simpson and H. D. Gooding to Corporal. Captain F. L. Krinks was transferred to the 32nd Battalion and Captain S. A. Railton relieved Captain A. Langan as Medical Officer. Lieutenant R. L. Cadden was sent to hospital as the result of a wound in the face. Major C. S. Davies (32nd Battalion) assumed command of the battalion during Colonel Clark's temporary absence.

Our next move was to Armentieres, the home town of the mythical mademoiselle. Nothing of note happened on the journey, the usual distances between units were observed as the battalion approached the forward area, and we duly arrived at "Half Past Eleven Square," so called by reason of the municipal clock having one day been put out of action by an enemy shell at the time indicated. At this time many of the inhabitants were still living in their homes, principally food shops and *estaminets*, which they were loath to leave partly for reasons of sentiment, but mainly because of the thriving trade they did with the troops. As most of the large buildings, former warehouses, were empty, no difficulty was experienced in obtaining good billets. Naturally, all ranks made the most of a fine evening in pleasant and comparatively safe surroundings. This was our first visit to a partially deserted city and strange was the sight of grass and weeds growing between the cobblestones of streets that once reverberated to the sound of busy traffic. The ruined and deserted railway station was also a mass of long grass, matted weeds, and rusted rails.

On the morning of September 22nd, we continued our march to the front line, taking over the right sub-section of the Houplines sector from the 9th Royal Scots. For some reason, which was not apparent, we marched across the River Lys into Belgium by means of a bridge which gave evidence of having suffered through much shelling and which threatened to give way under our weight, thence along the left bank of the stream for about two miles, when we re-crossed it per medium of another bridge that was equally shaky, and so on to our various positions in the defence system. While here, the battalion formed portion of the specially constituted "Franks" force, but, as our brigade remained intact, the change did not trouble us in any way.

The trench systems at Houplines were different from that to which we had been accustomed at Fleurbaix, inasmuch as they consisted largely of a series of strong-posts with unoccupied trenches between them. The whole position appeared to have been neglected and our men put in a strenuous week effecting repairs.

Houplines, which lay within a few hundred yards of our

trenches, had been a densely populated industrial suburb containing many factories.

Mute evidence of this was the number of chimney stacks that had been more or less damaged by shell-fire—some stood out like lone sentinels from which the adjoining buildings had been burned, some resembled gaunt tree-stumps after a bush-fire, some had been holed completely through, and large chunks torn from the sides of others revealed the sooty interiors. Nevertheless, many contrived to remain erect as though defiantly challenging the enemy to do his worst. The workmen's homes, hundreds of them built in terraces, had apparently been vacated hurriedly, for they still contained beds, washstands, mirrors, tables, chairs, carpets, crockery, and kitchen utensils mixed with broken bricks, masonry, and dust, curtains still clung to the shattered windows, and from the walls hung pictures and photographs. A feature of the poorer French home is the framing of birth, christening, marriage and other certificates, and many of these still intact, were hanging precariously from picture rails. The plight of these panic-stricken people hurriedly leaving their all behind them can better be imagined than described.

On September 28th we were relieved by the 29th Battalion and moved back into reserve, two companies being billeted in Armentières and two in Houplines. Incidentally, this was a black day for the city and its suburbs, as an extra heavy bombardment destroyed many buildings and killed a large number of civilians. On this day also Lieutenant S. W. Coleman and 143 reinforcements arrived and Captain Wark returned from hospital. Although the battalion was out of the front line, fatigues went on as usual, but, as the evenings were free to most of the men, the time was pleasantly spent.

Returning to the trenches on October 3rd, we relieved the 29th Battalion. The only diversion during this second "tour" was a release of cloud gas on the enemy trenches, followed by a heavy bombardment from our divisional artillery. Incidentally, this was the only occasion on which this form of gas was used by our battalion in the whole campaign, as subsequent releases were made per medium of shells and the deadly projector.

While the Royal Engineers who carried out these gas attacks, were installing their cylinders in our front line, we were somewhat perturbed at the possibility of some dreaded *minenwerfer* or high-explosive shells fracturing the containers, with dire results to ourselves. For the first few days gas masks were kept at the "alert," but as nothing of an unusual nature occurred the uneasiness soon wore off and all hands became interested in the new experience.

As a favourable breeze was necessary for the success of the attack, numerous weather-vanes and other novel gadgets were fashioned by the garrison and mounted above the shelters and on the breastworks. These weathercocks were studied by the troops with the calculating eye of a sea captain, as were the movements of rain clouds and the drift of smoke puffs from exploding shrapnel, especially when these were moving towards the enemy lines.

For several days perverse weather conditions prevailed, but finally, on the night of October 5th, a breeze of the necessary strength arrived from the correct quarter and it was decided to release the gas at 8 o'clock. Prior to "zero" all troops, with the exception of the engineers and a few sentries, were withdrawn to the subsidiary lines, and Lieutenant Barbour was appointed to act as official observer.

Barbour placed himself on one of the shelters from which to watch the progress of events and to notify any change of wind that might jeopardise the operation. The night was dark, and the engineers, distinguishable in the faint light by their brassards, completed their final adjustments just before "zero". At this hour the fighting zone remained strangely quiet, broken only by the sullen and continuous reverberations of the guns up Ypres way.

All watches had been synchronised, and promptly at 8 o'clock gas masks were donned and the gas released. From his elevated post Barbour obtained a view of the heavy mixture as, fanned by the breeze, it steadily rolled across No-Man's Land, keeping very low and resembling a thick fog. It soon filled shell-holes and ditches and folds in the ground, and apparently surprised and overwhelmed the German listening posts, as no evidence of life came from them.

Sixty seconds after its release the sentries in the German front line, apparently suspicious at the ominous silence and the sudden development of what appeared to be an early evening ground mist, sent up a number of flares. Their flickering haloes exposed in bold relief the eerie panorama of man-made fog beneath, relentlessly creeping forward, but it was not until five minutes after "zero" that the Germans fully realised its deadly significance and raised the alarm with sirens and the continuous clanging of gongs. They evidently anticipated an infantry attack, as, shortly after the alarm was raised, rifle and machine-gun fire was directed at our line.

Lieutenant Barbour subsequently reported every phase of the attack, which, judging by the number of stretcher cases and "walking" wounded observed shortly after daylight, must have caused the enemy many casualties.

On October 10th we were again relieved by the 29th Battalion, thus completing our front line service in this neighbourhood.

Battalion headquarters were situated in a much perforated *château,* which must have been a superb residence before the war. Its spacious halls, reception rooms, stairways, gardens, and parklands were wonderful to roam through even in their battered state. Remnants of glass-covered hot houses contained ripening grapes which, needless to state, were not left entirely to the birds. Our remaining days in this neighbourhood were spent in repairing a reserve trench that zig-zagged through the local cemetery. No skeleton was unearthed, but the broken headstones with their indecipherable inscriptions, while forming good material for strengthening the breastworks, caused one to reflect upon the futility of the human to memorialise his relations.

A more pleasant subject to dilate upon was the divisional baths, situated in an abandoned brewery. The hot water in which the men wallowed and splashed so comfortably was contained in large vats, which formerly held beautiful sparkling amber ale. Many and varied were the comments concerning the use, or misuse, to which these receptacles had risen or descended, but all agreed as to their suitability for bathing purposes. Lieutenant C. A. Backhouse — "Bacchus" to his fellow subs — was in charge of one of these parties, and whether the lines "To what base uses may we yet return Horatio," occurred to him is not known, but is highly probable in view of the appropriate soubriquet inflicted upon him. An impending detail for this job, by our sportive adjutant, was that of Lieutenant C. D. Beer, but a sudden move order spared the latter officer any humiliation which such a tour of duty might have involved.

On October 13th we were relieved by a New Zealand battalion and moved, by means of motor buses, to the neighbourhood of Strazeele, where we were billeted for four days prior to our departure for the Somme. The strength of the battalion at this period was 34 officers and 882 other ranks. Fifty-six reinforcements, including Captain George Wynne, Lieutenants Stephens, Wisdom and Thompson, arrived, and Captains Allen and Fullarton rejoined after recovering from wounds received at Fromelles. Captain Sloan was promoted to the rank of major and appointed to the command of "C" Company, Captain "Jim" Chapman taking over the position of adjutant. Some training was carried out at Strazelle, but most of the time was devoted to preparations for the move south and to voting on the conscription issue. Winter was approaching, and each man was issued with warmer underclothing and an additional pair of boots.

Our losses in the Houplines section had been light. Private W. J. Graham was killed, three others were wounded, and twelve were evacuated sick.

CHAPTER IX.

WINTERING ON THE SOMME.

THE move to the Somme on October 17th culminated in one of the most distressful episodes in the history of the battalion and, rightly or wrongly, further weakened the respect — so badly shaken at Fromelles — for the higher command. The exigencies of the new methods of warfare which necessitated the carrying of a box respirator and a steel helmet, in addition to a blanket, greatcoat, rations, ammunition, etc., had already increased the burdens of the infantryman, but with the issue of heavier clothing and an extra pair of boots at the approach of winter, the load was such that only a strong man could carry. In addition to the foregoing, certain company stores, including a Barr-Stroud range-finder, had to be carried by individuals alternately when on the march.

Leaving Strazelle at 6.30 a.m., we marched to Bailleul and at 10.30 entrained for Longpre, a village some twenty miles north-west of Amiens. The train accommodation provided was woefully inadequate, and much overcrowding took place, many men suffered from cramp, due to the cold conditions and inability to stretch their legs. It was long after dark when we detrained at Longpre, and heavy rain falling added to the general discomfort. The eight-mile march to billets in the village of Bussus-Bussuel will long be remembered by all who took part in it. The men were overloaded, cold, and hungry, the road was wet, uneven, and slippery. The C.O. was criticised for not halting at the usual time-periods, but, under the existing conditions, he undoubtedly did the right thing in keeping the battalion on the move. All would have gone well, and the men would have struggled on until daylight, but unfortunately the guide, confused by the wind and rain and the utter darkness, missed his way within less than a mile of Bussus, and led us along a road that diverged slightly to the right of the village. The result was disastrous. Very soon the metalled roadway gave way to an unformed one which led up a slippery incline. The C.O. soon realised that an error had been made, and halted the column while he consulted a map and probably abused the unfortunate guide. This error proved to be the last straw. Worn out by the strain of the march and with their morale broken, many men sank down on the roadside while others took cover in adjoining hedges and haystacks. The company officers, who for hours had been helping to carry the arms and equipment of their weaker men or some of the additional stores, did their best to rally them, but met with little success. However, the more determined men hung on and our billets were eventually reached. Shortly after daybreak search parties were organized, and by midday all the stragglers and most of the discarded equipment, principally boots and blankets, had been recovered.

After resting for two days at Bussus, the battalion marched on October 20th to Ailly, where it was picked up by a fleet of motor vehicles supplied by the French Army. This was to us a novel and much appreciated form of transport. Every tenth bus travelled empty, the idea being that, if one of the others broke down or sustained a puncture, the troops could immediately be transferred to the spare one, and the journey continued without undue delay. The overcoats worn by the motor drivers were made from untanned hides of Moroccan goats, the multi-coloured hair of the animals remaining on the outside of the garments. This led one of our wags to remark that "Joseph had nothing on these chaps."

The Somme country is more broken than that of Flanders, consisting largely of spurs and valleys, with numerous streams. The farmers, unlike the Flemish peasants, who live on their holdings, congregate in more or less insanitary villages, with the result that the countryside here is not nearly so picturesque as that farther north.

While the trip can hardly be described as a joy ride, we arrived without incident at Buire, an almost deserted village on the northern bank of the River Ancre, three miles from Albert. Here we were billeted for the night. The buildings allotted to us were of a very poor character, and barely sufficed to keep out the rain and wind. However, worse lay ahead.

The following day we marched through Dernancourt, Meaulte, and Albert to "Carlton Trench" (near the demolished village of Montauban), which our men quickly renamed "Hungry Hill," on account of the scarcity of rations and lack of shelter there. The roads were muddy and the great volume of outward traffic made marching difficult. Some men were forced to walk in the gutter, and, so as to lessen their difficulties as much as possible, frequent changes were made in the composition of the flank lines. The dashing past of staff cars splashing mud in every direction—ever a source of irritation to the infantry—also added to the discomfort of all ranks. Passing through Albert and almost beneath the great bronze figure (six tons in weight) formerly representing The Madonna holding a child towards heaven, but now pointing to the ground at an angle of about 45°, no doubt stirred feelings of resentment in many hearts, and strengthened resolves to bring the ruthless invader to book.

As we came within range of enemy guns, the usual distance between companies and platoons was observed. A much bedraggled battalion of the Coldstream Guards passed us on its way to the rear after a tour of duty in the front line, and this provided an opportunity for some good natured banter on both sides. The forlorn state of the country through which we had passed since reaching

WINTERING ON THE SOMME

the Somme, is vividly described in the following extract from Captain A. R. Ellis' "Story of the Fifth Division":—
"The whole area was one of indescribable desolation. Once a charming countryside, it had swelled upwards in a series of gentle undulations between the Somme and the Ancre River valleys, both of which were here about 150 feet above sea level. Between the rivers, the highest ground was the ridge connecting, with occasional depressions, Pozieres, Martinpuich, High Wood, Longueval, and Delville Wood, where the altitude maintained was nearly 500 feet. Before the war the area had supported the usual French agricultural populations and its fields were neatly kept and fertile, its villages numerous and quietly prosperous, its inhabitants diligent and content with their simple role in the scheme of things. The natural beauty of the landscape was enhanced by the woods and villages with which it was dotted, the former carefully kept and, in summer, green, cool and alluring, the villages, their houses half hidden by the trees and orchards about them, clustering snugly around their Gothic churches as if seeking security in the shadow of their soaring spires. Dainty roads wound, ribbon-like, between the villages connecting them all in a network of loving fraternity.

"A blast from the trumpet of war and all was changed; the idyllic landscape became in a few short months the most loathsome and appalling terrain in the world. No brush will ever paint, and no pen will ever tell, a tenth part of its repulsiveness, or of the sufferings of those who endured its horrors. A storm of high explosive raged over it night and day for many weeks. Millions of shells, each freighted with a hideous force of disruption, fell upon its fields, its woods, its villages. Chewed and masticated by the teeth of war, they lost all semblance of their former shapes. The fields became mere areas of dishevelled rubbish, the shell-holes filled with putrid water in which rotted the corpses of men and animals. The frames of gun carriages and of other vehicles, twisted into grotesque shapes, lay everywhere, and, even when the fiery breath of war had swept on to fresh devastation, death lurked for many in the unexploded shells and bombs with which the whole ground was littered. The villages were not merely destroyed. They were obliterated. At first they had burned. When that phase was over there were still standing the stout frameworks of the stone and brick edifices. These in turn had been shattered till they lay on the ground as shapeless heaps of brick and rubble. Not content with this, the storm of destruction had still fallen upon them, grinding and breaking and burying them until they were now scarcely distinguishable from the turbid seas of mud that had once been the meadows about them. But the transformation of the woods was more pitiable still. In them the resistance had been stoutest; on them, therefore, the fury of war had been the most concentrated. Their leaves had fallen prematurely; their boughs had been lopped off by flying fragments; their trunks, at first only scarred by shrapnel, had all in turn received the direct hit that had rent them asunder. Crashing to the ground, they had been hastily improvised as impediments to the relentless British advance, and meshes of barbed wire had held them for a space till the inevitable barrage came down once again. And then had come the infantry assault, when the surviving attackers met the surviving defenders in the grim shock of naked steel and clashing rifle butts, when, locked in a death embrace, friend and foe had wrestled desperately among the riven tree trunks and in the gaping shell-holes where their roots lay exposed. So that by now the once lovely woods were but a grim, silent concourse of the shattered boles of trees, standing stiffly there like a regiment of the dead on parade. And hundreds of the shell-holes among them were the sepulchres of unknown heroes and every broken tree trunk a memorial without a name. Delville Wood in October, 1916, was surely the most terrible spectacle that war had yet vouchsafed the world — Delville Wood, with its unburied corpses and its stinking trenches parapeted with dead Germans to protect those who yet lived. And perhaps some of the men who died in its foul recesses saw with the prophetic eye of death a future still unrevealed to those of us who are left. For a Tommy and a German, dying together in the same shell-hole, had smiled at each other before they breathed their last, and had clasped hands across some other bodies that lay there. Death had not parted the grip nor quite obliterated the expression of mutual goodwill and understanding that had accompanied it."

From October 22nd to November 5th half the battalion remained at "Hungry Hill" carrying out such training as the wretched weather conditions would permit. About a mile to the left was the battlefield of Pozieres, where for six weeks, from late July to early September, the 1st, 2nd, and 4th Australian Divisions had suffered heavily but won outstanding fame.

The transport lines were situated in a valley in rear of "Hungry Hill" and it was there, from the point of view of the transport section, that a tragedy happened. "Ginger," one of their favourite saddle hacks, sank in the mud and died. When in Egypt the transport horses broke from their lines, "Ginger" was the only one who did not join in the stampede. Lieutenant Barnett rode him almost continuously for three days rounding up the delinquents, and it is possible that his death may have been accelerated by those strenuous efforts. The sorrow of the transport men at his death almost equalled that which they felt when a human mate "went west."

Battalion headquarters, "C" Company (Major Sloan) and 'D" Company (Captain Cheeseman), moved up between Delville and High Woods to the Flers "Reserve Trench." It was amusing to see the men endeavouring—like a lady of the Victorian era—to hold up the skirts of their greatcoats from the mud, but as it became deeper this was impossible, and the tails were allowed to swish along behind. As the mud thus collected soon became too heavy to carry or drag along, the obvious thing was to remove it. A bright individual suggested that the most expeditious means would be to cut a foot or two off the bottom of the coat, an idea that was much acclaimed and speedily adopted. As neither tailors' scissors nor chalk was available, the cutting had to be done with blunt jack-knives. Hemming materials being also non-existent, the final effects caused quite a lot of merriment.

Flers Reserve Trench was in reality an irregular drain some six feet deep and eight to ten feet wide, which stretched across what had once been a potato field, but which was now a morass similar to a mangrove swamp when the tide is out. That we were in or on a potato field was soon evidenced by the fact that when a portion of the so-called trench fell in, tubers fell in also and were a valuable supplement to our food supply. Facing us some three miles away was the town of Bapaume, its church steeple and the tops of some of its higher buildings being in view Some distance on our left was the Butte of Warlencourt, and on our immediate right the ruined village of Flers. Every building in Flers had been levelled to the ground, but its cellars still gave shelter to a few small units. Running to the front was the awful "Fish Alley," a tortuous communication trench that will never be forgotten by those whose misfortune it was to use it.

On the night of October 31st we relieved the 32nd Battalion in the front line near "Factory Corner," and in turn handed over to the 21st Battalion (2nd Division) on November 3rd. By then we had almost reached the limit of human endurance, having been in practically open trenches for eight days.

Shortly after the 5th Division had entered the line orders were received for it to take part in an offensive, fixed for October 25th, across the valley in front of Bapaume. Continuous rain, however, caused the attack to be postponed from day to day, and in the end the 5th Division's task, greatly modified, was handed over to the 2nd Division,

"C" COMPANY SOMEWHERE IN FRANCE

WINTERING ON THE SOMME

which took the 5th's place in the line. The 2nd Division, attacking in the mud on November 5th and again on the 14th, and fighting under most difficult conditions, lost over 1,700 men without gaining any material advantage.

In the third volume of the Official History, Dr. Bean gives the following vivid description of the terrible conditions obtaining on the Somme battlefield at this time.

"On his journey into the trenches, each infantryman now carried his greatcoat, waterproof sheet, one blanket, 220 rounds of ammunition, and when fighting was in prospect, two bombs, two sandbags, and two days' reserve rations, besides the remnant of that day's 'issue'. Thus burdened, the troops dragged their way along the sledge-tracks beside the communication trenches, the latter—except in the actual front-system—being now never used. But the sledge-tracks also were by this time deep thick mud, which, especially when drying, tugged like glue at the boot-soles, so that the mere journey to the line left men and even pack-animals utterly exhausted. In the dark those who stepped away from the road fell again and again into shell-holes; many pack-animals became fast in the mud and had to be shot, and men were continually pulled out, often leaving their boots and sometimes their trousers. Three of the 25th Battalion had to be dug out of the 'jumping-off' trench on November 5th; a company commander of the 5th Pioneers was dragged out by a mule; a few weeks later a rescue party broke the back of an officer of the 2nd Division whom they were trying to haul from the mud. After each fight, i.e., November 5th and 14th, when the carriage of wounded across this area had to be performed almost entirely by stretcher-bearers, these men, working in four or five relays of six or eight to each stretcher, were quickly worn out; and, although detachments of the 21st and 24th Battalions worked devotedly as well as all the available bearers of the field ambulances, numbers of wounded, after being tended at the forward aid-posts, had to be left lying for twelve hours in the open without blankets for want of men to carry them. When sledges became available, single horses were often unable to drag them. A man of the 27th has recorded that when, after lying in No-Man's Land for five days with a smashed leg, he was eventually brought to the trenches by stretcher-bearers under a white flag, he had to be dragged thence over the mud area by three horses attached to a sledge.

"Coming into the trenches under such conditions, and starting their tour of duty in a state of exhaustion, the garrison of the front line usually had to stay there forty-eight hours before relief. At first the men tried to shelter themselves from rain by cutting niches in the trench-walls, but this practice was forbidden, several soldiers having been smothered through the slipping in of the sodden earth-roof, and the trenches broken down. If, to keep themselves warm, men stamped or moved about, the floor of the trench turned to thin mud. At night the officers sometimes walked up and down in the open and encouraged their men to do the same, chancing the snipers; but for the many there was no alternative but to stand almost still, freezing, night and day."

To describe in detail our method of getting back to "Hungry Hill" after being relieved by the 21st Battalion is somewhat difficult. Although officers were in front and rear, the movement could not by any stretch of imagination be called a march; it was just a case of each man picking the way that best suited him. One of those bringing up the rear remarked that the scene reminded him of a mob of cattle moving across a wide stock route; another, while approving the remark, suggested cynically that the word "sheep" be substituted for "cattle." The greatest danger to the individual was the concealed shell-hole, anything from two to four feet deep, which, filled with liquid mud, gave no indication of its existence.

These death-traps caught many men unawares, and, had help not been available, some—on the verge of utter exhaustion and weighed down by equipment and sodden clothing—would undoubtedly have perished.

The number of men suffering acutely from "trench-feet" was so great that the R.M.O. (Captain Railton) deserves the greatest credit for his almost superhuman efforts to get them back to Carlton Trench. The sight was a harrowing one for the rear-guard. The provision of transport was impossible, and it is doubtful whether all would have survived the ordeal of "Fish Alley" had it not been for the judicious issue of rum to those who became exhausted. Quite incapable of wearing boots, the afflicted "sloshed" painfully through the quagmire with pieces of sand bag wrapped round their tortured feet. Whale oil had been issued and orders given that each man was to rub his feet with it and so maintain the circulation of the blood, but as later events proved, it was not of much practical use. A prominent notice on each jar of oil, "Not to be used by Indian troops," indicated that the War Office had not forgotten the Indian Mutiny.

A new menace, "trench fever", of a previously unknown character was suspected when the medical officers failed to diagnose the illness of Corporal B. C. Smallcombe. He was forthwith rushed to England so that the disease could be fully investigated, but nothing of a disquietening nature was discovered, and subsequent patients, much to their disgust, were treated locally.

During the forenoon of November 5th, after the various parts of the battalion had been collected, we marched in more-or-less disjointed order through Bazentin-Le-Grand and Mametz to Fricourt, where shelter from the rain was obtained in improvised shelters, and after a liberal issue of rum and a good meal, a refreshing rest was obtained by all ranks. It was here that there occurred an incident for which some have not entirely forgiven our otherwise respected C.O. Some twenty cases of rum, forty gallons in all, had been dumped into our lines from a broken-down transport, and it was ours for the taking. The quartermaster, "Soldier Bill," had just completed loading the "windfall" on to a waggon, when the C.O. happened to come along and ordered it to be thrown off into the mud. Whether the C.O. of the unit following us did likewise is doubtful.

The following day we resumed our move to the rear area, reverting at last to something like march discipline. Some of the men were still weak from exposure, and it was good to see their stronger comrades carrying rifles and packs in addition to their own. At one period a sergeant was carrying three rifles. The march per boot ended at the miserable village of Buire, but its billets were quite acceptable after our recent experiences.

On the morning of the 7th, all were heartened by the arrival of a fleet of French motor buses by which we were whirled along to Vignacourt, a hamlet thirty miles behind the line, and within a short distance of Amiens.

Though dirty, Vignacourt was a welcome haven of rest and recreation for the following ten days. The early part was devoted to cleaning up and replacing shortages, principally bobbed greatcoats, discarded boots, and lost ammunition. Light-weapon training was carried out, supplemented by short route marches, one of which, in particular, through a small wood was much enjoyed. The many tinted autumn leaves were falling and forming a carpet on the ground that no pantomime stage could ever hope to equal.

The only matter for reflection was the fact that the scene portended the early approach of winter, which had been forecasted as one likely to be more severe than usual, and which, as it turned out, was the worst that France had known for sixty years. Among the happenings of this period were the completion of voting on the conscription issue, an inspection by General Birdwood, and a fall of snow, the latter a new experience for the majority of the battalion.

Our strength was now 36 officers and 949 other ranks. Lieutenants Adams and Levitt were away, having been

WINTERING ON THE SOMME

seconded for other duties, and 39 men were evacuated sick.

On November 18th, thoroughly rested, and reinforced by some new arrivals, we again headed for the front line. Buses conveyed us to within a short distance of Ribemont, a mile west of Buire, and we billeted there for the night. On this occasion there was an almost complete absence of the jollity and good-natured chaff that had characterized the journey forward the previous month. The novelty of being driven by hairy coated Frenchmen had now worn off, and the memories of "Hungry Hill," "Fish Alley," and "Factory Corner" were too recent to be forgotten. The march to Montauban was as strenuous as before. It is true that the volume of traffic had not lessened and the mud was, if possible, worse than ever, but the roads had been pushed slightly farther forward and the duck-board tracks improved.

A cluster of "Nissen huts" had sprung up at Montauban since our previous visit. These certainly gave shelter from the rain and the piercing wind, but as sixty men had to crowd into a space intended for forty, the conditions were most uncomfortable.

The only remnants of the village were a few broken stones and the twisted iron gates and broken tomb-stones of the old French cemetery.

The water for the "cookers" was brought from storage tanks in the village, and so bad were the conditions that six mules had to be used to draw each water-cart. One day one of the mules in a team delivering water to our cookers, becoming restive and fearful of the mud, kept plunging about, and caused the driver to drop his whip. He dismounted to pick it up, when the mule, still plunging, put its hoof on his foot, sinking him almost to the thigh. Naturally, the onlookers expected an outburst of profanity, but as the unfortunate man extricated himself he looked up into the mule's face and was dumb—the Australian language had failed him. On another occasion a mule kicked the nose-cap of a supposedly "dud" shell, and at once caused a vacancy in the animal lines.

It was at Montauban that the battalion lost the services of Captain Blair Wark, a most capable leader, who was transferred to the 32nd Battalion. Lieutenant Haviland left us also, being seconded to one of the divisional medium trench mortar batteries. Major Sloan and Captain Cheeseman were sent to the Fourth Army School at Flexicourt for a course of instruction. Fifty men were evacuated sick during our three days' stay at Montauban, thus reducing our strength to 34 officers and 899 other ranks.

At this time the whole countryside of the Somme was littered with discarded stores and equipment of every conceivable description, particularly the brass cylinders of 18-pounder ammunition. Thus it came about that regular salvage companies were organised in each division, and by the end of the war millions of pounds worth of material had been recovered and reconditioned and put to further use.

The next three weeks (November 22nd-December 12th) were strenuous ones. The almost invariable routine was to move forward in three stages to Trones or Bernafay Woods, thence to "Needle Dump" in the intermediate line, and finally, on to the front trenches facing Le-Transloy—remaining no longer than two or three days at each place. The backward movement to the Montauban "base" would then begin, for the conditions were such that front-line troops had to be frequently relieved.

After a few days' spell and the process would be repeated. Almost every day a few men were killed or wounded, but our greatest losses were due to sickness, and particularly to trench feet. From the latter cause alone fifty-five members of the battalion lost one or both feet, creating an unenviable record in the A.I.F. Private Archie Cox had both feet amputated, but, as he still contrives to win bicycle races in Newcastle, the artificial limb experts

WINTERING ON THE SOMME

must have excelled themselves in his case. The loss of toes was a common occurrence, one man losing all ten.

Whale oil for treatment of the feet was now discontinued and a powder issued in its place, but this, too, was of little use. Gum boots were issued, but not in sufficient numbers. The 13th day of December upheld its traditional reputation for bad luck, as on this day 142 of our men were evacuated sick.

The great offensive battle that had raged almost continuously since July 1st had practically ended, each side contenting itself with artillery, trench mortar, and machine gun fire. While there was available plenty of warm clothing, including numberless sheepskin vests, the almost continuous rain prevented the drying of clothing, hence the excessive sickness. It was at this period that the strength of the battalion fell to its lowest ebb, totalling less than 400 of all ranks. Higher authority, acting perhaps on the assertion that a change is as good as a rest, detailed us as "corps troops", and from December 12th to January 12th we were engaged in road construction and quarry work in "Sausage Gully", near Pozieres. The routine was monotonous, but afforded the great advantage of night-time rest.

Captain Jim Chapman's diary records that all hands enjoyed a good Christmas dinner in Montauban Camp—Jim was a teetotaler—but another record by Hubert Stinson stresses the fact that nothing stronger than tea was available, so to quote his words, "How could it have been a good Christmas?" For the information of the uninitiated, it may here be stated that rum was considered to form portion of the daily food ration and not at all associated with periods of conviviality.

The remainder of the division, including our transport, had by then moved back to Rainneville, Coisy, and Vignacourt, some eight or nine miles from Amiens, and on the authority of R.Q.M.S. Tom Fricker, real Christmas fare was obtainable in those villages.

Our artillery did their best to minimise the enjoyment

of the enemy's Christmas dinner. Punctually at 12.30 (German time), when probably he was enjoying his lager beer and plum pudding, greetings from every gun on the Australian Front were sent to him. Similarly at midnight on 31st December, he was given a reminder of the New Year by our gunners firing first a single shot, then, after a pause, nine in rapid succession, again a pause, another single shot, a pause, and finally seven in rapid succession, thus forming 1-9-1-7.

About this period the system of communication avenues to the front line gave place to duckboarded tracks across the open. These were quite as safe as trenches during the long hours of darkness and much more comfortable to walk upon. Moreover, pack mules could move along the duckboards, whereas they could not negotiate the communication trenches. Sandbags tied around a mule's hooves prevented his slipping and of his own volition he learned to put his foremost foot down steadily, feeling his way like a human.

The "corps" employment came to an end on January 12th, when, relieved by the 29th Battalion, we moved back to the Fricourt brigade camp and thence forward to Montauban, "Trones Wood," "Needle Dump," and the front line. We relieved the 53th Battalion in "Zenith," "Spring" and "Summer" trenches—inappropriate names at this period! On 26th we handed over our responsibilities to the 29th Battalion and by the usual stages crawfished back to Fricourt.

Training, such as weather conditions permitted, was carried out until February 6th. During this period heavy falls of snow occurred, followed by frosts. Trenches and shell-holes which were previously feet deep in water and slush were now frozen hard, and this made movement much easier. Methods in the conveyance of food to the front lines improved, a thermos method being used to keep it hot during the journey, and "Tommy cookers" were issued to troops in the front line. The carrying of coffee in petrol

WINTERING ON THE SOMME

tins was somewhat of a failure, as it was found impossible to eliminate the taste of the spirit. Men who wore moustaches, and particularly those with colds, were much inconvenienced by the icicle pendants which hung from their upper lip and, in consequence, many of them reverted to clean shaving.

Body armour was now issued for raiding purposes. The 57th Battalion tried it out, and, while it was not altogether a failure, the troops found it too heavy and cumbersome for ordinary trench work. The remark of a wag, who, after referring to the soldiers of the twelfth century, and the 96 lbs. of armour carried by Ned Kelly, that "men was men in them days" was not universally approved by his mates.

On February 7th the battalion moved forward again to Montauban and Pommier Redoubt, relieving the 31st Battalion on road and railway fatigues. A week later, on being relieved by the 60th Battalion, we went on to Delville Wood to engage in further pick and shovel work until the 20th. For about the twentieth time since our enlistment, divisional orders contained a reference to the non-saluting of officers. These were perfunctorily read on parade, but went absolutely unheeded, one Digger remarking—"If the heads cannot make us salute like soldiers, they certainly are turning us into good navvies."

Casualties, except those due to sickness, were light during the month. Very little change in personnel took place, our strength averaging 35 officers and 950 other ranks.

By the middle of February the thaw was commencing, fogs came down frequently, and the whole terrain once more became a quagmire. However, by reason of the improvements made in roads, tracks and railways, and the better methods of food supply, and, with the ever lengthening days, conditions were vastly superior to those of the previous four months. Canteens had been established in forward areas, and various organizations were combining to make the lot of the soldier more bearable. The Rev. Fred

Ward, of the 32nd Battalion, who, it will be remembered, was our Church of England Chaplain in Egypt, was particularly praised by men of all units for his efforts to provide hot coffee, biscuits, etc., to those returning wet, hungry and tired from the front line. Bob Mather tells a story to the effect that on one occasion he saw the padre busy with pick and shovel cutting steps down a slippery bank in the vicinity of his stall. Questioned as to the reason for this unusual activity, Ward replied: "I heard more bad language last night from men sliding down this beastly bank than I have previously heard in my whole life, and I am determined that it shall not recur to-night." Truly a practical method of reformation. Incidentally, our good padre, as these lines are being written, can be found at the following typically English address: Dorking Vicarage, King's Lynn, Norfolk, England.

On February 21st the battalion left Delville Wood, moving to Needle and Switch Trenches, where the mud, due to the thaw, was so bad that a number of men were in danger of smothering—some certainly would have died if help had not been at hand. Two nights later we relieved the 31st Battalion, having two companies in the front line, one in "Rose Trench" and one in "Miller's Son." Before daylight that morning, however, the German garrisons had withdrawn from most of their front line opposite the whole front of the Fifth British Amy (in which we were then serving). This was the beginning of the German retirement, which ended early in April, when the enemy took position in the formidable defences of the Hindenburg Line.

"The day which followed, February 23rd (says the Australian Official History) appeared to all troops on the Anzac front to be absolutely normal, . . . Early in the night of the 23rd, however, the attention of several battalion commanders was focussed on the German trenches facing their several sectors by reports very different from those previously received. From the right leftwards, in the 5th Division a patrol (of the 31st Battalion) reconnoitring Sunray Trench, which that division was to attack a few days later, found that it was empty except for a single enemy post; yet the

WINTERING ON THE SOMME

enemy was throwing an unusual number of flares. Patrols of the left brigade (12th) of the 4th Division found Stormy Trench full of movement till 8.30, but very quiet from that time on. Along the front of the 1st and 2nd Divisions almost every patrol brought back the news that, in contrast to its abnormal activity on the past few nights, the German front appeared to be almost dead. The known points from which machine guns usually fired were silent; flares were being thrown all along the front—but from positions well in rear of the trenches usually held."

This information, however, did not reach corps headquarters until midday on the 24th, but up to 5 p.m.:—

"These facts were assumed to have a purely local significance. At that hour, General White at corps headquarters telephoned to all divisions the news, just received from the Fifth Army, that the V. British Corps had found the German positions in Petit Miraumont and south of it empty. This, he said, combined with the reports of Australian patrols, suggested that 'a certain withdrawal of the enemy's forces has taken place or is about to take place.' "

"It is astonishing evidence (comments Dr. Bean) of the paralysing effect of the long, tense struggle in the Somme mud that the first general realisation of the truth should have come to the Australain divisions with this message. The only sphere in which the intelligence organisation of the corps had functioned usefully was that of the patrols. Their reports on the nights of the 22nd and 23rd were abundant and accurate in almost every detail; but patrols had only to rivet their attention on the narrow sector immediately in front of them. Unfortunately, almost every department of the staff behind them was doing the same. The leaders, having for months been matching their wits against those of the enemy in solving the problems of their own few acres of muddy front, had lost sight of wider considerations. With them the vital and absorbing matters were next week's raids, the coming offensives, the cutting of wire. Thus staffs, both higher and lower, which for forty-eight hours had vital items of intelligence actually lying on their tables, failed to recognise them and pass them on."

That night, our patrols entered Sunray Trench, meeting with slight resistance on the right. A block was established on both flanks and the position held. Our casualties consisted of Lieutenant R. Gaskill and one man was killed, Captain Ray A. M. Allen, Lieutenants Don Chalmers, C. J. Craker and nine other ranks were wounded. We were relieved by men of the 29th Battalion, now under the command of one of our old officers, Lieutenant-Colonel M. Purser, which exploited "Sunray" still further and were deservedly complimented on their activity. We worked back progressively to "Needle Dump" and "Trones Wood."

CHAPTER X.

(BAPAUME AND BEAUMETZ).

For another week the battalion reverted to pick-and-shovel work, and on March 8th moved to "Townsville Camp" where some useful platoon organisation and training was carried out. At the same time, a considerable number of all ranks were attending schools of instruction, specialising in various branches of the military art. But the long sojourn in the neighbourhood of Delville, Trones, and Bernafay Woods was drawing to a close, and, despite the mud, the battalion was in great heart.

On March 12th we relieved the 19th Battalion (2nd Division) in the reserve line near "Factory Corner", moving thence to the support line at "Yarra Bank." At this time the Germans were holding two strong lines (R.1. and R.11.) in front of Bapaume, though on the night of March 11th they had withdrawn from part of R.1., near Loupart Wood, north of the Bapaume road. All the previous week smoke had been rising from the town and the villages beyond it, and British airmen reported the wholesale movement of railway trains east and south in the German back area.

"Conjectures as to the German intentions (says the Official History) were confirmed on March 13th by the discovery, apparently in a dug-out in Loupart Wood, of two copies of orders of the 1st Guard Reserve Division. One, dated March 11th, contained instructions for the withdrawal on March 11th, from R.1. More important was the other, an earlier order of March 5th, laying down the procedure of the main retreat to the Hindenburg Line. This showed that it had been intended to carry out the whole retreat from the R.1. line to the Hindenburg Line in two main stages."

The all-important question was—on which day would the main retreat begin? After studying the captured orders, Sir Douglas Haig's intelligence staff came to the conclusion that the final withdrawal was already in progress, and that the R.11. line was probably held only by the German rearguard, which would be due to retire at 4 a.m. on March 14th or 15th. On the night of the 13th, however, the Australian patrols found the Germans holding their line in strength. The 31st Battalion entered the R.1. line through the 6th Brigade sector on its left, and on the following night advanced almost to a sort of "switch" trench connecting R.1. and R.11.; but all attempts to probe the R.1. line to the south of that point, opposite the whole of the 5th Division's front, were repulsed. Again on the night of March 15th the enemy was found to be exceptionally alert, and in the early morning of the 16th a bombing party attacked a post of the 31st Battalion. The patrols heard German waggons coming, as usual, towards the line, but observed that the drivers were shouting and making unnecessary noise, apparently with the idea of inducing their opponents to think that no retirement was in progress.

"Throughout the 16th signs were conflicting. The German sniping was in all parts noticeably keen," records the Official History, "but during the afternoon an aeroplane of the 3rd British Squadron which flew over R.1. in front of the 5th Division reported that, instead of the hail of machine-gun and rifle-fire usually turned upon probing pilots, only a single shot was fired at it near Grévillers. Yet, after dusk, when for the third night in succession strong special patrols of the 5th Australian Division reached the wire of that trench, they were met, as normally, by bombs and machine-gun fire."

"Such was the position when, at midnight, 'B,' 'C,' and 'D' Companies of the 30th Battalion relieved the 31st in

'Rye' and 'Bayonet' Trenches and the 'Yellow Cut,' opposite Bapaume.

"A warning had been received to keep close touch, as the withdrawal seemed imminent; the enemy was then firing machine-guns and throwing many flares, and the patrols reported the line held, but not, they thought, in strength. At 3.40 a small attack was ordered on the left against the German barricade in the switch between R.I. and R.II. After the Stokes mortars had fired a dozen rounds, a small party of 'C' Company bombed 150 yards up the trench, but found it empty, though some of the flare cartridges in it were still hot. At 4.30 the party halted and built a barricade. Till this hour German machine-guns were especially active, ripping the earth of the Australian parapets, but shortly afterwards a patrol on the right, under Corporal J. H. King, entered R.I. [here known to the Australians as 'Till Trench']. Learning of this about 6 o'clock, Lieutenant-Colonel Clark ordered a general advance, but, on being reminded of the activity of the machine-guns, agreed to send forward patrols first. They went out at 6.30 and found the enemy gone. The three front-line companies of the 30th then advanced in artillery formation, still preceded by their scouts, over the 1,200 yards of open crest intervening between them and the old town. Its high ramparts and deep moat, now grown with grass and trees, appeared a formidable obstacle if any rear party had held them, but they were silent."

Lieutenant A. C. White, commanding the centre company ("B"), and Lieutenant D. Vincent were the first to enter Bapaume. When Corporal C. E. Alcorn's patrol returned with the information that Till Trench was empty, they went forward with it, ahead of the company, crossing Till and the support line (R.II), the two of them entering the town together through the cattle-market. Naturally they were highly elated at the distinction which they had brought upon the battalion and particularly on "B" Company. As Alcorn was responsible for "B" Company getting into

Bapaume first, it was unfortunate that after all the members of his patrol had been sent back with messages, he personally had to take the final one from the outskirts of the town, which he did with "disciplined reluctance."

Shortly after 7.15 the left and centre companies had reached the main Péronne road running along the heights through the town. At its junction with the high road to Cambrai was a huge crater, recently blown, which they occupied. A large proportion of the houses had evidently been blown down by the Germans in the last few days, and many were burning, the smoke rendering it difficult to see down the streets.

Patrols were at once sent forward. One of these, under Lieutenant Gunning of the right company, moved swiftly through the north of the town, gaining touch with an officer of the 23rd Battalion (6th Brigade). Germans were sniping from houses and other vantage points, and a member of this patrol, Private R. N. French, was killed on the Vaulx-Vrancourt road, beyond Bapaume.

After a short spell, during which the troops experienced the great satisfaction of scraping the Somme mud from their clothing and equipment, the left and right companies ("D" and "C"), commanded by Captain T. C. Barbour and Lieutenant E. Adams respectively, were ordered to move forward 700-800 yards on both sides of the Cambrai road. As the companies emerged into the green intact country beyond the town, odd parties of Germans were seen running back across the open, and when fired on they disappeared. The leading platoons broke into skirmishing order and, for the first time, advanced as in open warfare. "D" Company reached its objective quickly, and for a time both flanks remained in the air. Shortly after dusk, however, "C" Company came up on the right and a unit of the 23rd Battalion made contact on the left. The German rear-guard facing them occupied an unfinished trench, known as the "R.IIa." or "Barbarossa" line, which was protected by a belt of wire.

A.W.M. Photo E373.

STRETCHER BEARERS, BAPAUME
Pte. W. H. Walters, (Pte. A. L. Bull). Pte. T. Donnellan.

STREET SCENE, BAPAUME

A.W.M. Photo E371.

The day's casualties in the battalion amounted to one man killed and nine wounded. Lieutenant Gunning got a bullet through the heel of one of his boots, apparently an Achilles attempt to wound him.

Captain Barbour in his report specially mentions the work of Lieutenants E. H. Richardson and H. J. Wells, Corporal D. Smith, Lewis Gunners J. J. Hill, R. McDiarmid, H. McDiarmid, and Runners E. Pockett, J. Ford, J. Wilson, G. Cooper and E. Robinson, during this period.

That night an accident occurred which nearly culminated in tragedy. Sergeant G. Haigh fell into a narrow well partially filled with water, and it was some time before he could be rescued. An attempt to pull him out with a strand of wire failed, as it broke when he was nearing the surface, and he was again precipitated into the icy cold water. Eventually a party in charge of the medical officer, Captain Railton, was despatched from battalion headquarters with the necessary equipment and restoratives, and on his being brought to the surface he was wrapped in blankets and hurried to hospital where, fortunately, he soon recovered.

Great was the delight of all ranks at finding themselves in such surroundings, with green fields and villages on all sides. Gone was the slush and squalor of the previous long winter and hopes of a speedy ending of the war arose in many a heart. Great care, however, had to be exercised, as the enemy had left many booby traps, in the shape of delayed mines, in dugouts and houses, and had also polluted a number of wells. At this juncture it must be recorded that the 31st Battalion had, during the previous four days, done much to pave the way for our advance, by keeping in close touch with the enemy and retarding his preparation for retreat. The casualties of the 31st during this period totalled 119.

"The occupation of Bapaume," says the Australian Official Historian, "aroused throughout the British Army in France a glow of elation whose warmth it is difficult to recapture in a written account. During half of 1916, while the British Army had been waging the most terrible struggle in its history, this town had been the goal. Staffs of corps and even of armies had tended to become engrossed in efforts to gain the few acres of mud and debris which led up to it; and tens of thousands of the flower of the British nation devoted the last weeks of their lives to an all-absorbing endeavour 'to reach Bapaume.' Consequently, when the news of its fall began to spread—staff officers, war correspondents, and official photographers began to stream to the place. On March 18th the tide of visitors flowed so strongly as to arouse caustic comment from the working parties of Australian pioneers toiling to bridge or fill-in gaps blown by the Germans in the Albert-Bapaume road."

During the afternoon of March 17th the commanders of the two Australian front-line divisions (2nd and 5th) each organised an advanced guard, to "act promptly and boldly against detached bodies of the enemy." In the 5th Division the advanced guard comprised half the 15th Brigade, with an attached squadron of light horse and other arms. About daybreak on the 18th it passed through the outposts, and, crossing the now empty Barbarossa (R.11.2) line, captured the village of Fremicourt on the Cambrai road, and the R.111 ("Beugny-Ytres") line, three miles beyond Bapaume. The following day it drove the Germans from Beugny, Lebucquiere, and Velu. The 30th Battalion moved forward one thousand yards to Bancourt, and dug in on a line selected by the brigade-major (Major R. G. Casey) and our adjutant, Lieutenant James Chapman.

On March 20th Lieutenant White and C. S. M. McKinnon captured a German in an abandoned sugar factory. When questioned, the prisoner stated that he had been left behind to blow up a mine in Fremicourt but that he had not yet carried out the job. He was accordingly bustled along to the village, and, on its being found that the mine had been exploded three days previously, his only explanation was that he must be suffering from loss of memory. White's comment was to the effect that he "looked like a dope who would go to sleep and be left behind." Anyhow, he was something of a novelty, as the battalion had not taken a prisoner for some months.

North of the Cambrai road this day the advanced guard seized the village of Morchies, but south of it was unable to drive the Germans from Beaumetz. Before dawn next morning, however, patrols found it empty, and it was at once occupied by our sister battalion, the 29th, which had relieved one of the attacking battalions (60th) of the 15th Brigade. Later, on the 21st, the 30th relieved the 59th Battalion in the Morchies sector, Colonel Clark being placed in charge of the outpost line of both battalions. Captain Cheeseman temporarily commanded the 30th.

March 21st and 22nd were spent in quietly consolidating the new position. On the night of the 22nd "C" and "D" Companies, on right and left respectively, were holding the battalion front, with "B" Company in support in a sunken road some 600 yards behind the right company. "A" Company was in reserve, and Captain Cheeseman occupied a dugout between "C" and "B". On account of the long front which "C" Company had to hold between the Cambrai road and Morchies, Lieutenant ("Yank") Adams had his men distributed in small posts save on the left flank, where a partially sunken road allowed two platoons being located together near company headquarters. The right post of the Company consisted of six men with a Lewis gun ensconced in a crater which the enemy had blown at the point where the Morchies-Beaumetz road crossed the main Cambrai Road. From this post to the first sentry group of the 29th Battalion on the right, was over 300 yards, while on its left there were no men of "C" Company for at least the same distance.

The night of the 22nd was quiet, but early on the 23rd a patrol from "C" Company, under Lieutenant Yeomans, came in and reported movement by the enemy in front.

Before dawn a scattered bombardment of field-guns and light howitzers fell on the Australian position, and the Germans suddenly advanced to the attack.

"There was a light ground mist at the time," writes an N.C.O., "and aided by this, the enemy advanced in mass, overwhelming part of the garrison of Beaumetz, including the small party in the crater, who put up a gallant fight. Their Lewis gun was heard firing, and an examination of their rifles afterwards showed that the little party had fought to the last, the Germans sustaining heavy casualties before they finally subdued the post with stick-bombs.

"A Boche machine-gun section then took possession of the crater, and a party of some 70 strong pushed on and enfiladed the remainder of 'C' Company's position from the right. Lieutenant Gunning of 'C' Company led a party against the crater, but was temporarily held up owing to the accuracy of the fire from the enemy machine-gun. Snipers on both sides were exchanging shots, when the German detachment was seen retiring in disorder, hotly pursued by two yelling platoons of the support company.

"The first intimation the O.C. of the support company (Lieutenant White) had of the enemy attack was the opening of the bombardment. The company was standing-to at the time, and one 4.2-inch shell fell very close to company headquarters, causing several casualties, and blowing Lieutenant Vincent and Corporal Alcorn off their feet. Almost immediately orders were received from Captain Cheeseman to hasten to the assistance of the front-line company. Vincent, though suffering badly from concussion, immediately went forward with one platoon, accompanied by Lieutenant Williams with another. Alcorn, who was also severely shaken, moved a platoon, which he commanded at the time, to the right flank astride the Bapaume-Cambrai Road.

"The platoons under Vincent and Williams swept up

Coy. Sgt.-Maj. GEOFFREY COWEN, BAPAUME

AT BAPAUME
Above: Pte. C. W. Marsh, and Pte. L. Dixon, M.M.
Below: Pte. T. H. Davis, M.M., and Pte. C. F. Cavanaugh.
A.W.M. Photo No. E374.
A.W.M. Photo No. E370.

the hill at the charge, coming immediately under heavy field-gun fire. The party of seventy Boche, who had penetrated the front line, advanced yelling 'Hoch! Hoch!' and throwing stick-bombs to intimidate them. Nothing daunted, the Australians advanced, also yelling, and the enemy first wavered and then broke and ran. The confusion spread, and those of the enemy's attacking force who had not been killed or wounded, hurriedly evacuated our positions, and, pursued by the concentrated fire of rifles and every machine-gun that could be brought to bear upon them, retired hastily to their own lines."

The position was thus restored on the front of the 30th Battalion, and about the same time the enemy in Beaumetz itself were driven out by a determined counter-attack made by the 29th Battalion, which, incidentally, recaptured the Lewis gun which had been lost at the crater by "C" Company. A special patrol, made up of headquarters details under the adjutant, Captain James Chapman, investigated the situation in Beaumetz and reported back to Colonel Clark, with all the reassuring details.

It is estimated that the Germans suffered at least 150 casualties during the action. They included a detachment of "storm troops," specially brought up from near Valenciennes.

Lieutenant Adams was awarded the M.C. for the coolness and initiative he showed on this occasion, and Sergeant B. O. Davies received the D.C.M. for his "conspicuous gallantry when in command of a Lewis gun section."

That night the 58th Battalion took over the line of the 30th, which marched back to Bapaume and commenced road fatigue. "No rest for the 30th" appeared to be the slogan.

A sensation was caused on the night of the 25th when the town hall was blown up by a delayed-action mine which killed a number of men, including two visiting French deputies. Large working parties, including some from the 30th, dug all night and the next day, and succeeded in rescuing six of the men who had been trapped in its cellars.

On March 27th the battalion relieved the 58th Battalion in the outpost-line, handing over next day to the 54th Battalion. The next three days were devoted to improving the inner outpost-line and repairing roads in the Bapaume area. In view of the fate of the town hall, brigade headquarters authorised the construction of shelters some distance from the main portion of the town. These were made from material obtained from the débris of ruined buildings, and, as the work was supervised by Lieutenant Adams, the place during our occupation of it was known as "Adamstown."

On April 1st—appropriate day for a hoax—the battalion was warned to be ready to move forward at an hour's notice to support the advanced guard. All were dressed up ready to go, when another order arrived cancelling the arrangement. For the next fifteen days the companies were engaged in pick-and-shovel work, repairing the Albert-Bapaume railway, but as spring was now with us, the time passed pleasantly enough. A guard of honour was provided for General Birdwood on one of his periodical visits, during which he presented Sergeant Davies with the ribbon of his D.C.M., and Privates E. H. Lester and W. A. Ward with that of the M.M.

A compromise between the spiritual and temporal authorities appeared to have been brought about on Sunday, April 8th, as two companies of the battalion attended church parade while the remainder filled the shovel and swung the pick as usual.

About this time Colonel Clark received his D.S.O. A number of changes had also occurred in the battalion. Lieutenants D. L. Brown, C. D. Button, H. Robertson, B. D. Rush, M. Griffin, and R. C. Chapple had reported for duty, and forty other ranks, including Sergeant A. W. Chivers, returned from hospital. Regimental Sergeant-Major A. H. E. Whipp, Company Sergeant-Major E. H. Richardson, and Sergeants F. A. Butterworth and T. S. C. Horgan were appointed to commissioned rank. Among those promoted to the rank of sergeant were Corporals H. J. Shepherd, N. J. Sutherland, A. D. Burns, F. McGovern, H. Doust, A. L. Warboys, and J. E. Penrose. Lieutenant W. E. Oakes was transferred to the headquarters Lewis gun section, Lieutenant Horgan was appointed signalling officer, Lieutenant C. D. Savage and Sergeant W. H. Huxley were transferred to the 8th Light Trench Mortar Battery, and Captain G. W. Wynne, Company Sergeant-Major E. G. McKinnon, and Sergeant E. H. Shipp sent for a tour of duty to the 8th Training Battalion in England. Captain A. P. Hext, Lieutenant F. Hamilton, Sergeants F. J. Daley and Grahame Sands, and Private P. Milgate were among those evacuated sick to hospital. In a batch of forty other ranks invalided home about this time were Sergeants H. H. Stevenson, F. J. D. Field, J. A. Bentley, and G. Evans, and Private P. J. Nankivell. Captain I. G. Fullarton was detailed to return to Australia for staff duties, and his going was a distinct loss to the battalion.

Accidents of the "didn't-know-it-was-loaded" nature occurred from time to time through men picking up live grenades and bombs. The C.O. took these misadventures seriously and issued a warning that was read on three consecutive parades. Further reference to non-saluting and slackness in dress was made about this time, without much result, one man remarking, "Navvies don't salute their gangers, so why should we?"

On April 15th, four days after the 4th Division's disastrous attack on the Hindenburg Line east of Bullecourt, the Germans, using 26 battalions, made a strong but costly sortie against the line of the 1st and 2nd Divisions from Noreuil to Hermies, temporarily overrunning the 1st Division's guns in the Lagnicourt Valley. The 29th and 30th Battalions were sent up to reinforce the 1st Division, if necessary, but were not called upon to enter the fight. Two companies of the 30th were attached to the 3rd Brigade at Morchies, while the other two and headquarters remained at Beugny. "C" Company under Lieutenant Adams was given the special job of consolidating a position in Louverval Wood, which it successfully accomplished after working all night and well into the next day.

Two days later the battalion moved back to Bancourt, and, on being relieved by the South Staffordshire Regiment, marched, by way of Beaulencourt, Gueudecourt, Flers, and Longueval to "Albury Camp" in the Albert area, where the 5th Division was to "rest" for the next four weeks.

A wonderful change had come over the whole countryside; what formerly were seas of mud were now light green fields, thus showing the fertility of the soil and the rapidity with which Nature reasserts herself when left alone. Green leaves were sprouting from the blackened stumps of once stately trees, and the undergrowth of Delville and neighbouring woods appeared to be trying to hide their scars from public view. Properly constructed roads had given place to corduroy and duckboard tracks and hutted camps provided ample accommodation.

The battalion remained here for eighteen days, undergoing strenuous training in all branches of infantry work. The perfect weather conditions no doubt contributed to the great improvement noticeable in discipline, deportment, and general appearance. Recreation was not neglected, two days being devoted to divisional sports at which the 8th Brigade won its share of prizes. The second day was devoted to a grand horse show, which created great interest and was largely attended. Driver W. Thompson won second prize in the entries for general service limbered waggon and pair of mules, and Driver L. Tripp gained third prize in those for travelling kitchen and pair of horses.

A piece of ground was cleared for football, and some excitement was caused when an enemy grenade, which had stuck in the mud some months previously without exploding, came to life when forcibly pulled from the ground by

BAPAUME AND BEAUMETZ

one of the players. Several men were injured and the game was postponed indefinitely.

Regulations concerning payments to men proceeding on leave or to schools were published about this time. Subject to their accounts being in credit, N.C.O.'s could draw up to £2 for each day of leave, whereas the private soldiers could draw but 30s. The maximum amount allowed to N.C.O's. was £20, to the privates £15. The latter could not understand the reason for what, to them, appeared to be an invidious distinction, their unanswerable contention being, "If my pay book is in credit, why can I not please myself as to what amount I draw." A notification in battalion orders to the effect that men proceeding on leave could have a bath and be issued with clean underclothing and towels on application to the sanitary officer in the Rue de Bapaume, Albert, was much availed of; but another paragraph, relating to the saluting of officers when on leave, was not generally approved.

Polling for the Federal Elections on Sunday, April 29th, was attended to very perfunctorily, as most of the men had lost touch with politics and were not much concerned as to which side won.

After receiving so many inoculations in Egypt it had been thought these had been finished with, but paratyphoid had still to be combated, and all ranks thus acquired a further dose of serum. The fact of being given twenty-four hours in which to recover from the local effects of the inoculation more than counterbalanced the slight inconvenience which the operation involved.

With the withdrawal of the Germans from the Bapaume ridge it became safe for the former inhabitants of Fricourt, Montauban, Gueudecourt, Flers, Bazentin, and other villages to return thither to search for treasures which they had buried ere fleeing from the advancing enemy years before. Many pathetic sights were seen when families, mostly women in mourning, vainly endeavoured to locate their one-time homes and in the end had to turn away disappointed. A notable exception is mournfully recorded by Private J. S. Bartley, who states, "One morning a French civvie unearthed a large hoard of gold and jewellery from beneath a tree under whose branches we had for some days played 'two-up,' little dreaming of the wealth that could have been ours for the digging."

Further promotions occurred during this period, Captain Cheeseman becoming a major, Lieutenants Macfarlane and White captains, and 2nd Lieutenants Brown, Craker, Button, Rush, Robertson, Hamilton, Williams, Whipp, Gunning and Richardson lieutenants. Regimental Quartermaster-Sergeant T. C. Fricker and Company Quartermaster-Sergeants K. Smithers and J. McDuff received commissions, Fricker being appointed quartermaster. N.C.O's. given a step in rank included N. J. Sutherland to C.Q.M.S., and E. J. Tysoe, R. Estell and E. J. Dunkley to sergeant. The following officers reported for duty—2nd Lieutenants H. W. Wedd, A. J. McCallum, F. W. Keen, G. Seymour, and W. R. Marler. Lieutenant A. H. Treloar was invalided to England suffering from trench feet, and after spending fourteen weeks in hospital, was transferred to the machine-gun school at Grantham. Sergeant D. Smith was awarded the Military Medal.

On May 9th the Hindenburg Line called again. In the previous week the 2nd Division had gained a foothold in the German stronghold and, after desperately repulsing three general counter-attacks, its brigades had given way to those of the 1st, which also withstood three formidable attempts to oust them. The 5th Division was therefore ordered up from rest to relieve the tired 1st. The 14th and 15th Brigades which had to take over the front line, moved by rail, the 8th Brigade following per boot. This circumstance took the minds of the old hands back to Egypt, when the 8th were the privileged train passengers from Tel el Kebir to Moascar, while the remainder footed it through the sand. The 30th Battalion, marching through Bazentin, Longueval, Flers, Gueudecourt, Beaulencourt,

Bancourt, and Fremicourt, took over a reserve position from the 57th Battalion in the "Beugny-Ytres" line. The following day was devoted to forward reconnaissance by the C.O. and company commanders while the men rested.

On the night of May 11th the battalion relieved the 2/12th London Regiment in a sunken road at Beugny. No shelter of any kind was available, but the weather was fine though cold. "B" Company became temporarily lost in moving in and had quite a thrilling time for an hour or two. Naturally the unfortunate guides had to shoulder the blame. The next move was to Lagnicourt, where the 30th acted as support until May 16th, being shelled almost continuously and losing about twenty men. Fortunately it was not required to reinforce the front line even on the morning of the 15th, when the Germans made their seventh and final counter-attack, which fell on the 54th Battalion (14th Brigade). On moving back to Vaulx-Vraucourt on the 16th, the battalion relieved the 59th Battalion in the reserve line. Hereabouts the country is somewhat elevated, and it was possible to see a long distance into the territory occupied by the enemy. The spires of churches and other tall buildings in the town of Douai were plainly visible.

For the next eight days the companies were employed in wiring and generally improving the position, and parties specially detailed, carried forward heavy gas cylinders for "Z" Company, Royal Engineers, which projected the gas into the German lines at 2 a.m. on May 24th. That night the battalion was relieved by the King's Royal Rifles (59th Brigade) and marched back to Bapaume, where it remained until June 15th.

The first half of this period was devoted to cleaning up, replacing losses, and general training, the latter half to road and railway construction under corps control. If the use to which these same roads were destined to be put a year later could have been foreseen the work would indeed have been heartbreaking; happily, no one then visualized the enemy again marching along them in columns of fours.

Gazing down upon the remnants of a score or more of villages that lay between Bapaume and Albert, one realised the enormous advantage in the matter of observation that the Germans had enjoyed during the previous winter, while we were floundering in seas of mud.

A real ray of sunshine in our sometimes monotonous existence was the appearance at Bapaume of the 8th Brigade band, which met us on our return from Vaulx-Vraucourt. The men of the 30th would not acknowledge it as the brigade band by reason of the fact that its leader, Les Wellings, and most of its members were originals of the 30th Battalion, looking upon it instead as part and parcel of our own unit. It will be remembered that prior to the Battle of Fromelles all bandsmen in the division were turned into stretcher-bearers—actually the real purpose for which they were enlisted—and their instruments returned to store. The story of the formation of the 8th Brigade band, as given by Wellings, is as follows:—

"After Fromelles the remaining members of the band carried on as stretcher-bearers for about two months. One day in the front line General Tivey enquired if I could get a band together for the purpose of attending a ceremonial parade at which General Plumer was to present decorations to members of the 5th Division. When I replied that I had not sufficient men left, he gave me authority to obtain them, if necessary, from all units of the brigade. Luckily I was able to scratch sufficient musicians together, but what a time I had in going into the front lines of each company to secure them. I felt that I was a special target to enemy snipers, as several bullets appeared to miss me only by inches. Was I glad when I gathered the mob together and told them to report to me on the following day at Sailly, where our instruments were stored? We had three days in which to get new equipment, polish up the instruments, and practise. Fortunately the parade was postponed for two days, during which we made good progress. The band performed creditably and was personally congratu-

B. COMPANY GROUP, BAPAUME

Among those shown are: Capt. W. H. Zander, Sgt. R. McKinnon, Cpl. F. McDowell, Pte. A. C. Walker, M.M., Pte. T. H. Davis, M.M., and Pte. H. Lahiff, M.M.

A.W.M. Photo E362.

lated by General Plumer, who was surprised to learn that we had just come from the trenches."

Subsequently this band was for a time attached to divisional headquarters, and it was only due to General Tivey's persistent efforts, that it was re-allotted to the 8th Brigade, where it remained until after the Armistice.

CHAPTER XI.

(SENLIS AND LE CROQUET).

On June 16th the 5th Division moved by train to the Rubempre area, north-west of Albert. The battalion occupied comfortable billets around Senlis, and until the end of June all ranks enjoyed a complete rest. The weather was glorious, the food good and plentiful. The whole countryside appeared to be a mass of red poppies, blue cornflowers, ripening fruit and waving crops of wheat, barley and rye grass. A reasonable amount of leave to Amiens was granted and all those due for furlough proceeded in batches to England.

An order was issued at this time that all clothing was to be put through a lethal chamber known as the "Foden destructor." One individual failed to carry out the order and was, in consequence, fined a day's pay. His defence was that he was not troubled by insects; the statement caused one Digger to suggest that the offender's skin must be too poisonous for anything to live on; another, possibly inclined to be more charitable, remarked that perhaps the real reason was that the culprit belonged to a society whose object was the preservation of wild life.

Social intercourse with the civil inhabitants was much appreciated by the troops, particularly the opportunity to enjoy again the conversation of womenfolk, who had not been seen by some of the men for about eight months. Naturally they were only too pleased to assist the farmers in the harvesting operations, which were now in full swing. A "statistician" at divisional headquarters estimated that the assistance thus given amounted to 30,046 hours, but he did not venture to assess the value in francs. Among the novel methods used by the peasants was the churning of butter by dog-power. The animal, usually big, strong and ferocious-looking, was placed in the inside of a hollow wheel from which he could not escape or even turn round, and on which were nailed cleats or steps. Stepping on these projections caused the wheel to revolve and as its axis was connected to a churn inside the dairy, the necessary circular movement was brought about. The dog appeared to know what was required of him, for, as soon as the trapdoor was closed, he would start to pedal vigorously, at the same time barking by way of protest. He seemed to know exactly when the cream was converted to butter, for he would stop suddenly and no amount of persuasion would induce him to continue, he simply stood stock still as much as to say to his tormentors, "I have done the job, now let me out." Wheat, oats, barley and other grains were threshed by somewhat similar means, but in this case the power was derived from a heavy draught horse endeavouring to walk up endless steps on an inclined plane, the principle being somewhat similar to that which obtains in the working of escalators on railway stations and in warehouses.

Sunday, July 1st, 1917, was a busy day for the battalion, the usual church parade being followed by a presentation of ribbons by General Birdwood in the presence of the divisional and brigade commanders, and Mr. W. A. Holman, then Premier of New South Wales. At the conclusion of the ceremony, the 8th Brigade marched past Lieutenant-General Sir Alex. Godley, and later a platoon of the 30th Battalion was detailed to give a demonstration of an attack, using live ammunition and bombs and being supported by Stokes mortar shells. This little diversion was well carried out and the platoon was congratulated on its effort. Colonel Clark records in his diary that the corps commander expressed himself as follows:—"I have never seen a finer body of men and their soldierly bearing could not have been surpassed by any troops in the world." The result of the fortnight's rest and recreation, combined with an issue of clean clothing and good food, was now apparent, all ranks settling down to solid work with the cheerfulness that is absolutely essential to the acquirement of military knowledge. Only those who have had practical experience in the training of men fully realise the futility of attempting instruction under adverse conditions, such as standing about in mud, wet feet, damp clothing, and partial hunger, which lower the spirits and produce a "fed-up" complex.

Schools for all branches of infantry training were established and a field firing range near Thiepval was acquired for practical work. Weekly route marches through the beautiful countryside, now looking its best, interspersed with attack, advanced guard and rear-guard schemes, filled in the time quite profitably. The latter exercises were often practised, the authorities apparently hoping to resume open warfare at an early date. One particularly pleasant route march which occupied two days, took the battalion through the town of Corbie—later the scene of many convivial memories for the A.I.F.—across the Somme by means of a pontoon bridge built by the 8th Field Company, a swim in the river during the midday halt, and on to the village of La Neuville, where the night was spent in billets. The return to Senlis the following day by the same route, was accomplished without any casualties.

On July 4th a divisional assault-at-arms was held at Henencourt Wood, and while the brigade as a whole was fairly successful—the 32nd Battalion was in great form—the 30th did not gain a place in any of the events. On the 12th the division held a military tournament in the presence of His Majesty the King. The 29th and 31st Battalions carried off the honours for the brigade on this occasion.

2nd Lieutenants H. E. Wonnocott and W. G. McDonald,

arriving with a number of reinforcements, brought the battalion up to its maximum strength of 45 officers and 1076 other ranks. It was about this period that Lieutenant R. D. Mulvey, who had been a temporary captain for some time, was promoted to the substantive rank of captain, as were Lieutenants W. H. Hind, F. A. Wisdom, E. Adams and C. H. Morrison. Regimental Sergeant-Major B. A. Bragg and Company Sergeant-Major S. H. Fisk were elevated to commissioned rank; Sergeant B. O. Davies to R.S.M.; Sergeants J. H. King, J. B. McGowan and R. A. Jelfs to C.S.M.; and Corporals E. W. Robinson and A. D. Burns to sergeant. In addition, several transfers took place. Captain John Chapman now became adjutant; Major Street temporarily left the 30th to take command of the 54th Battalion; Captain Barbour was seconded for duty with the 8th Training Battalion in England, and Lieutenant Wisdom received an appointment on brigade headquarters. Lieutenants C. D. Savage, D. Chalmers, E. E. Haviland and C. A. Backhouse were taken on strength from supernumerary and seconded lists. Lieutenant R. C. Chapple was accidentally wounded in the head while instructing rifle grenadiers, and had to be invalided to England.

As leave to England, Paris and Amiens had been taken by practically all hands during the seven weeks' vacation, the credit in most pay-books became very low, and not a few men experienced a feeling of relief when orders came for the division to proceed northwards to Flanders.

"It was at this stage," writes Dr. Bean, "that Australian soldiers—in particular, the infantry—came to be known, together with the New Zealanders, as 'the Diggers.' The term had occasionally been heard before, but hitherto had been general only among the New Zealanders, who are said to have inherited it from the gum-diggers in their country. It carried so rich an implication of the Anzac infantryman's own view of his functions and character, that it spread like fire through the A.I.F., and by the end of the

L

year was the general term of address for Australian or New Zealand soldiers."

Following a general clean-up and the disposal of odds and ends somewhat reminiscent of its last days in Egypt, the battalion entrained at Aveluy for St. Omer, arriving there at 3.30 p.m. on July 30th, and marching thence to billets at Le Croquet in the Racquinghem area. The railway arrangements differed widely from those which obtained on the journey south nine months before. On this occasion there was no undue crowding or overloading, and each train (twenty-four in all) carried a proportion of the battalion's transport waggons—evidence of the fact that at long last the higher authorities had awakened to the necessity for treating the men as human beings.

At this stage it may be appropriate to record the transfer of Major T. R. Marsden, from the position of brigade machine-gun officer to a higher appointment in the division with the rank of lieutenant-colonel. One of six members of the Australian Instructional Corps appointed to commissioned rank on the formation of the battalion in Sydney in 1915, Marsden did consistently good work during the whole of his service.

During the battalion's sojourn at Le Croquet, training continued to fit it for the great Passchendaele offensive which had opened on July 31st but was now practically held up by abnormal rains. A more elastic system of attack by infantry was practised, platoon and section leaders being given greater responsibility and more scope for their initiative. A thin line of scouts was followed by sections in single file moving behind their leader in "worm" fashion, with larger bodies moving up in rear in varying depths and distances. Another innovation was the firing of the light trench-mortar from a sling, thus obviating the necessity of fixing a platform for it on the ground.

The Germans, for their part, had ceased to man their front line by strong garrisons; instead it was held lightly by troops disposed in depth. And in waterlogged Flanders they had specially constructed numerous concrete blockhouses (afterwards known as "pillboxes" among British troops) across the landscape, each one so placed as to give the maximum support to its neighbours and yet not to mask the fire of those in rear. "Though fairly obvious targets, often easily visible to observers or on air-photographs, they would withstand the direct hit of all but the heaviest shells. Thus the garrison had a good chance of surviving even the heaviest bombardment, and of emerging with its machine-guns as soon as the barrage passed. Some blockhouses were loop-holed so that machine-guns could fire from within; but most were simply rectangular boxes of concrete, blind except for an exit at the rear. At such posts the machine-gunners had to hurry out with their gun, and mount it on the trench parapet, or on a concrete platform beside the blockhouse, or sometimes on the blockhouse roof. If they were quick, their action might hold up the advance in their neighbourhood. On the other hand, the new British platoon organisation was specially devised for fighting such obstacles—the rifle grenadiers and Lewis gunners being present to cover the riflemen and bombers while these worked round the blockhouse and took it in rear. This method, however, became impossible if the enemy held out in other supporting positions in rear and on the flanks." (A.O.H., Vol. LV., pp. 623-4).

CHAPTER XII.

(POLYGON WOOD AND PASSCHENDAELE).

ON September 14th "A" Company under the command of Captain P. Charlton moved up to the forward area where for ten days it was employed burying cable for the 5th Divisional Signallers, rejoining us at Chateau Segard. Three days later the remainder of the battalion—except a "nucleus" which was sent to the divisional reinforcement camp at Caestre—moved up to Steenvoorde. The practice of not taking the whole of a battalion into any particular engagement was first developed in the Somme battles of 1916. The second-in-command of each battalion and each company, together with about an eighth of the whole unit, remained at a divisional base, thus forming a nucleus on which to rebuild the battalion if it suffered heavy loss. In reality this was a practical observance of the proverb "Do not put all your eggs in the one basket."

On the 18th the battalion reached Vanoost Camp in the Abeele area, whence it moved to Chateau Segard on the 24th. Four days previously the British offensive had been resumed, eleven divisions (including the 1st and 2nd Australian) advancing on an eight-mile front from the Ypres-Comines canal northwards to the Ypres-Staden railway. The attack—officially known as the Battle of the Menin Road Ridge—was completely successful. The next stage, in which the 4th and 5th Divisions were to take part, was fixed for September 26th, by which time the massed artillery would have moved forward and registered its new targets. The task of the 5th Division, which had relieved the 1st on the nights of September 22nd and 23rd,

POLYGON WOOD AND PASSCHENDAELE 149

was to capture the whole of Polygon Wood and the German "Flandern I" line beyond it; the 14th and 15th Brigades were to make the attack, with the 8th in reserve. But the plans were nearly upset on the 25th, when the Germans launched a heavy attack against the line of the 33rd (British) Division immediately north of the Menin road and drove back its left brigade. After a day-long fight—into which General Elliott's 15th Brigade, holding the front on the left of the 33rd Division, was drawn, and lost heavily under incessant shell-fire—two battalions (29th and 31st) of the 8th Brigade had to be lent to Elliott for the morrow's attack. The 30th was warned to be in readiness to move forward at a moment's notice to support the 33rd Division. The various routes were reconnoitred and marked with luminous boards, but, as things turned out, the battalion was not required.

The attack met with overwhelming success, this being largely due to the effective creeping barrage of the artillery.

Subsequently the 30th and 32nd Battalions relieved their sister units in the newly won position and had the task of turning a mass of shell-holes into something approaching a defensive position. For a time the position was uncertain, but the line was gradually consolidated. At daylight on September 28th the posts of the battalion discovered a large number of Germans crouching in shell-holes in front of them. The S.O.S. was fired and the artillery opened; but the Germans, far from showing any inclination to fight, surrendered to a strong patrol. They were a poor looking lot—2 officers and 63 men of the 73rd Reserve Infantry Regiment who had lost their way in the dark. On their being interrogated, it was discovered that they had only recently arrived from the Russian front.

The following day and night the captured front was subjected to heavy artillery fire. This was accurately directed by German airmen, who dropped green flares over the various positions; and by it the 30th sustained a number of casualties. In holding the front-line the sections were distributed in artillery formation. Those actually in Polygon Wood camouflaged their shell-hole posts with branches of trees and scrub. "T" shaped sap-heads dug forward from them provided comparatively good cover from hostile shelling and it was mainly owing to this factor that the casualties were kept so low.

The 30th was relieved by the 8th Leicester Regiment on September 30th, and moved back to Dickebusch via Black Watch, Clapham Corner, Hooge, Halfway House, Shrapnel Corner, and Cafe Belge. Captain Charlton was left in the line with the Leicester Regiment. On rejoining the battalion the next day he reported that the enemy had that morning counter-attacked at Polygon Wood and had re-taken some ground on the right flank, but that the Leicesters, though badly enfiladed and with more than half their officers casualties, had hung on to their frontage.

At Dickebusch, Charlton was promoted to major and became second-in-command of the battalion.

On October 1st, the 30th moved from Dickebusch to a tented camp at Wippenhoek, buses conveying about 200 men, while the remainder marched. The nucleus, which had stayed at Caestre under divisional control during the Polygon Wood operations, now rejoined the battalion, which again became a complete unit. Though rather crowded, the accommodation provided was reasonably comfortable. Good baths were available at Poperinghe, a clean issue of clothing was made, and the all-important matter of pay was attended to. All small-box respirators were inspected by the divisional gas officer and a general overhaul of arms, clothing and equipment was made. Rain fell intermittently, but during the dry spells physical training, bayonet fighting, and route marches were carried out. Church parade was held on October 7th and the usual wail from divisional headquarters re non-saluting read out to the men.

A new method of sending reports by rocket was tried out here, but does not appear to have been successful.

POLYGON WOOD AND PASSCHENDAELE 151

The brigade report was to the effect that although the new apparatus sent a message some 600 or 700 yards, it became very hot in the process.

In the meantime, on October 4th, the most important battle of the offensive—in which the 1st, 2nd and 3rd Australian Divisions and the New Zealand Division played a leading part—had been fought and won. Broodseinde Ridge, from which the Germans had for two years, looked down on the Ypres flats, was now in British possession. Moving up to the "Swan Area" by 'bus, the 30th relieved the 4th Battalion (1st Division) in some dirty dugouts and crowded shelters. Rain was falling and winter conditions were rapidly approaching. The authorities, mindful of the havoc caused by trench feet during the previous winter, had made provision for the issue of extra pairs of socks and anti-trench feet powder, which was sprinkled in the socks. Due for another tour of duty in the front line, the companies were on October 9th met by guides of the 9th Battalion at Birr-Cross road and led forward. As each man was carrying 72 hours' rations in addition to his usual impedimenta, the journey through the mud was exhausting. Fortunately, the relief was effected without loss. The 30th occupied the left sector of the brigade frontage, the 32nd and 22nd Battalions being on the right and left respectively. "A" and 'C" Companies held the line with "D" Company in support of the forward slope of Broodseinde Ridge. "B" Company was in reserve at Tokio Ridge, and, though farthest from the front line, had the worst experience. Moving up in daylight just behind the 32nd Battalion and the 8th Light Trench Mortar Battery—both of which suffered heavily, Captain Roy Mulvey (a former officer of the 30th) being among the badly wounded—it reached its position—a line of shellholes—without loss, but thereafter suffered a severe battering from heavy howitzers, Sergeant George Lowbridge and Corporal Dave Price being among the killed.

The battalion's first patrol brought in four Germans of

the 448th R.I. Regiment. They were all young men barely out of their teens and appeared to be quite relieved on being escorted to the "cage" at "Shrapnel Corner." October 11th was a dark day for us, as Lieutenant Ken Smithers died of wounds, Lieutenant S. H. Fisk and six men were killed, ten men were wounded, and one was missing. Another patrol bagged a couple of the enemy, but this did not compensate for our losses. The whole position was a series of shell-holes absolutely devoid of shelter and very trying on all hands. A tape laid loosely on the ground led to the regimental aid post, and it was freely used during the hours of darkness. Where practicable, barbed-wire was placed between the shell-holes, the idea being to render the line a little stronger than when it was taken over, a practice not always observed by units when tours in the line were of short duration.

On the night of October 13th the 60th Battalion took over the 30th's line but, due to faulty staff arrangements, it was ten hours before the relief was accomplished. Parties of both units met on a single row of duckboard track behind Broodseinde Ridge, and were jammed there for hours. The Germans normally shelled this area but, for some unknown reason, they refrained from doing so on this particular occasion, otherwise the casualties must have been heavy. Some of the men essayed to walk off the duckboards but this was found to be impossible and numbers had to be rescued from the mud. In consequence, the battalion reached the hutted "Cornwall" camp at Ouderdom in a disorganised state. Coffee was issued at the Lille Gate, and a hot meal—the first for three days— was ready on arrival at the camp.

After three fairly comfortable days, during which clean underclothing was issued and bathing facilities availed of, the battalion again moved up to the forward area. Halting at "Half Way House," it was employed for four days in carrying duckboards and other material from Birr-Cross Road to dumps at Hannebeek and Garter Point, and the

POLYGON WOOD AND PASSCHENDAELE 153

cable head. A few men were evacuated sick, but great attention was paid to the feet and by rubbing in anti-trench foot powder casualties were kept within reasonable limits. Bombs dropped by enemy aircraft caused the death of Lieutenant D. L. Brown. Among the wounded was Lieutenant W. G. McDonald. A slight diversion was caused by the falling inside our lines of a Gotha, which one of our 'planes had put out of action.

On October 21st the 30th moved to the support line on "Anzac Ridge" and for five days experienced a very strenuous time. Little shelter was available, but food—thanks to the restless activity of Quartermaster Tom Fricker—came along regularly. Although the position was heavily shelled day and night, working parties managed to continue the work of duckboard laying, wiring, etc. Casualties were heavy, General Tivey being among the wounded. Colonel Clark temporarily took charge of the 8th Brigade and Captain Jim Chapman, being the senior officer of the 30th present, assumed command of the battalion.

It was here for the first time that our trench-mortars engaged low-flying enemy aeroplanes and, judging by the haste with which they flew away, and failed to return, the pilots must have been considerably scared. Incidentally, Private Jack Corlett, a Lewis gunner, in chopping a slice of wood from a wing of one of the 'planes—which was promptly appropriated by a nearby souvenir hunter—accelerated the departure of the enemy airmen.

Although the mud and slush were not quite so bad as on the Somme the previous winter, the conditions were awful, and it was with feelings of undisguised pleasure that the battalion learned that it was to be relieved and would move back to the area behind Ypres. The rearward journey commenced on October 25th and ended at "Winnipeg Camp," via Birr-Cross Road, Pioneer Walk, Derby Road, and Bullets, where, from October 26th to November 5th, the unit underwent another general overhaul, feet being attended to, clean clothing issued, and bathing parades, route marches, and training of various kinds carried out. Major P. Charlton, returning from leave, took over the command of the battalion from Captain James Chapman. Lieutenant-Colonel P. P. Abbott and a number of men—formerly of the 30th—from the disbanded 6th Division, arrived, accompanied by 90 reinforcements.

About this time Captain John Chapman—who incidentally had not yet reached his 21st year—was promoted to the rank of major (a majority prior to a majority), being probably the youngest officer in the A.I.F. to reach field rank.

During the three periods in the forward area the battalion's casualties amounted to 3 officers and 63 other ranks killed, and 2 officers and 195 other ranks wounded.

Both the 29th and 31st Battalions lost almost twice as many as the 30th, while the figures for the 32nd were the lowest in the brigade. Major Charlton, Lieutenant Rush, and the medical officer (Captain Railton) received the Military Cross, and the following N.C.O.'s and men the Military Medal:—

Sergeant	A. D. Burns	Private	A. May
,,	T. Eccles	,,	W. H. Parker
,,	R. T. Estell	,,	R. J. Pearse
,,	F. McGillicuddy	,,	C. W. Potter
,,	W. G. Smith	,,	L. J. Raynor
Corporal	H. D. Chapman	,,	B. G. Sayers
,,	W. F. Munday	,,	W. J. Smith
Private	E. L. Baker	,,	H. E. Williamson
,,	A. E. Costin		

In Routine Order 448 the C.O. expressed his appreciation of the services rendered by the undermentioned.

Sergeant	A. L. Anderson	Corporal	R. Southam
Corporal	W. E. Abbott	,,	T. W. Ford
,,	R. H. Cooper	,,	W. J. Burns
,,	L. B. Field	,,	F. Duncan

Corporal	L. S. Tisdell	Private	D. F. Rankin
Private	W. W. Butler	„	D. P. Rankin
„	A. G. Faulks	„	F. Simpson
„	R. E. Goldie	„	J. D. Smith
„	O. A. Hanley	„	J. F. Spencer
„	N. Hughes	„	A. W. Trappel
„	P. F. McLean	„	R. H. Whitton
Private	R. McGregor	„	C. E. Wiggins
„	A. A. Nicholle	„	G. E. Weiley
„	C. H. O'Connor	„	J. White
„	E. A. Roderick	„	B. W. Powe

It may be of interest to quote here two extracts from divisional orders which appeared about this time, one relating to the issue of rum, the other to the prevention of gingivitis.

"RUM ISSUE — It has been brought to notice that in some cases the issue of rum has been improperly used. Sufficient rum is to be drawn only for those men who actually drink it. Officers are responsible that no man receives more than his ration. Men who do not drink rum are not permitted to draw and hand it over to others. Commanding Officers are responsible that proper supervision is exercised when the rum ration is issued. Disciplinary action will be taken should any contravention of this order occur."

"GINGIVITIS, PREVENTION OF — A number of cases of ulcerative gingivitis have been reported by the S.O.A.D.S. (Staff Officer, Army Dental Services) in France, as having occurred among Australian troops. The complaint, which affects the teeth, appears to be infectious and can be transmitted from one man to another by use of drinking vessels, smoking pipes, spoons, etc., also by exchange of box respirators. Units will be warned that the exchange of these articles leads to infection and care should be taken to avoid the common use of drinking vessels, spoons, forks, etc., which should be carefully sterilised in boiling water. This also applies to officers' messes, in which cases have occurred in which the disease has been conveyed to almost all of the members. The exchange of S.B.R's. (small box respirators) in Gas schools and units will be avoided as much as possible."

As the second order contains no reference to the issue of rum in the line, when often only one receptacle was available, it may be inferred that "S.R.D." was too strong for the ubiquitous germ.

CHAPTER XIII.

(THE WINTER OF 1917-18).

THE 5th Division was now to relieve the 30th and 33rd British Divisions in the Messines-Wytschaete sector; and, in accordance with the programme laid down, the 30th moved, in stages, from "Winnipeg Camp" to Abeele, where it remained training until November 11th, thence to a hutted camp at Locre, and eventually to the support line near "Bristol Castle", relieving the 1st Queen's (Royal West Surrey Regiment). On November 14th it took over the portion of the front line held by the 2nd Worcester Regiment. The trenches showed signs of neglect, and in a number of places the sides had fallen in. The "cookers" were placed near Bethlehem Farm, and hot meals were sent up regularly after dark and before daylight. Inter-company reliefs between front and support lines took place at frequent intervals. It was here on November 17th that the battalion sustained a grievous loss. Captain H. Stephens, one of the most capable officers in the 8th Brigade, and a leader beloved by his men, was killed in his company headquarters, and Captain C. H. Morrison was wounded. Stephens was buried in La Plus Douve cemetery.

As mining activities were contemplated in this neighborhood, the brigade mining company was reconstituted, and to be known in future as the brigade works company. It consisted of three officers and sixty-five other ranks—principally miners and carpenters—and its role was to work in conjunction with the brigade field company of engineers, Captain E. Adams, of the 30th, being in charge.

The country was studded with concrete pillboxes, which

THE WINTER OF 1917-18

had been captured during the Messines battle in the previous June. These were found useful as company headquarters, strong-points, sentry posts, shelters, cook-houses, etc. A survey was made of these miniature forts in the brigade area, and a plan drawn up in which each was numbered and given a map reference, thus facilitating their allotment to the various units. The work of pumping out and draining them, constructing bunks, and otherwise rendering them habitable was expedited, the shelter thus provided being much appreciated by the troops. Some of the pillboxes were quite roomy and contained sufficient accommodation for a platoon; in one—possibly used as an officers' mess at some time or other—were found a piano, an electric transformer, and a considerable quantity of furniture. The question of connecting up these shelters by underground passages was under consideration, but the work was not carried out during the 5th Division's occupation of the line.

At this period the notice boards with regard to "dangerous winds", that is, the winds by which enemy gas could be carried over our lines, were withdrawn, as cloud gas had now been altogether replaced by that carried in shells. The shell-fire was constant night and day, and as the doorways of the captured pillboxes faced the enemy, his artillerymen appeared to aim at them, and in a number of cases they succeeded in gaining direct hits. On one occasion a 5.9 inch shell exploded a few feet in front of a pillbox which was being used as a cookhouse. The door was destroyed and the opening completely blocked with earth, but otherwise little damage was sustained. The brigade record of the incident ends by naively stating that the inmates—Lieutenant Whipp and twenty men of "A" Company—"were dug out after dusk."

On November 21st the 30th was relieved by the 31st Battalion, and moved back to "Pioneer Camp." After a week of digging, wiring, duckboard carrying, and dodging enemy shells as best they could, the troops thoroughly appreciated the relief. They also had the satisfaction of knowing that they had done their share in making the sector more comfortable than it was when they entered it. Companies went in turn to the Wulverghem baths, where all ranks were able to enjoy a thorough clean up and receive a fresh issue of clothing. At the end of seven days the battalion took over from the 31st, and for another week kept watch and ward on the right of the brigade sector.

About 3 p.m. on December 5th, a number of multi-coloured balloons, about 12 inches in diameter, floated across from the German lines, and from them, by means of some automatic device, dropped pamphlets relative to peace terms and the recent German successes in Italy. As our men were then resting snugly in the solid shelters, very little notice was taken of this propaganda. On the following day some copies of the *Gazette des Ardennes*, a German publication printed in French for the "benefit" of the inhabitants of the captured areas, fell into our lines. Naturally, they were "French" to most of us.

On the night of December 5th one of our contact patrols, consisting of two privates, R. G. Sterling and L. C. Barclay, had the misfortune to be ambushed and seized by a German patrol. Sterling, who tried to escape, was shot and dragged along for some distance by the Germans until, thinking he was dead, they left him in No-Man's Land. Fifteen or twenty minutes later he returned and reported the affair. This naturally caused a stir at brigade headquarters, as it was feared that the prisoner might be tricked into divulging vital information, including possibly, the hour at which the forthcoming relief was to take place, thus giving the enemy an opportunity of shelling the front line and communications during the change over. Consequently, the relief hour was altered from 5.30 to 11.30 p.m. But as the former hour approached and passed without any increase in the normal artillery fire, it was apparent that the Germans had no inkling of the relief.

The battalion's stay in the Messines area was coming to

an end. For seven weeks it had been intermittently moving from reserve to support, on to the front line, then progressively backwards, and anon repeating the process, meanwhile wiring, digging, draining and patrolling. Snow had fallen on several occasions, and been followed by rain, sleet, frost, and extreme cold. However, as food was plentiful, and changes of clothing and bathing facilities were available in the reserve area, the men remained cheerful. The number evacuated sick was not abnormally large, notwithstanding the subsequent discovery that a large number of German dead had been buried in our catchment area.

On being relieved by the 31st Battalion on December 12th, the 30th moved back to the vicinity of "Bristol Castle", remaining there on fatigue work until the 15th. The following day it marched to Rossignol camp at Kemmel, and thence to De-Kenneber siding, near Bailluel, to entrain for Desvres, a town a few miles from Boulogne, on the English Channel. The sixty mile train journey was uneventful. Snow covered the ground, giving the whole landscape a beautiful aspect. All ranks were looking forward to a great holiday and a merry Christmas, but the latter was somewhat marred by a shocking railway accident, a carriage being telescoped and sixty men of the 32nd Battalion killed or injured.

The billets provided for the men at Desvres were not of the best, the principal one being a dilapidated cement factory, which in its time had housed many troops. A large tank, perhaps better described as a small reservoir through which warm water flowed, was a great boon. As this water at a lower level was utilized for some manufacturing process, one of the conditions of its use as a swimming pool was that soap was not to be mixed with it. Needless to say, this instruction was not universally obeyed. The weather was cold, but as a full truck of coal was standing on the adjacent railway siding, conditions of warmth were soon brought about. As the fuel bore no distinguishing marks, the officials could only guess at its destination. Similarly the railway fence, composed of worn-out sleepers, gradually but surely disappeared. The problem of lighting was overcome by running extensions from the street electric wires, the various *estaminets* unwittingly supplying the necessary bulbs. One enterprising party of men "borrowed" a couple of tarpaulins from the railway goods shed and made quite a natty compartment for themselves.

The officers' billets, which, in accordance with accepted tradition, were more comfortable than those of the men, consisted principally of rooms in private houses. One of the best of these was allotted—whether by accident or design is not known—to "Dad" White, "Don" Chalmers, and "Dud" Vincent, their host being a Dr. Stopin, who had two charming daughters. A slight drawback (according to White) was the never-ending stream of callers, among them our staid C.O., who on special occasions was wont to oblige with a song at the piano.

Major F. Street rejoined our battalion here as second in command, after temporarily commanding the 54th, and "A" Company was again taken over by Major P. Charlton.

The days before Christmas were devoted to a general clean-up, and damaged uniforms were replaced by new issues.

Most of the men, despite the attractions of the *estaminets* and other places of amusement, rose to the occasion and paid more than usual attention to their personal appearance, thus increasing the respect of the civilian population for the A.I.F. The transport sections were particularly keen, their members voluntarily spending many hours in grooming horses, shining harness and buckles, and cleaning waggons and cookers, each unit of the brigade vieing with the other in bringing everything up to date.

Christmas and Boxing Days were naturally observed as close holidays in the back areas, and the meals were supplemented with delicacies purchased from battalion funds. A large parcel containing innumerable articles from the

THE WINTER OF 1917-18

battalion "Comforts Committees" in Sydney and Newcastle had arrived a few days previously, being practical reminders of the regard of the womenfolk for their men abroad. Full advantage was taken by all ranks of the opportunity afforded by the holidays to explore the great seaport of Boulogne, and doubtless some, looking from the cliffs towards England, remembered the pathetic story of Napoleon and the English sailor, so humanely portrayed by Thomas Campbell.

Interior changes about this time included the following promotions: Lieutenants W. A Thompson, C. D. Savage, and J. C. Rickard to the rank of Captain; Regimental Sergeant-Major B. O. Davies to 2nd Lieutenant; Sergeant A. H. Ellis to R.S.M.; Corporals H. D. Gooding, J. Hogg, and T. Eccles to Sergeant. Among those returning to the unit —from hospital, special duty with other units or formations, and from various schools of instruction—were Lieutenants D. Chalmers, W. T. Hanlon, G Haig, E. H. Richardson, H. R. Orpen, F. D. Beer, C. E. Harrold, V. W. Biddle, H. J. Wells, M. Griffin and D. Vincent, Sergeants M. F. Sinclair, A. E Rowlings, J. Penrose, T. Massey, A. H. Wilcockson, H. D. Shepherd and A. L. Anderson, and Corporal C. E. Alcorn. Major John Chapman was transferred to corps headquarters, for training in duties appertaining to "G" branch, and his brother, Captain James Chapman, to 14th Brigade H.Q., for staff training. Lieutenant W. Zander now became adjutant of the battalion.

At a brigade parade the ribands of the Military Cross were presented by General Birdwood to Captains A. C. White and F A. Wisdom and also to the Rev. F. G. Ward, our former C. of E. chaplain, who had made a name for himself as a coffee dispenser at Delville wood, of the Distinguished Conduct Medal to Company Sergeant-Major F. McGowen, and of the Military Medal to Sergeants R. J. Estell and F. J. McGillicuddy and Corporal J. E. Weiley. Lieutenant-Colonel Clark, Sergeant S. R. Murdoch, and

Private Don. Woodbine had recently been mentioned in Sir Douglas Haig's despatches.

Battalion, brigade, and divisional sports were held. The brigade series commenced on January 7th, when the 30th lost an "Australian Rules" football match to brigade headquarters. This was not surprising, since this game was little played by New South Welshmen. The battalion, however, had the satisfaction of beating the 31st the same afternoon in a Rugby Union contest. On the following day we won the three miles cross-country race and on January 11th the brigade Rugby final. Rugby apparently was the only game in which our men excelled, as the 30th's Soccer team was badly beaten in a match with brigade headquarters. On the 13th we annexed the putting-the-shot prize and the mile flat race, and came second in the 880 yards championship and the long jump. Ten days later No. 8 Platoon, under Lieutenant Whipp, won the brigade platoon contest. The 32nd Battalion won the brigade challenge cup, the 30th having the satisfaction of being runners up. The points allotted were as follows: 29th Bn. 284.75, 30th 338, 31st 227.25, 32nd 350.15.

The long period of rest and training came to an end on 30th January, 1918, when the battalion marched to Samer and thence proceeded by train to De Kennebek siding. Before leaving Colonel Clark appropriately expressed his feelings in the following order:

"The past months of rest have been of great benefit to the battalion, and, at the present moment, the spirits of the members have been seldom better. The training during the period has been only such as to keep the men fit, and this fact, together with the large amount of recreational training carried out, which, itself, created a great deal of interest and keen competition, are the main factors in bringing the unit to its present high standard.

"The strength of the battalion has been maintained well above establishment during the month, there being very few

THE WINTER OF 1917-18

evacuations through sickness and, of course, no battle casualties.

"Some considerable difficulty was experienced in obtaining new clothing and equipment but, at the present juncture, the equipment is practically complete, though a fair amount of clothing is still required.

"The state of the Transport Section is excellent and it is doubtful if its condition has ever been better.

"During the month approximately 150 men have been granted leave to the United Kingdom, while a large number of members availed themselves of the opportunity of visiting Paris. Leave to Boulogne was given daily.

"The discipline of the battalion has been good, by far the greatest proportion of offences being minor breaches of discipline.

"The six weeks' stay at Desvres has been perhaps the most enjoyable rest the battalion has had during its stay in France."

On January 31st the 30th took over part of the brigade frontage in the Messines sector from the 12th Battalion (1st Division), the 38th Battalion (3rd Division) being on its right and the 32nd on its left. Here it remained without change—other than inter-company reliefs—for about three weeks, during which nothing of major importance happened. Nightly patrols scoured No-Man's Land. Improvements to the front, support, and reserve lines went on continuously. Posts were strengthened, duckboards laid down, all ranks being kept as busy as possible. N.C.O's. obtained plenty of practice in report writing and sketching. Sergeant Fred. Duncan was an adept at sketching and some of his efforts are now preserved in the Australian War Memorial at Canberra. The weather was extremely mild, an agreeable contrast to that which had prevailed during the previous winter, and, in consequence, the health of the army was excellent. Socks were now changed daily, and the gum boots much appreciated.

Raids were undertaken by neighbouring units, the 30th

assisting where practicable. On one such occasion Lieutenant Cam Gunning operated a "Chinese" attack—that is, the raising of a number of dummies in No-Man's Land by means of wires and other devices—which apparently caused the Germans much consternation, as they wasted quite a lot of ammunition before knocking out their "enemy".

On being relieved by the 57th Battalion on February 25th the 30th moved back to Wulverghem camp in the reserve brigade area. During this period Colonel Clark was granted a month's leave to England for business reasons, and Major Fred Street assumed command of the battalion.

A circular which caused favourable comment from most of the men, was one threatening deserters with exposure in the Australian press. Although the threat was not carried out, it may have had a deterrent effect on waverers Fortunately, although not entirely exempt from such cases, the 30th Battalion had little trouble in this direction. The following is an extract from the circular in question:—

"As there has been, in some units of the A.I.F., a number of cases of desertion, and as it is considered essential that the opprobium attaching to such a matter should rest upon the individuals at fault and not upon the A.I.F. as a whole, it has been decided by the Defence Department that hereafter the names of the men convicted of desertion from the fighting line or after their units have been warned for duty in the line, thereby throwing extra work and danger upon their loyal comrades, will be cabled, together with their unit, place at which enlisted and sentence, to the Defence Department, Melbourne, who will arrange for their publication in the press throughout Australia. This decision has been arrived at after mature consideration of the matters involved.

"In the interest of the brave men who compose the mass of the A.I.F., it is necessary that steps be taken to prevent their inclusion in the general condemnation caused by the action of a few individuals.

"The spirit of fair play in the Australian Forces will understand this need. The man who deserts his comrades in a time of stress —who refuses to pull his weight and take his share of risk— thereby not only increases the danger and labour of the remainder, but, what is worse, he tarnishes the fair name which the gallant men who fought and died have built up for Australia.

BATTALION OFFICERS, DESVRES

FRONT ROW: Capt. W. A. Thompson, Major P. Charlton, M.C., Major James Chapman, O.B.E., Lieut.-Colonel J. W. Clark, D.S.O., Lieut.-Colonel F. Street, D.S.O., Capt. A. C. White, M.C., Capt. E. Adams, M.C.
SECOND ROW: Padre Smith, Capt. S. A. Railton, M.C., Lieuts. J. McDuff, G. W. Evans, A. H. Whipp, J. J. W. Flynn, M.C., H. J. Wells, M.C., F. Keen, G. Haig, B. A. Bragg, M.C., T. C. Fricker, W. T. Hanlon, M.C., D. Chalmers, M.C., H. W. Wedd, T. S. C. Horgan.
BACK: Lieuts. B. O. Davies, D.C.M., N. W. S. Hamilton, C. E. Harold, C. D. Beer, M. Griffin, J. C. Yeomans, D.S.O., E. E. Haviland, H. R. Orpen, W. E. Oakes.

*A.W.M. Photo E.*4510.

THE WINTER OF 1917-18   165

"It is only fair that any man whose actions tend to cast a slur upon Australia should themselves bear the shame and that their names should be made known to those at home to whom our individual and collective reputation is dear."

During the period spent at Wulverghem, February 22nd to March 15th, about half of the men were continuously employed in depening the defensive system. The idea, first developed by the German, was not to depend entirely upon the front lines, but to create successive strong areas some distance in rear. It was obvious that a German attack on a large scale was to be expected in the approaching spring, and measures were being expedited to combat it.

Each battalion was training strong raiding parties, the 30th consisting of two officers and sixty other ranks. Specialists in all branches were attending schools of instruction, the latest being one for training in the care, treatment, and feeding of carrier pigeons, and the attachment of messages to them, and for acquiring an all round knowledge of this branch of despatch sending. Runners were mostly detailed for this work, and were dubbed "Pigeoneers". The C.O's. batman, Sid Nightingall, suggested that a school for his branch of the army should be instituted, with the object of bringing about uniform methods in the polishing of boots, leggings, and leather equipment, the relative values of cleaning compounds, the adoption of uniform temperatures of shaving water, soda fountains, and allied subjects.

The observance of Sunday as a holiday was much appreciated as, after church services, football was freely indulged in. Other than a few men being evacuated through sickness, and the arrival of reinforcements, not much interior change took place in the Battalion during this period. Captain C. D. Savage returned from the 14th Training Battalion. Sergeant J. J. Casey was awarded the M.M. for conspicuously good work on the night of February 2nd. The silver cup won by "C" Company at Desvres was presented on a battalion parade.

Two cinema shows were within walking distance of the

camp and 150 free tickets were issued to the battalion. The Y.M.C.A. and the Salvation Army appeared to vie with each other in pitching their tents close to the front lines and also in supplying the needs of all ranks. The "Army" people were particularly good to the troops, and a "Digger" short of a silver coin was never denied a packet of cigarettes.

The quartermaster's report for February makes interesting reading. The meals sent up to the front line troops consisted of the following:—

Breakfast.	*Lunch.*	*Dinner.*
Porridge or Rice.	Brawn.	Stews, Dry Hash.
Bacon or Dry Hash.	Jam, Cheese.	Curried Rabbit.
Bread, Cocoa or Coffee.	Bread, Tea.	Curried Mutton.
		Cocoa or Tea.

For the men in reserve areas the food was rather more varied in character:—

Breakfast.	*Lunch.*	*Dinner.*	*Supper.*
Bacon.	Rissoles, Tea.	Roast Beef.	Soup.
Bread, Jam.	Rice & Custard.	Curry & Rice.	Biscuits & Cheese.
Tea.	Biscuits, Puddings.	Brown Stews.	Cocoa or Tea.
	Stewed Fruit.	Tinned Fruit.	
		Custards, Tea.	

If readers are inclined to query the correctness of the foregoing, particularly that relating to supper, which admittedly widely differs from the traditional "Soldiers' Supper", they are advised to communicate with Captain and Quartermaster Tom Fricker, who may be found at the pleasantly rural address of Masons Drive, Pennant Hills Road, Parramatta, N.S.W.

2,500 lbs. of fat were saved and sent to D.A.D.O.S., as well as a considerable quantity of waste paper. The master tailor and his assistants had repaired all articles of clothing torn by wire and other means, and the regimental shoemaker and his staff had ensured that boots were maintained in a serviceable condition. Steel helmets were covered with hessian, and the regimental painters were kept busy on the

THE WINTER OF 1917-18

bodies of the transport waggons and in providing notice boards.

An extract from the diary of the 31st Battalion may be appropriately quoted here. "Referring to the employment of our draught horses, it is desired to state that a number of them have been employed in ploughing an area of land in which it was intended to plant potatoes, but when a farmer came along and claimed the field, the project was abandoned."

The foregoing, apart from its humorous aspect, gives an indication of the static conditions prevailing on this part of the front at this time. On March 16th the 8th Brigade took over the 15th Brigade's sector of the front line and remained in occupation of it until the 24th. The frontage was divided between all four battalions, the 30th being on the right with the 32nd, 31st, and 29th in that order on its left. On the right of the 30th, which had relieved the 57th Battalion, was the 21st (2nd Division). As we had previously occupied this sector of the line, its strong-points, listening posts, and lay-out generally were familiar to us. Some of us naturally remarked that the defences had deteriorated during our absence, forgetful of the fact that enemy artillery activity had been continuous during our absence. The daily routine was much the same as before; stretcher-bearers rarely had more than a couple of hours' idleness, and the front line garrison was ever on the alert for enemy raiders and gas attacks. An activity shared by all units of the brigade was the digging in of 347 mortars, which at a later stage fired numerous gas-shells and caused great damage to the enemy, silencing a number of his "minnies" that had been troubling us for weeks.

On March 18th "C" Company headquarters was hit by a 5.9-inch shell, which killed Captain Adams and wounded Lieutenant Haviland. "Yank", as Adams was affectionately known, was one of the most popular officers in the battalion, his cheerful disposition, sheer ability, and generous outlook having enshrined him in the hearts of all.

At this period the enemy appeared to be paying more than usual attention to company headquarters, as that of "B" Company occupied by Captain White and his staff, was also shattered, the inmates, with the exception of one man, who was hit, getting clear in the nick of time. Incidentally, the next company commander to occupy this spot — a 14th Brigade officer — was killed. Investigation showed that the tracks leading from the line of shell-holes — which constituted the front line — and converging on company headquarters, stood out clearly on the aerial photographs, particularly when snow lay on the ground, hence the ease with which these important positions were located by the enemy.

The famous Warneton Tower, which overlooked practically the whole of the country in the vicinity of the River Douve, and was used by the German as an observation post, had always been a source of annoyance. During this period, however, it was destroyed by a few well-directed shots from one of our 15-inch guns located on the railway line near Wulverghem.

CHAPTER XIV.

(THE GERMAN OFFENSIVE—1918).

THE morning of March 21st, 1918, will long be remembered by the men holding the front line, as this was the opening day of the last and greatest German offensive. The whole of the 5th Division's area was deluged with gas shells and *minenwerfers*, as were those to north and south along the British front, but the garrisons stood up to the bombardment and easily repulsed the attempts of the Germans to raid the front.

A few hours later on the front of the Third and Fifth British Armies east of Amiens, the tremendous blow fell. That night, it is said, General Headquarters considered the situation satisfactory. "The news which arrived during the next few days, however (says the *Australian Official History, Vol. V.*), was such that, in spite of the hopeful tone of the *communiqués*, confidence began to give way to anxiety. There appeared in the daily bulletins village-names that were household words with the Australian Corps, scenes of famous fights in 1917 and 1916, far behind the British line recently held. On March 22nd it was stated that the Germans had broken through at Beaumetz, and were trying to pierce the line at Vaulx-Vraucourt; the Fifth Army was falling back on the Somme south of Péronne."

On the 24th the 3rd and 4th Australian Divisions, which were then resting out of the line, were ordered south, and by the 27th their troops were in action at Hébuterne, Dernancourt, and Morlancourt. In the meantime, on March 22nd, news was received that the 8th Brigade was to be relieved by the 5th Brigade (2nd Division), and rumour was rife as to the 5th Division's future movements.

The 30th Battalion was relieved on the 24th by the 17th Battalion, and moved back, first to Wulvernghem camp, thence to Wippenhoek—where Colonel Clark was appointed "O.C., Advance Column"—and Thieshouck, and finally, to Godewaersvelde to entrain for a destination known only to the higher command, which turned out to be Doullens. On arriving there at 3 a.m. on March 28th, a twelve-mile march had to be undertaken, through the villages of Orville, Sarton, and Authie to Bus-les-Artois, in the Vauchelles area, where the battalion went into billets.

In this area, north-west of Albert, the 5th Division remained until April 4th in reserve to the Third British Army. Training was continued. The whole countryside was in a disturbed condition. The French inhabitants were leaving their farms and villages and fleeing westward, utilising every possible form of conveyance, and driving or leading as many of their domestic animals as could be collected. As in the case of nearly all retreats, a certain amount of looting occurred, but the Australians, despite their supposed lack of discipline, took little if any part in it.

Colonel Clark being detailed to take charge of the 5th Divisional nucleus, Major Street assumed command of the battalion. Major Street's report for the month of March, given below, indicates the state of our unit:

"The end of March finds the battalion in a new area, forming part of the Third Army reserve and ready to move forward at an hour's notice. The unit has had a rather trying time during the month, as the sector it was recently occupying had become very lively, and for trench warfare our casualties have been fairly high. However, the battalion is up to full strength, while the health of the troops is remarkably good, and their morale splendid. There were very few breaches of discipline during the month, and the majority were only minor cases. On the whole, the discipline has been very gratifying. Owing to the length of time the battalion was in the forward area, the clothing has been subjected to hard wear; a quantity of new clothing has been received, portion of which is being retained with which to meet emergencies. The transport section has kept up its high standard, the animals are in splendid condition, and the turnout is creditable. With a few days' rest the battalion will be well prepared and equipped for the hard fighting it is likely to meet."

The report of the transport officer, Lieutenant McDuff —one of the greatest "characters" in the A.I.F.—is also appended.

"On the 26th instant (he writes) we moved to Godewaersvelde, I being in charge of the 29th Battalion and 8th Brigade transport as well as our own. We had some stiff hills to overcome, including Mont-Des-Cats, and we had to double bank on some of these hills. A staff officer (Colonel or Major) at one place wished to know why we blocked the road, and the only answer I could give was that, if he could show me a better way of getting out of the difficulty, I should be pleased to avail myself of it. I was then left to carry on in my own way. Entraining at Godewaersvelde we journeyed to Doullens, thence by road to Louvencourt, and after resting there for a few days, moved on to Vauchelles."

Those who knew "Mac" will be able to read between the lines of the foregoing, and visualise the retreat of the "staff officer"—for colonel, captain, or general, were all the same to McDuff.

At 6.15 p.m. on April 4th the battalion received orders to march to Louvencourt, where it would "embus" for Daours. The journey proved to be a tedious one, and, due to delays and slow travelling, Daours was not reached until 2 o'clock the following morning. Then, after a delay of more than an hour, it marched to Bois de Gentelles, where the troops bivouacked for a period before relieving the 41st Battalion (3rd Division) in the reserve line. The posts were simply hastily-dug lengths of trench, sited to give good fields of fire. No shelters of any description were available in the company posts, and, as it rained heavily throughout the night, the conditions were most miserable. The following day a supply of trench shelters became available and conditions improved considerably.

On April 9th the 30th marched through Fouilloy, thence along the south bank of the Somme, and across a pontoon bridge to the vicinity of Corbie, relieving the 58th Battalion on the left of the brigade's new sector. It was destined to remain in this neighbourhood for a lengthy period, and many of the most pleasant memories of the 30th Battalion are centred around this part of France. The great German effort to divide the French and British Armies and reach the sea had failed in this area. The breach in the Fifth Army's line had been filled and the Australians were proud indeed of the part they had played.

The 8th Brigade was now astride the Somme River, its 30th and 31st Battalions on the south side, and the 29th and 32nd on the north side. Brigade headquarters were comfortably ensconced in the Red Chateau in Corbie. (It was in this neighbourhood that "Dad" White and Lieutenant McDuff made their memorable inspection of the front line, which is described in Part II. of this volume). Although many minor changes of position and inter-company reliefs took place during the period under review, nothing of a sensational nature happened. A few casualties occurred almost every day, among them being Lieutenant Dave Brewster, who was put out of action for a few weeks.

Vigorous patrolling of No-Man's Land was carried out each night. Among the most active members of the 30th in this respect were Lieutenants Wells, Bragg, Haig, Hanlon, Beer, Backhouse, and Vincent; Sergeants Eccles, Bickley, Curran, Gooding, Hogg, and Wal. Smith; Corporals Stubbs, Forbes, Stinson, Begg, Crutch, Craven, Bromley, McWilliam, Wynne, and Ford; and Privates Kelly, Cook, and Collins.

One of our aeroplanes—ominously enough its number

N.C.O's AT DESVRES, 1917

FRONT ROW: *Left to right*: Cpl. K. A. Stevenson, Cpl. W. Table, Cpl. C. H. Pratt, Cpl. R. Southam, Cpl. G. McKenzie, Sgt. A. D. Burns, M.M., Sgt. L. H. Moore, M.M., Cpl. F. C. Florance, Sgt. E. E. Brown, Sgt. A. L. Anderson, C.S.M. L. B. Bickerton, Cpl. D. B. B. McViety, C.S.M. H. J. Shepherd, Sgt. G. Begg, Sgt. R. McKinnon, Cpl. A. Kirkby.

MIDDLE ROW: *Left to right*: Sgt. E. Robinson, Sgt. G. Cowen, Sgt. F. Garran, Cpl. W. Duncan, Sgt. A. H. Brown, Sgt. P. Ferguson, Cpl. E. Wilkinson, Sgt. G. E. Hard, Sgt. G. W. Wrapson, Cpl. J. Mills, Sgt. A. E. Turley, M.M., Cpl. J. Watson, Cpl. T. C. Grogan, M.M., C.S.M. J. B. McIowan, D.C.M., Cpl. W. Lloyd, C.S.M. E. G. McKinnon, M.S.M., Cpl. H. D. Ford, C.Q.M.S. E. F. Walker, Cpl. A. Goldman, Sgt. W. H. Elms, Sgt. W. F. Munday, M.M., Cpl. W. H. Webb, Sgt. W. H. Jackson, Sgt. E. R. McBride, Sgt. J. E. Penrose, C.S.M. R. H. Cooper, Sgt. J. Buttsworth, Cpl. J. E. Skene, Cpl. A. H. James, Sgt. F. McGillycuddy, M.M., Sgt. L. E. Watterston, Sgt. J. D. Dickson, Sgt. R. J. Estell, M.M., Cpl. H. J. Jarvis.

BACK ROW: *Left to right*: Cpl. H. Webb, Sgt. A. W. Chivers, C.Q.M.S. F. McGowan, Sgt. J. A. Hogg, M.M., Sgt. F. McCristal, Cpl. R. J. Ball, Sgt. P. J. Holder, Cpl. G. Ogle, Sgt. T. Eccles, D.C.M., M.M., Sgt. A. C. Stubbs, Cpl. G. J. Bromley, Cpl. C. E. Alcorn, C. de G., Cpl. R. E. Johnson, Cpl. W. J. Burns, Sgt. W. C. Abbott, M.M., Cpl. A. L. Smith, Sgt. G. W. Smith, M.M., Sgt. C. L. Ridley, Sgt. H. D. Gooding, Sgt. J. H. Brown.

A.W.M. Photo. No. E1621.

Lieut. D. T. BREWSTER WITH SIGNALLERS AND RUNNERS, BLARINGHEM

THE GERMAN OFFENSIVE, 1918   173

was "13"—conveyed a morning greeting at 8.45 on April 12th by dropping four bombs on the 30th's front line—as someone remarked, it was certainly an effective way of waking us up. It was in this neighbourhood also that the brave German airman, Manfred von Richthofen, met his fate on April 21st.

Mutual shelling went on almost continuously, and much gas was exchanged, particularly by the enemy on Villers-Bretonneux prior to its capture from the 8th British Division on April 24th. His occupation of the town was, however, of short duration as on the ensuing night the 13th and 15th Australian Brigades drove him out faster than he came in. At this time Captain White was acting as *liaison* officer between the 5th Australian and 8th British Divisions, and was a witness of the gallant attempts of the "Tommies" to hold their own against heavy odds. The 8th Division was one of those which had borne the brunt of the rear-guard action fought by the Fifth Army during the German onslaught a few weeks before—its total casualties during the war were over 60,000.

The retaking of Villers-Bretonneux is regarded by experts as being one of the most successful night operations in the history of the war. While the 30th Battalion had no part in this brilliant achievement, it may not be out of place to record that it assisted the 14th Brigade to hold the right flank during the enemy's occupation of the area throughout April 24th. In this engagement General von Falkenhayn lost his only son—an ensign in the German Army—who insisted upon carrying forward flares and bombs at a critical moment. This happening is somewhat reminiscent of the loss sustained by Lord Roberts in South Africa during the campaign of 1899-1902.

Towards the end of April enemy activity in sending over gas-shells became very pronounced. He appeared to devote special attention to the 30th's regimental aid-post, in charge of Captain S. A. Railton. On April 16th an 8-inch shell struck the temporary hospital in Hamelet, killing a patient.

The R.A.P. was naturally moved to what was considered to be a safer building, but on the 18th a 4.2-inch gas-shell of the yellow ("mustard") variety pierced the new post, striking Railton's bed, but fortunately causing no casualties. The next move was also disastrous, as the doctor and four of his assistants were badly affected by gas fumes which had been retained in the clothing of several patients hurriedly brought in for treatment. Railton continued to work on until he could no longer see, when he was compelled to give in, and was promptly evacuated by the 8th Field Ambulance. Major H. M. North became our medical officer for a few days and was in turn relieved by Captain G. O. Robertson. The latter is particularly remembered by some of the 30th on account of his kindness to animals—dumb and otherwise. Taking charge of a cow temporarily separated from its rightful owner, he carefully studied her comfort at his R.A.P., and, in consequence, was able to dispense whisky and milk to deserving cases, of which there were many.

Our patrols were doing great work about this time, Lieutenants Wells, Biddle, Bragg, and Flynn being especially active. One of the many raids may be mentioned here. On the night of April 28th/29th a patrol of normal strength under Lieutenant H. J. Wells, including Sergeant Eccles, Corporal Stubbs, and Privates Player, Collins, Mather, Kelly, and Wearne, encountered a patrol of two men almost face to face and within a few yards of the enemy wire. It was hoped to make a clean capture but the men were on the alert and, turning at an angle, raced for the German parapet, which they had almost reached when "Dad" Wearne's Lewis gun caught them. The noise of the firing so close naturally alarmed the Germans, who at once showed fight. Wells, with great presence of mind, threw two smoke bombs into the enemy wire, which enabled our patrol to escape. After reaching a place of safety one of our men remarked that it may have been a patrol from a neighbouring battalion they had encountered, and to verify the truth

THE GERMAN OFFENSIVE, 1918   175

or otherwise of this surmise, Player and Mather retraced their steps and recovered two blood-stained enemy rifles and equipment which had been perforated with bullets, thus proving that no mistake had been made. In the meantime the wounded men, or their bodies, had been taken to the enemy lines.

It was in this sector that a dog, which had been chased many times, was eventually shot by a man of "C" Company in the support line. It wore a comfortable collar and rug, which, on being examined, was found to contain a coded message written in French; but an extensive search for hidden civilians in the village of Hamelet with a view to discovering its owner proved unsuccessful.

A particularly weak attempt by the Germans to foment trouble between the French and British came to light here. A balloon, which had evidently been blown off its course, dropped over our lines a large number of pink papers containing a long account in French of the ill-treatment of France by the English nation, the principal theme being the martyrdom of Joan of Arc, of which most sordid details were given. Naturally, no reference was made to the Siege of Paris in 1870 or to the loss of Alsace and Lorraine, or to the more recent treatment of the Belgians.

The brigade summary for the month, quoted hereunder, makes interesting reading:

"During the month of April the brigade moved about considerably and proved beyond doubt that under any conditions it was very mobile and always ready for instant action. At one period we were guarding the right flank of the British Army, joining hands with the French near Hangard. At present we are holding a front of approximately 4,000 yards, and, considering the length of time, our casualties have not been excessive. Active patrolling has been carried out, but the Boche has no fight in him. Identifications have been secured at intervals and the work of the patrols has been very creditable. All our men are in great spirits, and when the Boche attack does come again, we will certainly acquit ourselves as in the past; and as we have reason to believe the enemy respects our fighting qualities at the present, so will his respect and fear become greater as time goes on."

The battalion summary adds that "all cellars occupied by H.Q. units in Hamelet are now protected and made gas-proof. All roads are picketed to stop stragglers and to prevent unauthorised people from wandering about the sector. Under battalion arrangements, a sock-drying room has been established and is working satisfactorily in Hamelet. The hot food is brought up each night at 9 o'clock and in the early morning. The whole of the battalion sector has been considerably improved during the past two weeks and is now in a fairly strong and satisfactory condition. Everything possible for the comfort of the men has been done and there is no one who has not shelter in any part of the front line, support, or reserve."

Showing: Lieut. W. Williams, Lieut. W. C. Abbott, Sgt. G. Lowbridge, Pte. G. S. Pavey, Pte. G. D. Jennings, and Pte. J. P. Ryan.

AT ZONNEBEKE

A.W.M. Photo No. E1120.

A.W.M. Photo No. E1042.

IN THE TRENCHES AT ZONNEBEKE

CHAPTER XV.

(MORLANCOURT).

THE period May 1st-16th was devoted almost entirely to improving the front-line positions and to intensive patrolling. On the 16th the 53rd Battalion relieved the 30th, which in turn took over from the 32nd Battalion in the reserve area. The companies distributed in well camouflaged posts commanding the Somme Canal and its approaches were employed largely in tunnelling operations and on the construction of deep dug-outs.

Enemy gas was becoming very troublesome and effective measures had to be taken to combat it. Ordinary buildings were found to be useless, hence the activity to provide deep gas-proof shelters. One of the daily reports says that a deep dug-out with gas-proof doors had been completed, and was now available for use as a battalion headquarters, and also that a well, 35 feet deep, in which water had not yet been struck, was being timbered.

The weather was now comfortably warm and swimming parades were held daily.

The nucleus, consisting of a hundred of all ranks, arrived from Pernois camp and were distributed to their various companies, relieving a like number who, under Major Street, moved off for the same camp to the accompaniment of the usual chaff from their comrades.

On May 31st the 8th Brigade was relieved by the 13th Brigade (4th Division) and thus went into corps reserve in the Rivery area. The 30th Battalion, which handed over to the 45th, marched without incident through Blangy-Tronville to billets in Glisy.

Major Street's report for the month reads as follows:—
"The end of May finds the battalion about to be relieved and move to Corps reserve. The first fortnight was spent in the same position as the month of April. During the latter half of the month the battalion has been in brigade reserve. Although the time spent in the forward area has been unusually long, the morale of the men is still high. Bathing in the lagoons and portion of the Somme was freely indulged in, and this, together with a clean change of underwear, has helped to eradicate the slight outbreak of scabies that threatened to become epidemic. The discipline on the whole has been excellent. A supply of new clothing was issued to those in need of it and the unit tailors and boot repairers have been kept busy. The transport animals are in good condition and the vehicles have been repainted."

The Quartermaster's report records, among other things, that his saving of fat—the standard by which he was judged by the "Q" branch of the Army—amounted to 1050 lb. during May.

Among those evacuated sick or wounded during this period were Sergeants E. D. Robinson, E. H. Huxley, A. C. Stubbs, and R. Estell, and Corporals Don. Woodbine and J. S. Bartley. Promotions included Sergeants Geoff. Cowen and A. J. McCallum to the rank of company sergeant-major. The following returned to duty from schools of instruction or from hospital—Lieutenants J. H. King, C. D. Button, and D. Stuart, R.S.M. Jim Hunt, C.S.M. Norman Jehan, Sergeants A. W. Chivers and L. H. Stuckey, and Privates E. Bannister and A. W. Baxter. About this time we lost again the services of Captain A. C. White, who was seconded for duty with the brigade headquarters as assistant brigade major. The Belgian Croix de Guerre was conferred upon Corporal C. E. Alcorn, and the Military Medal on Privates G. W. Burns and H. Whyatt, the latter subsequently acquiring a bar to his decoration. At this stage the narrative may be interrupted in order to recall some of the more or less irritating orders which were issued during this period, and for which some members of the 30th may have been partly responsible.

Dress of Men on Leave. It is reported by the A.P.M., Nice, that N.C.O's. and men of the Australian Force continue to arrive on leave in the Riviera without belts or bandoliers. C.O's. are held responsible that men proceeding on leave, to any locality, are properly dressed, and that they are warned before departure from the unit of the necessity for complying with orders on this subject.

Bounds. No one under the rank of Lieutenant-Colonel is permitted to enter Abbeville without a pass signed by his commanding officer. No leave to Abbeville is to be granted. Amiens is placed out of bounds to all troops. No passes are to be issued to anyone to enter the town except those proceeding on duty.

Looting. The brigade commander regrets to state that complaints are being received concerning looting by troops in the area occupied by this brigade. He directs that commanders of units take every step in their power to safeguard the property and interest of the civilian inhabitants.

Company and platoon commanders are to be held financially responsible for any loss or damage in the areas occupied by troops under their command, whether committed by their own men or others, as well as for damage and loss caused by their troops elsewhere, unless they can bring the offender to book.

Bounds. The French Army area is out of bounds to all troops other than those on duty, or belonging to units granted special permission to be quartered in the area. No leave will be granted to visit the French area.

Dress. It has been noticed that some men are wearing portions of civilian attire. O's.C. units will take immediate steps to put a stop to this practice.

Improper Use of Explosives. The use of explosives for the purpose of obtaining fish from the River Somme is forbidden, and units stationed near the river will be responsible for checking the practice. Drastic disciplinary action is to be taken against offenders.

Game Shooting. Complaints have been received of men shooting game and cases have occurred of men being wounded by rifle shots apparently fired at game. The attention of all ranks is called to the following G.R.O., No. 1297, which will be read on parade in every unit once monthly, and be republished in all unit orders:—

> "1297—As cases still occur of officers and other ranks pursuing and killing game, it is notified for information that the hunting, shooting or killing of game (which includes hares and rabbits) by nets, snares or other methods, is strictly prohibited."

Strong disciplinary action will be taken against all offenders.

Shorts. The practice of cutting down breeches and slacks at the knees is prohibited. C.O's. will take steps to ensure that this order is observed.

Damage to Crops. All ranks are reminded of the importance of safeguarding in every way the productivity of the land. It should be realised under what difficulties the country is being cultivated, and what splendid services the older men, the women, and children of Northern France are rendering to the Allied cause by contributing by hard and constant toil as much as is in their power to the food supply of France. Every kind of conduct is forbidden which might cause any avoidable damage to crops or sown fields, and severe disciplinary action is to be taken in regard to any conduct or neglect leading to such results. In particular, officers and men are forbidden:—

(1) To go when off duty either on foot or on horseback upon sown fields or crops, including clover and hay crops, of any kind.

(2) To allow horses to graze anywhere unless arrangements have been made with the farmer to whom the field belongs.

MORLANCOURT

Glorious weather prevailed during the month of June, and the battalion's stay in Glisy area, despite long distance shell-fire, was reasonably enjoyable. The first two days were devoted to cleaning up, inspection of small-box respirators by Lieutenant Backhouse, and reorganization generally. Company officers reconnoitred routes leading to the forward area, studied maps, and held their men in readiness to combat any break through which the enemy might attempt. Here the yearly anti-typhoid innoculation was carried out, necessitating a further forty-eight hours' exemption from work.

By way of diversion, all units, including brigade headquarters, prepared aquatic sports programmes, and our band added to its many thoughtful acts by playing a programme of music to the inmates of Rivery Hospital. Each battalion carried out its own swimming competitions and selected its representatives for the brigade carnival, which was held in the Amiens Municipal Baths in the presence of a large number of people. The 30th's representatives won the brigade championship and, naturally, the battalion was elated at their prowess.

Further honours were bestowed upon the battalion at this time, Lieutenant S. C. Butler being awarded the Military Cross, and Sergeant S. H. Murdoch (who had recently been appointed to commissioned rank) the D.C.M. Lieutenant T. S. C. Horgan and Sergeant H. H. Cox were mentioned in dispatches. Members of the 30th were also pleased to learn that Major B. A. Wark, who had formerly served with our battalion but was now with the 32nd, had been awarded the D.S.O.

At this period the authorities appear to have had some idea that the war was not likely to be indefinitely prolonged—Bishop Long, who had been appointed Director of Education in the A.I.F., in a short talk to the men outlined probable schemes of repatriation and distributed forms of application for training in various phases of civilian employment.

On June 14th the battalion moved by 'bus to the forward area, relieving the 28th Battalion (2nd Division) in the front line at Morlancourt. Two men were killed and three wounded during the relief. The front had changed considerably in the past month. This was due to the gradual nibbling away of the German line ("peaceful penetration", as it was generally called) by successive units. It thus took the 30th some time to adapt itself to the new surroundings. On June 15th the battalion helped the Royal Engineers to "put over" some 200 gas projectors into a valley in which were seen a large number of the enemy. The wind was favourable and, judging by the signals for stretcher-bearers, the operation was quite successful.

On the night of June 16th a patrol of twelve men, under Lieutenant Bragg, surprised a *minenwerfer* crew in the act of firing their mortar from a fixed base in No-Man's Land. Our men captured two prisoners and suitably disposed of the remaining six members of the German post. One morning about 4 o'clock Major John Chapman, who was now serving on 5th Divisional Headquarters, arrived in the front line with an American officer to whom he was showing the defences of our neighbourhood. What the Yankee thought of the friendly greetings which John received from all ranks is not known, but it certainly afforded him a practical illustration of the happy relationship which existed between the officers and men of the A.I.F.

A day or two later a party of five American officers and nine N.C.O's. were attached to the 30th for experience in front line work. They were particularly keen to learn, and, incidentally appeared to enjoy the Australian interpretation of the English language as much as the Diggers enjoyed their colloquialisms.

Throughout the night of June 19th-20th the German artillery and trench-mortars paid particular attention to the front and rear positions along the whole sector. About 11 p.m. the barrage, which had been heavy for an hour and a half, slackened, but at 11.30 it was resumed with intensity

MORLANCOURT

for an hour, gas shells being freely mixed with high-explosive, and from 2.30 to 3 a.m. it again came down heavily. The gas, however, was blown back to the enemy's lines.

In the 30th Battalion the casualties amounted to 12, including Captain Hext (O.C., "A" Company) and Chaplain W. J. Hicks. Hext, who died next day at the casualty clearing station in Vignacourt, had been standing alongside a dump in the support line when a shell landed, seriously wounding him and burying him among the debris of the parapet, small arms ammunition, bombs, and flares. The flares immediately caught fire and the bombs began to explode. It was then that Private Edward Dunn, with an utter disregard for his own safety, rushed in and extricated Hext, whom he carried forty yards to the shelter of a sap.

Two other men among the many who performed gallant work that night were Corporal William Tripp and Private Jack Hough. During the height of the bombardment Tripp came up in charge of five limbers, containing a hot meal and other rations, and two water-carts. Determined, however, to get the hot meal through to the garrison, he promptly made a reconnaissance of the route and then led the column to the dump without loss. At the dump two mules were killed but Tripp replaced them and got the column back through the barrage without further casualties. Hough, who was a stretcher-bearer, reorganised fresh bearer-teams as those working with him were hit, and when the saps became impassable, led them over the open to the regimental aid-post.

At this period so many raids and patrols were carried out that it is impossible to refer to them all. Two, however, call for special mention.

On June 21st a sergeant and five men went out at midnight, and were shortly afterwards observed by the enemy. Immediately withdrawing, they proceeded along the line centre and found themselves behind a post from which they were challenged in perfect English. The leader naturally replied that they were a patrol of the 30th Battalion. Immediately some words were spoken in German and the patrol realised that they had run into an enemy strong-point. Getting away as quickly as possible, under a fire of bombs, rifles and machine-guns, all reached our lines with the exception of one man who had been wounded. The sergeant immediately went out to search for him, but met his death after going a few yards. It was surmised that a sniper's bullet exploded a bomb in his pocket. The wounded man was recovered the following night.

On the night of June 22nd-23rd a raid was carried out by a party consisting of three officers — Captain Don Chalmers, and Lieutenants Bragg and Hanlon — and 72 other ranks. Hanlon's party, on the right, met no opposition until within a few yards of the enemy line, when some bombs were thrown at them. As soon as they jumped into the trench the garrison scattered in all directions, and after killing twelve Germans they returned to our lines with two prisoners, one of whom immediately died of wounds.

The left party, however, were heavily fired on by machine-guns shortly after getting into No-Man's Land, and by the time they had advanced 130 yards, and were still some 40 yards short of the German parapet, Bragg found that his numbers had dwindled to such an extent that it would have been folly to continue. He therefore fired the return signal (a green Verey light). "My men saw this," he reported, "and immediately started helping their comrades who were wounded, to get back. Flares commenced to go up from the Boche line and he had splendid targets. I estimated at least four guns firing on us from in front and some from left flank."

Stick bombs now began to fall among them. While trying to help back Lance-Corporal Darcy Wynn, who was badly wounded and could not walk, Bragg was hit in the left shoulder but managed to drag him to cover in a shell-hole. Bragg then went across to a sap in No-Man's Land to see what had happened to his Lewis gunners, who had been stationed there to protect his left flank and rear, and his bombers, who had been ordered to push along it and thus gain the German line. The sap, however, was completely blocked in parts, and was being swept with machine-gun fire and bombs. "I found my machine-gun crew at the end of a block (he says), covering approaches from the Boche side. Stick bombs were falling here. I placed the riflemen in position to cover our flanks in case of a counter-attack up the sap. Our bombs were used up and bombers were either casualties or had fallen back. My machine-gun could not locate Boche bombers."

The Lewis gun was in charge of Lance-Corporal Victor Lancaster, who had always set a fine example to his mates. This night he excelled himself. Shortly after Bragg reached the sap, a bomb burst in Lancaster's face, taking away his lower jaw. Despite this, however, and the fact that he could not speak, he resolutely stuck to his gun and continued to cover the retirement of Bragg's party until forced to give up through weakness resulting from loss of blood. He then handed the gun over to his No. 2, and made his way back to the Australian line, refusing to allow any of his team mates to assist him.

For his gallantry and devotion to duty, Lancaster was at once recommended for the Victoria Cross, but he was already dead when the award to him of the Distinguished Conduct Medal was gazetted.

Two minutes after "zero" the German artillery and trench-mortars retaliated on the 30th Battalion's front line, blowing in the trench in a number of places and causing several casualties. The losses sustained by the raiders amounted to 4 killed, 18 wounded, and 4 missing, mostly in Bragg's party. Among those who were outstanding in their efforts to rescue the wounded from No-Man's Land were Lance-Corporal G. E. Weiley and Private A. C. Walker, both of whom had been members of the raiding party and worked till dawn on their humane tasks. Lieutenant B. O. Davies, the intelligence officer, was killed by a piece of *minenwerfer* casing as he jumped out of the front trench to go to the assistance of a man struggling under the load of a wounded mate.

From July 1st to 15th the battalion was stationed in the Franvillers area, specialists being engaged in intensive training, principally in cable burying and work at the Bonnay sawmills. A number were also detailed for crop cutting, threshing and other farm work.

Returning to the Morlancourt sector on July 16th, the 30th relieved the 57th Battalion in practically the same portion of the front line as it had previously held. The front was quiet and most of the time devoted to patrolling and generally improving the position. Seven days later the 32nd Battalion took over the sector and we moved back to a reserve area at Ribemont. As the trenches here contained good cover, the "cookers" were brought up to the company lines, the transport section and the quartermaster's store remaining farther back in Adam Wood. The first day in the new position was devoted to rest and cleaning up the area; the succeeding days to trench digging in Maret Wood and the carrying of gas-projectors. On July 27th, on being relieved by an English battalion, the 30th moved forward preparatory to assisting the 29th and 32nd Battalions in an attack which had been planned to take place on the night of the 28th.

"B" Company was attached to the 32nd Battalion and "C" to the 29th, the remainder being detailed to hold the front line on its being vacated by the attacking troops. The operation was brilliantly successful. It was estimated that 200 of the enemy were killed, while 92, including an officer, were taken prisoner. A large quantity of equipment was also captured, including 23 machine-guns, 4 *minenwerfers*, ammunition rations, etc. Moreover, the newly acquired country offered a better command of the Morlancourt Valley and gave the 8th Brigade a good foot-

MORLANCOURT

ing on the high ground south of the Bray-Corbie road. The 29th and 32nd Battalions gave special praise to our attacking companies and also to "D" Company, which was engaged as a carrying unit.

The satisfaction of General Tivey at the result of the whole effort is summed up in the following memorandum, which he sent to each unit:

"I desire to place on record my appreciation of the splendid work done by the Brigade in the very successful operation in the Morlancourt section on July the 28th/29th, 1918. The attack was carried out in a skilful and gallant manner, which has won the admiration of Army, Corps, and Divisional Commanders, also the G.O.C., A.I.F. The results achieved were not only due to good training and discipline, but also to the high standard of moral *esprit de corps* of the units concerned. The Australian soldier has made a name that we all have reason to be proud of and your latest exploit is worthy of the best traditions of the Force to which we have the honour to belong."

Subsequently, in corps orders Captain T. C. Barbour and C.Q.M.S. J. H. Bond received well deserved recognition for the parts they played in the operation—Barbour for supervising all carrying parties to the new position, organising the work of consolidation in the captured position, and having the killed and wounded brought into the Australian lines; Bond for taking charge of the ration parties on the night of the 28th-29th.

On the night July 31st, the brigade was relieved by the 55th (British) Division, the 30th Battalion's position being taken over by the 7th Queens'. "B" Company was at first brought to the Clermont line, "C" Company to the Bunbury line, "D" to Cobar line, and "A" to Bourke and Cobar lines. When the relief was completed the companies marched back nine miles to Querrieu, the last company arriving at 5 a.m. on August 1st. Tom Dunkley, the sergeant-cook, had a hot meal ready, and all who could be spared from routine duties turned in for a rest.

An important change took place here, our C.O. being transferred to the command of the A.I.F. Training Brigade, England. Colonel Clark had led the battalion for over three years, and, with the exception of temporary service with higher formations and ordinary leave, had not been away from the unit for a single day. The officers assembled to bid him farewell, and it was with mutual respect that he parted from them to undertake the responsibilities of a higher position.

Major F. Street now took over the battalion, and at a later date was promoted to the rank of Lieutenant-Colonel and awarded the D.S.O. Lieutenant A. H. E. Whipp returned to the front after a term of service with the 14th Training Battalion in England, and naturally received a boisterous welcome.

CHAPTER XVI.

(THE BATTLE OF AMIENS).

FOLLOWING closely on the set-back they received at the hands of Generals Mangin and Gouraud in the south during the latter days of July, the Germans were destined to sustain yet another severe defeat at the hands of the Canadian, Australian and III. British Corps, in company with the French, in the great Battle of Amiens, on August 8th—"the black day of the German Army in the history of the war," according to General Ludendorff.

"Ten miles to the East of Amiens (says C. E. Montague, in *Disenchantment*) a steep-sided ridge divides the converging rivers of Ancre and Somme. They meet where it sinks, at its western end, into the plain. From the ridge there was, in pre-war days, a beautiful view. On the north the ground fell from your feet abruptly, a kind of earth cliff, to the north bank of Somme, about a hundred feet below. Southwards, beyond the river, stretched as far as eye could see, the expanse of the level Santerre, one of France's best cornlands. South-east, you looked up the Somme valley, mile after mile, towards Bray and Péronne — a shining valley of poplars and stream and linked ponds and red-roofed villages among the poplars. But now the Santerre lay untilled, gone back to heath of a faded fawn-grey. The red roofs had been shelled — the Germans possessed them; the Germans held the blasted heath across the river; other Germans held most of the ridge on this side . . . English troops were to carry the eastern end of the ridge and the tricky low ground between it and the Somme. Australian and Canadian troops were to attack on a broad front, out on the level Santerre, across the river . . ."

When the 8th Brigade moved back to Querrieu preparations for the attack were already in full swing. All details of its part in the operation were carefully worked out at daily conferences, at which representatives of all arms were present, at brigade headquarters in the Bois de Mai. Much reliance was to be placed on the new tanks, and the period spent here was principally devoted to ensuring that all ranks became acquainted with tank tactics and movements generally. Demonstrations of various kinds were given daily and feint attacks made illustrating joint action in the capture of front and supporting systems of trenches. A specially selected party of machine-gunners under Captain C. D. Savage was trained at the headquarters of the 5th Tank Brigade, the intention being that they should go forward in tanks in the final stages of the attack and exploit the success.

Meanwhile, in the battalion technical stores were being overhauled, hot-food boxes constructed, kits inspected, bathing parades held, and every detail attended to with greater precision than ever previously. In the forward area preparations were rapidly completed. Dumps of engineer stores, ammunition, and rations were made at selected points, and in addition store-tanks were loaded with material which it was to be their task to carry forward in rear of the assaulting troops. The fact that this was the first occasion on which the whole five infantry divisions of the Australian Corps were to operate together, unquestionably brought about a feeling of confidence and inspired each man with a determination to do his best.

On August 5th the battalion nucleus, under Captain Barbour, was sent to a camp near Allonville, while the transport and the quartermaster's store moved up to the vicinity of Blangy-Tronville. That night the remainder of the battalion proceeded to the support line in the Fouilloy area south of the Somme, reaching certain allotted dug-

THE BATTLE OF AMIENS

outs on the terraces at 1 a.m. Hot food was brought up and all were fairly comfortable. On the afternoon of the 6th, metal discs for communication with aeroplanes during the attack were issued as were ammunition, ground flares, success signals, etc., and an additional water bottle to each man. Boards painted with the battalion colours were sent to the tanks allotted to the 30th and these were attached to the rear of each tank, thus giving rise to a feeling of ownership and mutual dependence.

Foggy weather prevented much aerial work at this time, and the enemy was consequently kept in complete ignorance of the impending operations. On the British side of the line aeroplanes hummed continuously to and fro when visibility permitted of observation, for the particular purpose of watching our forward area and ensuring that no abnormal movement of troops or transport took place by day, such as would be likely to raise the suspicions of the enemy.

The attack was divided into two phases on the Australian Corps front. The 2nd and 3rd Divisions were to attack first at "zero" hour, the 4th and 5th passing through them when they had reached their objectives, and carrying the advance to the old French front line as it had stood before the First Battle of the Somme in 1916. The 8th and 15th Brigades were to attack on the 5th Divisional frontage, the former being on the left. As far as the 8th Brigade was concerned, the 31st Battalion would advance on the right flank and the 30th on the left. The 32nd Battalion was to be in support, with the 29th in reserve. By August 7th all preparations were complete.

Large numbers of field and heavy guns, brought up for the occasion, had been placed in position and camouflaged, and were to remain silent until the barrage opened on the day of attack. The supply tanks allotted to the 5th Division moved into a small orchard just north of Villers-Bretonneaux on the 7th. About midday, a small enemy shell happened to strike one of them, setting it on fire. Loaded as the tank was with ammunition and petrol as well as other inflammable material, it burned furiously until the inevitable explosion took place. The tank crews rushed up to get the other unwieldly monsters away to safety; but, in spite of their heroic efforts, only three tanks were saved out of the total of eighteen, the remainder rapidly taking fire and exploding with terrific detonations, thus rendering the work of the rescuers an extremely dangerous enterprise. The onlookers were thrilled to see the coolness and gallantry with which the crews persistently tried to stop the conflagration from spreading, in spite of continuous explosions which filled the air with jagged, flying shell-splinters and portions of the iron structures of the tanks. As it was not possible to secure any more tanks at the eleventh hour, hurried arrangements had to be put in hand for the making good of the stores that had been destroyed, and for their carriage by horse transport.

On the eve of the battle General Monash issued to the troops an exhortation which, regarded as a prophecy, is probably unique in the annals of the whole war. It reads as follows:—

To the Soldiers of the Australian Army Corps:

For the first time in the history of this Corps, all five Australian divisions will to-morrow engage in the largest and most important battle operation ever undertaken by the Corps.

They will be supported by an exceptionally powerful artillery and by tanks and aeroplanes on a scale never previously attempted. The full resources of our sister Dominion, the Canadian Corps, will also operate on our right, while two British divisions will guard our left flank.

The many successful offensives which the brigades and battalions of this Corps have so brilliantly executed during the past four months have been but the prelude to, and the preparation for, this greatest and culminating effort.

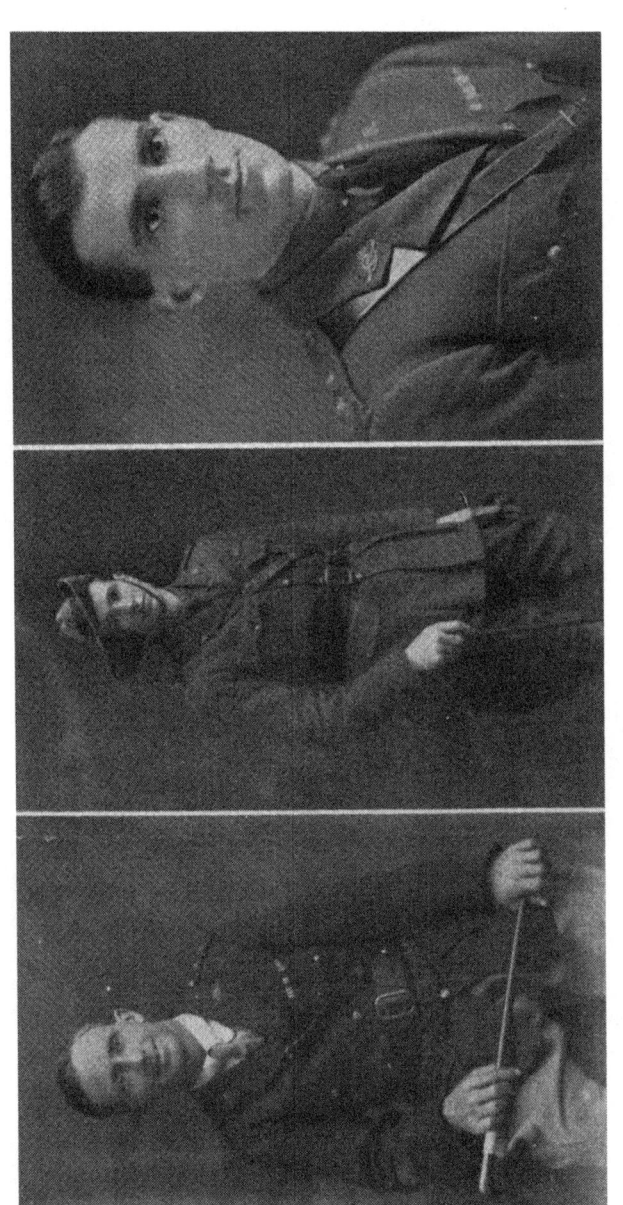

Lieut. W. C. ABBOTT, M.M.   Lieut. B. O. DAVIES, D.C.M.   Lieut. C. E. ALCORN, Belgian Croix de Guerre.

THE BATTLE OF AMIENS

Because of the completeness of our plans and dispositions, of the magnitude of the operations, of the numbers of troops employed, and of the depth to which we intend to over-run the enemy's positions, this battle will be one of the most memorable of the whole war; and there can be no doubt that, by capturing our objectives, we shall inflict blows upon the enemy which will make him stagger, and will bring the end appreciably nearer.

I entertain no sort of doubt that every Australian soldier will worthily rise to so great an occasion, and that every man, imbued with the spirit of victory, will, in spite of every difficulty that may confront him, be animated by no other resolve than grim determination to see through to a clean finish, whatever his task may be.

The work to be done to-morrow will perhaps make heavy demands upon the endurance and staying powers of many of you, but I am confident that, in spite of excitement, fatigue, and physical strain, every man will carry on to the utmost of his powers until his goal is won; for the sake of Australia, the Empire and our cause.

I earnestly wish every soldier of the Corps the best of good fortune, and a glorious and decisive victory, the story of which will re-echo throughout the world, and will live forever in the history of our home land.

The night of the August 7th was fine, but a dense fog came down soon after midnight, and persisted for several hours after the launching of the attack. Zero hour was fixed for 4.20 a.m.

"It needs a pen more facile than I can command to describe, and an imagination more vivid to realize the stupendous import of the last ten minutes," writes General Monash (*The Australian Victories in France in* 1918, *p.*

131). "In black darkness, a hundred thousand infantry, deployed over twelve miles of front, are standing grimly, silently, expectantly, in readiness to advance, or are already crawling stealthily forward to get within eighty yards of the line on which the barrage will fall; all feel to make sure that their bayonets are tightly locked, or to set their steel helmets firmly on their heads; company and platoon commanders, their whistles ready to hand, are nervously glancing at their luminous watches, waiting for minute after minute to go by—and giving a last look over their commands—ensuring that their runners are by their sides, their observers alert, and that the officers detailed to control direction have their compasses set and ready. Carrying parties shoulder their burdens, and adjust the straps; pioneers grasp their picks and shovels; engineers take up their stores of explosives and primers and fuses; machine and Lewis gunners whisper for the last time to the carriers of their magazine and belt boxes to be sure and follow up. The Stokes Mortar carrier slings his heavy load, and his loading numbers fumble to see that their haversacks of cartridges are handy. Overhead drone the aeroplanes, and from the rear, in swelling chorus, the buzzing and clamour of the tanks grows every moment louder and louder. Scores of telegraph operators sit by their instruments with their message forms and registers ready to hand, bracing themselves for the rush of signal traffic which will set in a few moments later; dozens of staff officers spread their maps in readiness, to record with coloured pencils the stream of expected information. In hundreds of pits, the guns are already run up, loaded and laid on their opening lines of fire; the sergeant is checking the range for the last time; the layer stands silently with the lanyard in his hand. The section officer, watch on wrist, counts the last seconds: 'A minute to go'—'Thirty seconds'—'Ten seconds'—'Fire'.

"And, suddenly, with a mighty roar, more than a thousand guns begin the symphony. A great illumination lights

THE BATTLE OF AMIENS

up the eastern horizon; and instantly the whole complex organization, extending far back to areas almost beyond earshot of the guns, begins to move forward; every man, every unit, every vehicle and every tank on their appointed tasks and to their designated goals, sweeping onward relentlessly and irresistibly. Viewed from a high vantage point and in the glimmer of the breaking day, a great artillery barrage surely surpasses in dynamic splendour any other manifestation of collective human effort."

Let us now turn to C. E. Montague's description of the battle (given in *Disenchantment*) as he viewed it that morning: "The mist in billowy, bolster like masses, wallowed and rolled about at the touch of light airs; at one moment a figure some thirty yards off could be seen and then a thickened whiteness would rub it out; down the earth cliff we looked into a cauldron of that seething milky opaqueness. Of what might go on in that pit of enigma the eye could tell nothing; the mind hung on what news might come through the air. We knew that there was to be no prior bombardment; the men would start with the barrage and go for five miles across the Santerre if they could, pushing the enemy off it. The stage was set, the play of plays was about to begin on the broad stage below, only, between our eyes and the boards there was hung a white curtain. Up the cliff, fumbling and muted, came the first burst of the barrage. Now the men would be rising full length above earth and walking out with smoking breath and bejewelled eyebrows into the infested mist. Then our guns, for an interval, fell almost silent—first lift of the barrage—a chance for hungry ears to assess the weight of the enemy's answering gunfire. Surely, surely it had not all the volume it had had at Arras and Ypres last year. And then down came our barrage again, like one rifle-bolt banging home and all thought was again with the friends before whose faces the wall of splashing metal, earth, and flame had just risen and moved on ahead like the pillars of fire and cloud.

"Hours passed, bringing the usual changes of sounds in battles. The piece that had started so rapidly on the piano slowed down, the notes spaced themselves out; the first continuous barking of many guns slackened off irregularly into isolated barks and groups of barks—just what you hear from a dog whose temper is subsiding, with occasional returns. That, in itself told nothing. Troops might have gained a few hundred yards in the old Flanders way, and then flopped down to dig and be murdered, or—but one kept a tight hand on hope. One had hoped too often since Loos. And then the mist lifted. It rolled right up into the sky in one piece, like a theatre curtain, almost, suddenly taking its white quilted thickness away from between our eyes and the vision so much longed for during four years.

"Beyond the river a miracle—the miracle—had begun. It was going on fast. Remember that all previous advances had gained us little more than freedom to skulk up communication trenches a mile or two further eastward, if that. But now! Across the level Santerre, which the sun was beginning to fill with a mist-filtered lustre, two endless columns of British guns, waggons and troops were marching steadily east, unshelled, over the ground that the Germans had held until the dawn. Nothing like it had ever been seen in the war. Above, on our cliff, we turned and stared at each other, we must have looked rather like Cortes' men agape on their peak. The marvel seemed real; the road lay open and dry across the Red Sea. Far off, six thousand yards off in the shining south-east, tanks and cavalry were at work, shifting and gleaming and looking huge on the sky-line of some little rumpled fold of the Santerre plateau. Nearer, the glass could make out an enemy battery, captured complete, caught with the leather caps still on the muzzles of the guns. The British dead on the plain, horses and men, lay scattered thinly over wide spaces; scarcely a foundered tank could be seen, the ground had turf on it still; it was only speckled with shell-holes, not disembowelled or flayed. The war had put on

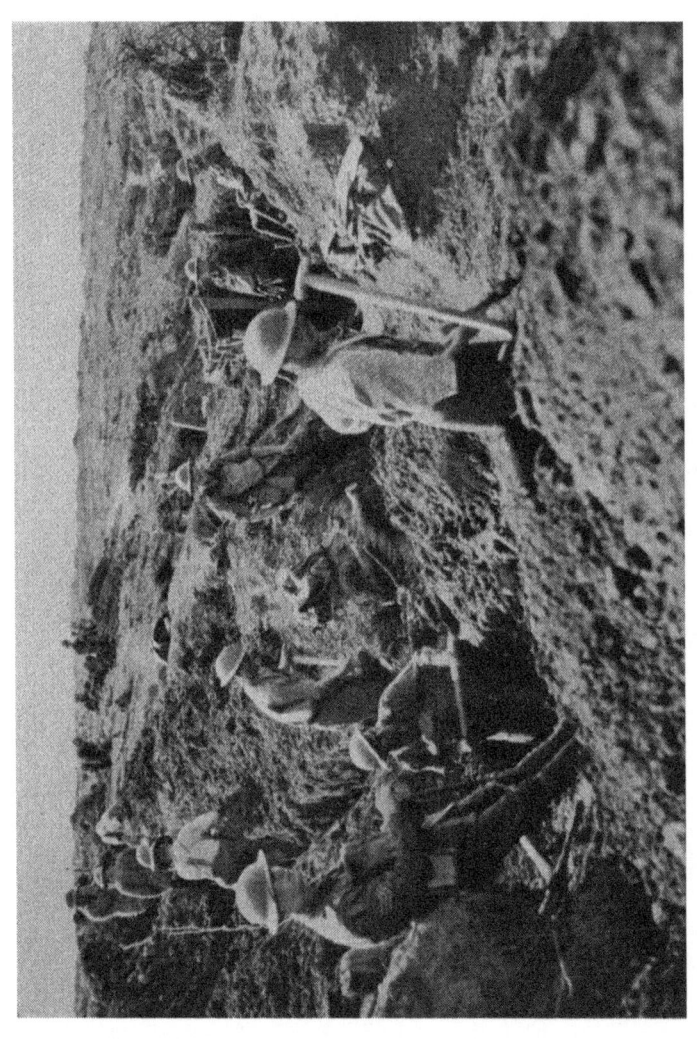

A. COMPANY, WESTHOEK RIDGE.

Showing: Lieut. S. Murdoch, D.C.M., Lieut. S. H. Fisk, Sgt. V. H. Drake, Sgt. F. Buttsworth, Sgt. W. C. H. Jackson, Pte. D. Sinclair, and others.

A.W.M. Photo No. E803.

a sort of benignity, coming out gallantly on the top of the earth and moving about in the air and the sun; the warm heath, with so few dead upon it, looked almost clement and kind, almost gay after the scabrous mud wastes and the stink of the captured dug-outs of the Salient, piled up to ground level with corpses . . . for a moment, the object of all dreamt desire seemed to have come; the flaming sword was gone, and the gate of the garden open."

The following account of the 8th Brigade's part in the battle is from the pen of an officer of the 30th: "After what prisoners subsequently described as a 'terrible three minutes' (he says) the barrage lifted off the enemy's front line, and the cheering assault battalions of the 2nd and 3rd Divisions rushed the German positions. Prisoners commenced to come in immediately; they stated that they had been taken by surprise and were unable to withstand the joint persuasiveness of our infantry and tanks.

"The attack swept on without a check on the Australian front, and at zero plus one hour the 8th Brigade moved forward. The fog, aided by the smoke and dust caused by the barrage, formed now an almost impenetrable veil. Company officers, however, moved by compass bearings, and at no time was there any confusion nor did one unit ever lose touch with another. Thanks to the wonderful counter-battery work of the heavy gunners, the enemy shelling, in spite of the frantic calls for barrage fire by his infantry, was scattered and ineffective.

"On passing through the village Warfusee-Abancourt it was seen that the enemy must have been thrown into a state of the wildest confusion—everywhere was to be seen equipment of every description which the harassed Germans had hurriedly cast aside in their frantic rush to get away from the oncoming Australians. The 30th and 31st Battalions advanced steadily, and, in spite of the continuing density of the fog, which rendered the operation doubly difficult, formed up on the line laid down for them, and punctual to the second moved forward in the second phase of the attack, supported by that barrage of such ferocious intensity. A few German gunners tried vainly to hold up the advance by pouring shell into the Australian ranks at point-blank range, but the majority of them were so demoralised by the tornado of high-explosive which descended with such pitiless accuracy on their positions, that they fled in confusion.

"Bayonvillers fell to the 31st Battalion and the troops on their right. In a sunken road near the village was a battery of German 77-mm. field guns; the gun crews made a desperate attempt to stop our advance, and, firing at point-blank range, succeeded in knocking out five tanks. It was only the individual bravery of the "Diggers" of the 31st that enabled them to overcome the determined resistance offered by this battery. Advancing in rushes through a veritable hail of high-explosive and shrapnel, they made their way into the sunken road, outflanking the surviving German gunners, who promptly fled, abandoning their artillery. Farther on the left, the 30th Battalion, advancing as though on parade, swept all before them and speedily beat down the resistance of machine-gunners, artillerymen, and riflemen alike.

"A huge railway gun, which had been employed principally in bombarding Amiens, continued firing until the infantry were within a few hundred yards of it, the fog being so dense that the crew were quite unaware of the extent of our advance. The whole train was captured by the 31st Battalion, complete with engine and several truck loads of ammunition. The smoking remains of two complete trains which the enemy had endeavoured to pull away testified to the good work of our airmen. Booty of all sorts was captured; the complete horsed transport of a German battalion was but one of the items secured by our men. Even searchlights and ambulances were abandoned by the panic-stricken Boche.

"Reaching the Morcourt Valley, the 30th and 31st Battalions skirmished round the depression, from which were subsequently taken over a hundred prisoners. It was here that a complete regimental canteen was found, and in addition, stores of all natures came into our hands. Enemy machine-gunners for the greater part quickly surrendered, but in this valley several apparently isolated parties put up a strong resistance, and were only overcome by the dash and resource of the eager Australians.

"At the exact time laid down, the infantry reached their objective; cases are on record where our airmen actually landed to tell infantry commanders personally what they had seen. All laid great stress on the fact that the rout of the enemy was complete, the roads leading eastwards being crowded with traffic hurrying panic-stricken from the battle-field.

"Our new positions were rapidly consolidated, and all preparations were made should the enemy attempt a counter-attack; the night, however, passed fairly quietly, and shortly after dawn on the 9th orders were received to take the village of Vauvillers, which was strongly held by the enemy. This task was entrusted to the 29th Battalion. At 11 a.m. the 29th, led by their C.O. (Lieutenant-Colonel J. McArthur) moved to the assault, assisted by seven tanks. The attackers were met with withering blasts of machine-gun and field-gun fire which sadly depleted their ranks, and knocked out most of the tanks. With the assistance of detachments of the 31st Battalion on the left, the gallant 29th, although suffering terribly from the fire of hidden machine-guns, advanced resolutely and drove the Germans before them at the point of the bayonet. Early in the operation armoured car detachments and cavalry pushed out well ahead and did splendid work, spreading confusion in the Boche back areas and blocking roads by shooting up horse transport. One armoured car planted the Australian flag in Proyart, some miles in advance of the objective, and in addition to other exploits, distributed bursts of machine-gun fire amongst the startled occupants of an officers' mess in the same village.

"After the fall of Vauvillers, the 8th Brigade consolidated

the new position and shortly afterwards the 2nd Division passed through to continue the attack. In the two days' engagement the total number of prisoners taken by the brigade was 831, in addition to a huge quantity of war material."

Considering the depth to which the battalion had penetrated the enemy lines, its casualties were not heavy, but among the killed were Major C. J. Wells (R.M.O.) and Lieutenant S. Haig. Lieutenant T. S. C. Horgan was wounded and subsequently lost an arm. Captain C. D. Savage, Corporals E. Wilkinson, P. Ashenden, F. H. Pickering and A. H. James, and Privates F. C. Colgate, C. R. Dawson, F. H. Barnes, J. Morrison, R. McGregor, and R. G. Buchanan were congratulated by the corps commander.

CHAPTER XVII.

(FOUCAUCOURT AND PERONNE).

ON August 10th the battalion moved back to the Aubigny area and was accommodated in dug-outs and trenches partially covered with tarpaulins; the men were very tired, but a hot meal was ready and they soon settled down. The following day was devoted to rest, cleaning up, and swimming in the Somme canal. Mistakes made in the open warfare of the two previous days were pointed out and preparations made for a further advance. The brigadier visited the battalion and complimented the troops on their recent achievements.

Six days later we were again on the move and marched to Morecourt Valley, taking over shelters from the 53rd and the 60th Battalions. The heat was considerable, but very few men fell out en route. Colonel McArthur, of the 29th Battalion, having been wounded the previous day, Major Charlton was detailed to take his place temporarily. As it was expected that raiding parties would soon be required, volunteers were called for to commence training; many more than were required were forthcoming, and eventually a party of 52 was selected, the officers being Lieutenants H. J. Wells, J. J. W. Flynn, and H. S. Grimwade.

On August 21st the battalion moved back to Aubigny, once more enjoying a complete rest and plenty of swimming in the canal. The battalion war diary records that a full issue of beer was made from the battalion's comforts fund.

Interior changes about this time included the following: Lieutenants A. H. Ellis, H. S. Grimwade, and W. I. Daniel taken on strength immediately after graduating from a cadet training school; Captain W. H. Zander posted as second-in-command of "B" Company, and Lieutenant H. W. Wedd in his place as adjutant; Corporals G. W. Paterson and F. A. Deffell promoted to the rank of sergeant, the former being attached to battalion headquarters for special duty.

Three divisions were to participate in the next attack—32nd British on the right, 5th Australian in the centre, and 2nd Australian on the left. An important alteration in the method of attack was now brought into operation, thus illustrating the extent of the enemy's demoralization. The deliberate operations hitherto adopted, namely, to reach an objective and stay there, were abandoned and follow-up tactics introduced. The 30th Battalion again moved forward to Morcourt Valley, this time taking over from the 7th and 8th Battalions (1st Division). "D" Company was on the right, "C" Company on the left, "B" in right support, and "A" in left support. Brigade instructions were to the effect that, following a concentrated artillery shoot, the 30th would attack the village of Foucoucourt, which was accomplished in great style, as is shown in Lieutenant-Colonel Street's report to brigade headquarters:—

"On the morning of the 27th, 'C' Company was ordered to straighten out its line and make a general line running from M20 central to left of 'D' Company. At 12.50 p.m. a message was received relating to an artillery programme with instructions that the battalion would act at the conclusion of the bombardment, with a view to the capture of the village. 'C' Company commenced to straighten its line at 2 p.m. and they were further instructed to bulge their line towards the village and threaten the rear of the village. The actual attack took place at 2.15 p.m.

"The dispositions at this time were 'C' Company working north of the village and 'D' Company frontally and south of the village. 'C' Company moved much quicker than 'D' Company, owing to better ground and made good progress

FOUCACOURT AND PERONNE

against very heavy machine-gun fire. The artillery gave this company excellent support. 'D' Company was working two platoons past the south of the village with one platoon holding frontally. The attack of this company was very formidable and the machine-gun fire very deadly. Notwithstanding this, they made ground and at 6 p.m. the two companies gained touch in front of the village. Rifle grenades here proved to be very valuable against machine-guns.

"The captures included one officer, 34 other ranks and 16 heavy and light machine-guns. It is estimated that the enemy lost at least 20 killed and several wounded. Most of the killed were bayoneted during the attack of 'D' Company. Corporal J. C. Ford, of that company, was with the platoon attacking frontally, which was held up by machine-gun fire, and after some delay he remarked: 'This is no good to me, I'll get that cow!' and rushed the gun, killing all the crew but one, whom he brought back with him. The platoon was then able to get on.

"During the attack the enemy put down an extremely heavy barrage, which interfered considerably with communications. Lines could not be maintained and the runners were called upon to do very heavy work. Unfortunately, many of them were killed and thus some messages were not delivered. Among those killed was Private J. Wilson, of 'D' Company, who, during a long period of active service as a runner, had earned the respect and admiration of all who knew him. I also particularly commend the work of Captain C. D. Savage and Lieutenant H. J. Wells, O'sC., 'C' and 'D' Companies respectively."

Next day the advance was continued, a start being made at 5.45 a.m. by "C" Company. A few minutes later the whole battalion line was in touch and advancing. Contact was maintained throughout the advance with the enemy, whom it was noticed were mounted on cycles with machine-guns attached. They were thus able to get well away before our troops and Lewis gunners could approach them. Steady progress was maintained, likewise good touch, and what had once been the village of Estrees was passed with little opposition. By 2.30 p.m. when the line was well clear of Estrees, a halt was called, as the men were thoroughly fatigued. The 31st Battalion, in support, received instructions from brigade headquarters to pass through the 30th, which it did at 5.45 p.m., continuing the advance until darkness set in.

The 30th now became the right supporting unit. A suitable spot was chosen on which to bivouac and a hot meal was brought along at 8 o'clock. The enemy refrained from shelling the place, with the result that a good night's rest was obtained. The country over which the advance had been made was exceedingly rough and broken, being nothing less than a maze of trenches and shell-holes. The battalion casualties during the past three days had been heavy: 14 killed in action, 14 died of wounds and 60— including Lieutenants J. J. W. Flynn, V. W. Biddle, C. D. Button, and H. S. Grimwade—wounded.

At 5 a.m. on August 29th the 30th moved forward in support of the 31st Battalion, reaching the west bank of the Somme at 8.30, and taking up a position astride the main Amiens-Péronne road west of Villers-Carbonnel. On this road was an enemy field-gun, which had evidently been wrecked by a German mine; its crew was lying dead around it. Several casualties were sustained, among them the medical officer, Captain L. E. W. Roberts.

As usual, a hot meal came up from the "cookers" at dusk and, despite enemy shelling, all ranks passed a reasonably comfortable night. Next morning the battalion moved back to a valley near Fontaine-les-Cappy, where it remained two days before proceeding to the divisional reserve area in the vicinity of Flaucourt.

Prior to our attack on Foucoucourt, and during our advance towards the Hindenburg Line, Major John Chapman was acting as brigade major of the 8th Brigade, and naturally took a great interest in the progress of his old

B. COMPANY GROUP. BAPAUME

Pte. D. Rattray, Cpl. C. L. Boland, Sgt. R. McKinnon, Pte. A. Page, Cpl. F. W. McDowell, Cpl. W. H. Linsley, Sgt. M. Arkell, Pte. A. C. Walker, M.M., Cpl. Alcorn, Croix de Guerre, Belgium.
A.W.M. Photo No. 361.

FOUCACOURT AND PERONNE

unit. For his activity during this period, he was awarded the D.S.O.

The month of September, while destined to be the last month of actual fighting as far as the 5th Division was concerned, was also one of very great strain and many casualties. But the end was in sight and all gave of their best. Foch was in supreme command and his slogan, "Attack"—"Attack", was thoroughly approved by the men in the ranks. The enemy was on the move, they said, so keep him going.

On September 1st the 8th Brigade again went forward, and on the 3rd the 30th Battalion, tired but in high spirits, reached the Somme near Péronne. At this point the river —looking upstream—turns almost at right angles to the south; hence, as the enemy was being pushed eastwards, it was again necessary to cross it and the adjacent marshes. The permanent bridges having been destroyed by the Germans, the passage had to be made by means of hastily constructed foot-bridges. As the 30th crossed during the daylight hours—5 a.m. to 5 p.m.—it had to move by sections at considerable distances apart. However, all eventually crossed the marshes and were allotted to trenches in the neighbourhood of Halle, which had formerly been portion of the enemy's defences of Péronne. The new area was very congested, a fact which the German airmen evidently noted, for about dusk there descended upon it a heavy bombardment of high explosive and "green cross" gas. All hands were compelled to wear their gas-helmets for upwards of three hours, and the hot meal which had just arrived from the "cookers" back at Fontaine, could not be eaten until the gas had dissipated. Two fine young officers, Lieutenants B. D. Rush and S. H. Murdock, were killed by one of the high-explosive shells and fourteen other ranks either wounded or gassed.

On the following day the 30th relieved companies of the 59th and 60th Battalions, and proceeded to straighten out and strengthen the position in the vicinity of "Darmstadt

Trench". On the right was the 57th Battalion, on the left the 32nd. On September 5th the 30th and 32nd pushed on, and without encountering much resistance, reached "Silisie Trench", near Bussu, some distance in front of Mont St. Quentin and about a mile and a half east of the Somme. Relieved here by the 3rd Division at 11.30 p.m. on September 5th, the battalion marched some six miles south through Péronne to trenches in the Le-Mesnil-Bruntnell area, arriving there at 5.30 a.m. All ranks were extremely tired and were looking forward to a rest; this, however, was not to be, as they had to take part in a further advance, parallel to the one described above. The 8th Brigade, having been given the role of advanceguard, had attached to it certain mounted troops and specialist units, and when, at 6 a.m. on September 7th, it moved through the outposts of the 14th British Brigade, its composition was as follows:- -

VANGUARD.

One squadron, 13th Light Horse Regiment (less one troop).
31st Battalion, on right.
29th Battalion, on left.
One section of field artillery attached to each battalion.

MAIN GUARD.

One Troop of Light Horse.
30th Battalion, on right.
32nd Battalion, on left.
8th Field Company, 8th Machine Gun Company Engineers.
8th Light Trench Motor Battery.
5th (Army) Brigade, Royal Horse Artillery (less two sections).
298th (Army) Brigade, Royal Field Artillery (less two sections).

This formation was maintained for the ensuing three days, and although not much resistance was met with—for

FOUCACOURT AND PERONNE

the enemy was hurrying back to the shelter of the Hindenburg line—marching across shell-torn country was very trying on the men, many of whom reached the verge of exhaustion. During this six-mile advance the 8th Brigade captured the villages of Hancourt, Vraignes, Bernes, Flechin and Poeully.

On September 10th the 8th Brigade was relieved by the 13th Brigade (4th Division) and moved back to the Le Mesnil area. The men of all battalions were thoroughly exhausted and were looking forward to a reasonable rest in a clean area; but instead, it seemed that they would have to make the best of extremely dirty trenches. In the neighbourhood, however, were dumps of timber and iron which had been abandoned by the enemy; and the men, individually or in groups, soon made themselves secure from the wind and rain. One bushman remarked that the "township" which sprang up reminded him of the habitations on the opal fields of White Cliffs and Lightning Ridge. The quartermaster was never far behind with hot meals, and the rum issue never failed. The men's packs, additional blankets, and other stores were brought forward from Aubingy, some twenty miles away. Clean clothing was provided and improvised baths constructed, the most effective method being to line a deep shell-hole with a tarpaulin, weighting or pegging the sheet down around the rim and thus preventing the escape of the water.

Seventeen days were thus spent in comparative comfort at Le Mesnil. Though out of sight of the enemy, the place was not beyond the range of the German artillery, which along with his airmen, almost every day caused a few casualties in the brigade. Training was carried out in the mornings, the afternoons being devoted to sport. The band was brought up and it, of course, contributed very largely to the contentment of all ranks. A brigade sports competition was held on September 23rd, at which our battalion won its share of the prizes.

During this period of rest Lieutenant N. W. S. Hamilton

was seconded for duty with the 14th Training Battalion in England, and Lieutenants W. E. Oakes, M. Griffin, H. E. Wonnacott and C. E. Alcorn returned to duty from hospital or schools.

Four popular—though largely Scottish—N.C.O's.—Company Sergeant-Major E. G. McKinnon and Sergeants A. J. McCallum, W. C. Abbott, and M. F. Sinclair—were raised to commissioned rank. Among others struck off the strength by reason of wounds or illness was Company Sergeant-Major Geoff. Cowen.

The Rt. Hon. William Morris Hughes, Prime Minister of Australia, paid a visit to the brigade at Le Mesnil. Few realised then the great part that he was destined to play at the Peace Conference, and in the repatriation of the A.I.F.

The following notification from A.I.F. orders received a mixed reception, one man remarking that the pay office authorities were very liberal with the other fellow's money:

"Approval is given for members of the A.I.F. who so desire, and who have sufficient credit in their paybooks, to draw amounts of pay not exceeding a total of Five Pounds (£5) in excess of the prescribed scales for pay issue, for the purpose of purchasing Christmas gifts."

The period of rest came to an end on September 27th. At 3 p.m. that day the battalion nucleus marched out—always an indication of an impending operation—to the divisional reinforcement wing at La Chappelette and the attacking troops moved off in the direction of Hervilly at 5.45. Packs, valises, blankets, and all surplus stores had previously been collected and placed in brigade dumps.

CHAPTER XVIII.

(THROUGH THE HINDENBURG LINE).

THE move of the brigade to the assembly position in the Hervilly area was a slow process, due to the great congestion of traffic, and it did not arrive at its bivouac until nearly midnight on September 27th.

An important operation, no less than the breaking of the Hindenburg line, and an advance of some four miles beyond it, was contemplated, hence tanks, guns, and supplies of every description were being pushed forward along all the available roads and tracks.

The 5th Australian Division was to co-operate with the 30th American Division on a two-mile frontage, the 32nd British Division being on its right, and the 3rd Australian, co-operating with the 27th American Division on its left. The 5th Division's frontage would be divided between the 8th Brigade on the right and the 15th Brigade on the left, the 14th Brigade being in reserve. In the 8th Brigade the attack was to be launched by the 29th and 32nd Battalions (the latter on the right), with the 31st Battalion in support of the right flank and the 30th Battalion in reserve. Such was the position on the morning of September 29th.

In this sector the Hindenburg line ran parallel to, and a short distance in front of, the St. Quentin Canal, which connected the river systems of the north-east with those of the north-west, thus making it possible for barges to proceed from Paris to Brussels or Antwerp, an idea carried into effect by the Emperor Napoleon in the early part of last century. To cross the watershed dividing these river systems, it had been necessary to construct a tunnel some three miles long, the course of which was indicated on the surface by a high mound known as the "tunnel embankment", through which air shafts had been dug at regular and frequent intervals. As the ordinary flow of water in the canal had been blocked by numerous dams, the whole length of the tunnel which was electrically lit, was available for barges which rested on the bottom and afforded accommodation for a large number of men and a vast quantity of stores.

The excavation was also largely availed of for cooking purposes, and it was from one of these improvised kitchens that the "cock-and-bull" story of a corpse boiling-down establishment subsequently emanated. The 30th American Division was to break through the Hindenburg line and advance some distance beyond it, after which the 5th Australian Division would pass through and advance to the Beaurevoir line some two miles farther east. Although both trench systems were eventually captured, considerable confusion occurred for a time, our allies losing heavily through lack of experience in exploring deep dug-outs and particularly the canal tunnel, from which the enemy emerged in force and attacked them in the rear.

At 8 a.m. on September 29th the 30th Battalion moved off from its bivouac area and with certain variations, maintained its role of brigade reserve throughout the ensuing three days' operations.

Crossing the Villeret ridge and approaching the jumping-off line it came under scattered shell-fire but sustained little damage. The morning was misty and this, combined with the smoke from our artillery, made it difficult at times to maintain direction. Approaching Bellicourt several casualties occurred, but losses were minimised by the fog which, up to this point, enveloped the landscape. By the time the eastern outskirts of the village were reached, visibility had improved and it was possible to see at least a mile ahead.

It was now realised that the American troops had not reached their allotted objectives, as considerable enemy movement could be seen in and around Nauroy, and machine-gun and anti-tank fire was being directed at the brigade. At this period a large gap opened up between the two leading battalions, due to the 29th being held up while the 32nd was enabled to continue forward. This necessitated the halting of the 30th and its taking up a position in a trench-line and shell-holes on the southeastern outskirts of Bellicourt pending developments. While here it was seen that an anti-tank gun was causing great havoc among the tanks, nine of which were destroyed in attempting to locate machine-gun nests.

Responding to a message from the C.O. of the 32nd Battalion (Major B. A. Wark), who stated that his left flank was in the air, our C.O. sent forward two fighting patrols under Lieutenants J. C. Yeomans and A. H. Forbes with the object of ascertaining the position in the village and, if possible, dealing with the destructive anti-tank gun. The patrols entered the Le Catelet-Nauroy trench and there managed to cut off a party of the enemy, killing eight and capturing eighteen.

About this time two tanks succeeded in approaching Nauroy from the south and, co-operating with Yeomans and Forbes, cleared the village and adjacent wood. Two posts established east of Nauroy were handed over to the 29th Battalion on the arrival of its right flank. Having accomplished the task allotted them, the patrols returned to battalion headquarters. The dash and resource of their leaders was highly commended. Yeomans received the D.S.O. for his action, the particulars of which are set out in the following extract from the citation which accompanied the award:—

"The front line troops having failed to reach their objective, and the position being very obscure, this officer led a patrol of 25 men forward to ascertain the enemy's dispositions in and around the village of Nauroy. The approach being under direct enemy observation, it was continually swept by field-gun and machine-gun fire, but by skilful leadership he worked rapidly forward without casualties. Nearing the village he noticed a tank, and leaving his sergeant in charge of the patrol, he entered the tank, which made into the village and ascertained that it was strongly held by the enemy with numerous machine-gun nests. With the aid of the tank, Lieutenant Yeomans decided to attack the village and the Le Catelet-Nauroy trench immediately in front, and so successful was his plan that the trench and village were mopped up with heavy losses to the enemy, in addition to 18 prisoners and 7 machine guns being captured. This officer himself rushed a machine-gun, personally killing the crew of four and capturing the gun. Then, with great dash and daring, he led his patrol through a network of trenches, bombing and bayoneting many of the enemy. Having cleared the village and its defences, he then established two posts north-east of the village, and held on in spite of heavy fire from field and machine-guns, till he handed over to the front-line troops, who from these posts were enabled to establish a line, which rendered safe the capture of the village by our men.

"The brilliant leadership and initiative displayed by this officer helped considerably to relieve a very critical situation, and the example of gallantry and utter disregard for personal safety was most inspiring to those under his command."

Lieutenant Forbes was highly commended for his capable leadership, and reference must also be made to the work of a Lewis gunner, Private A. E. Knight, who, moving into the open regardless of danger, silenced an anti-tank gun which would probably have accounted for our remaining tanks. For this action he deservedly received the Military Medal.

Although the 31st Battalion had been withdrawn from its former position and was placed in the widening gap between the 29th and 32nd, it did not completely occupy the frontage. Late in the afternoon, therefore, "B" Company under

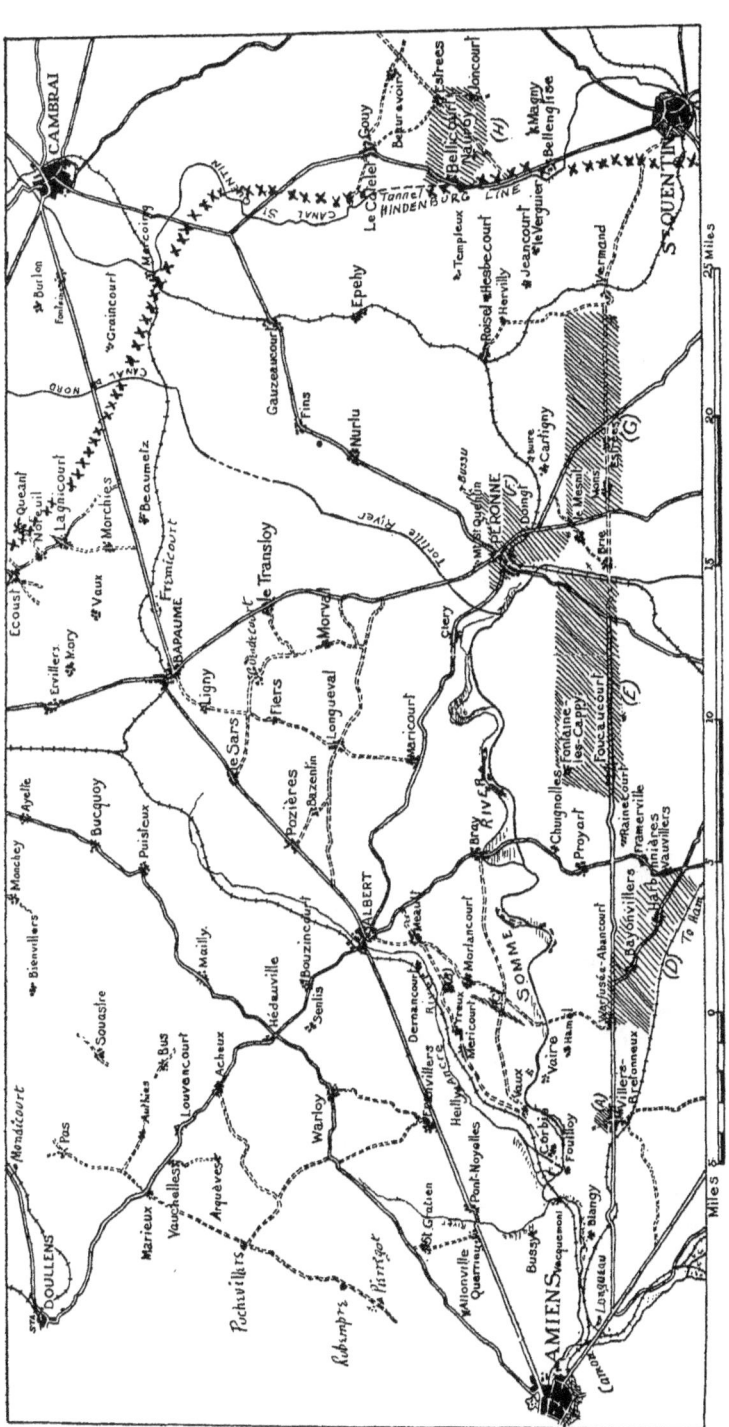

THE FIFTH DIVISION'S SECOND SOMME CAMPAIGN

The shaded areas are approximately those captured by the 5th Australian Division.

(A) Taken by 15th Bde., 24th-26th April; (B) Taken by 15th Bde., 4th July; (C) Taken by 8th and 14th Bdes., 29th July; (D) Taken by 8th and 15th Bdes., 8th-9th August; (E) Taken by 8th Bde. as Advance Guard, end August; (F) Taken by 14th, 15th and 8th Bdes., 1st-5th Sept.; (G) Taken by 8th Bde. as Advance Guard, 6th-9th Sept.; (H) Taken by 8th, 14th and 15th Bdes., 29th Sept.-2nd Oct.

(Reproduced from "The Story of the Fifth Australian Division" by permission of Captain A. D. Ellis, M.C.)

THROUGH THE HINDENBURG LINE 213

Captain Zander was sent forward to fill the vacant space, and, coming under orders of the 29th Battalion, was employed during most of the night in consolidating a position east of Nauroy. Here it remained until 5 a.m. on October 1st, when it rejoined the reserve. The company experienced a very trying time and suffered many casualties, Lieutenant H. Doust being killed by a sniper's bullet. In the meantime, the remainder of the battalion stayed in reserve until at 1 a.m. on October 1st, when orders were received to despatch two companies to participate in an attack on the Beaurevoir line. Accordingly, "A" Company was sent to the assistance of the 31st Battalion, to which it acted as support company. "D" Company, which was allotted to the 32nd Battalion, followed the barrage. An account of its activities, written by Captain Barbour, is given in Part II.

At 12.30 p.m. "B" and "C" Companies and attached details moved forward in support of the 31st Battalion and were about to assist in the exploitation of the position won, when orders were received for our relief by the 5th Brigade (2nd Division). An advance party was at once sent back to the neighbourhood of Malakoff Farm to prepare "Triangle Wood Trench" for the reception of the battalions.

The relief took place about midnight and the 30th reached what had once been a farm about 2 a.m. Although all ranks were on the verge of exhaustion, shelters were improvised and a little sleep was obtained. The total casualties suffered by the 30th in three days' operations amounted to one officer and fourteen other ranks killed, and three officers and 68 other ranks wounded. General Tivey came along during the morning and, in accordance with his usual custom, spoke encouraging words to groups of men here and there.

It was a weary and worn brigade that struggled back to the neighbourhood of Roisel, six or seven miles on the other side of the Hindenburg line, on the morning of October 3rd.

The fighting and exposure of the previous days had been most exhausting, but all ranks had the satisfaction of knowing that they had driven the enemy an appreciable distance towards his homeland and had restored a further strip of country to its rightful owner. The men who had come face to face with the enemy felt, as far as individuals were concerned, that the war was nearing its close, and that they had fought their last engagement. This view was not altogether shared by the higher authorities, who, of course, knew more about the enemy's resources; but the feeling of an early cessation of hostilities was too strong to be entirely ignored. As subsequent events proved, the men were right.

On arrival at the bivouac area all hands busied themselves with the building and improvising of shelters, for which there was no lack of material, as timber and iron from ruined buildings was easily obtainable. By nightfall all were fairly comfortable, and for the first time in four days undisturbed sleep was indulged in. The medical officer and his staff were the last to obtain rest, as, although all the wounded had been evacuated to ambulance and casualty clearing stations, a number of men were suffering from blistered feet and other minor ailments.

Five days were spent at Roisel, the time being devoted principally to rest and reorganization. The daily sight of considerable numbers of prisoners, passing to the rear areas under escort much heartened all ranks, and gave tangible evidence of the success of the units which had relieved them. The weather was turning cold, pointing to the approach of another winter, but one happily destined to be spent under much more pleasant conditions than those of the two previous years.

The quartermaster's store and the transport section, as well as the nucleus, rejoined the battalion here; and, while some of the nucleus expressed their disgust at having been denied the opportunity of participating in the breaking of the great defensive line, it is not unlikely that they were secretly satisfied at having escaped the fatigue of the enterprise.

The men's packs and blankets and other gear were now returned to them from the divisional dump. Battle stores, such as extra water-bottles, were returned to store; shortages were made up and clean clothing supplemented by a cardigan jacket was issued to all ranks, who availed themselves of the improvised baths that were set up. A well-stocked canteen was opened on October 5th, which was much appreciated and largely patronised.

At 4 a.m. on October 8th, exactly two months since the commencement of the victorious advance from Villers-Bretonneux, the battalion set out for Péronne to entrain for the Oisemont area near Abbeville, some eighty miles distant. The few days' rest at Roisel, together with the feeling which the completion of a faithfully discharged task engenders had worked wonders, and, although a much longer period was essential in order to regain fighting efficiency, the nine miles to Péronne were traversed in slightly less than three hours. After a hot drink at the railway station, the entraining was quickly and quietly accomplished, and at 11.15 the train started slowly on its western journey.

Because the eulogies of high commands were too often of a fatuous nature, they have not been recorded to any extent in this narrative, but it is felt those of Generals Rawlinson and Monash on the final achievement of the 3rd and 5th Divisions, were thoroughly genuine, and should therefore be reproduced.

FROM GENERAL RAWLINSON.

"The tasks carried out by the 3rd and 5th Australian Divisions in clearing the main Hindenburg system in the neighbourhood of Bony and Bellicourt have greatly assisted the operations, and I wish to thank both these gallant divisions for their endurance and tenacity in carrying out a most difficult and intricate operation."

FROM GENERAL MONASH.

"Please convey to all commanders, staffs and troops of Third and Fifth Australian Divisions my sincere appreciation of, and thanks for, their fine work of the past three days. Confronted at the outset of the operations with a critical situation of great difficulty, and hampered by inability to make free use of our artillery resources, these divisions succeeded in completely overwhelming a stubborn defence in the most strongly fortified sector of the Western Front. This was due to the determination and resources of the leaders, and the grit, endurance and fighting spirit of the troops. Nothing more praiseworthy has been done by the Australian troops in this war."

When the whole of the Australian Corps had been withdrawn from the battle-front after the capture of Montbrehain on October 5th, Sir Henry Rawlinson made a point of sending to it the following congratulatory message:

"Since the Australian Corps joined the Fourth Army on the 8th April, 1918, they have passed through a period of hard and uniformly successful fighting of which all ranks have every right to feel proud.

"Now that it has been possible to give the Australian Corps a well-earned period of rest, I wish to express to them my gratitude for all that they have done. I have watched with the greatest interest and admiration the various stages through which they have passed from the hard times of Flers and Pozieres to their culminating victories in Mont St. Quentin and the great Hindenburg system at Bony, Bellicourt Tunnel, and Montbrehain. During the summer of 1918 the safety of Amiens has been principally due to their determination, tenacity and valour. The story of what they have accomplished as a fighting army corps, of the diligence, gallantry and skill which they have exhibited, and of the scientific methods which they have so thoroughly learned and so successfully applied, has gained for all Australians a place of honour amongst nations and amongst English-speaking nations in particular. It has been my privilege to lead the Australian Corps in the Fourth Army during the decisive battles since August 8th, which bid fair to bring the war to a successful conclusion at no distant date. No one realises more than I do the very prominent part that they have played, for I have watched from day to day every detail of their fighting, and learned to value beyond measure the prowess and determination of all ranks.

"In once more congratulating the Corps on a series of successes unsurpassed in this great war, I feel that no mere words of mine can adequately express the renown that they have won for themselves and the position they have established for the Australian nation, not only in France, but throughout the world. I wish every officer, N.C.O., and man all possible good fortune in the future and a speedy and safe return to their beloved Australia.

H. RAWLINSON (General),
Commanding Fourth Army."

The decorations won by the battalion during the period August 8th-September 1st are as follows:—

DISTINGUISHED SERVICE ORDER.
Lieutenant-Colonel F. Street.
Lieutenant J. C. Yeomans.

MILITARY CROSS.
Lieutenant H. J. Wells.
Lieutenant J. J. W. Flynn.
Lieutenant V. W. Biddle.

THE PURPLE AND GOLD

DISTINGUISHED CONDUCT MEDAL.

Sergeant E. C. E. Amps.
Sergeant W. A. Dowd.
Corporal J. C. Ford.
Sergeant E. H. Mathews.

MILITARY MEDAL.

Sergeant W. C. Abbott.
Corporal P. Ashendon.
Private E. H. Baker.
Private G. Bredhauer.
Sergeant R. A. Case.
Private W. E. Collins.
Private C. F. Davis.
Private L. Dixon.
Corporal A. G. Faulks.
Corporal F. W. Ford.
Private R. Gilchrist.
Private G. Gillingham.
Private G. Glover.
Private A. Gordon.
Private G. Gott.
Corporal P. F. Grant.
Private R. Hartly.
Private F. M. Heslewood.
Sergeant J. A. Hogg.
Private W. H. Huxley.
Private J. Jones.
Private H. H. Joyce.
Private A. E. Knight.
Corporal J. W. Laing.
Sergeant T. M. Massey.
Private R. Mather.
Private W. McDermott.
Private H. T. McFarlane.
Private J. McMahon.
Private P. Milgate.
Sergeant L. H. Moore.
Private J. G. Morgan.
Private J. W. Motbey.
Corporal F. North.
Corporal F. H. Pickering.
Private G. W. Pittaway.
Private W. Player.
Corporal B. Powe.
Private H. Prowd.
Private D. P. Rankin.
Sergeant J. Regan.
Corporal C. Sander.
Private T. Shepherd.
Private C. S. Smith.
Private R. Smith.
Corporal R. J. Thomas.
Corporal A. E. Turley.
Sergeant G. E. Weiley.
Sergeant W. W. Watts.
Private P. Weston.
Sergeant D. Woodbine.
Private H. Young.

MENTIONS IN DESPATCHES.

Lieutenant-Colonel F. Street.
Captain C. D. Savage.
Lieutenant H. A. Grimwade.
Lieutenant C. E. Harrold.
Lieutenant H. W. Wedd.
R.Q.M.S. S. G. Sneesby.

CHAPTER XIX.

(ARMISTICE AND REPATRIATION).

THE train journey to the rest area was a slow one, but this was not a disadvantage, as it enabled all ranks to obtain glimpses of the country over which they had marched so laboriously during the previous months. The sight of Villers-Bretonneux and Amiens was particularly pleasing. As an advance party had preceded the battalion, no time was lost in reaching the allotted billets in and around the villages of Foucaucourt-hors-Nesle and Lignieres. Incidentally, the former place should not be confused with the village captured by "C" and "D" Companies on August 27th.

Here the 30th remained for several weeks, its strength being built up to 37 officers and 690 other ranks. Some of the late reinforcements were disappointed at their lack of opportunity to fire a shot at the enemy.

In common with all the contending armies, due to failing man-power, the 8th Brigade commenced to disintegrate on October 12th, 1918, when the 29th Battalion was amalgamated with the 32nd. It was undoubtedly a great blow to a fine unit and must have caused much heartburning. "The disbanding of the battalion (runs the final entry in the 29th's war-diary) is keenly felt by the officers and men, many of whom have been with it since its inception on 8th August, 1915. This battalion left Australia as a unit of the 8th Brigade on 10th November, 1915, and has always been well to the fore in fighting, in parade work, and in sport. . . . At no time in the history of the battalion has the spirit of *esprit-de-corps* been higher than at the time of disbanding." Major Charlton, who had commanded the 29th during Lieutenant-Colonel McArthur's absence, returned to the 30th at the end of the month and resumed duty as second-in-command. It may here be recorded that Lieutenant-Colonel McArthur had been a member of the 29th Battalion since its inception, and had served in all capacities from adjutant to commanding officer.

The locality in which the brigade was billeted consisted of small, widely scattered villages. The buildings allotted to the men were of poor character, and after recovery from the exhaustion of recent operations they became a bit restive. Efforts, however, were made to break the monotony: sports were organised and held each afternoon, a picture show was opened at Foucaucourt, and the following announcement, which appeared in routine orders, indicates the activities of the divisional concert party. Incidentally, it will be noticed that the location of the theatre was unmistakably indicated:

"The 5th Divisional Concert Party is now showing in the New Theatre, near canteen in Boulevard Abbeville, starting at 8 p.m. nightly. Prices: 4, 3, 2, and 1 franc."

Sport soon predominated over training and lectures, and many interesting football matches between units were arranged.

The following paragraph in divisional orders brought joy to the hearts of A. J. McCallum, J. Urquart, R. McDiarmid, H. McDiarmid, S. Jordan, A. McGilvary, J. McDuff, M. F. Sinclair, R. Mather, D. Stuart, T. J. McCann, T. Wallace, A. Grahamme, N. W. S. Hamilton, P. Aitken, G. Kirkpatrick, J. McWilliam, E. C. Robertson, F. McGowan, A. D. Burns, W. G. McDonald, D. Lynn, T. Storey, R. Southam, "Rab" Hartly, Don McDonald, and other Scotsmen in the battalion.

"SCOTTISH NATIONAL EMBLEM. It is the desire of the St. Andrew Society (Glasgow) to take advantage of the recent War Office Order which authorises sailors and soldiers to wear in their caps national emblems in honour of their National Saint's Day. This society has accordingly

ARMISTICE AND REPATRIATION

arranged to send as far as possible to every Scottish soldier a miniature National Scottish flag to be worn on St. Andrew's Day next. In order that indication may be given as to the number required formations and units will submit, not later than 15th inst., a return showing the approximate number of Scottish soldiers who will wear the emblem."

An order as disconcerting to those of Irish descent, as the foregoing notification to Scotsmen was pleasant, was the prohibition of further leave to Ireland, which caused Lieutenants Eugene O'Sullivan and Jack Witton Flynn simultaneously to ejaculate, "Another injustice." Their opinion was doubtless shared, among others, by Tom Donnellan, Jim Hunt, Vic. Walsh, Barney Donovan, Mick Minouge, Frank Brennan, Larry McGrath, Billy McDermott, Jim Clyne, Mick Maloney, Dan Lynch, Harry Hartigan, Mick Scully, "Gus" Gavin and Fred Daly. The ban was due to the sinking of the *Leinster Castle*, the principle passenger boat plying between Holyhead and Kingstown. Fortunately, the stopping of leave to Erin was of short duration, traffic being resumed when the service was reorganised.

An appreciation of the attitude of the British soldier to his fallen enemy is well illustrated by the following order issued on October 14th which, though probably right from an army point of view, certainly does not harmonise with humanitarian principles:

"It has been noticed that British soldiers, and in many cases officers, crowd round prisoner of war cages and talk and fraternise with the prisoners.

"This practice is to cease forthwith and the officers in charge of cages are held responsible that this order is carried out.

"Sentries posted round the cages are to be clearly instructed that they will be severely punished if they fail to enforce this order.

"German prisoners have also been seen wearing articles of British uniform, caps, greatcoats, puttees, etc. This is to cease forthwith.

"The army commander directs that in view of the orders which have already been issued on the subject, it should not be necessary to again have to call attention to them, and any further slackness in this respect will be made the subject of severe disciplinary action."

The last review of the 5th Division by its commander, General Hobbs, took place at Villeroy on October 29th. The numbers on parade were, of course, smaller than on any previous occasion, but the determination to fight on if necessary was quite apparent. All preparations were made for further effort, but as things turned out, the Armistice intervened and so the Australian Corps was not required to go into action again.

The news of the Armistice was naturally hailed with delight by the troops and they joined with the local populace in celebrating the joyous occasion, but as was the case towards the end of all periods of rest and training, pay books were light, and the wherewithal to purchase good cheer was quite limited. Prior to the great news being promulgated, time had begun to drag somewhat heavily, the weather was cold, poultry had become scarce and difficult to obtain either by purchase, or more direct means, the few fish remaining in the streams had become detonator shy, and winter supplies of firewood on the farms—particularly that stacked in the open—were fast diminishing, therefore any change, even a return to the front line, was not unwelcome.

It was some days before the full significance of the German defeat was fully realised by numbers of the men, due perhaps to the fact that for the past three or four years their minds and actions had been subjected to the will of higher authority, thus obviating the necessity for the ordinary exercise of independent thought. Sitting around the braisiers in the evenings, all manner of ideas were exchanged. "What did an Armistice mean? Would we go to Berlin? When would we be likely to reach home? What did the future hold for us?" While many other questions came up for discussion, deep down in the hearts of all was an unexpressed feeling of thankfulness that the strife was over, and many mental pictures were made of the changes that time had probably brought about in our former surroundings in far away Australia.

ARMISTICE AND REPATRIATION 223

As we were practically on the west coast of France, some disappointment was expressed at being so far in the rear. It required a considerable stretch of imagination to visualize the great German army moving slowly eastward and our greater army as slowly but relentlessly following. However, some fourteen days later we commenced our long march towards Belgium and the tension caused by comparative idleness at once ceased. Among the many changes immediately brought about was the departure to England of General Hobbs, Brigadier-General Tivey becoming Divisional Commander, and Colonel C. S. Davies taking charge of the 8th Brigade.

Our first day's march was a short one of about six miles to Huppy, thence on successive days to Bussigny and Mazinghien, halting at the latter place for eight days. On December 9th we moved a further stage forward to Favril, where we remained another eight days, thence on to Beugnies, where we were destined to remain until February 28th, 1919, thus dispelling the hope, which many cherished, of marching to Germany.

Although the billets were of a very indifferent character, all ranks were so elated at the prospect of an early home going that minor disabilities were considered of little consequence, and with their customary adaptability to circumstances the men soon settled down. Christmas Day was celebrated more heartily than on any previous occasion, the preparation for which, as detailed in the following order, makes interesting reading and will surely be appreciated by those readers who participated in the handling of the shovels and assisted at the vegetable harvest.

"*Duties and Training—22nd December, 1918.*

"The following duties will be carried out by companies to-morrow: A party of 1 N.C.O. and 6 men from each company to clean up the hall where the Xmas dinner is to be held. Shovels may be obtained from the Q.M. store. A party of 1 N.C.O. and 6 men from 'B' Company to report to Sergeant Dunkley at Q.M. store at 9 a.m.

"1 N.C.O. and 10 men from 'B' Company to report to Lieutenant Brewster at Battalion H.Q. at 9.30 a.m.

"1 Officer, 1 N.C.O. and 10 men from 'C' Company to work on cleaning up of lecture halls. The officer detailed, to report to the adjutant to-day for instructions.

"Each company to detail a party not exceeding ten in number for wood and vegetable collecting. Remainder of companies will be taken out under an officer for route marching, not exceeding five miles. Fatigue dress will be worn.

"One hour's P. and R. training will also be carried out."

The village was of a non-descript character and had been stripped of everything in the shape of machinery, metal and fixtures of use to the enemy. Although the people had recovered from their ebullitions of joy at the retreat of the invader, they appeared to appreciate our presence to a greater extent than those whom we had left behind in the Oisemont area. They were extremely poor and most of them had been on the verge of starvation many times. An act of charity on the part of the members of our battalion, which gave mutual satisfaction and will long be remembered by all who participated in it, was the provision of a Christmas treat to the children some eighteen days after our arrival. The particulars of this treat are set out by Private J. S. Bartley in Part II. of this narrative, also a vivid description of the celebration of Christmas by the troops. The following is a translation from the local newspaper regarding the entertainment of the children:—

CHILDREN'S FETE DAY AT BEUGNIES.
AUSTRALIAN BRIGADIER-GENERAL DISTRIBUTED TOYS TO FRENCH CHILDREN.
(Translated from *L'Avenir Liberal*).

"It is a tradition at Beugnies that at Christmas a distribution of gifts and good things be held. It was formerly the "Ladies' Patriotic League" which organised the festival, but war disturbed things. Who was now to take the matter

BATTALION OFFICERS, FOUCACOURT, NOVEMBER 1918

ARMISTICE AND REPATRIATION

up, seeing that the war was over? Good luck came this year in the shape of the 30th Battalion, A.I.F., which was billeted in the village.

"M. l'abbe Dubelle, parish priest, had hardly expressed his regrets at the disappearance of the old traditions, when Captain Chaplain S. J. Gwynn, hinting at the situation, the matter was at once taken up by the men of 30th Battalion and a resolution to renew the old custom was taken and executed.

"Would it be too much to do? At any rate, the 30th would do their best. The sum of over 1000 francs was donated voluntarily and the purchase of all that was necessary was made at the Grand Bazaar, Boulevarde Anspach, at Brussels.

"Friday, 11th January, in a large room of the fabrique des Produits Céramiques, decorated by the soldiers who were happy to make others happy, was held the distribution of toys, cakes and chocolates. What a day for the children after four years' bondage with the Huns! There were about 150 of them with their parents and sisters. They regarded with open eyes the array of toys intended for them and forthwith gained an imperishable souvenir of the Australians. The fete was under the patronage of the Brigadier-General, C. S. Davies, whose presence at first lent rather to the children's inquietude, for necessarily they were a trifle timid, but this was quickly dissipated as the General kissed the first of the recipients after presenting them with their toys.

"The children rendered 'God Save the King' in English, thus winning the hearts of their Australian auditors. These valiant soldiers joined in the singing of the 'Marseillaise.' After singing several French songs, the children were regaled with refreshments and the distribution of presents was commenced by the General.

"The exclamations and cries of joy and surprise cannot be expressed. It was necessary to have been an eye-witness to fully appreciate the happiness of these youngsters, among whom were also the children of the Orphanage of the

Sisters of Charity. After the distribution, a moving picture show was taken of the gathering in a field nearby. The children, held high in the arms of soldiers and shewing off their toys, were snapped by the photographer. Several were wearing the popular Australian hat and one youngster was seen to have made prisoner of the General's cap.

"This day will be an epoch in the annals of the history of Beugnies, and the youngsters will always have the liveliest recollections of the Australians, as a proof of which we have the fine letter of thanks sent to the commanding officer of 30th Battalion by the school-teachers and parents."

The letter referred to in the previous paragraph reads as follows:—

"Sir,

"We are very pleased with the warm sympathy which you have expressed us this day.

"On behalf of our parents, our school mistresses, and also in our own name, we wish to express our gratefulness and sincere thanks.

"During their four years of occupation, the boches tried without success to win our affection by their caresses and flattery.

"We have been anxious to keep our thoughts entirely for the French and their brave Allies—the Australians.

"Happy and proud, we offer these to-day full of love and admiration.

"We preserve a very lasting remembrance of your rest amongst us and we feel assured you will never forget your little friends of Beugnies."

Many and varied were the devices employed to relieve the monotony for the troops, pending their transfer to England for embarkation homewards. Leave to Paris, Nice, Brussels, and other cities was freely given, conducted motor-bus tours to Brussels, Ostend, Zeebrugge, Charleroi, Bruges, Antwerp, and other towns of France and Belgium were arranged, educational and industrial classes in many sub-

ARMISTICE AND REPATRIATION

jects formed, concerts, dancing classes, sports meetings, boxing, football, and competitions of various kinds encouraged. Needless to say, the game of "two-up" also contributed to the fortune or misfortune of its votaries. Furthermore, the huge Repatriation and Demobilisation Department which was formed in London, under the directing brain of General Monash, found temporary employment for many members with professional, business, and manufacturing firms in England and Scotland. In some cases, the positions thus found have been retained to this day, cases in point, as far as our unit is concerned, being those of Lieutenants H. J. Wells and T. S. C. Horgan, who are doing well in London, also Bruce Thomas, who on becoming a benedict made his home in the county of Fife, Scotland.

An essay competition, having for its subject "Australia's Part in the War," and for which the principal prizes were donated by Colonel Street and Major Charlton, deserves more than passing mention. The competition was divided into two sections, officers and other ranks competing separately. The first prize in the officers' competition, a trophy valued at £3 3s. od., was won by Lieutenant Bragg; the second prize, valued at £2 2s. od., by Captain Zander. In the other ranks section, Corporal J. Graham carried off the first prize—£3 in cash and a trophy valued at £3 3s. od. The second prize (£3) went to Private R. Mather, and prizes of £2 each were awarded to Lance-Corporal N. Hughes and Privates J. K. Conway and J. Pullen.

Among the many changes promulgated in routine orders during this period were the appointment of Major John Chapman as Brigade Major, 5th Brigade; the arrival from the officers' training school of Lieutenants C. H. McClosky, S. D. Dickson, F. C. Sharman, B. Thomas, and C. E. Hard; the return from hospital of Lieutenants B. A. Bragg and V. W. Biddle; and the departure for London of Captain Don Chalmers, who was attached to the Finance Section at

Horseferry-road for training in pay duties on transport vessels.

The following notices, which appeared in routine orders, may awaken the memories of survivors:—

"Lost in Beugnies on Sunday, 16th instant, an 'Aussie' wallet, containing papers and 225 francs in French paper money and 2 English £1 notes. Reward on returning to Sergeant E. Huxley, 30th Battalion.

"The Belgian authorities have arranged that the Restaurants economiques' Brussels provide British military authorities proceeding to that town with meals at cost price. Bread tickets for men on leave can be obtained from Compte de 'L'agglomeration Bruxelloise' on application."

As repatriation generally commenced with those units whose members had seen longest service in the A.I.F., it was not until January 24th that the first contingent from the 30th, comprising 123 N.C.O's. and men, left for England. Acting on the foregoing principle, those who had left Sydney on the *Beltana* in 1915 were given preference, and among them were: Sergeants E. J. Dunkley, W. Barrett, R. H. Hudson, W. Lethbridge, H. D. Gooding, G. Begg, Corporals J. W. Laing, H. D. Ford, T. W. Ford, E. Race, A. L. Smith, J. McWilliams, N. Hughes, Lance-Corporals S. Nightingall, E. H. Baker, R. McDiarmid, Drivers H. W. Turner, J. Joyce, W. H. Smith, N. Garaty, and Privates D. S. Hotchkiss, H. J. Stevenson, S. G. Evans, J. Brockbank, H. Bennett, P. Ryan, E. W. Pockett, W. McBride, S. W. Strike, H. H. Hughes, P. Milgate, R. T. Gibson, E. V. Green, H. J. Gavin, L. F. Dobie, E. H. Bannister, R. R. Buik, G. F. Armstrong, H. Diller, F. Millwood, W. H. Claydon, R. C. Trimmingham, and S. Murrell. With their departure the battalion was reorganised into two companies ("A" and "B"), to which the following officers and senior N.C.O's. were attached:—

"A" COMPANY.

O.C.   Capt. T. C. Barbour.
2nd-in-Command   „   C. H. Morrison.

Subalterns
Lieut. W. E. Oakes.   Lieut. E. G. McKinnon.
„ C. D. Button.   „ M. F. Sinclair.
„ A. H. Forbes, M.M.   „ G. E. Hard.
„ A. H. Ellis.   „ C. H. McCloskey, D.C.M.
„ R. H. Jelfs.
C.S.M.   107 Sgt. A. D. Burns, M.M.
C.Q.M.S.   1225 C.Q.M.S. N. J. Sutherland.

"B" COMPANY.

O.C.   Capt. C. D. Savage, M.C.
2nd-in-Command   „ W. H. Zander.
Subalterns
Lieut. F. Hamilton.   Lieut. F. D. Beer.
„ H. R. Robinson.   „ V. W. Biddle, M.C.
„ C. H. Backhouse.   „ A. J. McCallum.
„ W. R. Marler.   „ W. C. Abbott, M.M.
C.S.M.   335 C.S.M. E. G. Bailey.
C.Q.M.S.   2401 C.Q.M.S. F. McGowan.

On March 1st the 8th Brigade moved on to Sars Poteries, remaining eleven days, thence across the border into Belgium, halting in the Yves-Gomezee area. The conditions were much the same as those which obtained in the French villages, and much the same routine was followed. The units had gradually become reduced in size, and so, a week later the 30th absorbed the 32nd Battalion, the latter forming "C" and "D" Companies. Thus passed out the unit of the 8th Brigade which had been formed from men drawn from South and West Australia of whom there were few compeers and no superiors in the whole of the A.I.F.

The unit remained in this area until April 2nd. In the meantime, Captain James Chapman was transferred as Brigade Major to the 14th Brigade, and Lieutenants E. F. O'Sullivan and P. B. Hayman were taken on strength from training schools. Further screeds regarding non-saluting were received, as were additional warnings aaginst the killing of game and the unorthodox methods of catching fish. As the officers were accused of being as guilty as the men in this respect, an assertion not indignantly refuted, these dire threatenings only added zest to the sport.

A Soccer team drawn from units of the 5th Division went into training prior to a contest with the 3rd Division. Its personnel was as follows, but, sad to relate, our division lost the match.

Lieut. M. F. Sinclair (Capt.).	Lieut. D. Brewster.
Lieut. A. H. Forbes.	Sgt. A. McLennan.
Sgt. A. H. Brown.	Sgt. A. Burns.
L/Cpl. A. Collett.	Pte. E. Wittaker.
Pte. E. Roderick.	Pte. W. H. Brown.
Pte. R. Turnbull.	Pte. W. Tittley.
Pte. J. McKenzie.	

Among the most regretted incidents at this period was the breaking up of the band, which, after many vicissitudes with brigade, division, and corps, had at last returned to its parent. Les. Wellings and his men had earned the respect of all with whom they had come into contact, both in and out of the line, and now that the time had arrived for them to depart for home, there were few who did not feel that they were suffering a personal loss. Among the original members accompanying their leader were: C. S. Cryer, L. J. Hough, J. K. Lewis, P. Lawson, C. S. May, C. W. Peters, W. H. Sharp, H. H. Sharp, and R. A. Sproule. In the same draft were Sergeants "Wal" Smith, E. H. Matthews, and C. S. Johnson.

In bidding farewell to our bandsmen it may be appropriate to quote an order concerning dogs which was promulgated on March 13th, and which, no doubt, reminded them of the pet—referred to in an early chapter of this history—they had smuggled from Australia but were compelled, almost in tears, to abandon in Egypt.

"Any member who owns a dog and is desirous of getting the animal back to the British Isles will forward application to this

ARMISTICE AND REPATRIATION

Office by 18.00 to-morrow giving the following information:— (a) Rank, name and address of owner. (b) Age of dog. (c) Sex of dog. (d) Breed of dog. (e) Colour. (f) Recognition marks. (g) Period in possession of present owner."

On March 21st further amalgamation was brought about, the remnants of the brigade being formed into a composite unit, known as the 8th Brigade Battalion, under the command of Lieutenant-Colonel Street. The composition of its companies was as set out hereunder, each one retaining its original distinctive colour patches:—

"A" Company, 29th Battalion. O.C., Captain C. E. Davis, D.S.O., M.C.

"B" Company, 30th Battalion. O.C., Captain T. C. Barbour.

"C" Company, 31st Battalion. O.C., Captain V. L. Morrisett.

"D" Company, 32nd Battalion. O.C., Captain J. H. Allen, M.C.

On April 3rd the composite battalion moved to the Marcinelle-Haies area, in the neighbourhood of Charleroi, where its size gradually dwindled as further batches of men left for home. The last entry in our unit diary reads as follows:—

"May 4th, 1919. Quota No. 47 consisting of 37 officers, 20 sergeants, and 373 other ranks, marched out to Corps Wing, Charleroi, ready to entrain to-morrow. This quota, commanded by Lieutenant-Colonel F. Street, D.S.O., absorbs all personnel of the 8th Brigade."

EPILOGUE.

They were great days and the 30th Battalion, A.I.F., played its full part in them.

To those of us who are left, twenty years after the signing of the Armistice, memory lingers upon the many good comrades who "passed over", and as we see the sufferings of the survivors, some from physical disabilities, some from economic duress, we may sometimes wonder whether it was all worth while.

The situation was, however, not of our making. We were inexorably drawn in, and our hands are clean. In the absence of that sacrifice, who can say what may have been the lot of Australia to-day? And where stands the member of the A.I.F. but cherishes a pride that is almost divine for his participation? It was the price of Australia's freedom.

General Monash has recorded the loathing that every day filled his mind at the sacrifice of men and material that means war, but sounded the inevitable conclusion that if our heritage is to be retained, we must be prepared to defend it.

It was surely an inspired suggestion that the honours and traditions of the A.I.F. should not be allowed to pass, but should be identified with the militia units of the Commonwealth for ever. To the 30th Battalion, A.M.F. (the New South Wales Scottish Regiment) has been entrusted our battle honours and the colours that bear them, and the pride be ours that they are in such safe keeping.

Anzac Day, 1938, has passed. An unforgettable day of

memories when nearly 700 men of the "old unit"—the largest number it has ever mustered for the Anzac Day March, and the largest it will ever muster—was led by the Pipe Band of the New! The ever rolling stream flows on.

"The main host lie buried in the lands of our Allies who have set aside their resting places in honour for ever."

PART II

CONTRIBUTIONS FROM MEMBERS OF BATTALION

THE COMFORTS COMMITTEES.

(By Lieut.-Colonel H. SLOAN).

To refer to the activities of the Comforts Committees of Sydney and Newcastle (and the scores of women helpers whose names it is impossible to record) as an "incident" in the life of our battalion, is to inadequately describe the four long years of continuous effort on the part of that devoted band of workers, nor is it possible to estimate their share in indirectly contributing to the defeat of the nations with whom we were at war. While this expression of appreciation is somewhat belated, it is none the less sincere; unfortunately it will not be seen by a number of men and women who after rendering great services to their country have since passed on.

Comforts Funds Committees were formed in Sydney and Newcastle about the same time, and the work of each was equally praiseworthy. Unfortunately most of the records of the latter body have been lost, which is not surprising in view of the length of time which has elapsed since their activities ceased.

In the case of the Sydney Committee the initial meeting was held at the Sydney Town Hall on 27th October, 1915, and was attended by officers, mothers, wives, and friends of the members of the unit. The Chair was occupied by a staff officer from Victoria Barracks. The principal speaker was Mrs. R. R. S. Mackinnon, a leader of the Red Cross Society, who outlined the objects of the movement. Briefly, these were to collect, make, and send comforts to the troops overseas, and to establish a centre where their relatives could meet and discuss matters of mutual interest.

This centre later became a meeting place for returned members of the battalion who received assistance in various ways.

As the result of this meeting a committee was formed which met for the first time on 10th November, 1915. It consisted of Mrs. J. W. Clark (wife of the C.O.), President; Mesdames Austin Chapman, A. W. Meeks, S. S. Cohen, F. G. Waley, A. Winn and Lady Ewing, Vice-Presidents; Miss N. Sloan, Secretary; Miss E. Riley, Treasurer; Miss E. Rixon, Assistant Secretary; Mesdames Beardsmore, McCall, Eedy, Purser, Davidson, McFarlane, Sloan, Stinson, Allen, Vale, Payten, Jardine, Smithers, Marks, Spain, Denham, Gilderthorpe, Wark, Hamilton-Smith, Cross, Kaleski and Miss McFarlane.

Great assistance was rendered by the firm of Winn's Ltd., who provided a workroom, depot, telephone, packing and transport facilities, and also by the Bellambi Coal Company Ltd., which at the instance of its General Manager, Mr. F. G. (later Sir Frederick) Waley, gave the use of its board room for meetings. The depot was open for business and work from 9 a.m. to 5 p.m. on three days in each week; numbers of women, domestically handicapped, took the work to their homes for completion. Special mention must here be made of Mr. (later Sir Austin) Chapman and Mr. Winn, who, with the Secretary, Miss N. Sloan (now Mrs. George Rudd, of Inverell) constituted the backbone of the movement and supported the committee from the beginning to the end.

An idea of the activities of the Committee may be formed from its annual reports, the first of which, dated 6th November, 1916, shows that the year's receipts from various sources amounted to £1,550/5/0. From this goods to the value of £1,260 were sent overseas, as well as £250 in cash. Among the many gifts that were turned into money by means of raffles, etc., was a diamond ring, donated by Mrs. Austin Chapman, which realised £268/13/3. Later a Jervis Bay Estate Company, in which Mr. Chapman was

CONTRIBUTIONS FROM MEMBERS 239

interested, presented a block of land at Jervis Bay, the sale of which netted £432. Another item worthy of mention is that of £150 collected by the Sydney employees of Winn's Ltd.

As a result of the four years' effort, the total receipts amounted to £5,734/1/4. This provided 4,360 shirts, 3,206 pairs socks, and tinned fruits and puddings to the value of £300. In addition £1,650 was remitted overseas.

An item of disbursement worthy of mention was the allotment of £30 to provide a bed in the Waley Home for shell-shocked soldiers, which was presented to the Commonwealth by Lady Waley.

The last meeting of the Committee was held on 3rd November, 1919, when a sub-committee—Messrs. Winn and Langan, Mesdames Cross, Payten and Evans, and Miss Riley—was appointed to wind-up the affairs of the main body and dispose of the surplus monies. These consisted of £729 returned by Lieutenant-Colonel F. Street, D.S.O. (who latterly commanded the battalion), and £561 remaining in hand. This sum (£1,290) was finally disposed of in grants, varying from £50 to £100, to 17 members of the 30th Battalion who had suffered double amputations.

The office-bearers of the Newcastle Committee consisted of Mrs. C. J. Winn, President; Mrs. F. W. Lusk and Miss E. Street, Joint Hon. Secretaries; and Mrs. W. Humble, Treasurer.

Depots and workrooms were placed at the disposal of the Committee by W. Winn & Co., who also carried out the transport work free of charge. David Cohen & Co. assisted considerably in the matter of cutting out the garments, thus lessening the work of the various helpers.

As before stated, the records of this Committee are incomplete, but an idea of its achievements may be gained from the balance sheet for year ending 31st October, 1917, which shows receipts £872/9/5—the principal contributions being W. Winn & Company's employees, £52/16/8;

W. Winn and Co., £32/17/3; Mayfair Girls' League, £25/5/0; A. Southwood and Co., £25/14/0; A. Southwood and Company's employees, £23/14/0; Wattle Day League, £20; and per Mrs. Shearman, £10/16/0. The principal items on the disbursement side of this balance sheet are wool, flannel, and clothing £508/19/8, tobacco and pipes £140/7/11, and groceries and Xmas cheer, £125/3/5.

In addition to the foregoing, the Committee, working in conjunction with other organisations, raised the following sums during the year under review:—France's Day, £91; War Chest Day, £110/1/0; Red Triangle Day, £40; "Our Day," £34/1/7—Total £275/2/7. Also, in answer to the War Chest appeal for socks, it provided 350 pairs.

On the conclusion of activities the balance of monies in hand was devoted to the endowment of a cot in the Newcastle Hospital which serves as a lasting monument to the efforts of the women of this district in the great cause.

"LITTLE WILLIE".

(By Lieut.-Colonel M. Purser).

One of the most outstanding characters of the 30th was Sergeant-Cook McDuff, who later became battalion transport officer.

From the time of the battalion's arrival at the Show Ground camp until its departure in the *Beltana*, "Mac" and the camp medical officer did not seem to get on well. Every soldier knows how seriously (and quite rightly) M.O's. regard the presence of flies, and, when the camp M.O. saw the butcher's block in the 30th Battalion's cookhouse literally covered with them he roared: "What are those flies doing there?" McDuff did not reply, but walked slowly towards the block. As he approached, the flies

C.S.M. GEOFF COWEN. D.C.M.

Sgt. F. McGILLICUDDY, M.M.

Pte. P. MILLGATE, M.M.

Cpl. F. C. NORTH, M.M.

gradually flew off until only one remained. Shaking his finger at it, "Mac" said: "Willie, you naughty boy—what are you doing there? You know you have no right to be there." The M.O. exploded and threatened "Mac" with arrest, but the latter managed to talk himself out of it, as he usually did.

After that there was peace, or at least a truce, between the two for a time, but on the day before embarkation "Mac" went to the M.O., and, after referring to the friction which had occurred between them, asked in a humble voice and without the flicker of an eyelid whether, on the eve of his departure for the front, the M.O. would do him a favour. On the latter's replying that he would do so if it was within his power, "Mac" handed him a matchbox with the request that he would "take care of Little Willie." On opening the box and finding that it contained but a solitary fly, the M.O. was apparently unable to find words for the occasion and could only say, "It's a good job for you, McDuff, that you are leaving to-morrow."

A VERY OLD SOLDIER.
(BY R. MATHER).

ONE group of the 3rd reinforcements of the 30th Battalion had for a musketry instructor a staff sergeant-major who had served 21 years in a celebrated kilted regiment. He was that type of drinker that was never really drunk and yet never sober. He would set the rifle up on a tripod and explain briefly what we were supposed to be discussing, lest some officer should come along, then we would exchange all the latest stories. At the end of the course our combined knowledge of musketry could have been written in large print on the back of a postage stamp.

It can be imagined that there was consternation in our ranks when we had to proceed to Long Bay for some real shooting, and learned that only those whose marksmanship was up to a certain standard would be in the next draft for the front. This was serious. Comradeships had been formed and we all wanted to go through the great adventure together. The old soldier alone remained unperturbed. He took a swig from the flask in his hip-pocket and addressed us. "You all want to get away, don't you?" We agreed. "You know nothing of musketry," he continued. And again we agreed. "Well, pay me 5/- a man, and I'll fix it with the markers at the butts." We all paid, and we all passed. No trouble at all.

FRUIT.

(By Lieut.-Colonel M. PURSER).

As no orders were forthcoming and no one in authority seemed to know or care that the 30th Battalion had arrived at Suez in H.M.A.T. *Beltana,* the C.O. (Colonel Clark) decided to send the Adjutant (Captain H. Sloan) ashore for orders and to despatch mails and cables. The captain of the ship at first demurred about sending a boat, but finally agreed on condition that it was manned by a crew from our "A" Company (who were ex-naval reservists) and that one of his officers was in charge.

We were proud of our boat's crew, which, in A.I.F. uniform, and rowing in approved navy style, received an ovation from the siege battery, nurses and passengers on an Orient boat which had arrived just ahead of the *Beltana* and was lying closer inshore.

After conducting his business, Captain Sloan found the crew all present at the time arranged, which was doubtless a great relief to him. I believe that Captain N. McCoy, M.C. (formerly of "A" Company) has stated that, when ordered to heave, some of the crew certainly did, but not on the oars. This was probably due to the manner in which they had spent the £1 given them by Captain Sloan on landing, and doubtless had an important bearing on the decision of the ship's officer to sail back.

Colonel Clark watched the adjutant and the boat's crew come up the gangway, and noticing that some of the latter were carrying cases, asked, "Is that liquor coming aboard?" I was standing near him and said, "It looks more like fruit," and Captain Sloan quickly added, "Yes, fruit, sir." Colonel Clark swallowed it—the explanation, not the "fruit"—and that night, at Captain Sloan's invitation, some of us swallowed the latter served in glasses with soda water.

GENESIS OF 30TH BATTALION TRANSPORT.
(By DRIVER N. GARATY).

THE first member of the transport section was a self-appointed sergeant, splendidly uniformed. He wore a tram driver's jacket, with three expensive gold stripes, a pair of "issue" riding breeches, leggings, and ornate swan neck spurs—he was known to the troops as "Diggley Bones," and he was gifted with the knowledge of a very old soldier. One morning, however, "Diggley" was found to be A.W.L., evidently having attached himself to a unit where he was more appreciated.

After a few weeks at Liverpool, we moved by road to the Show Ground at Sydney. We were fortunate in having secured men who had been trained as farriers, wheelwrights, and tradsmen of various kinds.

The section embarked on the *Katuna* (A13), which had been fitted as a horse ship. Adelaide was the only port of call—more horses were taken on there during a few hours' stay, after which the voyage was continued to Suez. In spite of having no veterinary officer on board, the ship landed all its horses in Egypt, having successfully weathered an equine epidemic of some kind while crossing the Indian Ocean.

Near Serapeum the section detrained and was ordered to picket its horses at a spot quite close to the railway. A whistling engine was responsible for a stampede, most of the horses breaking away. Captain Barnett gives an amusing account of the experiences he had in trying to recover his straying "neddies"—in fact, it would appear that a large portion of Northern Africa was combed, the area searched extending southward almost to Abyssinia!

After having collected every animal lost, plus a few others, the transport section camped on the Canal.

While here Captain Barnett transferred to the 5th Divisional Artillery—his own horse, which led the stampede, was ridden by him throughout the campaign in France.

A SAND BLAST IN AN OUTPOST.
(By Capt. T. C. BARBOUR).

For some weeks the battalion occupied portion of the chain of outposts situated several miles east of the Suez Canal, running parallel with the 90-mile watercourse. As the Turk was rather loath to come to close quarters since his initial repulse on the canal banks near Ismailia, life in these lonely outposts became very monotonous, although the British yeomanry regiments on our northern flank found the monotony relieved somewhat when the sons of Islam paid them a surprise visit one dark night in April, 1916.

After a week or so of tenancy of the desert outpost, during which calm weather prevailed, word was received that General Tivey, in charge of our brigade, would be liable to visit the post at any moment. Preparations were made, with a special clean up of the trenches, and when it was finished, Sergeant Whipp declared, "There isn't a speck of sand out of place."

Unfortunately, a violent sand blast arrived unexpectedly. The strength and fury of the wind came as an unpleasant

CONTRIBUTIONS FROM MEMBERS 245

surprise to the tiny garrison. A few spots of rain, and then the wind rushed down, snarling and tearing at anything above ground. It drove the sand forward in dense masses like hail, soon burying the trenches and those optimists who had excavated shelter pits in the sand! Some of our minor structures erected above ground were momentarily shuttlecocked about, then uprooted to disappear like wraiths in the blinding gloom. The sun, which had been shining like a ball of fire, disappeared as though in a dense fog. The power of the wind exceeded anything the troops had previously experienced, and in a few hours all our labour had gone for nothing.

With Sergeant Whipp I was entombed in an excavation used as platoon headquarters. It possessed a canvas cover supported on props which disappeared in a flick. As the fury of the blast gradually filled the excavation with sand like running water, we pulled ourselves out to successive levels until it overflowed, leaving most of our possessions buried beneath. After our first short experience we readily understood how cities and monuments of the past became lost in the shifting sands. Finally, when the storm died down, we discovered that the whole of the defences had disappeared.

Privates J. Hill, P. J. Nankivell, the McDiarmid brothers, and other members of the platoon, who had erected special posts controlling selected fields of fire, discovered that the drift sand had so altered the contour of the locality that new posts had to be sited to govern the altered conditions.

After the rifles and S.A.A. had been cleaned of the dust, the platoon set to and worked like beavers to restore the defences, under the direct rays of the pitiless sun, which again came to light, and a certain amount of progress was made.

While engaged in supervising the work, my attention was drawn by the sentry on duty, an ex-seaman with a protruding jaw, to a string of horsemen halted on the distant landscape, their silhouettes cutting the skyline like a Grecian frieze. They appeared to be studying maps. The ex-seaman, who was the worst rifle shot in the platoon, proposed by way of challenge to pump a few shots across their bows, but was restrained from carrying out his intentions. After a few minutes, the cavalcade advanced towards our posts, and before long General Tivey and a number of staff officers put in an appearance. The general had taken advantage of the lull in the storm to make a round of visits.

"Well, Barbour," he inquired, in his soft modulated tones, as he halted practically on the site of one of the submerged posts, "where are your trenches?"

I replied, "Your horse is standing over one at the moment, sir." A flicker of a smile relieved the general's features, and then, after giving an appraising glance at the surroundings, he again inquired in his soft drawl, "What do you propose to do if the enemy attacks?"

I promptly replied, "Capture as many prisoners as possible, sir, and set them to work to rebuild the trenches."

Judging by his quiet chuckle, I think General Tivey gave the proposition his blessing. The cavalcade then departed to visit other posts.

A RECONNAISSANCE IN EGYPT.

(By Lieut.-Colonel M. PURSER).

ONE evening in December, 1915, I was informed by the adjutant that I was to proceed the following morning with an escort of Bikaner Camel Corps to reconnoitre Hill 353, with a view to the establishment of a post, which had to be manned by my company ("C").

Next morning a lance-naik (lance-corporal) and three men of the Bikaners reported with a spare camel, and I think the whole battalion turned out to see me fall off as the camel rose after I had mounted. Thanks, however, to the fact that I did not have to ride Arab fashion—as the Bikaners use a saddle (a double one with two seats and

CONTRIBUTIONS FROM MEMBERS

two sets of stirrups)—I found myself on the camel instead of on the ground when my mount stood up. Having accomplished that much, however, I found myself unable to lead off, having not the slightest idea of how to make a camel start, or of controlling or guiding him with the one rope attached to the wooden peg in his nostrils. I therefore signed to the lance-naik, who was aware of our destination, to move off, and I found that, as I had assumed, my camel, having received army training, conformed to the movements of his companions.

Walking and trotting alternately, with the N.C.O. alongside me and the other three scouting ahead, we had proceeded some distance when we heard the roar of a bursting shell, and a pillar of smoke and sand rose from "Target Hill" on our right front. H.M.S. *Minerva*, lying in Lake Timsah, was engaging in gunnery practice.

Nearly unseating me as he swung sharply to the left, my camel set off in pursuit of the escort, who were putting distance between themselves and Target Hill. They had a fair start, but my camel had a good turn of speed and soon caught up with the rest of the field, and by the time the next shell landed we had covered a considerable distance, and were riding stirrup to stirrup. Although I did not know whether such things could be used on a camel, I would have given much for a pair of reins and a bit. I was quite unable to control my mount, and could not get the Bikaners to stop, and I began to wonder how many miles we would cover before they considered it safe to do so, but, after we had gone a couple of miles they gradually eased the pace to a walk and resumed their original positions. It was, to put it mildly, very annoying that, being unable myself to speak their language nor they mine, I could not express my opinion of them.

The remainder of the day was without incident, and I returned to Ferry Post with the knowledge that I had taken the star part in one of the war's comedies—an officer sent on reconnaissance with a mount he could not handle and with men to whom he was unable to give instructions.

A PLACE FOR EVERYTHING.
(By K.30).

On board the old *Beltana* during our voyage to Egypt it was the duty of the "one-pip artists" to deliver lectures on various military matters to their platoons. One lecture delivered at length by "Tim", and accompanied by a practical demonstration, was on the "web equipment"—how to put it together and what the various parts were for, laying particular stress on the ammunition pouches.

We had just crossed the Suez Canal and were about to move out and occupy the various bastions. To facilitate the issuing of ammunition the troops were lined up with their ranks facing inwards, the C.Q.M.S. ("it's a matter of life and death") dropping 150 rounds of S.A.A. into each man's hat.

The job completed, we were ready to move when a "dopey" individual called out, "Where will I put my ammunition, Mr. ——?" Like a flash came the reply from "Tim", "In your —— water-bottle, where else would you put it."

IT HAPPENED AT FERRY POST.
PART I.
A "MAJOR" INCIDENT.
(By CYRIL LAVENDER).

We wondered on one particular occasion what brand Major Holford favoured or whether he mistook the Suez Canal for the Red Sea and us the Israelites, when he chose an objective to march to by night from Ferry Post—our first night march.

Most of us unreasonably blamed Major Purser for losing us, but after all, he wasn't the Almighty. Major Holford had picked an object on the other side of the Canal. What the Major called the Major afterwards, we never heard. They probably both called the mess orderly.

CONTRIBUTIONS FROM MEMBERS 249
PART II.
THE EXPLANATION.
(By MUIR PURSER).

In accordance with orders, I reported with my company one night in December 1915 at the third of the line of incinerators situated on the roadside of the staging camp at Ferry Post, and received orders from the second-in-command (Major C. J. Holford) to march from there on a compass bearing of so many degrees. He would neither say how far I was to march on that bearing nor what my objective was, but told me that R.S.M. Jackson would accompany me and let me know when I had reached the objective. This was a new one on me, but I set my compass and moved off with my second-in-command alongside me, checking my direction.

We marched until we reached the bank of the Canal near Bench Mark, but although the R.S.M. was satisfied that I had marched correctly on the bearing given, he was puzzled by his inability to find either Major Holford or the object on which the bearing had been taken. The absence of Major Holford was due to the fact that after starting us off he had received a visit from Captain Holland and had remained in camp to entertain him.

A short march along the Canal bank would have brought us to our camp, but the R.S.M. asked if, as a check, I would return on a back bearing. I agreed, worked out the bearing, set my compass and led the company back to the identical incinerator from which we had started. This apparently excellent marching by compass added to the R.S.M's. bewilderment, but he did not know that on the return journey I had not bothered about my compass but, aided by a slight moon, had led the company over the track we had made on the outward trip.

The following morning Major Holford pointed out the objective which it was intended that I should reach—a flagpole apparently at Bench Mark. As I could not remember the existence of a flagpole at that place when I had visited it some weeks earlier, we rode across the desert and found that, when halted on the previous night, "C" Company was heading straight for the flagpole but could only have reached it by swimming, or by a repetition of the happening recorded in the fourteenth chapter of the book of Exodus. The flagpole in question was on the other side of the canal!

PART III.
THE CHARGE.
(By JAMES PAYTEN).

Scene: Orderly Room, "C" Company, 30th Battalion.

Place: Ferry Post, Egypt.

Time: 10 a.m. next morning.

Players: Major Purser (Major), Corporal Layton (Corporal), Privates Lavender and Payten (L. & P.).

Major: "You are charged with being absent from parade."

Corporal: "Sir, I was orderly corporal last night, and just before the company returned to camp I went through the lines and found these two men lying in their tent. I struck a match and asked why they were not on parade, and said I would crime them."

Major: "Did they speak to you?"

Corporal: "No, Sir."

L. & P.: "We were on parade, Sir."

Major: "Did you answer your names at the roll call?"

L. & P.: "There was no roll call, Sir."

Major: "Where did we go and what did we do?"

L. & P.: "We went on a night march, Sir, and got lost in the desert."

Major: "Tell me some more of what happened."

L. & P.: "We had to sit down for some time while you checked your bearings and some of the men thought dawn was approaching and commenced crowing like roosters. You stormed at some of them for lighting cigarettes and said certain things and——"

Major to Corporal (impatiently): "These men were evidently on parade. Is anything the matter with your eyesight? Do your glasses need changing? Case dismissed."

PART IV.
REMINISCENCE.
(By CYRIL LAVENDER).

Scene: Martin Place, Sydney, 20 years later.

Pate: "Good day, Lav. Where's the nearest? Have you seen anything of Charlie Layton since he crimed us on the Canal?" (Laughter).

Lav.: "Yes. He said he had his glasses checked in the meantime and found them quite all right, but I admitted nothing."

Pate: "I wonder whether Major Purser ever knew the strength of the matter. Let me see. Where were we that night? Have another. Good fun, Jim."

L. & P. carry their minds back. "Recollect there was to be a night march that night and we had the afternoon off to rest? Quite innocently we crossed the Canal and couldn't resist joining a limber as a 'working party' bound for Ismailia. No harm in the outing. (We'll be back before the march—that's all that matters). Better hop off here and have a couple of spots. Mustn't have too many, though. Cripes, this Gyppo whisky's strong, or do we only think so because we have been off it for some time? Two more only and home we go. Just about time to make it for the march. Homeward bound. Better keep Lav. in the middle. He's not too clever. Hullo, Pate's 'gone to the pack'. Blank spaces for several hours. Pitch darkness. We came to on the banks of the fresh water canal, cold as frogs, shivering and very groggy. 'That "Skee" must have been doped Pate. What's the time? Some swine's pinched the wristlet watch my girl sent me.' 'Mine, too, with all that was worth taking with it.' We'd been 'ratted'—not a red cent. left. 'Here's a Tommy cookhouse.' 'Have some soup, choom?' The soup was good and pulled us round a little. 'Better make back—might miss the march.' Remember, Lav., we had a night march all on our own and walked miles to cover the last few hundred yards. Got to the tent and dropped. Faint recollections of the angels saying, 'Lavender and Payten, I'll crime you in the morning.' We didn't speak. We couldn't. How the blazes did Bill Grahame make it? Good job he did and tutored us. We weren't missed, and no roll call. Surely that was enough to go on and keep the red ink out of the pay book."

ALL'S WELL ON THE LEFT OF THE LINE.
(By Major JAMES A. CHAPMAN).

EARLY on a December morning in 1915 the 30th Battalion marched from the "aerodrome" camp at Heliopolis, entrained at Helmieh, and travelled to Moascar, where it bivouacked for the night. Marching through the pretty town of Ismailia the following morning, it crossed the Suez Canal by a pontoon bridge manned by the Royal Australian Naval Bridging Train, and relieved the Ghurkas at Ferry Post, a sand-bag fort on the banks of the Canal. There were also stationed here at the time the Ayrshire Battery of the Royal Horse Artillery, the Bikaner Camel Corps, and the Hyderabad Lancers.

Each night in turn the companies went on outpost duty beyond the bastions. A horse would draw a log along the bank of the Canal from Ferry Post to Bench Mark, three to four miles to the north, thus making a smooth track in the sand, which was examined before dark and again at daybreak, any footprints showing on it being matters for immediate investigation.

It was "D" Company's turn to go on duty, and Sergeant Zander brought me the list of the N.C.O's. and men detailed to the various posts to be occupied by No. 16 Platoon, of which I was then in command. These posts included two or three dredges moored in the Canal—posts much sought

CONTRIBUTIONS FROM MEMBERS 253

after by the men—the camp of the conscripted Egyptian Labour Corps, and the lighthouse at Bench Mark.

It was my invariable practice to accompany the first patrol in the evening and generally the last one in the early morning. On this occasion, after giving instructions for the men to move to their posts, I donned my equipment, saw that my rifle (platoon commanders at that time being armed and equipped similar to the rank and file) was handy, and awaited receipt of the password for the night. This was brought to me by Lieutenant Couchman, the second-in-command of our company, who expressed his intention of accompanying me on the patrol. I, therefore, did not rouse the two men who would otherwise have gone with me, and Couchman and I set off between 8 p.m. and 9 p.m.

We visited the various sentry groups, exchanged signals with those on the dredges, passed the "Gyppo" encampment with its chattering, ghost-like forms, and climbed the lighthouse hill, having then only to connect with the troops at Bench Mark. While crossing a small sand dune on the way we were greatly surprised to see a small party on the banks of the Canal with what appeared to be a dimmed light. Couchman and I came to the same conclusion—that a small Turkish patrol had managed to gain the Canal and were about to mine it. Hurrying forward to obtain better observation, we discerned four dark figures in loose garments. One was holding the light over the water while another seemed to be prodding or depthing the water with a pole; the other two had a small dark object attached to a pole. The latter, we concluded, was a small mine which was about to be placed in the Canal. We decided to capture the party.

Having a rifle, I moved into position to cut off the party's retreat, while Couchman went forward to investigate. In six or seven minutes I was as close as I could get to the party without disturbing them, and a minute later Couchman approached along the bank. Several times the members of the party put their hands into the water, but they had not yet lifted the "mine" in. We were in time.

Suddenly they stopped what they were doing, put down the "mine" and looked in Couchman's direction, and I immediately covered them with my rifle. Couchman then gave the signal to close and I moved in cautiously. The "Turks" proved to be four friendly little Ghurkas on a fishing expedition. The one with the light had held it over the water to attract the fish, the one with the pole stunning and placing them in what we had thought to be a mine but was actually a bucket. They conducted us to their O.C., who had not seen a white officer for some time, and we celebrated the meeting in time-honoured fashion. Couchman returned with one of my patrols at dawn, and we reported "All's well on the left of the line."

AN INCONVENIENCE.
(By R. MATHER).

LIEUTENANT-COLONEL J. W. Clark, addressing the battalion at Moascar prior to its departure for France, said, "All that we have undergone hitherto cannot be regarded as hardships but merely inconveniences." This is a tale of one of the inconveniences.

Rab Hartley, from Cessnock, was the Scotch comedian of No. 16 Platoon. When I first met him he was entertaining a group of recruits awaiting the arrival of the doctor at a hall in West Maitland. His song went something like this:

> Drums were beating loudly,
> Highlanders were marching proudly
> To embark upon a ship bound for the war.
> And the lass I'd vowed to love for evermore.
> The pipes were skirling,
> When I left the toon o' Stirling,

CONTRIBUTIONS FROM MEMBERS

As the River Forth at Stirling is little wider than Cook's River at Undercliffe, it was difficult to visualise any troops embarking there, but the audience was not critical.

Rab continued to entertain us in more ways than one, until late in 1918 he was severely wounded and returned home with the somewhat doubtful compensations of a Military Medal and a pair of German field-glasses. His funniest act was put over at Hog's Back in the front-line trenches several miles east of the Suez Canal. Hog's Back was not a place from which to send home even post-cards. The daily routine had become as monotonous as the scenery, and the weather was as hot as a furnace-breath. One quart of water was the daily allowance, and from this most of us reserved a 2oz. tobacco-tinful for shaving and washed out our eyes and ears with the shaving brush.

When Rab announced that he intended to have a bath, his mates touched their foreheads significantly. "Sunstroke," said some. "Too soft for this country." Rab, finding himself the centre of so much interest, announced where and when the great event would take place. He had salvaged a spare water bottle and by the exercise of a rigid economy had saved a few fluid ozs. daily until he had a whole quart to splash about in. Promptly at the appointed time Rab appeared in his birthday suit and received an encouraging cheer. He scooped out a large hole in the sand, pressed his waterproof sheet into it, and pegged down the four corners. Pouring the water into the cavity he proceeded to sponge himself thoroughly, and ignored the running fire of ribald comment. "Cripes, you can count the hairs on his chest." "Lucky you wasn't in the Black Watch, Scottie, and having to wear a kilt with those knees."

Meanwhile old Sol from his chariot of flame was shedding his effulgent rays on Rab's naked torso. Many of the spectators began to drift away, but the more observant noticed that the water seemed to be disappearing. Having soaped himself all over, Rab realised that it was an odds-on race to get the soap off. The water-proof sheet was now as hot as a sheet-iron roof in mid-summer, and the water vanished while the soap caked around the hairs on Rab's legs.

AN UNOFFICIAL MEDICAL INSPECTION.
(By H. H. STEVENSON).

DURING our first sojourn at Ferry Post in late 1915 one of the most monotonous duties was to pull a large vehicular punt back and forth across the Suez Canal by means of wire ropes. The traffic was heavy and continuous, particularly during the mornings and evenings, when hundreds of "Gyppo" labourers employed in making roads into the Sinai Desert had to be ferried over. But it did not take our men long to persuade the "Abduls" to pull themselves over and, as they sang at their work the Diggers enjoyed the morning and evening entertainment.

One day a "Gyppo" came aboard with a hand bandaged up, which he tenderly rested in his voluminous one-piece garment. Our men naturally exempted him from duty on the rope and for this practical expression of sympathy he appeared to sing more loudly than his toiling comrades. The following day, when Lieutenant "Jim" Chapman's platoon was on punt duty, the usual request to get on the ropes was made to the "Gyppos," but quite 40 per cent. of them produced bandaged hands from the recesses of their dirty flowing robes, and with gestures indicated their inability to assist in the work of propulsion.

This abnormally large "sick parade" somewhat surprised our men, who, never slow to size up a situation, held a hurried conference and decided on a plan of action. Quickly waving the Gyppos aside and seizing the ropes, they started the punt on its voyage, the sons of Allah meanwhile chattering and grinning as though enjoying the situation. On reaching the centre of the Canal, however, work on the ropes was suspended, and the punt, never hard to

Left to right and down: Pte. E. L. Baker, M.M., Pte. H. E. Williamson, M.M., Sgt. J. Regan, M.M., Sgt. D. Woodbine, M.M., Sgt. J. C. Ford, D.C.M., Pte. Geo. Gott, M.M.

CONTRIBUTIONS FROM MEMBERS 257

stop, came to a standstill. The "patients" were lined up at one side of the vessel and ordered to remove their bandages. Soon all was confusion. Those who could not produce a sore hand were promptly dumped overboard, their more or less white gowns forming balloon-like shapes and tending to keep the wearers from sinking. After some half-dozen had been summarily dealt with in this manner the remainder tore their camouflage to pieces and frantically rushed to the ropes, and, in their eagerness to escape a ducking some pulled one way and some another, causing the punt to swing in all directions. As some of those floundering in the water were in danger of drowning, a few of our men dived after them and soon all were hauled aboard and the voyage was resumed.

The Gyppos evidently took the lesson to heart, as from that day forward no further trouble was experienced and punt duty was looked upon by the troops as one of the cushy fatigues of Ferry Post.

THE LANGUAGE UNINVITING.
(By K.30).

At Tel-el-Kebir an order was promulgated to the effect that the G.O.C. of the Corps desired the use of bad language to be cut out. "The two words he specially refers to are .... and .... as he understands that these two words are not used in Australia."

A voice from the back of the parade: "The .... has never been there."

AN OUTSTANDING "CHARACTER".
(By CYRIL LAVENDER).

Well I recollect our first trip into the front line. Fritz was tickling the parapet with shrapnel. Of course, we had the "wind up" and crouched beneath the parapet. A huge friendly rat (of the variety known only in Flanders) quite unconcernedly ran along the top. Reub. Patterson was heard to exclaim, as we again ducked our heads, "They talk about the brave Anzacs, the rats are the gamest things I see about the place." That eased our mental strain.

It was not long after that "Patto" thought he was "back home" as the result of a lump of H.E. that ricochetted from the dead centre of his steel helmet, crumpling it up and sending it skimming for yards. He was never afterwards seen near the line without a tin hat.

"Patto" was instrumental in creating battalion history. The most anxious member to see real active service, he was in consequence the first member of the 30th to be wounded by a bayonet. It should be noted that this happened at Tel-el-Kebir. Armed guards with fixed bayonets were child's play to "Patto".

TURNING OVER A NEW LEAF.
(By Lieut.-Colonel M. PURSER).

From the day of its formation until I left it a year later to become second-in-command of the 32nd Battalion, there was no serious "crime" in "C" Company of the 30th. There were, however, a few whose appearances at orderly room for minor breaches of discipline were rather frequent, and I remember an occasion at the R.A.S. Showground when one of them was cheered on his way to orderly room by the company singing "Auld Lang Syne."

This story concerns one of the "regulars" whom I shall call Ernie, and who, a couple of months prior to our departure from Egypt for the Western Front, developed the habit of appealing against every punishment I awarded him. He was, in fact, so ready to appeal that on one occasion when I said "case dismissed," he could not help blurting out "I appeal."

About a fortnight before we left Moascar to embark at Alexandria, Ernie and his friend Tom appeared before me on a charge of being absent from the company lines at tattoo roll call. Not considering this very serious, I awarded them two days' confinement to camp, which really meant nothing. Nevertheless, I heard the familiar "I appeal" from Ernie. Doubtless from a sense of loyalty to a pal, Tom also appealed.

The following morning I took the two of them before the C.O., to whom Ernie explained, "I have been getting into a lot of trouble lately, Sir" ("Yes, you have," said the Colonel) "and have decided to turn over a new leaf, so I went to the Y.M.C.A.—and I know no better place to go, Sir—but there was such a crowd that I could not get out in time to be in the lines at tattoo." Tom grinned sheepishly, and half-heartedly supported Ernie's story.

The C.O. confirmed the sentence I had given them, pointing out that it was very light. But when the two had left the tent he remarked to me, "If that man is trying to turn over a new leaf, Major, I wouldn't be too hard on him." "Surely you did not swallow that story, Sir?" I asked. When he replied that he saw no reason for disbelieving it, I informed him that when awarding the punishment I knew Ernie's story to be untrue, as during the evening in question it had been reported to me by the company orderly officer, Lieutenant Fullarton, that he had seen Ernie and Tom at the Y.M.C.A.—not inside at the concert, but outside running a two-up school!

Ernie made the supreme sacrifice at Fromelles, but Tom is still very much alive.

THE HEADQUARTERS LEWIS GUN SECTION.
(By A. E. WEBB).

DURING the reorganisation of the A.I.F. in Egypt early in 1916 many changes in organisation took place, including the transfer of the Vickers machine-gun sections from battalion to brigade control. Battalions were now armed with the new Lewis gun; and on March 20th our own Lewis gun section came into being. This consisted, in the first instance, of thirty men and four guns only under Lieutenant A. H. Treloar.

Save for a few occasions rendered necessary by military exigencies, the section carried on as a separate entity, with its own billets, its own parades and activities, and its own cook. In the days of its early "teething" Arthur Treloar's smiling outlook on life, and almost youthful enthusiasm for the job, helped greatly to smooth out the initial difficulties encountered by the new unit. Later, when we had "crossed the Rubicon" in France and had passed from an eager anticipation to a chastened reality, he remained, under the tremendously changed conditions, not quite so buoyant within himself, but always an approachable and considerate O.C. Then, during the dark and stressful days of the first Somme campaign, he transferred his affection from the Lewis to the Vickers gun.

While we were still speculating, amid the mud and misery of Montauban, as to the possible outcome of a change in our command, we were caught up in the firm and friendly grip of a new chief—Lieutenant W. E. Oakes, from "C" Company. An immediate and intuitive feeling of confidence was reawakened within the section, and but little contact with our new O.C. was sufficient to convince us that it had not been misplaced. "Wes" Oakes had found his metier and we had found a leader. From that day to the end of our fighting activities there existed between us a bond of understanding and trust that grew closer as time went on. Always by his unwavering sense of duty, his quick grasp of new situations, his fearless example in emergency, and his innate gentlemanliness, were we inspired to give of our best in return.

And so, as the Lewis gun organisation grew, our activities expanded with it. The four headquarters guns in time were increased to eight, while the companies were ultimately equipped with one to each platoon—an enormous advance on the original fire-power of a battalion.

The instruction of a growing stream of fresh gunners, their supervision in the line, the replacement of spare parts, and the maintenance of our own teams in the trenches, became the routine responsibility of the headquarters section. Answering all demands made on them, "the Gunners" retained to the last their reputation for efficiency and service.

In the process they evolved between themselves a cameraderie and unity of purpose which remain to this day fast and unshakable. Never at any time far removed from the wider activities of the battalion itself, the gunners wove into the larger pattern a history all its own—a record of zeal and performance of which all are justly proud.

Looking back now, across a span of two decades, on the highlights of those stirring and stressful war days, I see them still with staggering clearness. Faces and figures, familiar and cherished, live again to play their part, and rekindle a welter of varied feelings.

Taking them at random, they come and go across the vista: attitudinous "Mick" Lister, the Section's "O. Pip.," as likeable as he was lofty, and as staunch; "Jackie" White, the mighty "atom," matching an outsize in packs with a wide and permanent grin; "Charlie" Westbrook, cheery, open-hearted, and carefree ever; "Harry" Martindale and "Ernie" Brown, straight and clean and level-headed; fair-haired "Freddie" Sharman, voluble and vehement, champion of the section's cause; "Harry" Myles, willing and cheerful; "Bunny" Humble, precursor of Wallace Beery, and famous for his "bunch of fives"—speech with him was fluent, colourful, and automatic; "Freddie" Scholes, "Smacker" Aimes, and "Brig" Dawson, a tough bunch of warriors, full of "fruity" anecdote; George Gibson, one of the whitest of men, cool, calm, and capable; "Stump" Short, "Ted" Bannister, "Joe" Heskey, and "Harry" Hitchens, from day to day playing their part without fuss or fireworks; "Gus" McDiarmid, frolicsome and fearless, swimmer, runner, and gunner; Ray McDiarmid, brother, sponsor, and adviser to "Gus," wise in his silences and dependable as the sun; "Mat" Baxter, slight and fair and mischievous, leader of the "troubadors"; "Freddie" Millwood, "Herb" Taylor, "Lorry" McKinnon, George Sykes, and "Basher" Sweeny, a youthful quintette, wise in their generation and apt to exploitation; "Joe" Hill, sturdy, hard-headed marksman, who loved his gun like a brother; "Jimmy" Balfour, from South Australia, with his "hollow legs" and priceless humour; "Mo" Duncan and "Charlie" Sullivan, self-possessed and capable always; "Norm" Winn, whose happy nature gravitated towards the funny side of every situation; "Tom" Perkins, whose quiet, tolerant nature was seldom ruffled; "Handy Bill" Taylor, with a practical eye that saw through most difficulties; "Bill" Daniel and "Vic" Batten, both with plenty of balance and rich in facile humour; young Percy Collier, a bright and wholesome lad, full of promise; George Jones, steeped in sober judgment, playing well an earnest part alongside "Harry" Glanville, stoically taking things as they came, and—last, but not least—the keen-eyed and trusty "Mike" Hogan.

Then, in the wake of all these good fellows, the one and only "Paddy." Blue-eyed, and fresh looking as Ireland's verdant hills, he had an unimpeachable "brogue," an aptitude for very mixed metaphors, and an unfailing propensity for figuring in the farcical. These heaven-sent qualities of his took the sting, for us, out of many a dismal situation, and no circus with its star-turn clown was ever more replete than was the section with its "Paddy." Volumes would be needed, indeed, to extol his virtues as a comedian and to encompass the full round of his exploits. Yet, withal, he had a heart of gold, and the working strength of a bullock. His willingness to help in the cause of the general good, and the energy he must have expended in carrying out some

of his self-imposed tasks, were truly phenomenal. For— to cite one instance, every gunner of the 30th will recall how often we hailed with joy the clattering thud that shook the hut as "Paddy" arrived with a full sack of coal "salvaged" from a "Froggie" train five kilometres off!
Long live "Paddy" Ryan!
Long live the Gunners!

THE 30th's FIRST RAID IN FRANCE.
(By LIEUT.-COLONEL M. PURSER).

THE raid under the command of Lieutenants Macfarlane and "Yank" Adams at Fleurbaix is generally believed to be the first carried out by the 30th Battalion, but it will be noted from the following that at least one preceded it by a couple of months.

We officers of "C" Company were not popular with Madame at our billet in Morbecque—our first one in France —because we washed on the back step in cold water drawn from the pump into a canvas bucket and only purchased from her a jug of beer each night to have with our supper of biscuits and cheese, whereas some English officers who had previously been billeted there had been in the habit of purchasing from her hot water in which to wash, and coffee and cakes for supper.

One night, however, we thought we would improve our fare, and asked Madame to sell us some eschalots. She did—about a dozen for a franc, which at that time was worth 9d. Our remarks regarding her rapacity were very rude, but, nevertheless, on the following night we again decided to have eschalots. Lieutenant "Ted" Haviland promptly volunteered to obtain them, and returning a few minutes later with a large bunch, was asked, "How much did you pay for that lot, Ted?" His reply explained the mud on his boots and the soil adhering to the "violets." "Pay," he said, "stone the crows, we paid for these last night." He had successfully raided Madame's garden.

HOW THE 30th WAS PUT TO ROUT.

(By Colonel J. W. CLARK).

I HAVE more than once referred with pride to the fact that the 30th never lost a position it was holding, nor lost practically one yard of trench. I think, however, it is due, to those members of the battalion who were not present, to unfold the murky tale of how we were once put to rout, not by the enemy, but by a mule.

We left the peaceful little village of Morbecque, after three very happy weeks there, to make our first move towards the front, all being in full marching order and carrying a little extra. It was a warm, muggy day in July when, about 10 a.m., we started off. Before we had marched three miles, some of the brigade commenced to fall out, but up to 1.30 p.m. the 30th had lost only eight men. A halt for lunch should have been made before entering Merville, but higher command ruled otherwise. So we did not halt until the rear of our column had cleared the town, by which time a lot more casualties had been caused by a mile-long stretch of cobblestones.

Our march was through very flat country along a narrow road bordered on each side by ditches full of mud, water, and slime. Movement to a flank was impossible, owing to the width of the ditches. I rode at the head of the 30th with my adjutant, Captain Sloan. "A," "B," "C" and "D" Companies followed in that order, with intervals of some 200 yards between each, and close on the heels of "D" Company came the R.M.O., Captain Langan, mounted on a sorry looking nag ("Calamity Kate"), with our chaplain, Father King, walking alongside the doctor's steed. Just behind them came the A.M.C. cart, piled some eight feet high with medical stores and officers' valises, etc., and drawn by a big rawboned mule, fresh after several weeks' spell. Its driver was a lad of about 16 or 17 years, who weighed under 7 stone and was usually called "Little Tich." Though small, he was full of grit.

We had great difficulty on the narrow road in passing a large steam-roller, which drew up to the side to make room for us. Suddenly, as the tail of our column, to wit, the A.M.C. cart, came abreast of it, the man in charge of the roller started his engine with a fearful burst. Our mule gave one jump, grabbed the bit in its teeth and bolted.

Dr. Langan, whatever other athletic prowess he possessed, was no rider. And, although "Kate" had been specially selected as proof against anything within reason, she became absolutely mad when the shaft of the mule-cart, which also knocked the Padre over, struck her in the rib. She also bolted, dislodging the doctor.

The mule and cart continued their victorious career right through "D" Company, who had no time or room to get out of the way. Dozens jumped or were knocked into the ditches, feet deep in water and slime. "Tich" stuck manfully to the reins, even though pulled full length along the shaft. I had just ridden back to see how the rear of the battalion was progressing, when the affair happened; the shaft missed my back by inches; my horse tried to bolt, and I hung on, wondering how in the devil I could get out of the way. By now the cart had reached "C" Company and commenced to scatter them right and left in the same way until about half-way through the company a brain wave seized one of its members, Private Murphy. Swinging his rifle he struck the mule an awful blow with the butt right between the eyes. It blinked, shook its ears, and decided to stop, and "Tich" then regained control.

Roars of laughter went up from the lucky ones on the road, as they saw the men in the ditches searching for rifles, etc., and being dragged out wet through and covered with mud.

Finally the march was resumed, but all the ginger had gone out of the unlucky ones, and our numbers dwindled considerably before we reached our billets in the town of Estaires.

INTIMATE PICTURES OF NO-MAN'S LAND.
(By Capt. T. C. BARBOUR).

WHEN in the middle of 1916 the 30th Battalion reached the fighting zone in France, the war had long since reached that stage when the embattled nations gazed at each other across No-Man's Land, a land of romance for the newcomer. During July, "D" Company entered the front line for the first time in the vicinity of Bois Grenier, an obliterated hamlet, disclosed by a pin point on army maps, just east of the shell-gutted village of Fleurbaix. It was considered a quiet sector, a "nursing" ground for the breaking-in of raw troops. It lived up to its reputation.

At night the expectant garrison gazed across the high breast-works for their initial peep into No-Man's Land, which was flanked by belts of corroded wire erected by the Tommies and their opposite numbers during the stalemate of 1914. To assist their observation it was brilliantly illuminated with star shells and Verey lights. These flares were ejected from a heavy brass pistol possessing a kick like a mule and, needless to say, much erratic shooting took place with it. Scores of flares, despatched serenely skywards, fell in No-Man's Land close to our wire and defences; others dropped in the rear of the breastworks to expose the newcomers in dazzling relief.

While this demonstration of vertical shooting was in progress, a wiring party, of which I was placed in charge, emerged through a sally-port to commence their first humble task on the Western Front. We were frankly dubious about tackling the proposition until our industrious flare boys, after much practice, attained a measure of success in directing their flares towards enemy territory. The party then settled down with cutters and gloves to their allotted task, being covered by Corporal Gooding and a small detachment.

Engrossed in their work, the men forgot the presence of the haloes of light and the romance associated with No-

Man's Land, particularly when they surveyed at close quarters a homely selection of discarded socks and "armour-plated" biscuits, a glorious aggregation of bully-beef and jam tins, and long stretches of barbed-wire and trip hurdles, liberally festooned with discarded portions of soldiers' underwear.

My duties this night also included a patrol of the company front and an inspection of the condition of the defences, so, taking advantage of a quiet spell, I left Sergeant Hunt in charge of the wiring party, and commenced my tour. Armed with a heavy service Webley, and by contrast, a light automatic (loaned for the occasion by our first reinforcement officer, Lieutenant E. A. C. Macfarlane) I felt quite confident to deal with any pork-pie caps I might encounter.

During this lone patrol, through waist-high grass and weeds, I found our numerous star-shells useful for my survey, but rather disconcerting when they fell to sizzle at one's feet. One particular halo of light appeared to trail me relentlessly. I had a vague impression that it must be emanating from some budding flare-king interested in my welfare, for it illuminated my surroundings with monotonous frequency.

After a somewhat lengthy tour I decided to shake my feet of the delectable area, with its grisly accumulation of relics, and make for home. Mounting the wide breastwork I flopped down on to a firing-step of one of the bays, where, much to my alarm, I was greeted by a hostile sentry. In spite of my furnishing the password, he insisted on pressing his bayonet against a rather frail button on my tunic, between times levelling a copious flow of unprintable adjectives at me. As I was wearing a Digger's tunic and pants much perforated by the wire, with strips of protecting hessian dangling round my puttees, I must have presented a sorry spectacle, and I had considerable difficulty in overcoming his scepticism as to my identity. He maintained I wasn't one of their "b—— blokes."

During this colloquial interlude a Digger was despatched to locate the officer on duty. Finally, Lieutenant Alan Mitchell, the tallest and leanest subaltern in the 30th and proprietor of the broadest smile, arrived to verify my identification. It appears that I had overstepped "D" Company's domain, and patrolled into the area of "C" Company, an unpardonable sin according to the rigid code of No-Man's Land. Even after my identification was established, the belligerent sentry hesitated to lower his weapon. It almost seemed that he was disappointed at not taking the opportunity to indulge in a little bayonet practice earlier in the proceedings.

On rejoining Sergeant Hunt's party in No-Man's Land I found that the wiring task had been completed. Reinforced with elements from Corporal Gooding's detachment —wise individuals blessed with a delicate sense of smell— they had assembled like Druids of old at the lone and somewhat shell-shocked, but still perpendicular, tree that stood surrounded by a luxurious carpet of grass in a fold of the ground some distance from the breastwork. Under these idyllic conditions—a near approach to a No-Man's Land paradise—the warriors were enjoying a rest, rising occasionally to carry out a quaint form of tribal ritual, by paying homage to a portable earthenware shrine, on which were printed the mystic initials "S.R.D." This jar, a symbol of efficient service, was a thoughtful contribution from that uncrowned King of the "Q" Branch, Sergeant James MacDuff, a legendary figure in the life of the battalion, and one famed for his spacious girth, ready wit, and winning smile.

During my meanderings Lieutenant Macfarlane's small automatic had been lost, and, although I made a diligent search of No-Man's Land the following night, I could not locate it. Mac accepted his loss philosophically and dismissed the subject of indemnity with a hasty gesture. When he led the battalion's first raid he took a heavy Webley into action and he considered it was his salvation.

CONTRIBUTIONS FROM MEMBERS

PERCY AND HIS "PIPPINS".

(By LIEUT.-COLONEL M. PURSER).

ON returning to the front line a few days after the Battle of Fromelles the remnants of "A" and "C" Companies were combined under my command, with Captain (later Major) Percy Charlton as second-in-command. At the time "pippin" rifle-grenades were in rather plentiful supply, probably because they were comparatively cheap (I think I am right in saying they cost about 1od. each). Of the percussion type, they would be very nasty bursting in a trench—they were certainly nasty to handle, a good percentage of them being exploded by the shock of discharge. For this reason they were usually discharged from fixed rifles, fired by a string from behind a sandbag breastwork or similar protection.

Captain Charlton entered whole-heartedly into the job of transferring these "pippins" from our trenches to the enemy's line and the men he selected as his assistants were no less enthusiastic. Improving upon the usual method of using fixed rifles, they mounted a couple on a trolley which ran on rails laid parallel to the front line, and, trundling this along the company front, discharged their "pippins" in the direction of the enemy from various points at all hours of the day and night, especially in the early hours of the morning.

Seldom were we disappointed in our expectation of enemy retaliation, and on one occasion a battle in miniature developed. Charlton and his men had been particularly busy during the night, and the number of grenades they had landed in the enemy trenches evidently annoyed the Germans, for in the early hours of the morning "Swish" —"bang" came the first of a number of "pineapple" bombs, which we had never previously experienced. We replied with "pippins", but the "pineapples" continuing to arrive, I called a battery of field artillery into action. The guns did not at that period have many shells to play with, but their shrapnel was soon bursting over the enemy trenches. Then "c-r-r-r-ump", "c-r-r-r-ump", and his artillery was delivering quantities of "ironmongery" in the neighbourhood of battalion headquarters.

We watched this "strafe" with interest and, as none of it was coming near us, with a certain amount of amusement. But our turn was to come. Apparently Colonel Clark's beauty sleep was disturbed, for when he visited the line after breakfast he "strafed" us for causing, "with twopenny-halfpenny grenades," a bombardment of battalion headquarters with heavy stuff. He seemed in no way appeased when I remarked that no damage had been done to our line nor had we suffered any casualties, whereas the Germans had wasted a lot of shells in the bombardment. Neither did he seem in the slightest degree impressed when I pointed out that our "pippins" were helping, although admittedly in a small way, to win the war.

Percy Charlton and his merry men derived a lot of fun from their "pippins", and, anyhow, why should they worry if battalion headquarters was shelled? Were they not harrying the German and had they not a lot of "pippins" to get rid of? "Too right" they had, so they ignored the C.O's. "strafe", and continued to send a large quantity of grenades across No-Man's Land each night. I would not, of course, suggest that they secretly hoped for another bombardment of battalion headquarters, but they were still carrying on the good work when on August 6th, 1916, I left the battalion to take over the duties of second-in-command of the 32nd.

MEMORIES OF FROMELLES.
(By R. MATHER).

ALTHOUGH a native of old Caledonia, I must confess that the sentiment expressed in the popular Scottish toast:

"Here's tae us,
Wha's like us,
Deil the yin,"
is one that I have always regarded with faint amusement. Scotland's geographical situation may be partly responsible for this superiority complex. A glance at the map will show that it is right on top of England.

As the first wave launched its attack on the fatal field of Fromelles, No. 12 Platoon of the 30th Battalion, under the command of Lieutenant Jack Chapman, was in the shelter of "Cellar Farm Avenue" close to the front line, awaiting any contingency that might arise. Walking wounded were already on their way out and showed amazing fortitude. One fellow badly hit on the knee was progressing rearwards in a series of hops. He was clutching his knee with both hands, which were covered in blood, and as he passed he called out, "I'm one of the b—— lucky ones I s'pose."

Lieutenant Chapman shook the falling dirt from his steel helmet with a toss of his head, and remarked, "We'll get some backsheesh to-night." A stretcher party was approaching, "Snowy", the diminutive kettle-drummer, toiling between the handles. "Make way for the stretcher," I called out, and its occupant, recognising the accent in my voice, reached out his hand and grasping mine said: "Remember you're Scotch the nicht." "I'll try," I faltered doubtfully.

Every soldier knows that the period of waiting for something to do is the worst ordeal he has to undergo. All the traditions, legends, tunes, and songs of Scotland's story did not seem much of a help to me at that moment, and I wondered idly how my fellow Australians were feeling. Little did I know then that I was to live to see them (to use the words of Sir John Monash) "by their deeds in battle, earn for themselves a place in history which none can challenge."

STEAK AND ONIONS FOR SIX.

(By LIEUT.-COLONEL M. PURSER).

WHILE billeted in an *estaminet* in the Rue de Quesne, Fleurbaix, the officers of "C" Company lived mostly on "tinned stuff" purchased there, but as some of them were likely to "go West" in the coming fight (the Battle of Fromelles) they decided to have a real meal on the night before the battle. They, accordingly, arranged with Marie, the daughter of the *estaminet*, to provide for them 1 lb. of steak and 1 lb. of onions per man, accepting her assurance that she knew how to grill steak and fry onions.

After waiting till late in the evening, they had given up hope of getting the grilled steak and onions, and were just about to purchase some tinned food when Marie announced that the cooking was completed, and they sat down in anticipation of a really good square meal. Alas, they did not then know, as they came to learn later, that the cooking ability of the French *estaminet* keepers was apparently limited to eggs and chips, omelettes, etc. Our 6 lb. of steak, tough and anaemic looking, was served in one uninviting piece, and to this day I have never been able to decide how it was cooked—it appeared to be partly boiled and partly baked; the onions, served whole, were partly boiled and partly raw. Our disappointment can be imagined.

The same party never again sat down to an evening meal, for in the next night's fight five became casualties: Lieutenants A. Mitchell and J. Parker killed; Captain B. A. Wark and Lieutenants I. G. Fullarton and E. E. Haviland wounded.

COMPANY RUNNERS.

(By CAPT. T. C. BARBOUR).

To the uninitiated, the runner is invariably pictured as an apostle of speed streaking hell-for-leather, despatch in

Sgt. R. J. ESTELL, M.M.

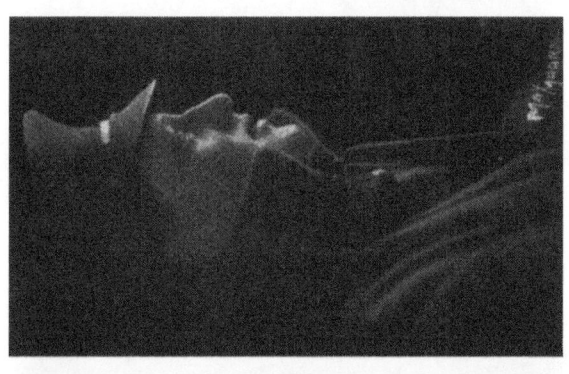

Bandmaster L. C. WELLINGS, M.S.M.

Sgt. C. H. McCLOSKEY, D.C.M.

hand, across a shell-swept landscape. Paradoxical though it may seem, a runner rarely ran. Prevailing conditions, especially in winter, precluded any excessive bursts of locomotion, and delivery of routine despatches from the front line hardly justified any spectacular effort or waste of his reserve of physical energy; but at least on one occasion Private J. Ford (later Sergeant J. Ford, D.C.M.), who had a long spin as a runner, had to run like the devil under the eyes of German sharpshooters in order to save his own life.

The long drawn out months of the 30th Battalion's service in Egypt were mostly months of placid inaction, so far as the runners were concerned, but, shortly after their arrival in northern France, they were unceremoniously pitchforked into the Battle of Fromelles, from which they emerged with flying colours. During the heat of that holocaust a platoon of "D" Company penetrated an isolated post in the German support lines—more aptly described as ditches—to find themselves up to their waists in water and with both flanks in the air. Runners were entrusted with various messages and requests for reinforcements, and they never hesitated to pass through the heavy barrage of enemy shells and flanking machine-gun fire. Some survived the ordeal, others, like the gallant McKillop, an emergency runner, were killed.

The epic story of Private P. J. Nankivell, M.M., which is related in Dr. Bean's Official History, illustrates the heroic conduct displayed by all runners engaged on the Fromelles battlefield. Many hours later, when the engagement had died down, Nankivell was discovered amongst the battle debris, a mass of shrapnel wounds—portions of the shell could be seen sticking out. He made no mention of his terrible plight, but was anxious to let me know he had delivered the message I had given him in our advance post. Nankivell survived, and was invalided to Australia, but never recovered sufficiently in strength to rejoin his unit. He well deserved his decoration, one of the first gained by the battalion.

T

"PADDY" OF THE LEWIS GUN SECTION.

(By F. C. SHARMAN).

AFTER the ghastly night of Fromelles, the boys of the 30th Battalion "keeping the peace" in the Fleurbaix sector were eager for anything in the way of promiscuous relaxation. So when, into the midst of a Lewis gun team in the front line wandered the inimitable Paddy, the Lewis gun officer's batman, the gunners were quick to seize an opportunity for diversion.

Paddy was quaint, unsophisticated, and refreshingly Irish—proud of his Waterford birthplace. His contacts with the common enemy, however, had been very remote, for scarcely ever had he been further forward than battalion headquarters. It was but natural, therefore, that he evinced much curiosity as to the nearness of Fritz and the location of the handiest communication trench. These artless enquiries supplied an immediate cue as to the course which should be followed, and Paddy was soon being "well drummed up" in the art of front-line observation.

Persuaded eventually to have a peep over the parapet at the Germans opposite, he wormed his way with infinite care and stealth to a promising sandbag, flashed a hasty glance over the top, then clattered down into the trench. Thus was he presented with his first blurred out "dinkum" glimpse of No-Man's Land.

Elated by this achievement he was easier "meat" now for the *bon mot* hatched in the minds of the grinning gunners. "Have a shot, Pat—here's my rifle," was the warm invitation now extended. Urged on by each of the gun-team in turn, he gingerly took the rifle which, for safety's sake, had been loaded with one cartridge only, and prepared to "have a go".

Then the wag, that emerges on all such occasions, found a stray screw from an ammunition box, slipped it into the muzzle, and explained that it was an excellent way of giving Fritz a "double-barreller". This was all a bit beyond

CONTRIBUTIONS FROM MEMBERS 275

Paddy's mental grasp, but the momentary hesitation he evinced was soon "ironed out" under a barrage of intensified persuasion.

Receiving elaborate instructions as to aiming and firing, he once more mounted the fire-step. His excitement was by now as intense as the gunners' anticipations were lively. After much shuffling and squirming below the crest of the parapet he finally slid the rifle forward—still with the screw down the muzzle—crouched behind it, squinted along the sights, took a flurried aim, and pressed the trigger. Bang-g-g! went the business with the roar of an 18-pounder, and Paddy was jerked backwards, almost into the bottom of the trench, tin-hat, rifle and all. Trembling with excitement, but beaming with pride and pleasure he hastily handed the rifle back, murmuring the while something about giving the so-and-so's "one to go on with!"

Amid the general laughter that followed, the owner of the rifle paid little attention to the state of his weapon. His lingering chuckles were turned to dismay, however, when at length he noticed its sorry condition. The rifle that had been so much his care and pride, now had a kink on the barrel like the spout of a kettle. With loud imprecations on the heads of all and sundry, he looked around for Paddy in particular. But that worthy, still enjoying the thrill of his adventure, was by then making good headway down the communication trench towards B.H.Q.

Quite unwittingly, indeed, had he given someone "something to go on with!"

THE PILGRIMS OF THE SOMME.
(BY CAPT. T. C. BARBOUR).

AFTER patiently enduring many months of their first winter campaign on the Somme, where the only vista was a tormented horizon of mud and dissolving trenches, the battalion was overjoyed at the golden opportunity of quitting the area and helping to speed the retiring German host across comparative virgin green country to the fastnesses of the Hindenburg Line. This unexpected transition from a morass of stinking mud and battle debris to a verdant landscape of firm ground with miles of rolling downs was received with an exhilaration of joy and wonder like that experienced by Xenophon's men, when, after the end of their trials and long journey, they first glimpsed the sea.

After a period of semi-open warfare, the Diggers were again overjoyed to receive the glad news of a long-promised rest in a back area, and, conjuring up visions of restful *estaminets* and romantic *mademoiselles*, they cheerfully "about-turned" and faced the west. Headed by the battalion band, under the command of genial Les. Wellings—a gallant soldier, who inexplicably missed his commission, and whose story, "Bandmaster and Stretcher-Bearer," has yet to be penned—the troops marched countless miles, only to receive a galvanic shock, when, weary and footsore, they again entered the desolate belt of mud which they had recently vacated.

Not a hamlet, not a home, not a blade of grass. A few splintered posts, all askew like drunken telegraph poles, advertised the remains of Mametz, Deville, High, Trones, and other once leafy French woods; and, in lieu of brick and mortar, which had been entirely demolished by the shattering force of high-explosive, the only shelters available were abandoned Nissen huts, the lining of which had long since been used as firewood. The site was officially verified by the presence of an army sign post, an isolated spectre in the sea of mud, on which was painted in large block-letters—large enough to upset the apple cart of any Doubting Thomas—the legend, "This is Montauban."

In this forsaken billetless area, far removed from the comforts of *estaminets* and *beaucoup vin*, the sorrows of the Diggers were added to by our excellent M.O., Doc. Railton, who performed much overdue work with the needle.

CONTRIBUTIONS FROM MEMBERS

The troops were now employed as battlefield scavengers, salvaging abandoned stores, ammunition, rifles, and bayonets, cleaning up the debris, and burying numerous German dead. Apart from regular musters of "souvenir kings", worried C.S.M.'s. reported a lack of enthusiasm for and dwindling attendances at the latter function. Much to the delight of the old hands, a number of reinforcements were duly honoured with the future custody of all graveyard operations.

Daily these men set out under their leader, facetiously dubbed "O.C. Stiff-'uns", and, as Old Sol gradually warmed up, the job became more irksome and operators correspondingly restive. At last a young warrior complained that he was fed-up with the endless spade work, also that he had enlisted to fight the Germans, not to act as a "b—— undertaker."

"Old Bill," a survivor of Fromelles, who had seen some twelve months' service in France without a break, patiently listened to the tirade, but, when "our hero" reiterated his intention of dumping his spade and violently assaulting Fritz, "Old Bill" slowly assumed the perpendicular, and after offering the young blade a rifle and bayonet, pointed in the direction of German territory, and adjured him in no polite terms to get a move on and do a "little killing," and, he concluded, "I'll follow you up with a b—— trowel."

A PRISONER OF WAR.
(By D. B. STOREY).

On regaining consciousness after my wounds at Fleurbaix on 19th July, 1916, I was helped along by a German until we met two other Aussies, the three of us continuing to the rear of the German lines to join many Tommies and Aussies who had been caught in the same stunt. Thence we were marched to Lille, where our wounds were treated by a matron, after which we had a slice of black bread and some coffee—the first food I had had for 30 hours—and put ourselves to bed. Sleeping till 6 a.m. I was awakened by a sparrow at the bars of the room. How I envied that bird its liberty.

After two days here, during which we received no medical attention—apparently the doctor detailed to us had been called away to attend to German wounded—we were told to dress. Entraining in cattle trucks, scantily furnished with straw, we made a two days' journey to Dulmen, in Westphalia, being jeered at by sightseers at every stop. On the way the guards supplied us with a bowl of soup, maintaining that they had scarcely enough for themselves, and at Dulmen we received more soup and black bread, which were greedily swallowed. Transported to camp by a civilian in a tip-dray, I was placed in a hammock to await a doctor —a Frenchman, who had been captured earlier in the field. He said I must look to God to put me right, there being no provision at Dulmen for operations.

Several weeks later a plan by some Aussies to escape by burrowing out of the camp was frustrated when a sentry fell through the rain-soaked covering of the tunnel. We were thereupon sent to the Schneidernuhl "strafe" camp in Poland, and were told that we could escape from here if we wished, but—like the others imprisoned there, some of them since 1914—we made no such attempt, for the Baltic Sea was on one side, the Black Forest was on another, and starvation faced us on all sides. Even the Germans were scantily fed, the main food being black bread, mangelwurzel soup, and black coffee. The British blockade was blamed for the shortage.

Some of our men, working on farms, placed broken needles in the feed of the cattle, which died as a result of their intestines being pierced. Consequently, needles were no longer allowed in camp.

My wounds breaking out in the winter of 1916, I was

marked for repatriation to Switzerland, but only after sixteen months was I sent there.

During our stay at Schneidernuhl the booming of Russian artillery was several times heard, raising our hopes of liberation, but, alas! Russia petered out. Thousands of captured Russians poured into the camp; food was almost unprocurable, and typhus raged. But for the Red Cross parcels we could not have survived.

HOODWINKING THE MINNIE KINGS.
(BY CAPT. T. C. BARBOUR).

DURING September-October, 1916, the 30th was brigaded with General Franks's force, and occupied the line at Houplines, near Armentieres. In this sector we took over from the redoubtable Royal Scots, the oldest regiment in the British service. These dour fighters, nicknamed "Pontius Pilate's Bodyguard", were here associated with a battalion of the Black Watch, who wore their picturesque kilts in the line.

Houplines possessed an evil reputation. It was the centre of a cloud gas area, and home of the heavy *minenwerfer* and their next-of-kin, the pestilential "rum jars". We gathered from our friends, the hairy Jocks, whose dialect was as broad and puzzling as the jig-saw blend of colours in their tartan kilts, that the century-old pastime of mortar throwing was extensively indulged in by the Germans here, and had caused quite a number of casualties to the garrison.

In retaliation for the mortar bombardments a squad of Tommies arrived and installed their "flying pig" mortar in a camouflaged pit, near the "Fry Pan". This projectile, which was designed on the familiar contours of a beer barrel, was hailed as the saviour of Houplines; but, to our alarm, the unruly "pig" proved to be as temperamental as a *prima-donna*, and as hard to handle as a mule.

Part of my job at Houplines was to furnish copy and digestible tit-bits for the breakfast table edition of that illuminating journal, *Comic Cuts*, and the sector proved to be a fertile field for obtaining the necessary material. On the completion of a conference with a sleek "brass hat", who dwelt on the alarming vagaries of the "pig", I decided to take up a strategic position and witness the demonstration from an extreme flank and so be free from any debris.

After considerable coaxing, and the Empire's formal blessing, the first "pig" was launched, at a somewhat low trajectory, in the general direction of enemy territory. It collapsed, however, in our own lines, uprooting the defences with a roar like the last trump. Fortunately, a discerning officer had made provision for such an event by withdrawing the restive garrison from the danger zone.

A judicious interval followed. Then another fully fledged monster was coughed skywards at a much higher altitude, where its portly outlines were seen to greater advantage. After experiencing a few seconds of aerial bliss, during which it disdainfully shed a fin, the mortar concluded its leisurely parabola, and gave up the ghost in No-Man's Land.

Following this baptism of the new infant, the Tommies, all hardened campaigners, promptly skedaddled. Their hasty departure spoke eloquently of a deep knowledge of German character, and synchronised with the arrival of the "backwash", which included a full measure of "minnies", intermingled with the thump of five-nines. A number of "whizz-bangs" also voiced their disapproval and searched for the home of the "pig".

Colonel C. S. Davies, who was acting as C.O. of the battalion at Houplines, was much perturbed at the growing damage caused by enemy canisters which daily thundered on our breastwork. These visitations confirmed the unsavoury impression conveyed to us by the sturdy Jocks on the night they vacated the premises.

Eventually Colonel Davies decided to try a ruse to draw the German fire without damage to ourselves. During daylight a small fire was made in a disused redoubt near the "Orchard", with an abundance of green shrubs heaped on top to create a pall of smoke. The colonel took up quarters in an observation post, in the subsidiary lines, to watch the results. These developed quickly, and were surprisingly productive.

Alert enemy observers promptly reported the location of the new-chum "cook house", and a copious supply of *minenwerfer* bombs took the air. These canisters were supplemented by a spiteful issue of "whizz-bangs", which arrived with gay precision to join in the joyful work of demolition.

To stimulate their efforts, the site of the "cook house" was periodically shifted, and much to our delight, the "minnie" kings cordially responded to these fleeting changes of address. On one of our special gala days German sleuths were elated to observe three "cook-houses" burning simultaneously—all were methodically extinguished by the opposition fire brigades.

During these prodigal displays of wasting ammunition, good work was done by our observers in marking down the retreats of the trench-mortar barons, and the map references were rushed piping hot to our friends the artillery, who immediately turned in on them. As retaliation from our front line an ensemble of Stokes mortar and "plum pudding" (68 lb.) bombs were pumped over No-Man's Land, also frillings in the shape of salvoes of our war-winning "pip-squeaks".

Altogether, Fritz experienced a rough passage at the hands of "Tivey's Chocs" at Houplines, and when further retaliation developed in the form of a nasty dose of cloud gas, ejected from the breastwork, the "minnie" kings of the other side lost much of their former zeal.

THE 30TH MEETS THE BLACK WATCH.

(By R. MATHER).

THE only occasion on which the 30th and the Black Watch ever met was on the 20th of September, 1916, when "Franks' Force"—a composite force, drawn from the 5th Australian Division and the 34th British Division—was sent to relieve the 51st (Highland) Division at Armentieres. As my brother was serving with the 15th Royal Scots, which was a part of the 34th Division, it will be understood why I was on French leave at the time.

Among the troops there were inveterate souvenir hunters who added fresh regimental badges to the collection on their belts whenever opportunity offered, and as the Scottish regiments in most cases had large and ornamental badges they were in great demand. I met two Jocks with a beauty for sale and, though I didn't collect them, I might have bought it had the price been reasonable.

"How much?" I enquired.

"Ten francs."

I looked at the two conspirators, and replied, "I was born north o' the Tweed masel."

One grabbed the other by the arm. "Come awa' Wallie, he'll put us in clink."

Fritz was shelling heavily as I proceeded to the Green Blind Factory in Armentieres, where the 7th Black Watch were billeted. He always did when I went visiting. The 7th had been the Territorial battalion in my home town of Dunfermline. "Where's Bob Sinclair?" I asked. "Wounded at Givenchy." "Where's Sandy Haxton?" "Wounded at Givenchy." One after another I named the men I had known, and soon gathered that Givenchy had been for them what Fromelles had been for us.

Presently one of the Jocks leaned across the table and whispered, "This is the driest b—— war I've ever been to." Being in funds, I took the hint. "Bring a few mates and let's slip out quietly," I answered. Then an argument ensued whether a red-headed one should accompany us. He was due to go on duty in an hour or two, but he refused to be left behind. We found an *estaminet* where *vin blanc, vin rouge,* beer, eggs, potato chips, and bread and butter could be bought. The place was crowded with Jocks and Aussies, chiefly of the 30th and 7th Black Watch, all out to make a memorable night of it.

There was a battered piano in the corner. The thirst of the pianist was apparently unequal to the supply of liquid encouragement he was receiving, for along the top of the piano was a row of drinks. Three women were being kept busy cooking and serving and they were being harassed by the clamouring crowd. The bursts of happy laughter were continuous and with the mixture of broad Scotch, English, and pidgin French, made the place a Towel of Babel. As the night wore on the redhead was being constantly reminded of his duty and the lateness of the hour. But he intimated that he had given years of his valuable time to the war and now it could wait. An hour later he would insist on shaking my hand and singing:—

"Here's a hand, my trusty friend,
And gies a hand o' thine,
Should auld acquaintance be forgot
And never brought to mind,"

which showed that he was getting things a bit mixed and, truth to tell, it seemed to me then that the brotherhood of man had at last become a reality. But we got a rude reminder that this was not so when Fritz started shelling. The womenfolk gathered the money hastily into a stocking and fled to the cellar. Two Jocks took charge of the egg-and-chip department and carried on business as usual while a big raw-boned Scot stepped up to the bar and called out lustily, "Name yer pizen, gents, name yer pizen." All of the money collected was placed in the till.

Taking advantage of the absence of the womenfolk, one Jock removed his kilt and displayed a large blue scar caused by a shrapnel wound on the fleshy part of his anatomy, just below the end of his back. We crowded round to see it and persuaded him to get up on the table where he piroutted before an admiring audience.

All goods things come to an end—but there was quite a number in that night's party whose recollections of how it did end are somewhat hazy.

LONGPRES TO BUSSUS.
(By J. S. BARTLEY).

EN ROUTE for the Somme on 17th October, 1916, the battalion received an unexpected order to detrain at Longpres. The night was heavy and black, and we scrambled out into pouring rain and rapidly assembled. Very soon, led by Colonel Clark, mounted on a gallant charger, we moved off, laden with full marching order and numerous additions, besides company stores.

Great coats rapidly became saturated and burdensome, causing inconvenience and discomfort owing to the oppressive heat. The first hour passed, followed by the second, without any prospect of the usual spell, and all the while the colonel's mount moved serenely along, setting the pace.

It was now realised that conditions had developed into a forced march, probably to try out the stamina of the men, and judging by the number of men who stuck it out, this test of physical endurance spoke volumes for the efficient training the old battalion had received in Egypt. Rain pelted down unceasingly. The only sounds audible were the rattle of accoutrements and the deadened sound of sodden boots.

The battalion moved along that old French road, up hill and down dale, kilo after kilo, leaving behind villages which stood out in the darkness like mute sentinels. By way of encouragement the officers began to call out the old army slogan, "Only one more kilo to go," but the strain was beginning to tell. Men began to rest just where they stood, some in pools of water, but after a brief spell rose up and plodded on. Others fell out and lay behind hay stacks in the pouring rain, the officers being kept busy rounding them up with torches.

The "one and only" kilo was long past. The march seemed endless, and no welcome order came for a spell. Officers were now seen carrying company stores, and the troops continued like a phantom army. No man spoke. Each plodded along with a grim determination to win through, not knowing how much further lay the welcome billets. Suddenly, as if emphasising the need for a spell, a shot punctuated the night, whistling high over the head of the column. But it failed in its effect as the colonel's horse paced serenely along without turning a hair.

Billets—never more welcome—were reached about 2 a.m. The march had continued without cessation and in pouring rain from ten o'clock the previous night. In the little Somme village of Bussus the battalion lay down to a well earned rest, whilst limbers were despatched back over the route to collect abandoned litter and help the stragglers back to the fold.

THE TEST.
(By R. MATHER).

"And when the snow is snowing
And it's murky overhead,
Oh: it's nice to get up in the morning,
But it's nicer to lie in bed."

So thought Jack Dykes at Vignacourt, with the result that he had to fall in on parade in a lamentable state of unpreparedness.

His rifle was encased in mud collected in the vicinity of Flers, and French mud is famed for its adhesive quality.

Major George Wynne, a newcomer to the company, gave the command, "For inspection! Port Arms!"

Here was an interesting situation, one that would enable the "other ranks" to decide as to the category into which Wynne should be placed. Casting a long, lingering look at Jack's rifle, he said: "It's all right, old chap. Don't bother to clean it. Next time we go in I'll get you a shillalah."

MUCH ADO ABOUT NOTHING.
(By J. S. BARTLEY).

COMING to the Somme from Armentieres, the battalion found itself on 27th October, 1916, at "Hungry Hill," close to the ruins of Flers and the wrecks of the first land battleships used in warfare—the tanks. Shelter for the night for No. 15 Platoon was a tarpaulin, but, after a series of turning movements by the whole platoon, George Gott, Doneger, and myself found ourselves definitely "on the outer." We therefore waited on Captain "Dad" White, who directed us to a small, rough shed in which were stored boxes of .303 and advised us to let no one turn us out. With a decent little fire going and the "Fray Bentos" sizzling in the dixie lids, our only regret was the absence of some S.R.D. to drink Dad's health.

Having turned in, our rest was disturbed by the R.S.M. of another battalion in the 8th Brigade, with whom we had had a spot of bother up north. He ordered us out of the hut and, on our refusing, drew our attention to his revolver. Counter-threats led to his withdrawal in some disorder, but he returned later with a "real" major of his unit—known to us as the "Mad Major."

Did he go "mad" when he saw our fire, which, it must be admitted, was scorching some of the boxes, whilst others had furnished the fuel? The engagement developed into a "major" operation, with the introduction of issues of jurisdiction between two Aussie battalions and rivalry between two Australian States. Surely a unique conflict even on French soil, the scene of many struggles for remarkable causes with strange adversaries.

Threatened with a charge of firing a dump, we demanded the attendance of our own officers. "Dad" and Lieutenant Coleman responded to our S.O.S. and raised many nice points, eventually requiring the R.S.M. to obtain maps and establish his battalion's claim to the position. By the time this had been settled—and the hut was outside our area—the night was well spent as far as we were concerned. We were content to escape arrest and huddle under the tarpaulin for a few hours. Fortunately—or otherwise—we never again ran up against that R.S.M. or the Mad Major.

"NO COMPREE."
(By GEOFF. COWEN).

It occurred on my first escort job. I had been sent to Boulogne with two others to bring back one of the battalion from the "clink" there. Despite a warning as to the brutal sort of prisoner I would have under my care, I found him a docile enough sort of "bird". We had no need to use "cuffs", or anything of that sort, and when we called at the Flemish estaminet for a "wet", our prisoner was invited to join us.

Sitting by the stove in the centre of the room was a very old grandma. A really beautiful young blossom came to take our order. Whilst she was producing the beer, a door on the other side of the room was opened and a middle-aged woman entered. In a very loud voice almost amounting to a shout, she addressed herself in Flemish to the old woman, who was evidently deaf.

Commenting upon this, one of the guard said to me, "The old girl's gone in the telephone, Corp," whereupon the mademoiselle immediately said in English, "Yes, Monsieur, Grandma is very deaf."

"Struth," remarked our prisoner. "You know how many beans make five, Mam'selle."

And believe me, she gave us the dinky-di soldiers' answer to that one, too. Yet these were the folks who would "No compree" for a week when it suited them.

AN ANGELIC VISIT.
(By R. MATHER).

LATE in April, 1917, after months on the desolate battlefield of the Somme, the battalion was resting in the vicinity of Bapaume, when someone passed the word that an Australian nursing sister was coming along the railway line. Soon the troops hurried to the scene—even the poker schools abandoned their games—and she became the cynosure of all eyes.

In other circumstances she must have thought our curiosity an unpardonable rudeness, but now, luckily for us, as we stood and stared at her, she seemed to understand something of what we thought and felt, and she went by with a word here and there, her lips every now and then enriching the smile her eyes had begun.

Could it be possible, we thought, that we had once lived in a world where such lovely creatures were our daily companions? Was it ages ago in some previous existence? Surely we had been unappreciative barbarians. Only after she had gone did it begin to dawn on us that we had behaved rather foolishly.

Ah well, C'est la guerre, as the French used to say.

NOT MENTIONED IN DESPATCHES.
(By E. F. O'SULLIVAN).

FRED, for his inches, was the best head worker in "B" Company. Detailed to a fatigue party which had to carry

30TH BATTALION, A.I.F. ASSOCIATION'S TREE OF REMEMBRANCE

Planted at the Melbourne Shrine by Secretary, H. Rogers (uniform), and Treasurer, D. B. Storey.

ammunition in boxes from "supports" in a sunken road to the front line near Lagnicourt, he wangled as his partner Percy, the heftiest member of the party, who, whom he thought, would bear the brunt of the burden. Fred, however, through being so much shorter, not only carried the load, but in the numerous falls in the mud and slush, due to broken and slippery duckboards and tracks, he was hit first by the "ammo" box and then by Percy. Each time that he was rescued his appearance and language became more foul, his references to Percy and his forbears more personal, and his comments on the army authorities more virulent. But he fairly seethed when "Ricketty", the sergeant in charge, broke the news that the guide was lost and told the party to keep quiet whilst he made a search.

Fred still continued to "pick" on his partner, and the mob, delighted that for once he had crashed, whiled away the time by pouring a little oil on the conflagration. The corporal's efforts to quell the noise were futile and the mob was delighted when the exasperated Fred took a crack at Percy, who, good-tempered like most big chaps, was content to stall and block in the subsequent box-on. This went on until Ricketty returned with the news that the party was in No-Man's Land, it having passed between two of the isolated posts constituting the front line.

The Aussies in the nearest posts, under the impression that there had been a clash between an Aussie and Fritzer patrol, had refrained from interfering, not wanting to wound their cobbers. Jerry, too, had apparently come to the same conclusion.

Fred still uses his head as a solicitor in a southern town in New South Wales.

BAPTISM AT BOIS-GRENIER.

(FROM THE DIARY OF R. E. LORDING).

LEANING against a wall, we are awaiting the major. A few cobbers are giving cheerful advice: "What kind of flowers do you want on your grave, Aussie?" "We'll write and tell 'em what you did in the Great War, Daddy." Yet, there's a "something" dinkum one feels in the air of this soldier's farewell. Here comes the major, he's been enjoying a little party. "Fall in and follow me, gentle flock," he says, and, laughing, we understand.

Walking in single file behind the major, he keeps us well entertained, and shouts us a drink at the last *estaminet*. We soon leave the cultivated fields behind. We are now in the shell-ploughed area, ruined houses and—bang! What was that? Only the bark of an 18-pounder from its cover a few yards away on our left. It silences us for a while. The sharp explosions of occasional whizzbangs become plainer, a large shell gives off much black smoke as it goes "crump!" on our right, and a few of ours whistle overhead. We come to some crossroads, lie back on our packs for a spell, and when the major's cane ceases its devil's tattoo on a cobble-stone it is again time to get on our way.

We are now treading along a duckboard track; the sides of the narrow winding sap are sufficiently high to give us cover. A few bullets sing gently over our heads and the burst of a shell sounds not far away. We have not long passed a support trench when we come to a halt. The word is passed back, "Keep low and run across!" The sap has been blown in. It comes my turn to run. I try to pull my tin hat down over my ears, and make a crouching rush across the open space. The smell of sulphur fumes indicates that the damaging shell has not long since burst. That short run, or perhaps the necessity for it, has quickened my pulse and breathing, and I am uncomfortably out of breath when we come to some sandbag works to left and right.

CONTRIBUTIONS FROM MEMBERS

This is the front line. Here we see three chaps "chatting." One remarks, "Here come the Marmalades!" Another calls, "Look out, Fritz! Here's Tivey's Chocs! Spare me blooming days!" We grin and try and think of a commonplace reply to these veterans of Jacka's Mob (14th Battalion). One of our number finds voice to say, "Hello! Where's this war we've heard about?"

"We've just knocked off for afternoon tea, sorry you're late," replies one of the "chatters," and they all laugh at our antics as a whizz-bang whistles over our heads.

Going to the left we see a notice, "Watson's Bay," which causes our smiles to look and feel more natural. After we cover about 300 yards of the front, two officers greet our major and we know that we have reached the company headquarters of the post. While awaiting instructions we lie back on our packs and watch the shells bursting round an aeroplane. We are debating whether it is one of ours or one of theirs. Whiz-z-z-! Instinct tells us that something solid is approaching from the sky. Smack! We all scramble. I rush into the nearest dug-out and am greeted with "What the Hell's the hurry, Grandpa?" by a signaller, who looks at me as though it was I who had just arrived from the clouds.

"What! Didn't you hear that chunk of shell?" I gasp.

"Cripes! That's nothing. You'll soon get used to that," he answers reassuringly. "If you're taking over C. 17 you've come to the right place. Better drop your pack and put your rifle over there."

He thinks I have "dropped my bundle." I make an effort to hide my fear. I carelessly throw my tin hat into a corner, ask the signaller what part of Aussie he comes from, and try to keep a steady hand as I offer him a cigarette.

"Hey! Look what's here!" he shouts, to wake the corporal on the sandbag bunk.

The corporal gives a grunt, stretches and rubs his eyes.

"What! The War Babies' Brigade! Thank God we've got a navy."

I make a few stinging remarks.

"Good for you," says the signaller, as he makes a bayonet swipe at a rat running near his 'phone. "That's the stuff to give 'im. Here! take a seat and make yourself at home."

"Seems a nice quiet place," I venture.

"Not bad," said the corporal, "till you stir up Fritz's hate."

With some display of indifference I manage to make a few inquiries and learn that except for mending busted cables and doing telephone duty—four hours on and eight off—the signaller's job in this possie is "sweet." The dug-out is almost shrapnel-proof; only a direct hit or a shell-burst near the opening can do any harm. They have not had many casualties. The tucker is pretty good, there is a cook-house in the line. My own observations tell me that rats and chats are numerous, and the smell of the place is anything but sweet.

While the corporal winds his puttees, the signaller gives me instructions how to plug the telephone to H.Q., C. 10, and artillery on their home-made switchboard. He is having a telephone conversation with some signallers of another post on the subject of Tivey's "Chocolates" having arrived at the war, when the corporal calls from outside, "Come on, young'un, I'll take you round the show!"

About ten paces from the dug-out we come to a parapet, and asking, "What's over there?" I step up for a look. I am roughly pulled down and fall in a heap at the corporal's feet.

"You silly young blighter," he says, "do you want to stop some lead? Fritz! That's what's over there. Here! here's a periscope; have a look at No-Man's Land." Then to prove his words and illustrate his meaning, he puts my hat on a stake and holds it over the top. Zip! the first bullet hits the parapet. Ping-g-g! the second ricochets off the target, and my respect for Fritz and tin hats is enhanced.

We visit Pyman's Corner and this inspires the corporal to call me Simon. "Come on, Simon!" he calls when I am trying to add a nosecap to the collection of metal that already fills my pockets, "you'll want a G.S. wagon to carry your souvenirs if you keep that up." We trace the 'phone cable along Sniper's Alley and I learn that the zip-zip-zip-zip! on the sandbags is the shooting of "Parapet Joe." "He's a dabster with the machine-gun," the corporal observes, and I feel that Joe can see us as we go along the sap.

It is almost dark. I keep close behind the corporal as he leads the way back. I have almost convinced myself that I am accustomed to the new surroundings, and am thinking how proud my people would feel if they could see me now when—flash! bang! right near my ear, and I fall flop on the duckboard.

"Ha! ha! ha!" I hear, and, looking up, see a chap preparing to fire another flare. "Ha! ha! That's the idea, sonny, you know how to duck. Ha! ha!"

I regain my feet, but fail to appreciate the joke, and decide that the vital question is to know when, rather than how, one should duck.

But for the moving illumination of flares, it is dark when we arrive back at C. 17. The corporal tells his signaller that I am getting on fine, and he advises an artillery officer sitting on the bunk that I have expressed a wish to go out spotting. That's news to me, but, remembering my resolution not to show any fear, I decide to give it a go, though I know nothing of the job. I am rather reluctant to leave my tin hat, but accept their advice and pull a Balaclava cap over my head.

"No! You won't want your rifle," says the corporal. "Take a bayonet for an earth pin. Here's your 'phone. Be careful where you lay the line."

"Prussian Guards over there," remarks the signaller,

with a grin; "you might collect a souvenir bonnet." He picks up a drum of cable, takes hold of his end and, giving me the drum, says, "Here you are, don't forget to bring it back."

They might have wished a man good luck, I think, as I pay out the cable and endeavour to keep close on the heels of the officer. He comes to a halt, says something to a sentry, and tells me to come on. We crawl through a little opening called a sally-port and, realizing that I am now in No-Man's Land, I follow him and, as far as possible, imitate his every action. I hold my breath and do not so much as move an eyelid when a flare lights up our surroundings. We come to our wire-entanglement, go to the left, and pass through an opening in the maze of wires. Going out half-right along a depression in the ground, I am anxiously trying to calculate the length of cable left on the drum when the glare of a flare temporarily blinding my vision, I stumble and fall into a water-filled shell-hole.

The cold water adds to my shivering condition, and my fingers tremble as I connect the 'phone when we establish ourselves in a shell-hole observation-post. The boss gives me the impression that he has been doing this kind of work all his life. Although he inspires some confidence, I stand at the alert with one eye cocked in the direction of Fritz and my kicking-off foot pointing towards home. The business of our mission seems quite simple. The boss scans the landscape ahead through his glasses, observes what he believes to be Germans mending their trench, and sends a range message to his battery. A shell or two come whizzing over and I can almost swear that I see bits of Fritzes in the flash of the explosion. It is some time before I am able to convince myself that the moving shadows caused by the flares are not a host of Germans. Our little game goes on into the night.

To the left I see a solid-looking figure moving, but am afraid to point it out to the boss in case he thinks I've got the wind up. Then I see two more in the same direc-

CONTRIBUTIONS FROM MEMBERS 295

tion—they seem to be coming towards us. The boss sees them, too, and we crouch down so as just to peep over the edge of our crater. I wish I had my rifle as I see a Fritz in silhouette against the light of a falling flare. But nothing happens. They disappear in the darkness that follows.

I am just beginning to kid myself that I like this game of pilgrims of the night when the time comes to go home. As we make our way back, an occasional burst of machine-gun fire breaks out and a few flares go up. In my endeavour to keep up with the boss I have trouble in rewinding the wire on to the drum, and I am sweating freely by the time we reach the sally-port.

"Thank you, corporal," says my companion of the night, as he presents me with a tin of fags. "Good night!"

The signallers are playing cards when I arrive at the dug-out.

"Well, how'd you like it, Simon?" asks the corporal.

"Oh! not bad—pretty tame," I answer.

"Simon! Struth! Ned Kelly, don't you mean?" remarks a signaller who is a stranger to me.

"Ananias, more like it," chips in the signaller of my acquaintance, and then proceeds to help himself and treat his cobbers to the gift tin of Gold Flake cigarettes I have placed on the table.

I am not slow to accept the corporal's offer of his bunk for a spell, nor is it long before I fall off to sleep.

THE BAPAUME "SPECIAL".
(By J. S. BARTLEY).

THE historic town of Bapaume was entered on St. Patrick's Day, 1917, after the famous patrol led by "Dad" White and Cec. Alcorn had cleared the way. Many jobs fell to the battalion and a week later a working party was detailed in conjunction with Canadian engineers, to repair the per-

manent way and re-lay the railway line from Albert. With
the continued severity of winter and eight to a loaf, the
job was no sinecure, particularly as the German gunners,
directed by a 'plane, were sending over those tall, shiny
steel, penetrating naval shells known to us as "rubber-
jacks."

One bright morning a lengthy and heavily laden train
was observed steaming up from Albert. Eventually it
could not make the grade and pulled up opposite our party
and some French linesmen who were repairing the telegraph
lines. We surmised that this would soon "draw the crabs".
Soon afterwards, another train consisting of an engine and
two luxurious carriages, came up. Its occupants disembarked and proved to be an inspection party of French
military and civil engineers. The former were in gay
uniforms, the latter in top hats and frock coats.

All was now set for the reception, which Fritz did not
fail to provide. While the second engine was pushing and
all hands were busily urging, over came a shell shrieking,
whistling, and roaring. Coming out of the clinch with
mother earth after the crash, we found Fritz had registered
a direct hit on the boiler of the first engine, which was
wrecked in a cloud of steam. It was fortunately a
"dud" and had buried itself in an adjoining bank.

The engine crew, who were badly scalded, were the only
casualties, but can you picture the babel and the panic of
the tourists? There was a wild scramble for the luxury
train and she was despatched *toute de suite* for Albert
with a full head of steam, amid cries of *allez allez, alle-
mand, boche, beaucoup bombard*. Some of the passengers
were left behind in the panic and they executed a war
dance to the amusement of the troops. The linesmen did
not trouble to put a hook into the poles in their descent
to join the exodus.

The "special" was never seen again at Bapaume during
our sojourn there.

THE QUARTER-BLOKE.

(By R. MATHER).

WHEN Sergeant Kenneth Smithers was appointed C.Q.M.S. he set an entirely new standard for the position. He treated all visitors to the quartermaster's store with a novel and unprecedented courtesy. If, for example, one applied for a new pair of boots and he was unable to supply them, he would look down at his own as if regretting that they were not the required size. In due course he would procure the boots, seek out the individual requiring them and deliver them personally. "Service and Satisfaction Guaranteed" seemed to be his motto.

Never was the satisfaction so evident as on the first occasion when he made the acquaintance of "D" Company. Despite the fact that we had been relieved from front-line duty, we were scarcely in an amiable mood. Our gumboots, which had been such a boon in the mud, proved a failure on ice-covered duckboards and, after a mile or two of slipping and sliding and many painful falls, we reached the reserve line nursing a grievance. The rest of the battalion was going out to Nissen huts at Montauban, while "D" Company's term in reserve was to be spent in the cramped dugouts of "Needle Trench."

Fate, however, had a salve in store for our injured feelings. Ken, anxious to make a good impression with his new company, had procured, in a manner which must for ever remain a mystery, a prodigous quantity of rum, and, as the company filed into the trench he took up his position opposite a little dugout which he had chosen as his own and began to issue it.

He was, however, unaware of the fact that this dug-out lay right opposite the centre of a large island traverse. The leaders, on receiving their issue, quickly sized up the situation and, circling the island, rejoined the queue in the rear and so began an endless procession. It was some time before Ken began to suspect that the company was one of unusual strength, but at last he somewhat timidly asked, "What company do you men belong to?" " 'D' Company, of course," came the reply, with a fine show of impatience at having the rum issue delayed. "Dad" Wearne's distinctive cast of countenance nearly spoiled everything, for Ken said presently, in the assured tone of one who is certain of his facts, "You have been here before." "Dad's" indignant denials would have been of no avail but for the weight of corroborative evidence from the rear and the assurances, in most emphatic, if impolite language, that "Dad", like themselves, had just arrived from the front line.

As he got towards the last of the rum, Ken cast an anxious eye on the endless line of men and now and then he estimated the weight of the fluid in the jar. At last, in desperation, he said, "Wait a moment," and disappeared into the dug-out. "Gawd! he's gone to put water into it," commented one fellow mournfully. This was exactly what he had done—we learned later that he had emptied his water-bottle into the jar.

When the supply came to an end and the last issue was served out, Ken received the surprise of his life, for instead of the hostility he had expected, he received a cheer from the crowd, who gathered round and explained the situation to him. Ken joined in the laugh against himself, and the company, now in singing mood, sang "For he's a jolly good fellow."

Later Ken received his commission, and fell at Ypres in 1917.

THE LE TRANSLOY GHOST.
(By J. S. BARTLEY).

No-Man's Land, in the Le Transloy sector, on a certain bitterly cold winter's night late in December, 1916, lay deeply buried in snow, the only beautiful thing about the

CONTRIBUTIONS FROM MEMBERS 299

place. Even that was being separated and blasted under the pernicious influence of a heavy double bombardment, ourselves and Fritz exchanging greetings by means of Stokes, "flying pigs," *minenwerfers* and "pineapple" bombs. The hour was midnight, and the whole place was an inferno. Flares, like beautiful elongated flowers, rose as if by magic, soaring high over the havoc, to fall spluttering and expiring in the snow.

At 2 a.m. both bombardments ceased as suddenly as they had commenced. Our raid took place and then a deep and profound silence fell on No-Man's Land, upon which a heavy frost was settling.

All France was frozen, and myriads of icicles hung down the side of the trench like so many ghostly fingers pointing out a warning of some hidden, impending calamity. I chanced to be the sentry on the post, and was occupied in turning over our stock of Mills bombs, to prevent them from freezing hard and fast, when suddenly some unexplained warning, some kind of instinct, compelled me to peer into No-Man's Land for a presence of which I was conscious, yet unable definitely to locate.

I could discover nothing to justify my curiosity, but a few seconds later my line of vision was caught by something which I shudderingly contemplated with unabated amazement and increasing horror, and also with a kind of protesting incredulity.

Admittedly I was startled, for creeping across my front there now appeared some mystifying unearthly thing, possessing neither shape nor form, developing into a shadow as it faded ghost-like into the night. This was ominous, if not supernatural, so summoning up courage I aroused the post, and we all stood-to-arms in various states of expectancy, as we had now reached a state of apprehension and fear. A startled cry from the trench was an indication that our mutual friend, the ghost, was about to pay a return visit.

There it was out in the snow, creeping along with transitory movements, and as we watched the Thing come closer, it merged into a series of moving legs, without bodies, and these legs moved as if seeking their dismembered bodies in the charnel house of No-Man's Land. Then as the apparition receded, it once again merged into a shadow, and vanished into its ghostly sepulchre, accompanied by the eerie shriek of a "whizz-bang" as a kind of death knell.

What Devil's spawn was abroad that night we could not guess, but, with its departure, the general impression was that we had all seen a ghost and that No-Man's Land was certainly haunted. If Fritzy saw the spook he certainly made no manifestation of being sensitive to the dread of the ghostly trespasser, and for that matter, neither had we.

We all returned to earth with the coming of daylight, when the dignity of the post fell to zero upon our learning the simple explanation of the phenomenon. Without our knowledge, our patrol had been abroad, and for the first time they were partly camouflaged in white. The omission to whiten their trousers and puttees created a fantastic effect as they moved along in the snow. Had the patrol been fully camouflaged, the chances are that they would never have been detected, and the joke would certainly never had been on the post.

In fairness to us on the post, I must say that not one of us had partaken, liberally or otherwise, of any S.R.D., and that we were all in our sober senses.

A DUD JOKE.
(By R. MATHER).

IT was mid-winter and No. 16 Platoon, recently relieved from the line, lay in their blankets around the sides of a Nissen bow-hut. They were dirty, unkempt, and unutterably weary with a weariness that was more than physical. Paddy Murphy alone remained by the brazier as if reluctant to leave its dying embers. I was a great admirer of Paddy as one admires those whose deeds of valour they may never hope to emulate, or those who have suffered in a great cause, for he had "Done his stretch for stoushing Johns." The fire flickered fitfully and cast its rosy radiance on his unusually thoughtful features.

"What's up, Murphy?" sang out Bob Goldie. "Are you working your nut to try to get out of it?"

"No," said Paddy, startled out of his reverie. "To tell you the truth, I was trying to figure out how the hell I got here."

At that moment the door flew open and a biting blast swept the hut from end to end. The cry of shut that —— door died in our throats as there entered the immaculate Captain Cheeseman, O.C., "D" Company, followed by Jim Hunt. "Bluey's" rubicund features were wreathed in smiles. He advanced towards the centre of the hut and began a lecture on his pet subject, *esprit-de-corps*. The morale of his beloved company was slipping, and he was attempting to fan the remaining sparks of our regimental pride into a blaze.

Intent on his task, he failed to notice that McDermott had risen behind him and was busily engaged in writing something on the back of the door. Fearful lest he should turn round and spoil the joke, which we felt sure was afoot, those of us facing "Bluey" assumed an attitude of rapt attention. "It is the pride of the Guard's division that 24 hours after they leave the line, they are ready to be inspected by anybody," he went on earnestly.

As he was about to leave the hut he turned to one side and spoke to someone, Jim Hunt threw the door wide-open and waited for the O.C. to precede him. Thus a whale of a joke was inadvertently spoilt, for on the door Mac. had written in large round hand:

> "The toad beneath the harrow knows
> Exactly where each tooth point goes.
> The butterfly upon the road
> Preaches contentment to the toad."

ONE WAY OF GETTING A RUM RATION.
(By W.A.T.).

I was dumped out of the leave train at Albert about dusk in mid-May, 1917, to find that the battalion was somewhere in front of Bapaume. As there were numerous lorries going in that direction, getting to Bapaume presented no difficulty; that of finding the battalion was resolutely put aside when I came across some old friends in the 4th Motor Transport Company, who fed and put me up for the night. After the evening meal the railway supply officer strolled in and was formally introduced. He look at my purple and gold (not blue and yellow) colour patches and began to laugh. On my inquiring the cause of his mirth he told the following story.

"A large dump of cases of rum had been established near his hut, and, of course, a sentry was put on guard over such a valuable cargo. The man was a Tommy, and conscientious. One day the R.S.O. overheard some Diggers, whom he now knew by my colour patches to have belonged to the 30th Battalion, asking the sentry to be a sport and look the other way while they obtained a little rum for their stomach's sake. The sentry indignantly refused. To the great surprise of the R.S.O., the Diggers went away without making any unseemly remarks, but gathered together again near his hut in earnest conversation. Wondering what was in the wind, he returned to the hut in time to overhear the last part of the conversation, which was, 'Oh, he'll never stop to look.'

"Away the Diggers went. Presently a Mills bomb was heard to explode some distance away, but near enough for some fragments to whistle high over the sentry's head, while at the same time another bomb, with the pin left in, rolled at his feet. He saw it coming, and vanished in quick time. Almost as quickly two Diggers with purple and gold patches also vanished, each carrying a case of rum."

"They had earned it, I thought," said the R.S.O., "for they certainly showed initiative."

CONTRIBUTIONS FROM MEMBERS

OEUF DANS LE CHAPEAU.
(By NOTRE BON AMI).

ONE day in a Flemish village we came across a group of children playing with a tennis ball. As they had no organised game, we introduced the art of playing egg-in-the-hat.

Immediate success, shrieks of laughter, terrible din; out came the *estaminet* Madame to see what was going on. Very interested was Madame, and she wanted to join the game.

But alas! The only "tit for tat" that Madame possessed was a faded sunbonnet. She was therefore advised to get some utensil of a more rigid nature.

Pourquoi pas, said Madame, and inside she rushed to return quite unabashed with a china vessel commonly associated with bedrooms.

A PRESENTIMENT.
(By L. COLWELL).

I HAD been "packing" to the line for three consecutive nights during the Passchendaele stunt in September, 1917, and was settling down to enjoy a night's rest when Gordon Scragg, who was going up to the line, came and asked me to take charge of his wallet and photographs, which in the event of anything happening to him (as he felt sure it would) he desired to be sent to the address given in the wallet. While trying to laugh him out of this mood and assure him that he would come through all right, I was myself, at the last moment detailed to accompany the "pack train". As Gordon persisted that he would not return from the night's job, I told him to leave his possessions in the keeping of "Jim", the section cook.

There were about a dozen of us in the "train", and on our way forward we were diverted to the switch road behind Ypres, which brought us out at Hell-Fire Corner.

Just as we reached that well-named and ill-famed spot Fritz commenced shelling the 60-pounders on the right of the road and one shell landed among us. "Tony" O'Connor, who was leading, was blown about twenty feet off the road into a shell-hole, from which he emerged unhurt but full of profanity and willingness to fight every —— Fritz gunner in France. I had been following him, my packhorse being "Old Bill", who at one time belonged to the O.C. of "C" Company, and was one of the finest walers that ever left New South Wales. Two of his legs were shattered and he was torn from flank to shoulder, as though a giant rake had been drawn along his underside. To put him out of his misery I got a British officer from the 60-pounder battery to shoot him, and with a heavy heart and a shrapnel splinter in my finger I returned to the horse-lines at Dickebusch.

All that I had seen when the shell burst were sparks on the cobbled roadway, men hanging on to frightened, plunging horses and trying to quieten them, and "Tony" O'Connor flying into the shell-hole; but when the roll was called it was found that Gordon Scragg's presentiment had come true. It was a saying among us Diggers that "you never heard the shell which was to get you." I wonder if poor old Gordon heard it.

MUSIK.
(By WAL SMITH).

On the morning of 28th September, 1917, we were called to arms by "Papa" Eugene O'Sullivan, who in no uncertain voice was lustily calling *Kamerad*, and through the mist we saw waves of grey uniforms climbing out of the ground.

Evidently "Sully" must have made some arrangement with the enemy, for they took to us most affectionately and we were fortunate enough to secure a bag of approximately 80 prisoners.

MAKING AND PACKING COMFORTS FOR MEN OF THE BATTALION

LEFT TO RIGHT: *Standing*: Mrs. Denham, Mrs. Allen, Miss Flower, Miss Mitchell, Mrs. J. W. Clark.
LEFT TO RIGHT: *Sitting*: Mrs. Stinson, Mrs Payten, Miss Fry, Miss Denham, Miss N. Sloan.
FOREGROUND: *Sitting*: Mrs. R. H. Beardsmore.

A.W.M. Photo. No. H16131.

The whole of No. 7 Platoon went into No-Man's Land and welcomed the little strangers in. We were soon joined by such stalwarts as the late C.S.M. Joe McGowen and Sergeant Bob Estelle, and we spent a very interesting quarter of an hour receiving tokens of esteem from our square-head friends, much to the annoyance of Lieutenant Williams, who threatened us with all sorts of summary punishment.

Presently Bob Estelle's keen optics lighted upon a brilliantly tabbed Fritzie uniform. Turning to me, he said, "Wal, this basket is a b——y general." Having visions of a glorified colour chart, or a nice "cushie" job at headquarters, we decided to apply the intelligence test, but were beaten from the commencement, as the only two languages we knew were trench French and the mother tongue. We decided to take a risk on the latter. Bob in his best Australian said: "Are you a general?" The Fritz, drawing from his pocket a mouth organ (something we had missed whilst going through him), played us a few stirring bars and then replied: "Me musik."

THE WRONG SIDE OF THE PILL-BOX.
(By Capt. A. C. WHITE).

OUT in front of Bailleul and almost on the Franco-Belgian border is a village which saw a good deal of the 30th Battalion towards the end of 1917 and early 1918. Some of the signboards averred that the name was Neuve Eglise, while others, apparently to avoid confusion, bore the inscription Nieuw Kerke.

Proceeding hence towards the line for a mile or two, one came to a collection of huts, heaps of bricks, and various remnants of houses incapable of use as fuel—according to the map this was Wulverghem, a most salubrious spot if you like, its beauty enhanced by a few gaunt, limbless trees scarred by much shell-fire. This was the position for the reserve battalion of the brigade holding the sector from Wytschaete Ridge to the River Douve further south. Beyond this again was a trench system accommodating the headquarters of the battalion on the right of the brigade front, in this case the 30th. Its reserve company was stationed near by at Bethlehem Farm (although all vestige of the "farm" had been most effectively obliterated). Close handy was an old German "pill-box" used as a cookhouse. Here meals for the front-line companies were prepared in the early morning and late afternoon, subsequently being delivered to the line in two-gallon petrol tins packed in sawdust containers—these, it might be said in passing, were most efficient contrivances indeed.

One uneventful afternoon was enlivened when enemy observers spotted smoke from the cooking operations in and about the pill-box. A period of comparative quietness was suddenly broken by the crash of heavy shells about the cook-house, which, having been built by Fritz, naturally, had its entrance on the "wrong" side from the point of view of the occupants. A very close shot blocked the doorway with a big bank of earth, imprisoning the faithful cooks, and also Lieutenant Whipp, of "B" Company, who happened to be paying a visit at the time.

The company at Bethlehem Farm watched the shelling with languid interest—they were not directly concerned, as their meal was not in jeopardy, and it was usually considered that unless a lucky shot penetrated the ground at the right angle, and burst underneath the pill-box, the tenants thereof were quite safe. In between the crashes, voices from the pill-box could be heard raised in song—under the baton of "Conductor" Whipp the imprisoned troops were whiling away the time with a little community singing. The bombardment eventually ceased, and a delegation sauntered over from the farm to assess the damage. In deference to urgent requests from those inside, shovels were procured, and Lieutenant Whipp and his fellow choristers were soon liberated.

The only casualties were several badly holed dixies, but substitutes were soon provided, and the boys in the line received their hot meal as usual as soon as darkness made it possible for the carrying parties to go forward.

"SCOTS WHA HAE."
(By R. MATHER).

THERE is a tide in the affairs of war which, if taken at the flood, leads to victory. That Sir Douglas Haig believed this tide to be at the flood became apparent early in September, 1918, when he issued orders that in all future attacks each unit was to push on to the limits of its power regardless of the position on its flank. The order ended with this significant sentence: "Risks which hitherto would have been criminal must now be incurred as a duty."

Lieutenant Bert Wells, O.C., "D" Company, and his second-in-command, Lieutenant J. J. Witton Flynn, appear to have come to the same conclusion some time in advance of the commander-in-chief. They led the right attacking company of the battalion in the attack on 27th August, 1918, which led to the capture of Foucaucourt and the advancing of our line beyond Estrees. As darkness fell Wells was supervising the consolidation of his newly-captured position while Flynn was similarly occupied half-a-mile distant. Dave Rattray volunteered to reconnoitre on the exposed flank of Wells' half-company, and set out alone in the darkness armed only with a revolver. It was a hazardous task.

"But little fear waked in his mind
For he was bred of martial kind."

Midway across the gap Dave encountered a party of Argyll and Sutherland Highlanders, under the command of a Lieutenant Galbraith. Finding themselves out of touch, they had taken up a defensive position facing the enemy, and no doubt Dave's appearance was doubly welcome as he was a brither Scot. "I was having a great old yarn to them," Dave explained later, "when Fritz handed us some 'iron rations' and smashed the officer's thigh." After attending to his wounds Dave pushed on, promising to send help as quickly as possible, and soon discovered the whereabouts of Lieutenant Flynn's half-company.

He notified Dan Lynn (another native of Glesca), and a company stretcher-bearer of the Scottish officer's plight. Dan tossed his stretcher on to the parados and leapt after it, to receive a wound that crippled him for life. George Gott and I were the next to be summoned. We placed the badly wounded officer on a stretcher and told four of the Jocks to be ready to follow us when we had attended to Dan Lynn. I approached Lieutenant Flynn and asked for two more men to complete our stretcher party. He was badly worried and now found himself in command of a much larger section of the Western Front than he could ever, even in his wildest dreams, have hoped to command. After a slight hesitation he detailed Tom Storey and Gavin to accompany us.

"How do you lift it?" asked the Jocks, looking helplessly at their stretcher. I replied in language that can't be written here, and the officer interposed the explanation that this was their first night in the line, that they were only boys, and added, "It's a damned shame, the mark of the school bag is still on their backs." In the darkness I had failed to observe their youthfulness. They called for a spell three times in the first quarter of a mile. Everything was quiet, but we had no guarantee that it would remain so. I explained this to them and also that the changing from the heavy end to the light end of the stretcher with its momentary relaxation was all the relief that was required.

"I suppose you are real Scotsmen," I taunted them. "If you are, you have something better in you than you have shown us yet, and if you have any sand in your craw now is the time to show it." It was a mile and a half over

CONTRIBUTIONS FROM MEMBERS 309

fallen tree trunks, ditches, trenches, and barbed-wire, to the 8th Field Ambulance dressing station, but they never again asked for a spell. The aid-post was in a brick tunnel and there we rested for a while. As the relay bearers approached to take over, Lieutenant Galbraith beckoned to me and, as he was being borne away, said: "I want to thank you, Aussie, for all that you fellows have done for us, and for the way you have looked after my boys." I shall never forget the look of amazement in his eyes when I replied in my broadest Scotch, put on for the occasion: "That's a'richt, we're a Jock Tamson's bairns."

THE BOX OF TRICKS.
(By Lieut. T. S. C. HORGAN).

It was the time when the battalion was in reserve in front of Corbie, and headquarters occupied what had been a "shooting box," consisting of two floors, both on ground level on account of the steep slope of the hill on which it stood. The lower, and safer floor was used as the mess and as the quarters of the C.O. and adjutant, etc., while the upper floor was shared by the R.M.O., Major John Wells, and myself.

The second night we were there Wells came in in great glee, followed by his batman and another man carrying a box-mattress which they had "souvenired" from a house in Corbie. Wells was easily the most fastidious man I met during my four odd years of active service. He had originally served with the light horse in Palestine, transferring to the infantry in France during the latter part of 1917. I invariably shared a dug-out with him when the battalion was in reserve and we became close friends, though it is true that he did his best to asphyxiate me on many occasions owing to his inability to occupy a dug-out without burning in it a "flare" or two to kill (or, at any rate, stupify) any parasitic "left overs" from the previous tenants. This process, on account of the absence of through draughts always left in the confined space a pungent tang that clung to it for days. However, Doc. Wells considered that it was worth while, and it gave him peace of mind, anyway.

But to return to the mattress. Wells crowed about his find, harping on the peaceful and comfortable night he was destined to spend, lulled into the arms of Morpheus by the gentle support of those springs which doubtless had served some uxorious Frenchman. My valise on the floor was good enough for me, anyway, and I dropped off to sleep to the accompaniment of sighs of contentment from Wells.

At 3 a.m. I woke to hear some pretty nifty cursing going on and, having shaken the sleep from my eyes, was amazed to see Wells, stark naked, picking brown objects off divers portions of his anatomy.

"What the hell....!" I ejaculated, and Wells growled, "Look at these b...b... bugs." I looked, and, having looked, roared with laughter, for he was literally covered with bugs, many of which had obviously tried to make up for the absence of "eats" from which they had suffered for so long. He had evidence of bites in plenty.

Between us we heaved the mattress outside and Wells spent the rest of the night scratching himself and giving me the itch too! In the morning an inspection proved that the mattress, which opened like a box, sheltered in its interstices thousands of flat starved-looking bugs, and I was surprised that Wells hadn't noticed the characteristic odour of the filthy things. (We used to become quite attached to "chats" on service, but bugs, ugh!)

That mattress with the remaining tenants went up in smoke, but many a leg-pull did Doc. Wells suffer. For a time I called him "Lousy", and this never failed to get a "bite", since he prided himself so on his cleanliness. (He used to wear his hair, which grew *en brosse*, close clipped, in case!!)

Poor Wells! I last saw him when he emptied the contents of a bottle of iodine into my forearm in a vain attempt to save that limb, and he ticked me off for puffing cigarette smoke into his face as he dressed the wound. He was killed next day, and the world was a poorer place from then on.

"BAD NEWS" FROM THE DIVISIONAL COMMANDER.

(By Capt. A. C. WHITE).

ONE of the "lousiest" sectors that men of the 30th Battalion ever donned gum-boots in was that delightful stretch of country, having as its right flank the River Douve, and enjoying the "advantage" (as the estate agents say) of being under direct observation from the famous Warneton tower. This well-known German observation post was somewhere opposite the divisional boundary; at this particular time the 3rd Division was on our right, across the Douve. To apply the term "river" to this doublet of water in a shallow valley full of mud was plainly ridiculous; still, it was so marked on the map. At certain intervals at night, patrols from the left company of the 3rd Division slithered across to our nearest post, and now and again we returned their calls.

In those winter months of 1917-18 darkness fell soon after 4.30 p.m., and morning mists and fogs were so frequent that visibility was often bad till after 10 a.m. This left approximately six and a half hours out of each twenty-four which the troops were free to spend in sleep and recreation. Just after being relieved by the 31st Battalion news went round the 30th that a raid was to be made on the German posts, roughly opposite the centre of the right company front of the 8th Brigade. "B" Company was in due course flattered to learn that the job was to be entrusted to them, and Lieutenants "Sandy" Bragg and "Bill" Hanlon, becoming convinced of the attractiveness of the idea, signified their willingness to assist. A complete raiding party volunteered, and for the next few evenings active patrolling was carried out by them in order to ensure that everyone became thoroughly acquainted with the enemy machine-gun and trench-mortar positions that were marked down for special attention by our artillery on the night of the raid.

As was usual in these cases, the 31st Battalion holding the line were vastly amused at the idea of some other crowd patrolling their front for them, and as it was of course necessary to get their permission every night before we went out "prospecting," we had to put up with a good deal of "mud-slinging," not always completely concealed by a very thin veneer of politeness. (Writing from memory I think it quite possible that "Bobby" Aland and Fred Drayton would remember something about this). However, final plans for the operation were drawn up and although the actual night for the stunt had not been fixed, it was felt by all concerned that it was not too far ahead.

The 30th was in reserve about Wulverghem, and one afternoon, as Sergeants Barrett and Wal. Smith were getting some of the raiding party together for the night's patrol work, General Hobbs arrived, and shortly afterwards I was sent for. General Hobbs greeted me thus: "Well, White, I've got bad news for you." I was commencing to register deep concern, as the thought flashed through my mind: "Good Lord, the raid must be on to-night." But the General went on to explain that the sole object of the raid had been to secure identification of the German division fronting us, and that several prisoners taken the previous night had provided the necessary information. "As I don't believe in raiding, just for the sake of raiding, your show will not now take place." This, of course, put a new complexion on things altogether, and, after suitably expressing my "deep regret,"

I withdrew to break the "bad news" to the remainder of the party.

Certain preparations had been made in order that the contemplated happy issue of the raid should be suitably celebrated, and, under the circumstances, it was decided that even if the raid had misfired, there was no reason whatever why the celebrations should be cancelled. So it came about that late into the evening the bosky wooded dells of Wulverghem echoed with boisterous approval of the divisional commander's "bad news."

THE INTENTION WAS GOOD.
(By R. MATHER).

IT was mid-afternoon on Ludendorff's "Black Day"—August 8th, 1918. The 5th Australian Division had reached the final objective on its whole front, and we of the 30th Battalion were in high spirits.

Considering the depth to which the enemy's positions had been overrun, we stretcher-bearers had had a remarkably easy day. After rendering first-aid to the wounded we had marked their position and left them to be picked up by the ambulance men following us.

Suddenly the familiar cry of "Stretcher-bearers, Stretcher-bearers" was heard. One of our boys, Peter Harrower, had just been hit in both heels by shrapnel. Ken Dunn, Ernie Pocket, George Gott, and myself comprised the stretcher party, and as each step now was a step nearer Aussie for Peter, we put our best feet forward.

The battalion aid-post had been established in a German casualty clearing station, and we reached there in time to see it hit by a 5.9, which killed the doctor and injured some of his staff. Deciding to push on to some other aid-post, we sighted one in a sunken road a mile or so further on but again, were just in time to see it receive a direct hit.

We stayed just long enough to see that there were enough survivors to attend to the wounded. We then plodded on rearwards, and it was a tired stretcher party that sighted an ambulance waggon by the roadside half-an-hour later. As we drew near, other stretcher-bearers could be seen loading it. They had already placed two stretchers inside, when we walked straight up to the rear of the waggon and deposited Peter in one of the vacant spaces. A storm of protest followed from our left, and on looking round we saw quite a number of other cases waiting their turn in a disused quarry. An A.M.C. warrant-officer came out, and I explained the situation to him. The doors were closed and the waggon drove off, and we congratulated ourselves on having given our patient a flying start homewards.

Eleven years later I learned from Peter for the first time that, having gone so far on his journey without skilled attention, the fact that he had not received an anti-tetanus injection escaped notice until the malady had him in its deadly grip, and a long uphill fight ensued to save his life.

Truly it's an evil road that is paved with good intentions.

MORLANCOURT—AND AN UNOFFICIAL ARMISTICE.

(By R. MATHER).

SOMETIME in July, 1918, "D" Company recently relieved, after a tour of front line duty in the Morlancourt sector, heard the joyful news that the battalion would be going out for a rest, and a touch of realism was added when "blanco" was issued. "Spit and polish" was the order of the day, and industrious N.C.O's. hurried to and fro accepting nominations for the various sporting events soon to take place far from war's alarms somewhere in a back area.

As darkness fell, however, a feeling of sadness came over the company when we learned that we were to move

CONTRIBUTIONS FROM MEMBERS 315

forward immediately to support the 29th Battalion in an attack at Morlancourt. We learned that an advance of 600 yards was contemplated—not far enough to capture even the trench-mortars—and that the artillery support available would be limited, as another attack by the 14th Brigade in the vicinity of Sailly-Laurette, was due to begin soon after ours. The members of "D" Company, which was commanded by Captain Barbour, were not enthusiastic as they moved up, for they felt they had been tricked into a "buckshee" stunt. Fortunately, they were not called upon to take part in the actual assault, their role being to occupy the front line as soon as the 29th hopped over and to supply carrying parties, etc.

Less than a minute after "zero" the familiar call of "stretcher-bearers" was heard—as things turned out the 29th suffered heavily, and it was not until sixteen hours later that the last of the wounded were brought in. One of the trench-mortar battery was the first to fall. George Gott and I were the regular bearers of Nos. 15 and 16 Platoons and having dressed his wounds, I approached Lieutenant Hamilton and asked for two additional men to complete the stretcher party. He detailed Privates W. Player and W. McDermott, men whose courage had been often tried and proved. Both were irrepressible humorists, and ideal mates for the ordeal which lay ahead.

The 29th had established a relay post as close as possible to the line, and from here the wounded continued their journey on wheels. For the first hour after the German S.O.S. went up the enemy shelling was continuous and heavy, but the attack by the 14th Brigade caused a lull. Equally dangerous if less nerve-racking to the stretcher parties was the period at the dawn of day, for Fritz was "windy" and kept up a deadly fire from rifles and machine-guns. When daylight arrived, however, he allowed us to work unmolested.

It was on this morning that I met the youngest German soldier I ever met. The ground between our old front line and the new one was strewn with wounded Germans, and as each stretcher party passed them their pleading was pitiful—although their language was not understood the look of entreaty in their eyes was unmistakable. My feeling for them was one of pity, but our own wounded had to be attended to first. As daylight broke I passed a German whose extremely youthful appearance caused me to look back. *Vater, Vater, Vater,* he pleaded. I handed him my water-bottle, and as he drank I thought it was only the uniform that conveyed the impression of manhood.

"How old are you?" I asked, scarcely expecting a reply.

"Fourteen," he replied.

"Oh, that be damned."

He produced his paybook, which gave the date of his birth as 3rd August, 1903.

"Is Germany so badly up against it that she sends her schoolboys here?"

I liked the way he replied, quick and straight his voice ringing with a pride he scorned to conceal, "I volunteered."

"Where did you learn to speak English?"

He answered in a quaint sort of way as if he were reading from a text-book. "I was educated at Hamburg and I learned to speak English there."

"Is your mother alive?"

"I have a mother and three sisters."

"All right, my boy, you'll see them again if I can fix it for you."

But I was in a difficulty. Duty and sympathy had clashed. I looked round for a rifle and bayonet amid the debris, intending to mark his position, but fate solved the problem for me. Just at that moment I saw not far distant a party of the 29th escorting prisoners to the rear. I called them over, improvised a litter from their overcoats, and had the satisfaction of seeing the boy bid farewell to the war.

It is seldom that amid the stark horror of war one experiences a real adventure, but a thrill was in store for us. Nearing mid-day we arrived at the front line, to find that there were no more wounded to be cleared except those who lay out in No-Man's Land, which was extremely narrow at this point. It appeared that a covering party had been thrown out in front in a semi-circle to protect the men consolidating the newly-captured trench, and that as they hurriedly withdrew at daybreak several wounded had been unable to return. It seemed to be taken for granted that these men would have to remain out unaided until after dark.

"Were their exact positions known?" we asked. We were shown two of them by the aid of a periscope which, incidentally, was the first periscope I had seen since the far off days of 1916 at Armentieres. We debated whether it was necessary to leave them until dark, as all wounded already evacuated from the front line had been carried out in full view of the enemy. What reason was there to suppose that he would not allow us to go a step further and complete the job.

It was decided that two men would be enough to try it out. The 29th produced a large red-cross flag, the first I had ever seen in the front line. I took the flag and McDermott the stretcher, and together we leapt over the parapet. A shot whistled past our ears almost at once. Often on patrol at night while standing stock-still in the glare of a Verey light I had heard a bullet pass equally close, though always with the comforting knowledge that ere another could be fired I would find refuge in the grass under cover of the darkness. On this occasion, however, there was nothing for it but to brazen it out and trust to providence. And providence was kind, for the enemy fired at us no more.

Getting a man on to the stretcher we carried him to the parapet, handed him over to others, and then returned to the job with another stretcher. When all but one of the wounded had thus been brought in, and we were within a few paces of him, another rifle-shot rang out and a bullet passed high over our heads. It was a warning that it would have been folly to ignore, so we resorted to a subterfuge. Dropping at once to our knees in the long grass, we pretended to be dressing a wounded man. While attempting to get closer to the Digger without being discovered I raised my eyes and was startled to see how close to Fritzy's line we had come. I looked at the line of sullen but interested spectators. I then stood up and by means of signs invited them to come out and rescue two of their own wounded who lay close at hand in the grass.

Presently a German N.C.O. sprang from the trench. He was well over six feet in height and built in proportion, a surly fellow with a poker face, none of the muscles of which moved in answer to my welcoming grin. I was disappointed in him. We were only a few paces apart, and had he shown any signs of friendliness I should have liked to shake hands with him, but, owing to his tremendous size and forbidding cast of countenance, I felt that distance, even a little of it, lent enchantment. He gave a gruff command, and some German stretcher-bearers appeared and so all the wounded were spared the ordeal of a long summer afternoon in No-Man's Land.

A VISIT TO GERMANY.
(By TOSH RIDLEY).

My last war experience was at Fromelles, where so many of my mates went west. Of my section of eight men who started to carry stores to the troops in the front line, five of us got through and did our little bit towards building up some kind of cover in the slimy ditches. Shortly after daybreak and just before we were surrounded, I was badly hit and for a time remained unconscious. When I came to my senses, I was alone and felt very sick and weak from loss of blood. I laid in a shell hole all day and towards evening started to crawl towards what I thought was our front line. I made very little progress, but on the following day as I was nearing a parapet of some kind, a German officer hailed me. He said, "Have you been out there all this time?" and I said, "Yes." He was a decent sort and told me that he had been in New Zealand for some years; he gave me a drink and a cigarette, and advised me to rest until a prisoners' escort picked me up. I was taken to Lille, where I spent the night in great pain. On the following day I was taken to a prisoners' hospital in Douai, where I remained until late in November. I was operated on several times and despite the dirty bandages and casual treatment to which the patients were subjected, I managed to recover and was sent to a prison camp at Ingolstad, where I was put to work and almost starved. I chummed with a 29th man named Vic Waite, and after we could stand our treatment no longer, decided to make a bid for liberty. We took the bold step of walking past the guard room as though we were going about our ordinary work, and got clean away. We crawled through a wire fence unnoticed, and after a time reached a forest, where we spent the night perched in a tree. We were very hungry and on the following morning decided to approach a farm house which we could see in the distance. We hid behind a hedge and were uncertain what to do, when fortunately the family—an old man, an old woman, and two children—came out of the house and walked towards a field. This was our chance; we rushed into the kitchen and were surprised to find lumps of pork, loaves of bread, and a stew simmering on the stove. We stuffed the pork and bread into our shirts, and emptied the stew into a kind of bucket and got away before the family returned. We spent that day and night in the forest, and after enjoying the good food, set out for Holland.

We dodged along for two days and were making good progress when we came upon a river, which apparently was being patrolled, and we were caught. We were each awarded 90 days' cells, and when our sentence expired, my mate Vic was sent to a camp near Berlin, and I was sent to Bavaria. At a later date I made another attempt to escape, but failed miserably and received another 90 days. I was classed as a bad character and given no further chance to escape, so I settled down and waited patiently for the wonderful day that eventually arrived, and I realised that I was free. When I entered Germany I weighed 11 stone; when I arrived in England I was down to 6 stone 10 lbs.

VIN ROUGE.

(By R. MATHER).

IT took place in broad daylight when the battalion was in the line between Hamel and Villers-Bretonneux. "Billy" Player, one of the company runners, having delivered a message to B.H.Q. in Hamelet, visited several of the village cellars and sampled various wines therein. This had an exhilarating effect, and turned Bill's thoughts to his less fortunate comrades in the line. From the window of the abandoned local chemist's shop he salvaged a gigantic glass vessel—some idea of its size can be gauged from the fact that its stopper was as thick as a man's wrist, and the vessel filled a chaff-bag. Having filled it with *vin rouge*, Bill next salvaged a push-bike. How he mounted it and started off will never be known. We first sighted a cyclist see-sawing across the road with a large load on his back and the end of a chaff-bag held firmly in his teeth. There was some shelling going, but Providence was kind. Bill got safely through and set the wine in triumph on the parapet. It was at this point that Lieutenant "Bert" Wells took a hand in the game. He detailed an N.C.O. to issue it out in such a way as to prevent any drunkenness and ensure that the war continued to be decently conducted.

CONTRIBUTIONS FROM MEMBERS

WAR IN RETROSPECT.

(By R. MATHER).

It is a curious coincidence that nearly every pair of brothers who served in "D" Company were parted by death.

"Wally" Smith lost a brother at Fromelles. Opposite the convent wall Cecil Dykes (of Kendall) was killed instantaneously by a sniper's bullet, while his brother Ernie carried on to the finish.

At Messines "Bob" Lewitz (of Wagga) was seriously wounded and had only partially recovered in "Blighty" when he succumbed to an attack of the deadly Spanish 'flu which was raging at the time. "Coon" Lewitz survived till the end.

"Paddy" and "Jimmy" Severs, fine types of Australian manhood, took part in a raid at Morlancourt in June, 1918, and, as far as I know, "Paddy" was never seen again, nor was his fate discovered. Jimmy and I carried a stretcher together after the raid and the fact that he was suffering all the agony of uncertainty did not deter him from helping others.

At Proyart Corporal "Davy" Hutton and Private "Bill" Curnow lay down to sleep. For them it was the sleep that knows no waking. Billy Hutton lived to return to Australia. (Curnow's brother, who served with the 13th Battalion, was mortally wounded at Anzac in August, 1915). At the same place on the following day young "Snowy" Wilson received a wound which caused him to be invalided home, and almost at the same moment his brother Jack was mortally wounded.

During our second Somme campaign the N.C.O's. of "D" Company suffered heavily. Sergeants Frank Curran, Peter Holder, and Dan McLellan were numbered with the slain. And in the very last stunt Sergeant Norman Gulson received a wound from which he died, leaving brother Eric to come home alone.

Both the Hartley brothers survived the war, but Wal.
perished in the Bellbird mining disaster soon afterwards
along with another of the 30th named Griffin. It was in
this disaster that "Jimmy" Self, who had also served with
the old battalion, distinguished himself in a vain but glorious attempt at rescue, with all that noble self-sacrifice which
is the miner's birthright.

We boast not of slaughter, nor praise war's deadly game
But those, who a tyrant did check,
Who fought not for glory, or honour, or fame,
But the tide of ambition and conquest to stem,
And died for humanity's sake.

While the waratah still shall adorn our hills,
    Or the wattle wave yellow in bloom;
While the fragrance of nature in dewdrops distils
Or the music of freedom is heard in our rills,
    Shall the laurel be green on their tomb.

While the sweet native roses yield their perfume,
    Or Beauty our poets inspire;
While the national symbol shall shed its red bloom
Or liberty kneel at the patriot's tomb,
    Shall their fame be a theme for the lyre.

While the ravage of winter shall nature deform,
    Or wrap her all lonely in gloom;
While the spirit that rides in his chariot of storm,
Or the dire threat of slaughter the nations alarm,
    Shall their laurels be vernal in bloom.

A PICKWICKIAN RIDE.
(By Capt. A. C. WHITE).

WITHOUT fear of contradiction, the 30th can claim that it
was the only battalion to have its front line inspected from
a sulky.

CONTRIBUTIONS FROM MEMBERS 323

After the 13th and 15th Brigades had brilliantly recaptured Villers-Bretonneux on 25th April, 1918, things were fairly quiet for a little time on the Australian front in that sector. The 8th Brigade was astride the Somme, with the 30th holding a line between the river and the foot of the spur which was surmounted by Villers-Bretonneux. Battalion headquarters were in Hamelet. No-Man's Land in this area was fairly wide, and consisted, on the 30th's front, of rolling fields of wheat.

I was temporarily attached to divisional headquarters at the time, as liaison officer to the division on our right. My duties were in nowise onerous, and the delightful warm weather prevailing at the time was an incentive to desultory wanderings over the hills and valleys on either side of the river. During one of these perambulations I called in at the 30th's transport lines and encountered that redoubtable transport officer, Lieutenant James MacDuff. Mac was undoubtedly one of the outstanding characters of the battalion, and his wonderful achievements in the way of commandeering transport whenever the 30th moved will always be remembered.

On this particular occasion Mac. was supervising the harnessing of a horse into a sulky which had been left behind when the French civil population fled before the advancing Germans a month or so previously. I accepted a pressing invitation to "come for a drive," and we were soon rattling down the road to Corbie which, although greatly damaged by shell-fire, still retained certain attractions for visitors. Mac. transacted some business with the staff-captain at brigade headquarters, and we made several other calls, being most hospitably received in all cases. Our efficient but non-military means of transport was most favourably commented on by all, and Mac., swelling with pride, suggested that we should, after dining, visit the 30th in the line in our most comfortable equipage.

So it happened that as soon as darkness fell, the sulky proceeded to Hamelet and battalion headquarters. Colonel

Street agreed with our respectfully offered opinion that it was a nice fine night, and, without giving undue publicity to our further intentions, Mac. steered the sulky for the front line. We met numerous ration parties and fatigues of all kinds proceeding on their diverse duties under cover of darkness, and it is quite possible that at times we may have been cursed for causing confusion by suddenly presenting ourselves in the front line itself in such an unorthodox manner. We drove in state along the line of posts (just behind them, be it said) until we reached Captain Chalmers, O.C., "B" Company.

It was hereabouts that the conveyance shed a wheel, and we were reluctantly compelled to leave the remnants on the spot. Captain Chalmers was most opposed to this course, and we understand that his objections bore fruit the following day, when an evidently perplexed German gunner persisted in sniping the sulky with a "whizz-bang."

THE BATTLE OF AMIENS.
TANKS AND ARMOURED CARS.
(By F. W. MILLWOOD).

My first experience of tanks came on August 4th, 1918, when, along with three other Lewis gunners under Lieutenant Haig, I was detailed to attend a School of Instruction some miles behind the front line on the lower Somme. Our principal training consisted of jumping from a tank—both while it was stationary and in motion—with our guns and ammunition, and running to a shell-hole or depression and opening fire on an imaginary enemy. Rumour that was then rife concerning a big attack was confirmed a few days later when we were directed to report to a Captain Luck (a name of good omen), in charge of one of the large-sized tanks. Walking behind the monster, we soon became aware that a great movement was in progress.

CONTRIBUTIONS FROM MEMBERS

Tanks, artillery, armoured cars, waggons crowded with men, ambulances, cavalry, and all manner of military vehicles appeared to be moving in the same direction. Towards dusk we discovered that our tank was following a white tape laid on the ground and that other tanks were gradually drawing closer to us. At last, when collisions appeared to be inevitable, the line was halted—we had reached our starting point.

Here we learned that we were attached to the last of three rows of tanks, and that at a later stage ours would "leap-frog" those in front.

This was to some extent consoling, as it indicated that we would not be in the initial attack. It was now about midnight and, on being told to sit down and await further orders, we got into a nearby shell hole, where we sampled our bully beef and biscuits and had a sip of rum.

I felt very cold and seemed to have just dozed off, when I received a rude slap on the shoulder accompanied by "Wake up, Fred, it's almost morning." A dense blanket of fog had come down, and the morning was unnaturally calm. Everyone began tightening equipment and making preparations to move. Suddenly a rumbling thunder came from our right, and in a moment hell seemed to have broken loose. The great moment had arrived. The enemy was slow in replying, but before long his gas was in evidence and we had to don our masks. Our tank started to move towards the German line, and we followed, keeping as close to it as possible. We soon came upon dead and wounded and, while it was impossible for the tank to avoid them all, we removed as many from its path as lay in our power. Prisoners and wounded were streaming back, and as we began to run into machine gun fire we were told to hop into the tank, which now moved much faster. From our cramped positions we could see practically nothing of what was going on around us, but we felt the concussion when missiles struck the tank and heard the rattle of machine gun and rifle fire. Fortunately, nothing of a heavy nature came our way, and the tank crew were able to keep their guns going when necessary. Thus we waddled along until dusk overtook us and another halt was called. "Get out, boys!" was the order, and out we came. Imagine our surprise when, instead of the endless shell holes and mud to which we had become accustomed, we beheld beautiful green fields all around us. Stranger still was the peaceful nature of our surroundings. We were told to make ourselves as comfortable as possible, as we would be off again at daylight, so we burrowed into a bank and, after another sip of our precious rum, fell asleep.

Morning came only too quickly. The tank engines were warmed up, and soon we were on the move again. Our experiences were much the same as on the previous day, the tank's job being to wipe out the machine gun nests of the German rearguard and to convey gun crews and their weapons to the forward areas. About noon we were somewhat startled when Captain Luck called to us: "Well, lads, this is where you play your part. When I stop, jump straight into a shell hole and stay there until you think fit to move forward. Good luck to you all." For a time we felt as if a mother had deserted us. We would have gladly climbed back into the tank, despite the heat and noise of her confined space, but she had done her duty, and like fledged birds we were left to our own devices. With Lieutenant Haig, we remained for some time in a large shell hole, endeavouring to become acquainted with our new surroundings, and in the meantime keeping our guns ready for instant action. Machine gun bullets were whizzing over us, but now and again we were able to gain a view of what appeared to be a railway goods-shed and yard containing stacks of timber. Suddenly Haig in a low voice said, "Keep still, a German armoured car is coming towards us." We could hear it coming nearer and nearer, when all at once the engine stopped. Waiting to be riddled with bullets our bodies were numb, until a Canadian voice rang

CONTRIBUTIONS FROM MEMBERS 327

out, "Hey there!" followed by "You sure are good actors." What a relief.

"Be very careful, boys," said the Canadian. "Snipers are everywhere, trees have been trailed across the roads. We could not get as far as we wished as all bridges have been blown up, and the town of Péronne, which is not far ahead, is alight from end to end. There are thousands of Huns further on, but all are retreating. Well, so long and good luck." We eventually left our friendly shell hole and ran to the goods-shed, which we reached in safety. The shed contained numerous guns and spare parts, and Lieutenant Haig remarked, "What a haul, we must chalk them 30th Battalion." These were probably his last words, as when my mate and I returned from examining some nearby dug-outs we found him lying dead. He had been shot by a sniper.

A SOMME SIDELINE.
(By J. F. SPENCER).

At the end of March, 1918, the battalion detrained at Doullens, and after considerable marching about the country, eventually reached Vauchelles. A hurried departure, however, was made from this village, and we arrived at Boves Wood just before daybreak.

Here we found a large number of British "Tommies" belonging to various units, inextricably mixed and all extremely tired and war-worn, owing to the strain of fighting a rear-guard action over a long period. Some of them said they had not had their boots off for a fortnight and were afraid that, if they took them off, they would not get them on again, as their feet were so swollen.

We soon made ourselves comfortable with the aid of some salvaged S.A.A. boxes and some straw, and by lacing together two ground-sheets. One North Coast lad borrowed an axe from the company cooks and, stripping the bark from a tree, built himself a hut.

The quick manner in which our boys settled down was an eye-opener to the "Tommies". That evening three fat cattle were located. One was shot, skinned, and dressed ready for the cooks to supplement our meat ration, and this was greatly appreciated by the troops.

Next day we moved up to the line just behind Villers-Bretonneux, which had been placed "out of bounds" to all troops. This did not prevent "souvenir" hunters from entering and exploring it, in spite of the intermittent shelling to which it was subjected by the Germans. The cellars of this small town proved to be a happy hunting-ground, and the numerous "finds", both liquid and solid, made many a heart the lighter coming home—as home to their cobbers they came, when their insatiable thirst was quenched.

"Diggers" in strange garb were a common sight during these days. A company cook, for example, attired himself in a frock coat and bell-topper, and walked about swinging a walking stick. Others showed a weakness for female apparel, which was put to uses never dreamed of by the original owners.

A MEAL FOR THE MAJOR.
(By Capt. C. H. MORRISON).

A COUPLE of weeks prior to the Armistice, as there were few field officers available, I was detailed to a Senior Officers' Gas Course at Le 'Touquet. The course, being for senior officers, was not an arduous one, and terminated on the 10th November.

The journey back on the first Armistice Day was memorable.

The remaining inhabitants in the small villages through which we passed were waving flags, dancing and shouting with joy.

As billets were always, for some foul reason, some

CONTRIBUTIONS FROM MEMBERS

distance from railtowns, I had to make my way, as best I could, from the nearest rail siding back to my battalion.

As I neared my company's village, I met an officer from another company, one of those rare ones who did not look upon the wine when it was red, or even white. He greeted me with, "About time you got back, Morrie. I have just left your company; they are all boozed. Even Tracker (Subaltern) is as bad as the rest. You have a job on hand." A nice welcome home for one stone cold sober.

I went on, and he was right. The local *estaminet*, one of very small dimensions, was full. The yard was full, the road was full, and so were the Diggers. The hostess was known to the troops as "Mrs. Had It." How or why this name was bestowed, I haven't the faintest conception. She was in tears and sought my aid. *"Oh! Monsieur Captaine, Les Soldats son tres mechant."* "They drink biere, cognac, rhum, but no pay." "Lieutenant Bloo-de-Dog (her pat name for Tracker) he very funny, but he pay beaucoup."

I saw Tracker and he saw me. He gravely saluted without a hat, and reported everything correct and in order. Knowing the extent of my individual power at the moment I went along to my billet. The cooks and batmen were quite tight, but they managed some sort of a meal for me. I asked where was the Major, and one of the cooks casually replied, "Joe is on a Court Martial." The Major, by the way, was an A. & I. Staff man, a good fellow, but very precise and dignified. About 4 p.m. the Major arrived, tired and hungry. He had a spot and said, "I must see if the cooks can dig me up something to eat." "Have had nothing since early morning."

A batman then wallowed into the room, and the Major told him his desires. The batman lifted up the window, and this conversation then ensued with the cooks.

"Old Joe's home."
"What's the old blanker want?"
"He wants his dinner."

"Tell old Joe to go to Hell. There's no dinner. He can get to ———."

"Mustn't talk like that about old Joe, he's hungry."

"Well, I'll see what we can do. Will he shout a *Vinblanc?*"

I did not look at the Major, knowing him as I thought I did, I expected threats of all sorts of punishments. The Major laughed, and remarked, "They seem to have been enjoying themselves." I just mumbled something in reply, and went out to try and catch up with those who were many drinks in front of me."

Somehow that incident appealed to the Major, and he often related, and probably still does, about the day when the cooks and batmen called him "Old Joe."

SIGNALLERS LEADING.
(By H. W. BARNFIELD).

"THE battalion will move off, signallers leading!" commanded the Colonel.

Who more worthy to lead the battalion—why, they even beat the band! "The intelligence wing of the battalion," as their original O.C., Stan Evers, was wont to term them. They never did fatigues and most had intelligence enough to transfer to other than infantry units upon the formation of the 5th Division in Egypt. This exodus left Sergeant Jack Facey, Corporal Tom Horgan, and Lance-jacks Eric Wright, Rowley Lording, Walter Crux, and Jim Sheehan to "lead" the battalion. But the nerve centre had to be complete if the body was to function. Communications demanded a full complement of ears and eyes. And so, Stan Hill, Alf Brown, "Bert" Stevenson, "Teddy" Wilkinson, Harry Campbell, Alf Edwards, and the writer were among those who rose from the ranks of the battalion to become members of its intelligentsia.

CONTRIBUTIONS FROM MEMBERS 331

Betwixt official parades and skirmishes on and over the desert in all battalion, brigade, and divisional stunts, when headquarters and outposts had to be provided with visual and telephonic communications, voluntary practice with the various instruments of their craft—flags, heliograph, Begby or Lucas lamps, D (Mark 1 and 2) telephones—occupied the sigs., while others enjoyed more frequently the pleasures of swimming in the canal or visiting the wet canteen. All who had the opportunity of attending the Imperial School of Instruction at Zeitoun returned with a first-class signaller's certificate. Incidentally, young Rowley took it upon himself to shanghai from the school three sigs.—"Chook" Fowler, "Lizz" Lamplough, and "Toc" Parker—who had been overlooked when the 2nd reinforcements were drafted to other units. How, without authority, they travelled dining saloon, detrained offside Moascar, evaded guards, crossed the Sweet-Water and Suez Canals, and were initiated in the dead of night into brotherhood of the 30th Signallers is but one example of the standard of initiative required of a signaller.

It was an efficient signallers' section that led the battalion aboard H.M.T. *Hororata*. A request from the naval escort for slower semaphore when, in response to a requisition for war news, a page of the *Egyptian Mail* was being transmitted, was the only hitch in communications between troopship and escorts on the perilous voyage across the Mediterranean. The high standard of signal service, maintained by watches from the bridge, was the subject of a complimentary message from the commander of a destroyer upon arrival at Marseilles. Other messages, mostly verbal, were received from the naval ratings. "What will you do with the Kaiser?" one shouted, and the reply—well, it might have been coded!

From Marseilles to Hazebrouck, two days and three nights' train journey, the signallers were again in the van —the guard's van mostly—when not exercising along the roof of the train. Following a brief period in billets, they were again on the march. And what a march! From Morbecque, and it was only about half a battalion the signallers led into Estaires. The reminder were left to find their own way over the rough cobble *pave*—one youthful signaller, with bare bleeding feet and a puttee trailing the road, acted as adjutant, or so it seemed, astride "Tod" Sloan's charger side by side with the Colonel. Thence to "Jesus Farm," and into the line at Bois Grenier, signallers leading. In their hurry to lead the battalion out of this possie, Alf Brown's rifle got excited; the bullet chipped the heel off the leading signaller's boot—it might have been his soul! And from the school billet, Fleurbaix, when Fritz put one through the roof, who led the rush? The signallers, with Wal Crux, as in the battalion sports, breaking even time.

The battalion got a bit split up in the stunt at Fromelles, the signallers being represented in all departments. Eric Wright, with "A" Company, got his issue of "iron rations" and transport leading to prison life in Germany. Young Rowley, in charge of "C" Company's signallers, got more than his issue and subsequently underwent some fifty operations that preceded his authorship (under the nom-de-plume "A. Tiveychoc") of *There and Back*. Jim Sheehan took the lead in volunteering to do a risky job of work. He, with so many battalion cobbers, "went west." They had to have a signaller and were fortunate to pick on Jim, who would lead them to a happy hunting ground. How about a message, Jim!

From Fromelles, the signallers led the battalion in many directions—over roads and duckboards, through mud and slush, into the line, out to billets—and, for the most part, under the able and fearless leadership of their debonair lieutenant, Tom Horgan, who was "winged" at Villers-Bretonneux. To Tom Horgan, and to his sergeants, Barnfield and Brown, and all members of the sect, communications were a religion, a religion demanding utmost devotion from its adherents. If it failed, the cohesion of the unit was gone, and the battalion could no longer exist as an entity capable of functioning as a united force. Night and day they worked in the mysteries and dangers of their craft: laying and maintaining those thin wires, operating intricate Fullerphones, and, when this means of communication was impossible (notably among the pill-boxes of the Ypres salient) signalling visually.

While Tom Horgan led the signallers, "Toc" Parker fed the "pigs". But once they went hungry. Because of a previous complaint, and to ensure an even distribution of the week's supply of mustard pickles, "Toc" dumped the issue into a stew (in lieu of his usual ingredient of grass). Figuratively, the pigs went to market; literally, all little signallers had none. "Toc" got his issue at Montauban—a dixie of boiling water. What a Blighty! And what a loss! "Toc" could always be relied upon for entertainment, the extent of his repertoire being *The Man from Iron Bark*.

However, the war went on, and the battalion with it, signallers leading, to the day of Armistice—the joyous yet bitter end. And, when regulation lines of communications were no more, to the field of fellowship dependent not on visible or audible signals, the battalion moved off—signallers leading.

WAS IT *JAMES* OR WAS IT *JOHN*?
(By Lieut.-Colonel JOHN A. CHAPMAN).

MEMBERS of the battalion, as well as others outside it, often became confused between two brothers, James A. and John A. Naturally, at first, in accordance with army's liking for abbreviations, they were known as J.A. and J.A. By a curious turn of fate John A., the younger, happened to come out of Duntroon slightly senior in grading to James A. Thus, to make matters somewhat more confusing, J.A. junior was actually the senior and J.A. senior, the junior.

They were lieutenants and captains together. James A. was adjutant of the battalion on two occasions and John A. on one occasion. Therefore, James A. was adjutant before John A., but he was also adjutant after John A.

When Colonel Clark became acting brigade commander during the period we were in the Anzac Ridge position, he left the battalion in charge of James A. John A. was then adjutant, but the C.O. thought it better that James A. should act as C.O. and John A. remain as adjutant, although the latter was the senior. He had apparently become a little worried over the J.A. and J.A. problem and had left it to the brothers to sort things out. So one day James A. would act as C.O. with John A. as his adjutant, and the next day the positions would be changed round. If a complaint arrived from a company commander the C.O. could always blame the adjutant—and by the time the investigation of the complaint was thoroughly in train, the C.O. had again become the adjutant. One could hardly prove oneself guilty. However, the battalion survived the brotherly combination.

Though James A. and John A. were not in Paris at the same time, they had leave in Brussels together. No! there was no confusion in either city between J.A. and J.A. The tales which reached the battalion were not all true. Many things were attributed to the J.A. brothers. Yes, but was it James, or was it John?

A CUP THAT CHEERED.
(By GEOFF COWEN).

ONE of the most pleasant spells we had out of the line was the one spent at Blaringhem in July, 1917, after the long months of duty on the Somme. Comfortable billets, good weather, decent *estaminets,* a fair proportion of leave to Aire, and better cooked food in consequence of some of

CONTRIBUTIONS FROM MEMBERS

our "babblers" having lately attended a cookery course, made life worth living.

As a diversion from ordinary drill with all its monotonous sameness for experienced troops, battalion sports and competitions were held, and great was the inter-company rivalry for the honours. No. 8 Platoon ("B" Company), not having any outstanding athletes, decided that, under Lieutenant Boyd Bragg, it stood a good chance of pulling off the "platoon-drill competition," and having so decided, entered into training with a zest.

Great were the preparations in our billet on the morning of the 24th. Boot polish and "blanco," with plenty of elbow grease, were the main items used in preparing our equipment and dress, while razor-blades were wielded with extra care so as to ensure a clean shave and no gashes.

Then the bugler informed us to "Dress for Parade." Could the original commander of No. 8, the late Lieutenant-Colonel "Bill" Cheeseman, who made soldiers of us at Liverpool Camp and the Showground, and on the desert in Egypt, have been there to inspect us as we turned out that day, I doubt if he could have found a fault with any of us.

And so to the parade ground to do our best for our new platoon commander. Here we found ourselves under the watchful eye of our company commander, Captain "Dad" White, with Colonel "Jimmy" Clark and several of the staff as judges. The day was beautiful and mild, a typical French summer's day, with just enough warmth in the sun to make one pleased to be able, with work, to raise an honest thirst.

Boyd, who had gained a working experience of our individual ability, plus our defects, received such a wonderful response from the platoon that the result of the competition was never in doubt. No. 8 won easily, the prize being a silver cup and 50 francs.

The parade over, and led by the proudest officer in the 30th Battalion, with the cup in the crook of his arm and the francs in his pocket, away we marched, *a la Guards*, back of the head well up, chin in, chest out, swinging the disengaged arm, and swanking it to beat the band. Passing the "official-stand," we chucked the judges a decent sort of "eyes-right" and marched off the ground.

Once out on the road, the order was given to "march-at-ease," upon which we immediately gave vent to our feelings by singing with loud if not tuneful voices: "What Ruddy Rotten Soldiers."

Down the road we went and on reaching an *estaminet* were surprised to receive the order "Right wheel!" In we marched, nearly frightening Madame out of her wits. *Oo! La-La* was about all she could say, until Boyd called out "*Toute Suite, Madam*, 50 *francs biere* and fill this cup up first."

Was it a merry party? Ask any of the old platoon that were fortunate enough to be with us that day.

CHRISTMAS IN BEUGNIES.
(By J. S. BARTLEY).

THE advent of Christmas, 1918 saw the battalion settled down in winter quarters at Beugnies in an area which for more than four years had been occupied by the German Army. The village was consequently dull and uninteresting, utterly devoid of comfort, life, or amusement, and the lot of the unfortunate population was not to be envied. Two extremely pleasant functions, however, took place during our stay there—a treat for the village children, and our own Christmas celebrations.

I believe that the padres arranged the first one. Each of us threw in a couple of francs, and a G.S. waggon sent to Brussels returned laden with toys. The function took place in an old pottery works on the Saturday afternoon before Christmas, in the presence of Brigadier-General G. S.

Davies, Colonel F. Street, and other distinguished officers of the 8th Brigade. The 30th band was in attendance and rendered selections.

With the assistance of the old village curé, every child was cordially invited to be present at the 30th Battalion's Christmas Tree, to receive entertainment, refreshment, and a gift of two toys.

Accompanied by their parents or guardians, hundreds of children, eager with anticipation, soon filled the old pottery works to overflowing. The sight of the various tables full of toys, sailing boats, dolls, kettledrums, etc., gladdened their hearts in no small measure, as some had never before received a Christmas gift. The children rendered musical items, concluding with the *Marseillaise*, at which all present stood to attention. As the last notes of the stirring anthem died away, the old village curé signalled all to remain standing. An element of surprise was now created; the children sang again, astounding us with three verses of "God Save the King!" in English, which the curé informed us had been learnt in less than three weeks.

After this, ice-cream, lollies, and drinks were handed out to them, creating quite a stir. Then followed the climax of the day—the distribution of the toys. This produced a scene of joy almost indescribable, as the little folks filed past the tables fondly holding their cherished gifts. The curé kept a watchful eye against double-banking, and assisted generally, which was a great help to all concerned. In the yard a photo was taken of them holding up their toys, many of them being hoisted shoulder-high by the Diggers; and a special photograph was taken of the war orphans. The children who, because of sickness or for other reasons, were unable to attend were not forgotten, the curé seeing to it that their gifts were sent on to them.

Christmas Day broke fine and clear, the whole place having been transformed into a veritable fairyland by a fall of snow the previous night. Old Sol shone out in all his grandeur and beauty, as if smiling on the first real

Christmas for years—since the echo of the guns had died away, peace and goodwill towards all men had a chance to reign once more.

Under such genial conditions, the whole battalion sat down to Christmas dinner, in the old pottery works, the portable contents of which had long since gone to Germany. Impromptu fatigue parties soon "souvenired" a piano and all available furniture that the village boasted; and, without a doubt, the dinner held the distinction of being the grandest spread we had during the whole campaign. Goodness only knows where the lollies, nuts, and other dainties which graced the table came from—but there they were, all creating a Christmas atmosphere. It looked like Christmas, it felt like Christmas, and it certainly was Christmas.

Thanks to Colonel Street and his worthy band of helpers, this pleasing function was greatly appreciated; and tribute is due to the efforts of the officers and sergeants who volunteered their services as waiters, thus contributing much towards the success of what was the last Christmas dinner that the lads enjoyed together. Many familiar faces were missing, and we experienced a feeling of deep and genuine sorrow as the toast of "Fallen Comrades" was honoured.

Round about Beugnies there were many fields that had been cultivated by the Germans. In them, cabbages, turnips, carrots and *pomme-de-terres* flourished abundantly, signifying that Fritz had showed poor judgment as to the probable duration of his stay there. The soup, therefore, was substantially "dinkum," being well thickened with the harvest from those fields.

Roast beef of Old England and vegetables made their appearance and the manner in which they were dished up was a lasting tribute to our worthy "babbling brooks." Then, lo and behold, came the plum pudding—served with custard, and good to look at. Last, but not least, old John Barleycorn stood in the corner in the shape of barrels from which copious draughts of good brown ale warmed the hearts of the men of the old battalion, who now indulged in a hearty sing-song, capable almost of bringing down the rafters.

After tea we staged a fireworks display, which greatly amused the villagers. A large dump of German flares was "souvenired," along with flare pistols and a couple of spring guns. The heavens were soon brilliantly illuminated with multi-coloured lights which made a grand show. Hissing through the air as fast as we could release them were the familiar red, double red, green, double green, the golden shower, and other well known signals. Thus ended a day that will long be remembered by those who were privileged to be present.

TREASURE TROVE.
(By R. MATHER).

SOME say that in pre-war days Private "Jerry" Rhodes was a prospector. There was evidence to support the notion, for he took an interest in all "mineral" formations wherever the strata happened to be exposed in railway cuttings or quarries.

But after all, "gold is where you find it," and Jerry's most famous discovery was made on a level stretch of green sward in the rear of No. 16 Platoon's billet at Beugnies during the post-armistice period.

The billet had been a large *estaminet*. Its owner, before the Germans occupied the village, had buried his stocks of spirituous liquors and apparently taken the secret with him when he "went west." Jerry discovered the cache when a mule put its leg through the turf. He had no time to peg out a claim; in a few minutes picks and shovels were procured and digging commenced.

Cognac, wine and liqueurs were quickly located and favourably commented upon. At first each new find was carefully examined, the bottles being cleaned and the labels read, but, as the troops reached the stage when one "stingo" is as good as another, it became customary to wipe only the neck of the bottle.

At nightfall one of the platoon had to be borne home on a stretcher. By the second day the news had spread and the digging became more extensive. French civilians were invited to join in the celebrations, but when they failed to return home the women folk invoked the aid of the military authorities.

A guard was therefore mounted and a sentry posted to prevent further digging, but he, finding the urge to become a prospector too great to resist, promptly stuck his rifle and bayonet into the ground, hung his equipment on it, and started to dig. Anyway, the war was over.

The punishment awarded for this dereliction of duty has, as far as I am aware, not been recorded.

THE 8TH TRAINING BATTALION.
(BY R. C. HOGAN).

IN January, 1916, shortly after the arrival of the 8th Infantry Brigade in Egypt, surplus troops from its units were formed into what was known as the 8th Training Battalion, through which passed practically all the subsequent reinforcements for the brigade. From Zeitoun the 8th T.B. moved in April to Tel-el-Kebir, and thence, in June, to England, where at first it was located at Lark Hill. Three weeks later it was transferred to Codford, but was finally sent to the fields surrounding Hurdcott House, a restored Jacobean mansion, which had originally been built in 1631. Here it remained until absorbed by another divisional unit in 1918.

The battalion occupied Nos. 8 and 9 camps at Hurdcott, and during the early period of its existence was commanded by Major C. F. Knight, the adjutant being Captain W. Room, and the quartermaster Captain W. Compton. With it was associated the 14th and 15th Training Battalions, the whole constituting a divisional group under a senior officer. The battalions were staffed by highly efficient groups of specialist officers and N.C.O's., who were carefully selected for their ability to impart the instruction gained at various schools in drill, musketing, bombing, signalling, physical training, bayonet fighting, etc.—which had been set up in various parts of England. The troops were housed in galvanised iron huts, lined with 3-ply pine and painted a dull red. Each hut accommodated about 30 men, and was fitted with a centrally situated Canadian stove for winter use. Wash houses, cook houses, mess huts, Q.M. stores, etc., were of a similar type.

A welcome innovation to new arrivals from Australia were the duckboard pathways, which kept the huts free from mud, and incidentally made the troops' footwear easier to keep clean. Spaces between the various buildings and other unoccupied areas of the camps were utilized for vegetable growing, the principal item being potatoes, of which some 70 tons were produced in the autumn of 1917, thus augmenting the somewhat meagre food ration. A feature of the cooking lines was the effort made to eliminate waste; separate receptacles were provided for each article of waste food, and even tea leaves were saved for dyeing purposes. The 8th T.B. was noted for its efficiently run "Regimental Institute," which was held up as a pattern to all T.B's. in the A.I.F. The battalion also possessed a brass band of exceptional merit.

All its instruments were donated by Sergeant "Mick" Maloney, a big-hearted, lovable personality, who was willing to back his patriotism with his cheque book. Strange to relate, some time after Mick returned to civilian life, he received a letter from a Commonwealth department advising him that, if he paid £120 Customs duty, he could obtain delivery of the self-same instruments, for which, apparently, a paternal Government had no further use! Life at the Training Battalion was never allowed to become monotonous—even the schedule of work was designed with the notion of making it interesting to all.

After the reinforcements had passed through various phases of their training and had gradually qualified in musketry, bombing, etc., they arrived at the stage when they were fit to be put "on draft" for France. Not the least important part of their training consisted of innumerable parades at the medical hut, where the R.M.O. inoculated them against various diseases which in previous wars had caused many casualties; judging by results, these inoculations, unpopular as they were at the time, were most effective and beneficial to the troops. In February, 1917, Major Sloan arrived from France to take over the command of the 8th T.B. from Major Steel. There was a good deal of pride and satisfaction at this change, since it meant that an officer of their own unit would be in charge of the camp.

On a day in April, 1917, all Australian troops on Salisbury Plains were reviewed at Bulford Field by His Majesty King George V. It was an unforgettable sight—27,000 men, rank on rank on a field of dazzling green, in that soft mellow light which is seldom absent from an English spring day; and as he passed along, the King was heard to exclaim, "What magnificent men, and what marvellous physique!"

Scattered around Hurdcott, within easy walking distance of the camp and "within bounds," were a number of small but charming Wiltshire villages. The most popular building in each was undoubtedly the village inn. These old inns, some of which are quaintly named—for example, "The Haunch of Venison"—were always well patronised by the troops. One of the most popular and picturesque was unquestionably the "Green Dragon" at Barford-St.-Martin. It will be remembered that Charles Dickens made this village the home of the impeccable Pecksniff, and it is in the "Green Dragon" that he introduces Martin Chuzzlewit to his readers. Here, a century later, Australian soldiers congregated to drink English ale and accept that same benevolent hospitality which has made the inn so famous.

CONTRIBUTIONS FROM MEMBERS 343

The spirit of the "Green Dragon" survives in New South Wales to-day, where the old feeling of comradeship and desire for social good fellowship have found expression in the "Order of the Green Dragon," an association of ex-members of the 29th, 30th, 31st and 32nd Battalions, who meet regularly three times a year in Sydney. The whole countryside is redolent with Roman, Saxon, Norman, and early British history. For example, Chiselbury Camp, an ancient Roman camp with a vallum eleven feet high in places, overlooks Compton and Hurdcott, and is connected with Old Sarum (Salisbury) by an old Roman road which runs along a high chalk ridge. It was on this ridge that Australian troops cut a huge map of Australia. The origin of this well known landmark was due to the initiative of Captain Room, who made a scaled outline from a weather chart in a Melbourne newspaper. The work was put in hand in conjunction with the group entrenching officer, and to various fatigue parties fell the task of carving the outline of their island continent on the ancient chalk downs of Wiltshire. A few miles nearer Fovant an excellent replica of the "Rising Sun" badge was cut into the hillside—another striking reminder to the English people of the days when the Diggers "invaded" the Old Country.

FORWARD TO THE HINDENBURG LINE.
(By Capt. T. C. BARBOUR).

THE 30th Battalion's rest near Péronne was one of short duration. While still licking their scars of battle, the troops, whose depleted ranks represented about one-third of their normal strength, were ordered to move forward to participate in the final assault on the Siegfried system, or Hindenburg Line, a section of which, shrouded in snow, we had glimpsed near Lagnicourt, in the early spring of 1917.

The attack, launched early on the morning of 29th September, 1918, proved to be one of the first magnitude. Two American divisions, the 27th and 30th, each bulging with virile young "doughboys," all eager to learn, were to lead the attack, followed by the 3rd and 5th Australian Divisions, whose task was to perform a graceful "leap-frog" through them, and storm the final objective.

The day broke with a familiar mist and, after the 30th Battalion had passed through the enemy's barrage to trail up the Yanks, it emerged through an artificial pall of smoke laid down by our own guns over the bottle-neck at the Bellicourt canal tunnel, only to discover that the Americans were held up. They were still fighting desperately in the formidable belts of wire entanglement, but, in spite of their gallant efforts and the magnificent gesture of numerous British tanks, their objective, which included the village of Nauroy, was not attained. The sacrifice of the "whippet" tank crews under the storm of shells, including anti-tank cannon and ponderous tank rifles (built on the lines of old-fashioned elephant guns), can justly be described as an epic of heroism. Practically all were knocked out or disabled and the unfortunate occupants of a number of them incinerated in the flames of their own petrol. A few escaped and ran to the shelter of our lines.

Captain J. C. Rickard, long associated with the 30th Battalion, a citizen soldier with a legal training and a firm believer in military etiquette and the *Manual of Military Law and Training*, was wounded in the head by a shell splinter from one of the advancing tanks. After calmly collecting and tabulating his personal effects, he made a courtesy call on Colonel Street in a nearby trench, apologised for his plight, formally handed over his command, and then, with the necessary equipment as laid down in regulations for the "walking" wounded, including a pack on his back, gave a punctilious salute, about-turned, and walked off the battlefield.

Slightly to our north the one-time peaceful village of

Bellicourt loomed up on the tortured landscape—a mass of flame. This rural hamlet, surrounded by stately trees and gardens of content, held the dubious honour of being a prominent landmark on a modern battlefield. Periodically it received weighty attention from the tireless German gunners. We watched detached buildings bulge and sway in an agony of movement and miraculously retain the crazy perpendicular of a tipsy reveller; others suddenly mushroomed, to collapse like a pricked tyre. Faint silhouettes scampered about like rabbits on the fringe of the village.

The destruction of Bellicourt was but a prelude to other such events, and, by the irony of fate, "D" Company, which helped to "pinch" another village nearby, received somewhat similar favours.

Although the 30th Battalion was in close contact at its prescribed zero hour, waiting, as per staff instructions, to perform its "leap-frog", it was deemed inadvisable to execute that movement until the situation became clear. For Colonel Street, whose battle headquarters were in "D" Company's trenches, the situation was a trying one, demanding not the exhilaration of hot blast and high spirits, but cold patience and disciplined sacrifice.

For some hours the battle raged unceasingly in our storm centre—rifle fire punctured with the din of high-explosive. A tingling drama unfolded before our eyes, the combatants being tossed to and fro under the stress of hand-to-hand fighting—slim figures in deep green tunics, including sundry distinct shapes in field grey. During this turbulent period, "walking" wounded of the 30th American Division on our front, when interviewed, were unable to shed much light on the situation, beyond the fact that the Germans had bravely defended their posts. Finally, it became apparent that the gallant Yanks, through inexperience, and because they lacked the technique necessary for dealing with innumerable nests of machine-guns posted in that tangled wilderness of wire, had paid the price of battle—a merciless one for those who surveyed the harvest, which was reminiscent of that of Fromelles.

Because of the general uncertainty our guns, totalling 1,000, of all calibres, had at first only fired intermittently, and then ceased altogether. Finally, General Monash decided that before the advance was resumed all the "doughboys" were to be withdrawn and Australian troops substituted in the line.

THE "CORPSE FACTORY".

When the noise of the great battle had died down, I found time to glance to the rear of our posts and take stock of the surroundings, including the mysterious tunnel over which we had blindly passed through a smoke barrage specially laid down to camouflage our movements. Beneath in the blackness of the tunnel—one of Napoleon's engineering triumphs, as he had to cut for some three miles through the high country, south to north, near the villages of Bellicourt and Le Catelet—ran the waters of a wide canal, connecting two river systems. This tunnel, a veritable fortress, gave secure accommodation for a large force. As I surveyed the superstructure, the pall of smoke intermingling with that of high-explosive and gas shells partially cleared away, and from one of the entrance shafts, an unarmed German soldier, wearing the symbols of the Red Cross, popped his head above ground, looking like a fundamentally healthy plant suffering from lack of light and air. After a hasty glance at the battlefield, he disappeared like a jack-in-the-box.

I felt curious regarding this scallywag's movements, and decided to take the first opportunity of making an inspection of the interior. Later on, "Doc." H. G. Downer, who had spent considerable time patching up numerous wounded Sammies, and I descended to explore the retreat of the Red Cross joker, and, with the aid of torches, negotiated a long flight of steps to emerge in Stygian blackness at the water level. Some faint smudges of light, like haloed glow-worms, could be seen in the gloom, and, on investigation, we were surprised to locate a large dimly lit barge at anchor. It was profusely festooned with red-cross bunting and crammed with wounded German soldiers under the care of an ambulance unit. Along the tow-paths could be seen the sinister outlines of machine-gun emplacements, eloquent testimony to the formidable nature of the defensive measures provided for the underground stronghold. Sundry enemy shells, falling above ground, kicked up a first-class shindy and sounded very close as the noise of their explosion reverberated hollowly in the still atmosphere of the tunnel.

After Downer had concluded a hasty examination of the patients, who appeared to be well cared for by their own attendants, we decided to quit the premises. Downer, who was short of bunting, retained one of the German flags, a red cross on a background of blue cloth, for use at the battalion aid-post.

Shortly after leaving the barge we noticed a small inner chamber, which, on investigation, disclosed one of the most unsavoury sights we had encountered during the long drawn-out years of the war. The place reeked with the pungent odour of human flesh and the acrid fumes of explosives. The interior was a shambles, the walls were spattered and dyed red, and several corpses and portions of human remains lay around. During our brief examination—carried out from the threshold of the charnel house, for we felt too creepy about the spine to venture farther in—outlines of vats were visible, giving the impression that the chamber had been used as a cookhouse or workshop. From its general appearance and the tang of powder, it was evident an explosion had taken place—maybe a chance shell had entered the vent and caused the havoc.

We lost no time in retiring from the eerie scene up the long flight of steps, and emphasised the departure by purifying our lungs with copious draughts of the upper air. Even the most hardened dug-out king, lead-swinger, or A.W.L. "bird", would have jibbed at the prospect of lingering for even a short half-hour in that "delectable" spot, with its cadavers in the blackness of the tunnel.

Sometime later a number of American war correspondents located the gruesome chamber, and before long news, which created a deep sensation at the time, was flashed to the world of the discovery of the alleged German "corpse factory" or boiling-down works.

* * * * *

Finally, when the battle-line was adjusted and the Sammies had been temporarily withdrawn, the offensive was resumed. In response to a message received late at night by Colonel Street from the 32nd Battalion, which was operating somewhere in the southern sphere of the battle zone, I was despatched with "D" Company at a moment's notice to the scene of action.

During the rain-soaked night several "platoons" of gas shells had dropped from the void in our sector, and for some hours prior to our departure the members of "D" Company—furiously resentful at the shelling, and at their inability to express their feelings by spitting in their masks —experienced a very trying time. Looking like goblin monks, they had gadded about in the heavy atmosphere and gloom of a maze of trenches, seeking pastures new, with poor results. Twice the optimistic Company Sergeant-Major, T. Eccles, and some interested assistants, including the runners, moved company headquarters to what they hoped were more "hygienic" positions, but in vain. Needless to say, when the notification to proceed south came to hand, the troops promptly divorced themselves from this pestilential area.

Guided by men of the 32nd Battalion, who themselves should have been guided, and with cheerios from the colonel and our youthful adjutant, Lieutenant Wedd, the company set out on its forced march through an oily black night of slanting rain. We steered in the general direction of Magny-la-Fosse, to weave through a tangle of rusty wire and murky shell-holes, and gyrate over much smelly battle debris.

As we stumbled in the gloom, our amorphous shapes were sprayed by an obscure but affluent machine-gunner. Apparently stumped for target practice, other gunners periodically joined in the fracas and criss-crossed the fighting zone with a deluge that made the atmosphere lousy with lead. This fire caused some embarrassment to the troops, who were forced to prostrate themselves on the muddy ground or toboggan into slimy shell holes. Near dawn, however, they arrived, dog-tired, in the vicinity of Etricourt.

Our subsequent movements read like a page from the *Arabian Nights*. In the dull light we stumbled across a long line of vague human shapes, spaced with evident care at regular intervals, their heads towards the east. They were a company of the 32nd Battalion, under Captain J. H. Allen; in military jargon, they were "on the tapes," awaiting "zero" and the barrage before moving off to assault Mill Ridge, a German stronghold somewhere to the east. The barrage was due to fall in a few minutes.

At an impromptu conference, at which brevity was the keynote, it was decided that "D" Company would forthwith take the place of the 32nd's company on the tapes. The change over was quietly and quickly effected, the company of the 32nd taking up position in rear of the "jumping-off" line, ready to move off in the second wave of the attack.

The dramatic reshuffle resulted in the officers and men of "D" Company obtaining their first and only breather since their gruelling night march from the vicinity of Bellicourt. It was not a refreshing breather by any means, as sensitive nostrils were still aware of the clinging odour of gas on saturated tunics. Feeling rather empty about the belts, the troops adequately cursed their luck.

It was under these unique conditions that the barrage dropped from the skies, and in the dim light of approaching day "D" Company, which had had no opportunity for reconnoitring the locality, assumed the perpendicular and, with the 32nd Battalion in support, closely followed the thin wall of projectiles for several hundred yards, dislodged the Germans, and captured Mill Ridge. While advancing in the open without cover, the riflemen and Lewis gunners succeeded in driving off a low-flying German 'plane before the objective was attained. Conspicuous among them was Corporal C. S. Smith, M.M., who introduced an interesting variant to the proceedings by periodically halting and resting his gun on the shoulders of a companion while he ejected some convincing bursts into the bulky outlines of the inquisitive intruder, which presented an easy target as it flew parallel to our advance. The gunners claim this reconnaissance 'plane, which was driven down in the wire-entanglements in the eastern portion of the Hindenburg Line.

While hastily consolidating the ground gained, under fire from silhouettes and shadows which had bolted back in the gloom, the faint outlines of buildings standing among trees slowly developed ahead out of the early morning mist. These turned out to be the western fringe of the village of Joncourt, which the growing daylight revealed as being undamaged, with green hedges and gay red-tiled roofs and a sleek church spire peeping between trees. The restful scene only required a few holly bushes and a peppering of snow to complete the picture of a European Christmas card.

Under field-glasses, however, it became evident that the church spire was either a German sniper's post or an observation post. Away in the distance a lonely enemy "sausage" balloon showed out suspended between heaven and earth like Mahomet's coffin. It suddenly vanished in a column of smoke, and was the last of its kind seen by us.

After admiring Joncourt and its neat rectangular farms for some time from our exposed posts, we decided to attempt the capture of the village without artillery assistance. It was obvious that Mill Ridge, with its weak defences, would soon become untenable under shell-fire.

CONTRIBUTIONS FROM MEMBERS 351

Some lusty "five-nines" had already arrived to herald the work of demolition, and the fact that the troops never considered themselves at their best as targets for high explosive only hastened the decision to advance. The C.O. of the 32nd Battalion and the units on our flanks were at once notified of our intentions, the company runners carrying out their arduous tasks with marked gallantry, for very little cover was available in the battle-zone, which the Germans raked with machine-gun and rifle fire.

With "D" Company still retaining its formation, and the 32nd Battalion moving behind in support, the advance was continued, and at 10 a.m. on October 1st the village was captured. Shortly afterwards the Germans turned their guns upon it, and soon the houses were a mass of ruins. The church spire, from which we had dislodged some Germans, was snapped like a carrot. Salvoes of gas shells were also thrown into the village. Fortunately, a number of dug-outs were available, and by using these our casualties were reduced to a minimum. The heavy gas was our worst antagonist, for it searched underground like a blanket of fog. Seen through our masks above ground it was very deceptive, and it formed an unholy trinity with the fumes of high-explosive and the smoke from fires.

Our imperturbable Lewis gunners again came into prominence when, shortly after the capture of Joncourt, a German battery suddenly appeared on the scene, unlimbered in the open and feverishly pumped several rounds into the red-tiled village. Posted on the fringe of Joncourt, our gunners, who never laboured under the baleful influence of an inferiority complex even when opposed by field-guns, promptly responded to the hostile reception by swinging into action with some lively bursts from their "daisy cutters". They effectively silenced the battery, but not before the audacious field-greys had succeeded in locating their posts, and demolishing one with a direct hit.

We remained in the village until the following day, which brought forth a proposition to storm the village of Wancourt. However, owing to the depleted ranks in the 8th Brigade—particularly those of the 32nd Battalion, which had experienced heavy fighting in the vicinity of Magny-la-Fosse—the proposal did not mature, as far as we were concerned.

* * * * *

Prodigies of gallantry and sacrifice were performed by the 30th in their final engagement. Among our killed was Sergeant N. N. Gulson, a very gallant and popular N.C.O., who freely exposed himself and was shot during the advance while directing his platoon. Lieutenant C. E. Alcorn, who fell severely wounded and was incapable of much movement but was aware of a shortage of revolvers in the company, succeeded in unstrapping his Webley and giving instructions for it to be forwarded on—it was received as a welcome addition to the armoury of Lieutenant Sinclair, a conspicuous officer during the attack. The actions of Company Sergeant-Major Eccles, who gained his D.C.M., and of other members of the company, were inspiring; but I would also like to pay tribute to all the warriors of "D" Company who participated in the memorable advance of September 29th-October 2nd, 1918, the final engagement of the 30th Battalion in the Great War.

HOMEWARD BOUND.
(By R. MATHER).

THE curtain falls. The old 30th Battalion as a unit is disbanded, its detachments are scattered over various stages of the homeward journey.

Let us follow the departure of one draft as it sails from Devonport on the S.S. *Devanha*. The troopship passes along a line of grey man-of-war. The sailors are mustered on the decks to give us a send-off and they cheer as only sailors can cheer, their white-topped caps swaying

CONTRIBUTIONS FROM MEMBERS 353

in unison. We return the compliment, but ours is a feeble effort by comparison, though we do our best. We pass Nelson's *Victory*, then come alongside another warship, its band playing "Rule Brittania," its crew cheering lustily. This is one of life's memorable moments. It is really goodbye at last. Some, doubtless think of newly-found friends being left behind; some of the ties of kinship and ties of friendship which bind us to the Old Country; others are leaving their Native Land for the sunshine of the land of their adoption. Some perhaps think wistfully of brothers or comrades whom Fate has destined to sleep "neath Northern stars apart."

The Digger, however, never allowed serious thoughts to remain uppermost for long, and just as in moments of stress he had sung with sardonic humour

"Oh, my, I'm too young to die
I want to go home,"

so now Les Wellings gives the signal to his bandsmen, who strike up

"Goodbye-ee, Goodbye-ee,
wipe the tear, baby dear, from your eye-ee."

Later in the Indian Ocean we retired for the night, knowing that at sunrise we would be within sight of the Australian Coast. Few, however, troubled to get up early; when they did, they greeted their native shore with a casual "Hello, Australia, Comment allez vous?"

PART III
NOMINAL ROLL

NOMINAL ROLL OF OFFICERS.

* Killed in action or died of wounds.

Lieut.-Colonel Clark, J. W. (D.S.O.)
Lieut.-Colonel Street, F. (D.S.O.)
Major Beardsmore, R. H. (D.S.O.)
Major Bilton, J.
Major Chapman, John A. (D.S.O.)
Major Charlton, P. (M.C.)
Major Cheeseman, W. J. R. (D.S.O.), (M.C.) (Chevalier Legion d'Honneur)
Major Denham, H. K.
Major Holford, C. J.
Major Purser, M.
Major Sloan, H.
*Capt. Adams, E. (M.C.)
Capt. Allen, R. A. M. (M.C.)
Capt. Barbour, T. C.
Capt. Chalmers, D. (M.C.)
Capt. Chapman, Jas. A. (O.B.E.)
Capt. Flack, A. K. (M.C.)
Capt. Fricker, T. C.
Capt. Fullarton, I. G. (M.C.)
Capt. Hartnett, W. E.
*Capt. Hext, A. P.
Capt. Hind, W. H. (M.C.)
Capt. Krinks, F. L. (M.C.)
Capt. Macfarlane, E. A. C. (M.C.)
Capt. Marsden, T. R.
Capt. Morrison, H. L.
Capt. Morrison, C. H.
Capt. McClean, F. S.
Capt. Rickard, J. C.
Capt. Savage, C. D. (M.C.)
*Capt. Stephens, H.
Capt. Thompson, W. A.
Capt. Wark, B. A.
Capt. White, A. C. (M.C.)
Capt. Wisdom, F. A. (D.S.O.), (M.C.).
Capt. Wynne, G.
Capt. Zander, W. H.
Lieut. Abbott, W. C. (M.M.)
Lieut. Alcorn, C. E. (C. de G.) (Belgian)
Lieut. Backhouse, C. A.
Lieut. Barnett, M.
Lieut. Beer, F. C.
Lieut. Biddle, V. W. (M.C.)
Lieut. Bragg, B. A. (M.C.)
Lieut. Brewster, D. T.
*Lieut. Brown, D. L.
Lieut. Butterworth, F. A. (M.M.)
Lieut. Button, C. D.

Lieut. Butler, S. C. (M.C.)
Lieut. Cadden, R. L.
Lieut. Callam, A.
Lieut. Chapple, R. C.
Lieut. Clark, J. P. K.
*Lieut. Coleman, S. W.
Lieut. Colman, F.
Lieut. Couchman, F. M.
Lieut. Craker, C. J.
Lieut. Cudden, R.
Lieut. Daniel, W. I.
*Lieut. Davies, B. O.
  (D.C.M.)
*Lieut. Doust, H. (M.C.)
Lieut. Dickson, S. D.
Lieut. Ellis, A. H.
Lieut. Evans, G. W.
Lieut. Evers, G. W.
*Lieut. Fisk, S. H.
Lieut. Flynn, J. J. W.
  (M.C.)
Lieut. Forbes, A. H.
  (M.M.)
*Lieut. Gaskell, R.
Lieut. Gibson, G.
Lieut. Griffin, M.
Lieut. Grimwade, H. S.
Lieut. Gunning, C. L.
Lieut. Hall, C. E.
*Lieut. Haig, G.
Lieut. Hamilton, N. W. S.
Lieut. Hamilton, F.
Lieut. Harrison, F. W.
Lieut. Hanlon, W. T.
  (M.C.)
Lieut. Harrold, C. E.
Lieut. Hard, G. E.
Lieut. Haviland, E. E.
Lieut. Horgan, T. S. C.
Lieut. Hayman, B.
Lieut. Jackson, E. B.
Lieut. Jelfs, R. A.
Lieut. Keen, F. W.

Lieut. King, J. H.
Lieut. Leake, C. D.
*Lieut. Lees, J. S.
Lieut. Levitt, V.
Lieut. Macdonald, W. G.
Lieut. Marler, W. R.
Lieut. Mason, L. F.
Lieut. May, W. E.
*Lieut. Mitchell, A.
Lieut. Mulvey, R. D.
*Lieut. Murdock, S. R.
Lieut. McCall, J. J.
Lieut. McCallum, A. J.
Lieut. McDuff, J.
Lieut. McKinnon, E. G.
  (M.S.M.)
Lieut. McClosky, C. H.
  (D.C.M.)
Lieut. Nagle, G. B.
Lieut. Oakes, W. E.
Lieut. Orpen, H. R.
Lieut. O'Sullivan, E. F.
*Lieut. Parker, J.
Lieut. Richardson, E. H.
Lieut. Robertson, E. G.
Lieut. Robinson, H. R.
*Lieut. Rush, B. D. (M.C.)
Lieut. Rule, S. R.
*Lieut. Seymour, G.
Lieut. Sharman, F. C.
Lieut. Sinclair, M. F.
*Lieut. Smithers, K.
Lieut. Stirling, F. M.
Lieut. Stuart, D.
Lieut. Thomas, B. B.
Lieut. Treloar, A. H.
Lieut. Vincent, D.
Lieut. Walker, C. J.
Lieut. Webb, A. E.
Lieut. Webber, C.
Lieut. Wedd, H. W.
Lieut. Wells, H. J. (M.C.)

NOMINAL ROLL 359

Lieut. Whipp, A. H. E.
Lieut. Williams, R. J.
Lieut. Wilkinson, W. T.
Lieut. Wonnacott, H. E.
Lieut. Yeomans, J. C.
(D.S.O.).

MEDICAL OFFICERS

Major Langan, A.
Major North, H. M.
*Major Wells, J. C.
Capt. Downer, H. G.
Capt. Marolli, G. E.
Capt. Marshall, W.
Capt. Railton, S. A. (M.C.)
*Capt. Roberts, L. E. W.
Capt. Robertson, G. O.

CHAPLAINS

Capt. King, T.
Capt. Ward, F. C. (M.C.)

MENTION IN DESPATCHES.

Lieut.-Colonel Clark, J. W. (2)
Lieut.-Colonel Street, F.
Major Beardsmore, R. H.
Major Charlton, P.
Major Cheeseman, W. J. R.
Capt. Chapman, Jas. A. (2)
Capt. Mulvey, R. D.
Capt. Railton, S. A.
Capt. Savage, C. D.
Capt. Zander, W. H. (2)
Lieut. Grimwade, H. S.
Lieut. Horgan, T. S. C.
Lieut. Lees, J. S.
Lieut. Murdock, S. R.
Lieut. Wedd, H. W.
Lieut. Yeomans, J. C.
Pte. Arkell, M. K. D.
Sgt. Cox, H. H.
Pte. Crux, H. G.
Cpl. Eccleston, J. G.
Sgt. McDuff, J.
Sgt. Murdock, S. R.
Cpl. Nicholson, H. L.
Pte. Smith, H. F.
R.Q.M.S. Sneesby, E. G.
C.Q.M.S. Walker, E. F.
Pte. White, J.
Pte. Woodbine, D.

CONGRATULATED BY CORPS COMMANDER

Capt. Barbour, T. C.
Lieut. Harrold, C. E.
Pte. Anderson, J. J. S.
Cpl. Ashenden, P.
Pte. Barnes, F. H.
Pte. Barrett, W.
C.Q.M.S. Bond, J. H.
Pte. Buchanan, R. G.
Pte. Colgate, F. C.
Sgt. Cox, H. H.
Pte. Dawson, C. R.
Cpl. James, A. H.
Sgt. Lowbridge, G.
Pte. Morrison, J.
Pte. McGregor, R.
Cpl. Pickering, F. H.
Pte. Strong, J.
Pte. Thelning, W. P.
Cpl. Wilkinson, E.

NOMINAL ROLL OF N.C.O's. AND MEN

*Killed in action or died of wounds.

516	Cpl	Abbott, E. W.
3186	Pte	Abbott, H.
3355	,,	Abbott, H. E.
1517	Cpl	Abbott, W. C. (M.M.)
1195	,,	Abel, W. T.
1517	Pte	Adams, E. D.
2867	,,	Adams, D. J.
821	,,	Adams, D. R.
4977	,,	Adams, J.
1966	,,	Adams, P. A. L.
2567	,,	Adams, W.
824	,,	Adamson, H.
1343	,,	Addison, A. W.
2354	,,	Addison, B. L.
1035	,,	Adeney, K.
254	,,	Ahern, W.
1209	,,	Aibert, H. G.
1246	,,	Aird, P. J.
388	,,	Aitchison, P. K.
587	,,	Aitken, P.
1031	,,	Aitken, S. E.
1034	,,	Aitkinson, C.
1670	,,	Aitkinson, E. R.
520	,,	Albert, P. H.
*890	,,	Albertson, G. W.
1203	,,	Albiston, T.
3508	,,	Alborn, W. G. E.
4336	,,	Alchin, A. F.
2267	Cpl	Alcorn, C. E.
344	Pte	Alder, A.
3547	,,	Alexander, J.
*3991	,,	Alexander, R. G.
4337	,,	Allan, A.
2568	,,	Allan, E. J.
1023	Sgt	Allan, J. W.
4732	Pte	Allan, R.
3065	,,	Allan, A.
3509	,,	Allen, M.
4428	Cpl	Allinson, T. A.
*3752	Pte	Allsop, T.
2866	Pte	Amidy, A. C. D.
816	Sgt	Amps, E. C. E. (D.C.M.)
815	Pte	Anderson, A. K.
2570	Sgt	Anderson, A. L.
815	Pte	Anderson, A. N.
1667	Cpl	Anderson, E. R.
679	Pte	Anderson, G.
2880	,,	Anderson, J. A.
814	Cpl	Anderson, J. J. S. (M.M.)
*90	Pte	Anderson, P.
2569	,,	Anderson, R.
1198	,,	Andrews, W.
347	,,	Anlezark, J. L.
819	,,	Annis, A. E.
2269	,,	Ansell, R. J.
2556	,,	Archer, J.
*340	,,	Arkell, E. C.
*341	Sgt	Arkell, M. K. D.
4334	,,	Armagnacq, L.
3347	,,	Armitage, E. H.
4490	Pte	Armitt, J. A.
1966	,,	Armour, C. J.
1037	,,	Archbold, S.
822	,,	Armstrong, A.
3507	,,	Armstrong, E. E.
48	Dvr	Armstrong, G. F.
5474	Pte	Armstrong, J. B.
3003	,,	Armstrong, W. F.
1666	Pte	Arndale, E. L.
1968	,,	Arnott, C. H.
1969	,,	Arnott, K. A.
4642	,,	Arthur, F. A.
4632	,,	Arthur, R.
1668	,,	Arthur, R. C.
3996	,,	Arthur, W. J.
1972	Cpl	Artis, A. B.
1518	Pte	Ashby, A. J.
4978	,,	Ashby, H. A.

NOMINAL ROLL

4150	Pte	Ashdown, E. E.
2572	Cpl	Ashenden, P. (M.M.)
3998	Pte	Ashley, A. A.
1229	,,	Ashley, C. J.
1519	,,	Asselin, S. L.
*1571	,,	Aitkins, C. A.
1034	,,	Atkinson, C.
1735	,,	Atkinson, I. T.
818	,,	Attfield, W. G.
3751	,,	Attwell, G. L.
4241	,,	Atwood, J. P.
*3506	,,	Aubrey, A. A.
*1036	,,	Auld, H. W. J.
*1971	,,	Aulton, V. H.
593	,,	Austin, E. G.
2271	,,	Austin, H.
4979	,,	Awcock, E.
2884	,,	Awega, J. S.
13	Sgt	Axtens, J. W.
1575	Pte	Aylward, T. W.
813	,,	Aylward, W. J.
1973	,,	Bacon, A. G.
834	Cpl	Bailey, A. S.
335	,,	Bailey, E. G.
2202	Pte	Bailey, R.
*50	Cpl	Bailey, V. R.
1043	Pte	Baillie, P. S.
2886	,,	Bain, J.
1975	,,	Bainbridge, J.
1974	,,	Baird, T. H.
4498	,,	Baker, A. E.
2592	,,	Baker, A. R.
*2884	,,	Baker, C. E.
1520	,,	Baker, C. H.
2582	,,	Baker, C. J.
*2871	,,	Baker, G.
350	Cpl	Baker, E. H. (M.M.)
2272	Pte	Baker, E. L. (M.M.)
3510	,,	Baker, H.
3772	,,	Baker, J.
2876	Pte	Baker, L.
800	Sgt	Baldcock, W. J.
2488	Pte	Balfour, J. R.
4326	,,	Balkham, E.
351	,,	Ball, F. W.
1685	Cpl	Ball, R. E.
*4748	,,	Ball, R. J. T.
364	Pte	Ball, W. O.
*2274	,,	Balsdon, J.
2275	,,	Balsdon, J. T.
*2276	,,	Balsdon, R. H.
3999	,,	Bamber, S. W.
371	,,	Bannister, E. H.
2591	,,	Bannister, L. H.
2497	,,	Bangle, K. M.
2496	,,	Barbour, A.
1048	,,	Barclay, C. L.
5137	,,	Barclay, L. C.
4735	,,	Barfield, W. V.
2894	,,	Barfoot, F.
3756	,,	Barnes, A. A.
4980	,,	Barnes, A. P.
7436	,,	Barnes, F. H.
2488	Cpl	Barnes, H. C.
*1320	Pte	Barnes, L. E.
1324	,,	Barnes, H.
1321	,,	Barnes, R.
603	,,	Barnes, W. S.
3515	,,	Barnett, H. W.
354	,,	Barnett, W.
104	Sgt	Barnfield, H. W.
619	Pte	Barr, G.
4305	,,	Barratt, R. E.
*836	Cpl	Barrett, H. R.
1978	Pte	Barrett, P.
3358	,,	Barrett, S. F.
3769	,,	Barrett, N. P.
354	Sgt	Barrett, W. (D.C.M.)
1683	Pte	Barron, A.
610	,,	Barrow, J.
3755	,,	Barry, H. A.
*4982	,,	Barry, M.
2277	,,	Barry, W. G.

3348	Pte	Bartholomew, S. E.	1981	Cpl	Bell, R. T.
2880	Cpl	Bartley, J. S.	2281	Pte	Bell, W. M.
3196	Pte	Barton, C. F.	2547	Cpl	Bennett, G. E. A.
1022	Sgt	Barty, D.	*3522	Pte	Benfield, V. L.
1686	Pte	Barwick, H.	612	„	Bennett, H.
2278	„	Bateman, A.	2779	„	Bennett, J.
261	„	Bateman, C. E.	*2287	„	Bennett, W. A.
1678	„	Bates, J. A.	*840	„	Benson, G. V.
1303	„	Batten, V. C.	2282	„	Bentley, J. A.
1051	„	Batten, F.	2584	Sgt	Bentley, J. T.
1821	„	Battram, E. A.	1980	Pte	Bentley, P. H.
2593	„	Baxter, F. G.	4339	„	Berger, A.
2882	„	Baxter, M. E.	4005	„	Berkeley, J. D.
362	„	Baxter, M. S.	4984	„	Bernasconi, S. V.
4983	„	Baxter, S. A.	2570	„	Bernauer, R. O.
4008	„	Baxter, W. A.	1710	„	Berry, A. C. E.
108	„	Bayley, A.	4741	„	Berry, F.
1877	„	Bean, C. M.	65	„	Berryhill, J. A.
1049	„	Beanland, L. W.	1677	„	Bertholli, E. E.
4491	„	Beasley, C.	2290	„	Bertram, R.
2875	„	Beattie, W.	3230	„	Best, J.
2872	„	Beauchamp, N.	3523	„	Bevan, W. S.
2873	„	Beauchamp, V. C. G.	1673	„	Bewley, A. H.
4887	„	Beaumont, S. F.	1687	„	Bewley, S. G. B.
106	„	Beck, E.	4006	„	Bible, E.
3759	„	Beckett, G.	*2283	C.S.M.	Bickerton, L. B.
3758	„	Beddall, J.	613	C.S.M.	Bickley, J. F.
2279	„	Bedford, T. W.	1743	Pte	Bien, T. D.
4002	„	Beecham, E. S.	3199	„	Biggs, A. N.
1374	„	Beetson, G. T.	2291	„	Biglands, J. R.
604	Dvr	Begg, A. R.	2136	„	Bilson, E. J.
839	Sgt	Begg, G.	1674	„	Billingsley, B. L.
4747	Pte	Behan, P. F.	2574	„	Bingham, R. C.
3833	„	Beggett, T. A. C.	3768	„	Binsken, E. A.
1521	Cpl	Belcher, J. W.	2284	„	Bint, W. D.
3517	Pte	Belgre, H. H.	3190	„	Bishop, A. L.
365	„	Bell, A. A.	617	„	Bishop, J. R.
826	„	Bell, C. G.	3514	„	Bismire, H. J.
1982	„	Bell, H.	4003	„	Bisset, G.
1050	„	Bell, H. J.	3771	„	Black, C.
4000	„	Bell, L.	2889	„	Black, J. F.
2280	„	Bell, T.	373	„	Black, W. D.
			4497	„	Blackman, A. H.

4504	Pte	Blackman, N. B.	1038	Pte	Bourne, R.
2285	„	Blackwell, A. R.	1220	„	Bovard, J. A.
*3698	„	Blackwood, J.	2791	„	Bowdler, E. W.
2577	„	Blake, H. V.	844	Cpl	Bower, A.
1983	„	Blakemore, J. G.	2288	Pte	Bower, S. E.
847	„	Blattman, J. C.	1671	„	Bowling, T. B.
1680	„	Blaxlup, C. S.	1041	„	Bowman, J. A.
4633	„	Blizzard, H.	1522	„	Bowman, W. L.
4739	„	Bloor, R.	4496	„	Bowyer, F. D.
3763	„	Bloxham, O. E.	*3757	„	Boyce, J. A.
616	„	Boag, A.	4246	„	Boyd, N.
1523	„	Body, A. V.	605	„	Boyle, G. F.
4885	„	Bogan, J.	2289	„	Boyle, R.
358	Cpl	Boland, C. L.	606	„	Boyle, T. R.
98	„	Boles, J.	600	„	Boys, W. T.
2286	Pte	Bolin, A. P.	2586	„	Bradd, H. F.
2314	„	Bolger, H. H.	4507	„	Bradford, S. G.
*2874	„	Bolton, P.	2290	„	Bradley, A. E.
825	„	Bond, F. C.	363	„	Bradley, O.
356	C.Q.M.S.	Bond, J. H. (M.S.M.)	4001	„	Bradley, P. J.
			2298	„	Bradley, S. A.
110	Pte	Bone, C.	1688	„	Bradney, A. S.
2294	„	Bone, E. T.	846	„	Bradney, D. W.
3774	„	Bone, R.	2589	„	Bradshaw, F. C.
*3067	„	Boorer, J. B.	2487	„	Bradshaw, L. W.
372	„	Booth, B.	6603	Sgt	Bradshaw, N. Q.
837	„	Booth, H. C.	*2883	Pte	Bradshaw, R. M.
1044	„	Booth, J.	1977	„	Brady, J.
1220	„	Borard, J. A.	1681	„	Bramwell, C.
4882	„	Bossie, W.	1989	„	Bramble, E. R.
4897	„	Boswell, E. C.	1985	„	Brandon, A. H.
1344	„	Bottom, J. C.	359	Dvr	Brann, R.
4176	„	Bottron, E.	1691	Pte	Brannigan, J. H.
4890	„	Boulden, R. M.	4007	„	Brasier, H. J.
4242	„	Boulten, P. H.	835	„	Bray, R. J.
*4503	„	Bourke, E. A.	1748	„	Brearly, C. F.
1682	„	Bourke, H. G.	849	„	Brebner, J. S.
*1876	„	Bourke, H. J.	4127	„	Bredhauer, G. (M.M.)
2585	„	Bourke, L. R.			
4496	„	Bourke, P. J.	355	„	Bremmell, C. F.
4494	„	Bourlet, J. J.	3189	Cpl	Bremner, J. B.
*4463	„	Bourne, A. M.	1161	Pte	Brennan, F. J.
5130	„	Bourne, C. H.	3191	„	Brennan, R. J.
*1994	„	Bourne, O. A.	*4223	„	Brennan, W.

4743 Pte	Brett, P. V.	
3770 „	Brett, W. H.	
2291 „	Brettle, F. G.	
2292 „	Brewer, H. N.	
2396 „	Breen, F. H.	
2888 „	Bridge, L. W.	
4126 „	Bridge, W. A.	
1524 „	Bridgefoot, J.	
*602 „	Bridgement, E. S.	
4127 „	Bridger, W.	
4255 „	Bridle, W. J.	
1201 „	Brien, A. C.	
49 Dvr	Brien, F. H.	
357 Pte	Brien, H.	
3199 „	Briggs, A. N.	
599 „	Briggs, D. M.	
830 „	Bright, S. J.	
1199 „	Brimmell, A. E.	
1329 „	Brisbane, J. J. R.	
*1986 Cpl	Briscoe, L. L.	
2293 Pte	Broadbent, E. J.	
1180 Cpl	Brock, S. J.	
1525 Pte	Brockbank, J.	
1296 „	Brocklehurst, G.	
3520 „	Brogan, J.	
3519 „	Brokenshire, H. W.	
366 Cpl	Bromley, G. J.	
832 Pte	Bromley, O.	
4004 „	Brook, L. H.	
1996 „	Brooker, G. R.	
3055 „	Brooks, E.	
*3912 „	Brooks, F. E.	
1526 „	Brooks, H.	
4989 „	Brooks, J. R.	
4736 „	Brophey, W.	
614 Sgt	Brown, A. H.	
98 „	Brown, E. E.	
618 Pte	Brown, E. C.	
1675 „	Brown, F.	
2294 „	Brown, G.	
4446 Cpl	Brown, G. E.	
*3521 Pte	Brown, G. T.	
1040 „	Brown, H. G.	
1672 Cpl	Brown, H. K.	
601 Pte	Brown, H. W.	
2868 Sgt	Brown, J.	
3518 Pte	Brown, J.	
607 „	Brown, J. F.	
833 Cpl	Brown, J. H.	
607 Pte	Brown, J. T.	
*1208 Cpl	Brown, O. D.	
2299 Pte	Brown, R.	
608 „	Brown, W.	
3073 „	Brown, W. C.	
2576 Sgt	Brown, W. H.	
2596 Pte	Brown, W. J.	
3359 „	Browne, W. G.	
4502 „	Browning, A.	
1039 „	Browning, R. S.	
2594 „	Bruce, C.	
4495 „	Bruce, G. E. B.	
1991 „	Bruce, J.	
2207 „	Bruderlin, A. J.	
*1671 „	Brudelin, L. B.	
4506 „	Bryan, R. J.	
368 „	Bryan, S.	
1988 „	Bryce, J. N.	
361 „	Bryden, J. A.	
2296 „	Buchanan, N. A.	
1992 „	Buchanan, R. G.	
1984 „	Bucham, S.	
3761 „	Buck, N.	
3512 „	Buckley, A. R.	
4340 Sgt	Buckley, L. E.	
3676 Pte	Buckton, W.	
1993 „	Buddle, W. H.	
1190 „	Buik, R. R.	
*3516 „	Buist, W. M.	
22 „	Buglin, A. V.	
2297 „	Bull, A. T.	
1527 „	Bull, J. L.	
4500 „	Bullock, L. C.	
842 „	Bunn, A. H. C.	
*4245 „	Bunting, C. R.	
2869 „	Burgess, B.	
2794 „	Burgess, C.	
*1047 Cpl	Burgess, C. B.	

NOMINAL ROLL 365

841	Pte	Burgess, L.
609	„	Burke, W.
*3360	„	Burke, W.
360	„	Burn, J. E.
4891	„	Burn, L. H.
2575	„	Burnicle, S.
2298	„	Burns, A.
2580	„	Burns, A. A.
107	Sgt	Burns, A. D. (M.M.)
*621	Pte	Burns, A. J.
3916	„	Burns, G. W. (M.M.)
4888	„	Burns, R.
2489	„	Burns, S. G.
2578	„	Burns, T.
*3356	„	Burns, W.
4501	„	Burns, W.
827	Cpl	Burns, W. J.
1684	Pte	Burt, J. W.
3511	Cpl	Busch, J. A.
*3915	Pte	Butcher, A. E.
105	„	Butcher, R. G.
2879	„	Butcher, W. A.
*2597	„	Butler, A. J.
1984	„	Butler, A. M.
5120	„	Butler, D.
*1045	„	Butler, G. A.
375	„	Butler, M. J.
2793	„	Butler, R. J.
2551	„	Butler, W. C.
2595	„	Butler, W. W.
3762	„	Buttell, F. A.
4244	„	Butter, H. J.
1249	Sgt	Butterworth, F. A. (M.M.)
4128	Pte	Button, T. A.
1989	„	Buttrell, A.
3765	Sgt	Buttsworth, J. L.
374	Pte	Byrne, G.
4016	Pte	Callaghan, G. M.
*1995	„	Callaghan, J. P.
2614	„	Callagher, E. J.
*241	Pte	Callan, W. H.
2679	„	Calthorpe, R. E.
855	„	Camac, R.
4344	„	Cameron, C. J.
1996	„	Cameron, D. P.
3526	„	Cameron, V. J.
*3753	„	Cameron, W. J.
4347	„	Campbell, A.
630	„	Campbell, A. C.
850	„	Campbell, D.
4516	„	Campbell, F. O.
856	„	Campbell, G. A.
392	„	Campbell, H.
3525	„	Campbell, L. H.
1810	„	Campbell, W. C.
*631	„	Camps, V. A.
1058	„	Cann, H. H. E.
3776	C.Q.M.S.	Cann, G.
1529	Pte	Cannon, R. G.
2599	„	Caplice, D. J.
1123	„	Carlyle, J. E.
903	„	Carney, J. P.
4352	„	Carney, P. A.
3213	„	Carr, A. V.
2610	„	Carr, G.
*3055	„	Carr, K. J.
4994	„	Carrall, W.
*1531	„	Carthan, H.
1530	„	Carrington, F.
1701	„	Carter, C. G.
851	Sgt	Carter, J.
622	Pte	Carter, J.
1997	„	Carver, C. H.
16	Dvr	Carnegie, W. L.
1946	Pte	Carver, D. B.
1053	Sgt	Case, R. A. (M.M.)
14	Pte	Catt, J.
1300	Sgt	Casey, J. J. (M.M.)
2605	Pte	Casey, P. R.
132	„	Casson, R. O.
632	„	Casson, T. G.
2612	„	Castle, A. G.

3361	Pte	Castle, V.	638	Pte	Clare, C. M.
*397	„	Caswell, D.	4999	„	Clark, D. T.
*860	„	Cather, A. E.	2309	„	Clark, F. M.
128	„	Cather, R. J.	2310	„	Clark, R.
4160	„	Cavanough, S. C.	2905	„	Clark, R.
134	„	Cawood, C.	2891	„	Clarke, A.
3667	„	Cawsey, F. G.	2009	„	Clarke, E. G. R.
4179	„	Creney, J.	2601	„	Clarke, E.
4996	„	Chamberlain, M.	395	„	Clarke, H.
4519	„	Chambers, H. D.	4315	„	Clarke, E. B.
4750	„	Chambers, W. J.	4462	„	Clarke, G. W.
1330	„	Champion, J.	383	„	Clarke, R. H.
4009	„	Champion, F.	4899	„	Clarke, R. M.
637	„	Champion, C. H.	1709	„	Clarke, S. W.
2271	„	Champness, L.	3524	„	Clarke, T. J.
1699	„	Chamney, W. W.	2606	„	Clarke, V.
3389	„	Chain, R. G.	133	„	Claydon, W. H.
1533	„	Chapman, J.	*51	Dvr	Clayton, C. K.
3365	„	Chapman, G. H.	4310	Cpl	Cleland, A. J.
2600	Cpl	Chapman, H. D. (M.M.)	4350	„	Cleland, V. A.
			394	Pte	Clements, H. K.
623	„	Chapman, J. L.	1333	„	Cliff, W. A.
1203	Pte	Chapple, T.	73	„	Cliff, W. G.
*1999	„	Chapman, J. W.	3200	„	Clifford, K. G.
4010	„	Chapman, T. H.	7108	Sgt	Clifford, W. G.
857	„	Chandler, E. C.	1173	Cpl	Climo, W. L. H.
605	„	Charge, V. E.	3778	Pte	Cloak, R.
1534	„	Charters, W. S.	4510	„	Close, J.
380	„	Cheeseman, H. J.	386	„	Clough, W.
1255	„	Cheeseman, R.	1998	„	Cloutt, P. J.
4636	„	Cheevers, J.	1703	„	Clyoe, A. R.
4648	„	Cheyne, R. G.	1462	„	Clyne, J.
3364	„	Chesterfield, R. W.	*137	Sgt	Coady, E.
			1702	Pte	Cobcroft, R. H.
1295	Sgt	Chivers, A. W.	*2902	Pte	Coggan, C. G.
2300	Pte	Christian, E.	389	„	Coghlan, E. J.
1054	„	Christian, J.	1695	„	Cohen, A.
852	„	Christie, D.	2895	„	Cohen, S.
*635	Sgt	Church, C. C.	1694	„	Colton, G.
4107	Pte	Churchill, I. A.	453	„	Collins, E. W.
*382	Cpl	Churchill, W. E.	1697	„	Cobley, C.
2604	Pte	Chynoweth, J. S.	15	„	Collier, C.
1331	„	Clancy, F. J.	4016	„	Colbran, S. L.
396	„	Clanes, A.	4311	„	Colburn, C.

NOMINAL ROLL 367

2000	Pte	Coleman, O.
1052	„	Coleman, S. J.
4754	„	Coleman, W. A.
388	„	Coleman, W. J.
628	„	Coles, F.
2307	„	Colgate, F. C.
377	„	Colless, C. N.
1179	„	Colley, E. A.
*1057	„	Collier, P.
3202	„	Collier, S.
853	„	Collins, E. V.
2302	„	Collins, G. E.
571	„	Collins, J. C.
3784	„	Collins, M. B.
4894	„	Collins, W. E.
		(M.M.)
391	Pte	Collins, W. G.
4465	„	Collins, W. H.
1535	C.Q.M.S.	Colman, F.
907	Pte	Colmer, C. K.
3206	„	Colmore, G. P.
2611	Dvr	Colwell, L.
4749	Pte	Connelly, W. M.
2890	„	Connolly, F.
3782	„	Connolly, J.
3532	„	Conolly, R.
*130	„	Connors, W. J.
4020	„	Conway, J. K.
2602	„	Conway, L. V.
2896	„	Conyers, R. R.
140	„	Cook, A.
3218	„	Cook, A. J.
3825	„	Cook, E. F.
2903	„	Cook, H. K.
399	„	Cook, K.
2303	„	Cook, J. J.
*3780	„	Cook, W. H.
2901	„	Cooke, A.
4355	„	Cooke, A.
4151	„	Cooke, N. H.
859	„	Cooke, O. F.
4011	„	Coomer, E.
4248	„	Cooper, A. F.
2204	Cpl	Cooper, A. J.

*141	Pte	Cooper, C. W.
*1251	„	Cooper, E.
4013	„	Cooper, C. G.
4895	„	Cooper, J. W.
2881	„	Cooper, L. C.
*393	C.S.M.	Cooper, R. H.
789	Pte	Cooper, S.
*633	„	Cooper, S. J.
2349	„	Cooper, T. E.
*387	Cpl	Cooper, W. H.
1055	„	Cooper, W. H.
2906	Pte	Copeland, F.
4758	„	Copland, J. C.
4129	„	Condick, W.
4753	„	Connell, G. W.
1250	„	Connor, W.
*130	„	Connors, W. J.
2602	„	Conway, L. V.
5001	Cpl	Corbett, J. W.
*5002	Pte	Cork, H. H.
1319	„	Corkhill, N. B.
2002	Cpl	Corlett, J. W.
*296	Pte	Cormick, J.
4521	„	Corne, P.
*3528	„	Cornford, H. G.
3777	„	Cornish, A. H.
854	„	Comerford, P.
2135	Cpl	Cosh, T. M.
2001	Pte	Conn, C. A.
17	„	Cosgrove, N.
79	„	Coote, L. S.
2898	„	Costello, H. E.
4666	„	Costello, J.
*2304	„	Costello, J. L.
4667	„	Costello, P.
4019	„	Costin, A. E.
		(M.M.)
*3208	„	Cotterill, A. S.
629	„	Cotterill, P.
131	„	Court, R. C.
*2613	„	Coutie, H.
1764	„	Cowan, G. A.
2004	„	Cowan, H. A.
3775	„	Coward, G.

4760	Pte	Cowcher, E.	2904	Pte	Crowfoot, P. L.
398	C.S.M.	Cowen, G.	2612	,,	Crowley, J.
	(D.C.M.)		400	,,	Crowsen, W. J.
1878	Pte	Cowling, A. J.	4511	,,	Croydon, A.
4012	Pte	Cowley, V. E.	4346	,,	Cruickshank, J. S.
*1842	,,	Cowie, A. J.			
2306	,,	Cox, A.	2313	Cpl	Crutch, C. E.
390	,,	Cox, R.	384	Pte	Crux, H. G.
*624	Sgt	Cox, H. H.	75	,,	Crux, W. C.
39	Pte	Cox, J.	1231	,,	Cryer, C. S.
*3779	,,	Cozens, F. J.	1226	,,	Cullen, R. W.
*2309	,,	Cracknell, D.	4901	,,	Cullen, A.
*1025	Sgt	Cracknell, R. B.	861	,,	Cullen, G. C.
3669	Pte	Craddock, A. W.	2897	,,	Cullen, D. A.
1696	,,	Craig, S.	1700	,,	Cullen, T. H.
*921	,,	Crain, H.	2625	,,	Cullen, D. A.
858	,,	Cramb, R.	4893	,,	Cullen, J.
2607	,,	Crameri, L. H.	1707	,,	Culley, R.
5003	,,	Crampton, T. W.	4515	,,	Cummings, J.
637	,,	Crammond, A.	306	,,	Cunneen, J. A.
1537	Sgt	Craven, H.	*1539	Sgt	Curran, F.
1695	Pte	Crecker, F.	4015	Pte	Curran, W. B.
3781	,,	Creagh, J. B.	1706	,,	Curson, E. E.
1316	,,	Creamer, F. E.	2314	,,	Curtis, S.
1538	,,	Cregan, F. J.	3785	,,	Cusack, P. R. B.
1251	,,	Creney, J.	3786	,,	Cusack, W. R.
2907	,,	Creswell, E.	4247	,,	Cushing, A.
4014	,,	Crew, A. B.	3207	,,	Cusick, H. W.
4349	,,	Crispo, C. H.	4522	,,	Curnow, W. I.
1162	,,	Croft, F. D.	4522	,,	Curry, A. S.
*2006	,,	Croft, G.	1706	,,	Curson, E. E. (M.M.)
4512	,,	Croft, W. H.			
*2010	,,	Croker, H.	1540	,,	Cuthbert, H. L.
2005	,,	Croker, R.			
2598	,,	Cromack, A. R.	2315	,,	Daborn, J.
2007	,,	Crosbie, C.	1713	,,	Dallaway, J.
3214	,,	Cross, C.	3218	Cpl	Dale, A. V.
3215	,,	Cross, S. G.	3759	Pte	Daley, J. W.
3349	,,	Cross, V. J.	4357	,,	Dalmer, F.
636	,,	Crossland, W. W.	*2011	,,	Dalton, C. B.
			*867	,,	Dalton, W. K.
1536	,,	Croudace, H. M.	3794	,,	Daly, D. E.
1639	,,	Croudau, H.	3535	Sgt	Daly, F. J.
2908	,,	Crotty, H. A.	4022	Pte	Daly, H. W.

NOMINAL ROLL 369

308	Pte	Dan, C. F.
4024	,,	Daniel, A. J.
1054	,,	Dankin, J. H.
4356	,,	Danswan, C. K.
5801	,,	Davey, G. R.
*4174	,,	Davey, O. C. T.
2913	,,	Davies, A. A.
415	,,	Davies, A. G.
3348	Sgt	Davies, B. O. (D.C.M.)
2317	Pte	Davis, C. F. (M.M.)
4767	Cpl	Davies, E. J.
4023	Pte	Davies, E. R.
3538	,,	Davies, F. G.
4661	,,	Davies, F. H.
*412	,,	Davies, H. R.
3793	,,	Davies, R.
401	,,	Davies, D. H. (M.M.)
2624	,,	Davies, W.
1278	Cpl	Davies, W. F.
2623	Pte	Davidson, H. J.
2616	,,	Davidson, J.
4025	,,	Davidson, N.
2910	,,	Davidson, W.
415	,,	Davis, A. G.
4900	,,	Davis, C. H. R.
1020	Sgt	Davis, C. J.
640	Pte	Davis, C. M.
309	,,	Davis, C. F. (M.M.)
2318	,,	Davis, H. C.
4668	,,	Davis, L.
2917	,,	Davis, L. C.
1336	,,	Dayment, P.
4766	,,	Daws, H.
1714	,,	Dawson, J. W.
145	,,	Dawson, C. R.
1541	,,	Dawson, L. J.
2012	,,	Dawson, J. T.
*52	,,	Day, L. W.
2625	,,	Dayes, L.
1542	,,	Dean, C. A.

1604	Pte	Dean, R. S.
868	,,	Dean, T.
*1543	,,	Deane, A. J.
2015	,,	Deards, S. A.
1062	,,	Deayton, A. G.
4036	,,	Dee, N. V.
3536	Sgt	Deffell, F. H.
1059	Pte	Dellar, R. B.
1716	,,	Delaney, A. N.
4525	,,	Deoberitz, A. M.
2641	,,	Dench, C. H.
2322	,,	Denholm, A. E.
147	,,	Denison, W. J.
3225	,,	Denning, A. J.
643	,,	Dennewald, A. W.
3226	,,	Denton, J.
3823	,,	Derkin, A. J.
3795	,,	Desmond, J. P.
2023	,,	Dettman, G. R.
2014	,,	Dexter, W.
2619	,,	Devine, H.
3792	,,	Dewe, G.
4764	,,	Dewhurst, W. R.
863	Sgt	Dewick, G.
2628	Pte	Dewley, G. L.
2627	,,	Dhu, J.
4765	,,	Dick, J. S.
2916	,,	Dickens, W.
2911	,,	Dickman, H. A.
*2634	,,	Dickson, J. W.
1544	Sgt	Dickson, S. D.
2632	Pte	Dickson, D.
2316	,,	Difford, G.
874	,,	Dike, J. B.
644	,,	Diller, H.
3537	,,	Dilworth, L. D.
3791	,,	Dingle, J. W.
3797	,,	Ditcham, O. L.
411	,,	Dix, M.
2319	,,	Dixon, L. (M.M.)
*649	,,	Dobbie, J.
416	,,	Dobie, L. F.
1026	,,	Dobson, J. H.

z

648	Pte	Dodds, C.	1545	Pte	Duffery, C.
149	Sgt	Dodds, F.	1545	„	Duffey, C.
1717	Pte	Dolan, J.	413	„	Duffy, E.
2492	„	Dolan, W. D. P.	2024	„	Dufty, E.
2742	„	Donald, J.	4657	„	Duffy, V. C.
2016	„	Donald, G.	1718	„	Dumbrell, C. A.
2618	„	Donaldson, J. A.	3533	Sgt	Duncan, F. de R.
2912	„	Doniger, H.	2323	Pte	Duncan, J.
1253	„	Donohoe, H. B.	2796	„	Dunbar, R.
2320	„	Donne, A.	2020	„	Duncan, R.
150	„	Donnellan, T.	*1060	„	Duncan, R. G.
3534	„	Donovan, B. W. A.	1328	Sgt	Duncan, W.
			646	„	Dunkley, E. J.
2621	„	Dormer, J.	647	Pte	Duncan, A.
*4027	„	Douglas, H. W.	4638	„	Dunn, C. H.
4253	„	Douse, C. D.	1235	„	Dunn, E. (M.M.)
1281	Sgt	Doust, H.	146	„	Dunn, E. E.
1252	Pte	Dowd, A. J.	3787	„	Dunn, J.
1464	„	Dowd, J.	*2130	„	Dunn, J. J.
148	Cpl	Dowd, W. A. (D.C.M.)	402	„	Dunn, K. W.
			2626	„	Dunn, L. A.
615	Pte	Dowlan, G. H.	409	„	Dunn, R.
*3541	„	Dowling, S. J.	*2322	„	Dunn, T. P.
872	„	Downs, N. H.	3796	„	Dunne, F. W.
*869	„	Doyle, J. T.	2320	„	Dunnicliffe, R. D.
151	„	Doyle, B.			
2017	„	Doyle, F. B.	1710	„	Duprey, G. E.
873	„	Doyle, F. M.	642	„	Dunstan, J. L.
2620	„	Drake, T. E.	645	„	Durall, J.
*1196	Sgt	Drake, V. H.	3790	„	Dunstan, T.
1061	Pte	Draper, T.	4026	„	Durbin, T. L.
2617	„	Drake, W. W.	3223	„	Dwyer, J. F.
2935	„	Drayton, A.	3224	„	Dyer, V. C.
4414	„	Drew, D. C.	*2021	„	Dykes, C.
4413	„	Drew, L. W. E.	2022	„	Dykes, E. G.
4255	„	Drinkall, T. W.	3222	„	Dyson, W. O.
2600	„	Drinkwater, J.			
4898	„	Drinkwater, W. J.	*3228	„	Earl-Yates, E. W.
497	„	Druery, J. G.	*2325	„	Easlea, R.
*406	„	Dryburgh, L.	4028	„	Eason, E. J.
864	„	Drysdale, W.	2335	„	Easten, R.
3221	„	Dubos, R.	*2026	„	Easton, T.
*4526	„	Dufferin, P. F.	5009	„	Eather, R. J. L.

NOMINAL ROLL

3798	Pte	Eaton, G. K.
2921	„	Eaton, J.
2634	„	Eaton, T. F.
877	Sgt	Eccles, T.
		(D.C.M.) (M.M.)
*157	„	Eccleston, J. G.
18	Pte	Edgar, A.
2637	„	Ede, E. F.
1065	„	Eden, F. G.
2027	Cpl	Edmonds, W. M.
*2326	Pte	Edmunds, C. E.
1293	Cpl	Edmunds, T. P.
1721	Pte	Edmunds, N.
156	Cpl	Edwards, A. C.
4534	Pte	Edwards, A. E.
338	„	Edwards, A.
*2328	„	Edwards, J.
3545	„	Edwards, J.
1547	„	Edwards, J. P.
3544	„	Edwards, J. V.
1547	„	Edwards, T. P.
2922	„	Egan, E. J.
4530	„	Eirth, H.
3227	„	Elbourne, W.
4680	„	Eley, F. G.
5011	„	Elliott, C. H.
4359	„	Elliott, F. W.
1276	Cpl	Elliott, N. A.
1720	Pte	Elliott, S.
650	„	Ellis, A. H.
576	„	Ellis, C. E.
1245	„	Ellis, F.
1244	Cpl	Ellis, R. D.
*1066	Sgt	Elms, W. H.
3801	Pte	Elmslie, J. A.
1245	Cpl	Eltis, F.
*4258	Pte	Ely, E. J.
3824	„	Elyard, H. J.
3799	„	Elyard, W. A. G.
3802	„	Emery, G.
5012	„	Emmitt, J.
4256	„	Endacott, E. J.
1548	„	Endicott, R. A.
2029	„	English, C. C.

3231	Pte	Enright, J. J.
1215	„	Erickson, F.
1346	„	Errington, W. A.
4257	„	Esmond, J.
136	„	Eshman, A. E.
155	Sgt	Estell, R. J.
		(M.M.)
3543	Pte	Etherington, M. R.
2920	„	Evans, A. H.
6	Sgt	Evans, E. C.
4535	Pte	Evans, H. A. K.
417	„	Evans, S.
1067	„	Evans, S. G.
2030	„	Evans, W. J.
2636	„	Eveille, E. J.
19	„	Ewing, C. R.
4533	„	Eyeington, T. W.
*2328	„	Eyles, H. J. P.
1272	„	Eyles, W. D.
20	Dvr	Fabry, M. P.
3578	Pte	Faddy, H. S.
3550	„	Fahey, E. P.
4540	„	Fairbrother, R.
2927	„	Falconer, J.
3368	„	Falconer, J.
*2645	Cpl	Farmer, A. G.
652	Pte	Farley, F. H.
3803	„	Farlow, C. V.
1549	„	Farrar, N. T.
4262	„	Farrell, O. J.
2329	„	Faulds, R.
3548	Cpl	Faulks, A. G.
		(M.M.)
2643	Pte	Favelle, A. E.
*3805	Cpl	Fawcett, C.
4537	Pte	Felley, A. J.
4541	„	Fegan, S. R.
2031	„	Fellowes, W. B.
5902	„	Felton, T.
*882	„	Fenwick, R. G.
1724	„	Ferrie, A. L.

3554	Pte	Ferguson, C. B.		1294	Cpl	Ford, H. D.
2926	Sgt	Ferguson, P.		883	Sgt	Ford, J. C.
*2032	Pte	Ferris, T. J.				(D.C.M.)
3370	„	Ferry, G.		654	Cpl	Ford, T. W.
*1550	„	Fidding, C.				(M.M.)
675	„	Field, B. A.		4773	Sgt	Ford, W. H.
676	„	Field, F. C.		4029	„	Fordham, H.
331	Sgt	Field, F. J. D.		*3804	Pte	Fordham, L. O.
3806	Pte	Field, L. B.		*5019	„	Foster, A. P.
4032	„	Finlayson, M. A.		2697	„	Foster, C. A.
584	„	Finlayson, R.		420	„	Fox, J. H.
3803	„	Finnigan, C. J.		*519	„	Fox, W.
2330	„	Finch, J. J.		1723	„	Fowler, W. F.
3232	„	Firth, V. V.		2034	„	Francis, A.
2925	„	Fish, A. N.		418	„	Francis, B. J.
2924	C.Q.M.S.	Fisher, C. A.		656	„	Franklin, S. G.
				5684	„	Franks, L. G.
4538	Pte	Fisher, F. J.		4514	„	Fraser, G.
3236	„	Fisher, J. J. F.		5020	„	Fraser, H. J.
2918	„	Fisher, P. J.		3552	„	Frazer, E. F.
4771	„	Fisher, P. W.		3552	„	Freame, W. C.
2331	„	Fisher, T.		1322	„	Freeman, I.
164	Cpl	Fisk, S. H.		4360	Cpl	Freeman, S. R.
3551	Pte	Fitzgerald, G.		343	Pte	Freeze, G.
2646	„	Fitzgerald, J.		2366	„	Freemantle, A. R.
3073	„	Fitzgerald, M. J.				
653	„	Fitzgerald, W. J.		4772	„	Frewin, A. M.
12	Sgt	Flack, A. K.		4291	„	French, A. E.
2332	Pte	Flack, J. W. A.		4412	„	French, F. J.
*5015	„	Flanagan, W.		881	„	French, F. S.
4031	„	Flatman, F. C.		1410	„	French, P. V.
886	„	Fletcher, L. M.		*885	„	French, R. N.
3547	„	Flood, E. E.		*2644	„	French, T. R.
4030	Sgt	Florance, F. C.		2638	„	Frew, W.
1551	Pte	Flinn, R. McL.		2333	„	Friend, S. H.
659	„	Flynn, D. A. B.		2036	„	Frisby, J. A.
421	„	Fogo, J.		3367	„	Frost, A.
2033	Cpl	Foley, J. F.		2035	Cpl	Frost, A. C.
*4475	Pte	Foley, J. F.		*2602	„	Funnell, A.
880	Sgt	Forbes, A. H. (M.M.)				
				1266	Sgt	Garran, F.
1726	Pte	Forbes, F.		3558	Pte	Gage, C. A.
3368	„	Ford, A. R.		2334	„	Gain, A.
*3369	„	Ford, A. W. J. J.		2336	„	Gallagher, A. J.

NOMINAL ROLL 373

3556	Pte	Gallagher, H.
3562	„	Galli, C. J.
422	„	Gallienne, E. A.
4038	„	Gammey, M.
53	Dvr	Garaty, N.
		(FRENCH CROIX DE GEURRE)
2337	Pte	Gardem, H. L.
943	„	Garden, H.
*889	„	Gardiner, H.
663	„	Gardiner, V. A.
4034	„	Gardner, W.
5	Sgt	Gardner, W. J.
*2308	„	Garland, C. S.
5022	Pte	Garland, A.
3372	„	Garland, W. P.
5800	„	Garrick, N.
2338	Cpl	Gates, R. R.
893	Pte	Gavin, A. J.
3818	„	Gearey, J. P.
3241	„	Gee, W. A.
2146	„	Geddes, T.
3564	„	Geeves, J.
657	„	Gehlken, H.
*1337	„	Gelling, P.
2930	„	Geoghegan, J. T.
1280	Cpl	Geraghty, J. P.
*2039	Pte	Germon, G. T.
890	„	Gettens, W. B. B.
4548	„	Gibb, A.
1737	„	Gibb, J.
2040	„	Gibbs, J.
4365	„	Gibbett, W. J.
425	Dvr	Gibbes, W.
1274	Sgt	Gibson, G. L. A.
2933	Pte	Gibson, H.
667	„	Gibson, R. T.
2341	„	Gibson, S.
4039	„	Gibson, T.
4545	„	Gibson, T.
2041	„	Giddy, J. J.
1304	„	Gilbert, C. J. G.
3810	„	Gilbert, R. A.
2342	„	Gilchrist, E.
2343	Pte	Gilchrist, R.
		(M.M.)
2046	„	Gilchrist, W. H.
171	„	Gilderthorp, G. F.
1072	„	Gillespie, F. P.
4543	„	Gillett, S. A.
1206	Sgt	Gillies, R. T.
*3816	Pte	Gillies, J. J.
5024	„	Gillingham, G.
		(M.M.)
1553	„	Gillingham, W.
4774	„	Gilmore, H. W.
3211	„	Gileson, H. M.
2648	„	Gillmour, D.
*1074	Cpl	Gladstones, G.
1075	Pte	Gladstones, V. T.
1554	„	Glanville, H. R.
3880	„	Gleeson, T.
3808	„	Glen, T.
*1291	Cpl	Glenn, F. J.
1216	Pte	Glover, G.
		(M.M.)
3815	„	Glynn, J. F.
1555	„	Godfrey, D.
865	„	Goddard, S.
1069	„	Godwin, W. A.
21	Sgt	Goff, A. W.
5694	Pte	Gofton, J.
1243	Dvr	Golp, A. N.
4130	Pte	Goldie, R. E.
1073	„	Goldie, R. W.
3811	„	Golding, S. J. W.
66	Cpl	Goldman, A.
4421	Pte	Goldman, V. J.
1605	„	Goldrick, C. R.
1729	„	Gonsalves, S. F.
1068	„	Goode, G. P.
*887	Cpl	Goodhead, T.
1279	Sgt	Gooding, H. D.
2045	Pte	Goodman, M.
666	„	Goodsall, J.
4544	„	Goodsell, F. H.
668	„	Goodsir, J.

894 Pte	Goodwin, D. C.	
1556 „	Gordon, A. (M.M.)	
2649 „	Gordon, W.	
3074 „	Gorman, R.	
2929 „	Gott, G. (M.M.)	
199 „	Gould, G. A.	
5026 „	Gow, C. H.	
4033 „	Gow, L. E.	
*3559 „	Gowing, B. G.	
4040 „	Gowing, D. A.	
3087 „	Grace, W. G.	
74 „	Graham, J. M.	
892 „	Graham, A.	
1071 „	Graham, J. W.	
*4041 „	Graham, W.	
1308 „	Graham, W. C.	
*2043 „	Graham, W. J.	
660 „	Graham, W. H.	
661 „	Grahame, A.	
664 Cpl	Grahame, J.	
4366 Pte	Granger, G. A.	
3243 „	Grant, K.	
4043 „	Grant, D. W.	
*5093 „	Grant, F. T.	
3556 „	Grant, H. M.	
3813 Cpl	Grant, P. F. (M.M.)	
2934 Pte	Grant, R. H.	
3244 „	Grant, S.	
669 Cpl	Grant, S. R.	
4131 Pte	Grant, W. O.	
4549 „	Gray, A.	
3561 „	Gray, C. S.	
175 „	Gray, G. G.	
1024 Sgt	Gray, G. G.	
47 Dvr	Grey, F.	
1070 Pte	Green, A. J.	
1096 „	Gregory, G. H.	
2201 „	Green, C. A.	
662 „	Green, E. V.	
3371 „	Green, F.	
2345 „	Green, F. A.	
4329 „	Green, O. D.	
4036 Pte	Green, P. S.	
3239 „	Green, R. W.	
2344 „	Green, W.	
2932 „	Greesham, S. M.	
*938 „	Gribble, G. E. J.	
423 „	Grierson, H.	
665 Cpl	Grieve, W. J.	
423 Pte	Grievson, H.	
2349A „	Griffin, J.	
2348 „	Griffin, W. A.	
2347 „	Griffiths, D.	
5027 „	Griffiths, J. E.	
2350 „	Griffiths, W. H.	
4037 „	Griffiths, W. J.	
1557 Cpl	Grogan, T. C. (M.M.)	
4621 Pte	Grosvenor, T.	
427 „	Gruther, J.	
4547 „	Grumley, T. J.	
3809 „	Guest, D. G.	
2906 „	Gulson, C. E.	
*888 Sgt	Gulson, N. N.	
*2341A „	Gunn, H. W.	
426 Pte	Gunther, J.	
3817 „	Gunton, P. S.	
1740 „	Gutteridge, F. A.	
80 „	Guy, J. A.	
4042 „	Guy, R.	
3812 „	Guy, W. T.	
2052 „	Hackett, A. L.	
*2351 „	Haddrell, F. G.	
1230 „	Hadfield, C. B.	
2937 „	Hadfield, J. E.	
807 Cpt	Haig, G.	
3126 Pte	Hain, R. J.	
2053 „	Hain, W. E.	
*3825 „	Haines, E. J.	
683 „	Haines, W. R.	
4051 „	Hakanson, F.	
907 „	Hales, E. W.	
1083 Sgt	Hale, F. H.	
23 Pte	Hall, E. G.	
684 „	Hall, F.	

NOMINAL ROLL 375

898	Pte	Hall, R. E.
182	„	Hall, W. A.
1081	„	Hall, R. B.
2938	„	Hallett, J. R.
3567	„	Halliwell, J.
1558	„	Halliwell, R.
3823	„	Halsall, R. C.
677	„	Halpin, H. J.
1755	„	Hambleton, J. S.
*439	„	Hamence, E. G.
184	Sgt	Hamilton, F. A.
2654	Pte	Hamilton, J. J.
429	„	Hamilton, M.
2352	Cpl	Hamilton, W. H.
4776	Pte	Hammond, W. M.
1752	„	Hampton, W. H.
3820	„	Hampson, G.
2357	„	Hancock, K. E.
436	„	Hancock, W. H.
*2137A	„	Hanley, A.
1080	Cpl	Hanley, F.
2049	Pte	Hanley, J.
902	„	Hanna, E.
1757	„	Hanna, W.
2244	„	Hannan, L. E.
1801	Sgt	Hanleon, C.
2660	Pte	Hamahan, M.
2952	Pte	Hensen, A. H. A.
2946	„	Hansen, D. A.
1744	„	Hanson, E.
1085	Sgt	Hard, G. E.
4323	Pte	Harding, H. T.
2659	„	Harding, K.
1415	„	Hardy, J.
*2665	„	Hare, J.
3376	„	Hargraves, W.
5031	„	Harland, W.
4047	„	Harley, J. D.
3572	„	Harlow, W.
4552	„	Harman, H. W.
1756	„	Harper, E. C.
*2663	„	Harper, E. G.
3569	„	Harper, J. J.
2054	Pte	Harragon, E. E.
2055	„	Harragon, F. E.
2948	„	Harre, A. R.
24	„	Harre, F. W.
1078	„	Harrigan, J. E.
2054	„	Harrigon, E. E.
3573	„	Harrington, G. A.
681	„	Harris, J. W.
1238	„	Harradine, F. S.
1211	Sgt	Harrison, F. G.
1027	„	Harrison, F. W.
183	Pte	Harrison, W. J.
1560	„	Harrison, F.
671	„	Harrison, W. J.
1255	„	Harrison, L. T.
5697	„	Harrower, P.
*190	„	Hart, J.
5114	„	Hartigan, H. L.
2050	„	Hartley, R. (M.M.)
2051	„	Hartley, W.
430	„	Harvey, C. J.
1749	„	Harvey, S. H.
808	„	Hassall, R. L.
76	„	Hast, R. A.
*188	„	Hawcroft, C. H.
3824	„	Hawke, J. V.
1219	„	Hawkey, W.
3377	Cpl	Hawkins, V. M. C.
*2944	Pte	Hawksford, T. H.
2355	„	Hawley, J.
1400	„	Hayes, A. A. E.
680	Sgt	Hayes, E. B.
2650	Pte	Hayes, J. H.
2654	„	Hayes, J. H.
1275	„	Hayes, M. F.
4375	„	Hayes, T. C.
1751	„	Hayes, R.
2058	„	Hayler, E. J.
*192	„	Hayman, W. F.
683	„	Haynes, W. R.

191	Pte	Hazzledene, W.
25	,,	Heber, V. E.
1746	,,	Healey, P. J.
2653	Cpl	Heathcote, H.
4368	Pte	Hearnden, H.
5053	,,	Hearne, A. H.
*186	,,	Hedges, L. J.
443	,,	Heeger, E.
384	,,	Hem, E. B.
2945	,,	Henderson A.
2356	,,	Henderson, J.
1177	,,	Henderson, J.
2350	,,	Henderson, R. S.
*4052	,,	Henderson, T. W.
2664	,,	Hening, H. J.
2817	Cpl	Henry, A. G.
2664	Pte	Henning, H. J.
2357	,,	Henwood, R. C.
*2056	,,	Hepple, M.
4054	,,	Herbert, E. E.
3349	Sgt	Herriott, W. M.
*4370	Pte	Herman, M. P.
*1561	Sgt	Herps, R. H.
3254	,,	Heskey, J. M.
4372	,,	Heslewood, F. M. (M.M.)
4053	Pte	Hetherington, E.
4777	,,	Hewson, W. W.
*4059	,,	Heycox, E. C.
3566	,,	Hibbert, R. T.
1084	,,	Hibbert F. E.
678	,,	Hitchen, W. J.
1324	,,	Hickey, J.
2359A	Cpl	Hicks, O.
903	Pte	Hickey, A.
*2358	Cpl	Hicks, H.
672	Pte	Hicks, H.
1077	Cpl	Higgie, W. C.
2787	Pte	Higgins, F.
1562	,,	Higgins, J. T.
*196	Dvr	Higgins, W. B.
4324	Pte	Hill, A. E.
3827	Pte	Hill, A. J.
*3374	,,	Hill, A. J.
4553	,,	Hill, F. S.
4046	,,	Hill, G. R.
2943	,,	Hill, G.
2060	Cpl	Hill, J. J.
438	Pte	Hill, S.
*4050	,,	Hill, T.
1754	,,	Hills, L. G.
673	,,	Hills, P. A.
4056	,,	Hillier, W. E.
1745	,,	Hinde, F. N.
900	,,	Hine, F. J.
3568	,,	Hinchey, S. W.
2360	,,	Hinchliffe, D.
*2655	,,	Hindes, G.
4512	,,	Hinkley, G. M.
2912	,,	Hirst, W. D.
2651	,,	Hird, H. McD.
3255	,,	Hitchcox, F. P.
2361	,,	Hitchins, H. J.
5128	,,	Hoad, A. E.
2068	,,	Hoare, P.
1753	,,	Hobbs, F. W.
3571	,,	Hobbs, R. R.
3375	,,	Hobby, H. G.
2363	,,	Hodge, J.
2063	,,	Hodgins, H.
1197	,,	Hodgson, H. J.
1323	Sgt	Hogg, J. A. (M.M.)
2063	Pte	Holbert, W. J.
682	,,	Holder, A.
*904	Sgt	Holder, P. J.
4764	Pte	Hogan, W. U.
4044	Sgt	Hogan, R. C.
185	,,	Holgate, J. M.
1563	Pte	Holliday, A. M.
906	,,	Hollows, J.
2915	,,	Holloway, F.
1563	,,	Holliday, H.
4057	,,	Holliday, H.
194	Dvr	Holliday, W.
441	Pte	Holmes, R. T. C.

NOMINAL ROLL 377

2915	Pte	Hollaway, F.
2467	„	Holloway, S.
2064	„	Holbert, W. J.
2062	„	Holmes, A.
189	„	Homesby, H. A.
*2939	„	Holt, B. P.
3570	„	Hood, A. L.
1750	„	Hood, B. B.
5034	„	Hooklyn, F. U.
3033	„	Hookey, A. H.
674	„	Hopper, C. L.
2349	„	Hooper, M. V.
3069	„	Hooper, S. C. H.
1748	„	Horendene, H.
1352	„	Hornby, W. J.
3246	„	Hornby, J.
3822	„	Horney, E. P.
1015	„	Hoskins, C. H.
1565	„	Hotchkis, D. S.
1564	„	Hotchkis, J. H.
*895	„	Housdon, D. J.
2657	„	Hough, J. (M.M.)
1290	„	Hough, L. J.
*2362	Cpl	Howard, A. E.
1016	Pte	Howard, E. A.
1256	„	Howard, L. E.
1401	„	Howard, R. C.
435	„	Howard, V. N.
440	„	Howes, T. C.
3247	„	Howcroft, B.
4373	„	Howes, W.
2947	„	Hoy, R.
4367	„	Hoye, R. C.
675	„	Hoye, T. G.
1566	„	Hudson, C. H.
46	Sgt	Hudson, H. R.
5037	Pte	Hudson, J.
2365	„	Hudson, R. L.
3379	„	Hughes, H. C.
2638	„	Hughes, L. H.
1397	„	Hughes, H.
2366	Cpl	Hughes, H. H.
432	Pte	Hughes, N.
901	Pte	Hughes, N.
1567	Sgt	Hughes, F. W.
1017	Pte	Hughes, W. J.
2364	„	Hugo, R. J.
*5038	„	Hulls, H. W.
2066	„	Humble, J.
3577	„	Hume, H. G.
4783	„	Hunt, A. B.
437	„	Hunt, E. W.
806	R.S.M.	Hunt, J.
195	Pte	Hunt, O. O.
442	„	Hunter, J. G. (D.C.M.)
3378	„	Hunter, H. C.
*1079	„	Hunter, R.
679	„	Huntington, W. S.
*2936	Pte	Huntriss, A. H.
1232	Cpl	Hurst, J. T.
187	Pte	Hurst, W. D.
5039	„	Hurcombe, H. G. S.
3565	„	Hutcheson, C.
2539	„	Hutchins, F.
4778	„	Hutchings, F. S.
3245	„	Hutchinson, G.
1221	„	Hutchinson, P. J.
3373	„	Hutchison, W. H.
*2065	Cpl	Hutton, D. M.
4045	Pte	Hutton, V. E.
4786	„	Hutton, T. E.
3137	„	Hutton, W. N.
4048	„	Hutson, F. C.
4049	„	Hutson, J. H.
4076	„	Huxley, A.
2652	Sgt	Huxley, E. H.
2656	Pte	Huxley, F. W.
2940	Cpl	Huxley, W. H. (M.M.)
1082	Pte	Hydon, W. V.
1871	„	Hyde, A.
*4055	„	Hyde, J. A. J.

378   THE PURPLE AND GOLD

909	Pte	Ings, P. E.		444	Pte	Johnson, C. H.
*686	,,	Ingles, W.		446	Sgt	Johnson, C. S.
4554	,,	Irlam, F.		910	Cpl	Johnson, J.
1338	,,	Irwin, R. J.		2368	,,	Johnson, J.
199	,,	Irvine, D. G.		2961	Pte	Johnston, J. A.
1086	,,	Israel, E. V.		445	,,	Johnson, J. J.
381A	,,	Ivory, C. H.		1571	,,	Johnson, J. R.
				2958	,,	Johnson, O.
2670	,,	Jacobs, H.		2072	Cpl	Johnson, R. E.
2367	,,	Jacobs, V. E.		3579	Pte	Johnson, S. B.
2665	,,	Jacobs, P. A.		688	,,	Johnston, E. W.
2671	,,	Jacobs, W.		2667	,,	Johnstone, J. B.
447	,,	Jack, A.		67	,,	Johnston, J. G.
4063	,,	Jackett, J.		2635	,,	Jomartz, E. H.
1568	,,	Jackson, A.		911	,,	Jones, B.
1270	,,	Jackson, A. A.		*2075	,,	Jones, E.
1760	,,	Jackson, F.		*3259	,,	Jones, E. J.
*451	,,	Jackson, F. H.		3258	,,	Jones, E. R.
*4061	,,	Jackson, J. W.		2079	,,	Jones, F.
2069	Sgt	Jackson, W. C.		912	,,	Jones, G.
1313	Pte	Jackson, W. J.		450	,,	Jones, G. A.
4265	,,	James, A. F.		*448	,,	Jones, H.
689	,,	James, A. H.		*2370	,,	Jones, J. (M.M.)
691	Cpl	James, A. H.		*2955	,,	Jones, J. A. V.
*1569	Pte	James, A. M.		3380	,,	Jones, J. E.
2666	,,	James, C.		5709	,,	Jones, J. R.
1088	,,	James, E. W.		1761	,,	Jones, J. W.
913	,,	James, J.		449	,,	Jones, L. S.
4062	,,	Jamieson, W.		1271	,,	Jones, P. J.
1297	,,	Jardine, R. T.		4064	,,	Jones, R. H.
3260	,,	Jarvis, F. E.		3828	Sgt	Jones, S. B.
2353	Cpl	Jarvis, H. J.		3346	Pte	Jones, W. T.
1234	Pte	Jeater, W. D.		2953	Sig	Jordan, E. D. R.
4676	,,	Jeffrey, R. C.		2371	Sgt	Jordan, S. J.
3257	,,	Jefferies, W. H.		2668	Pte	Jordan, W.
1170	C.S.M.	Jehan, N. B.		2960	,,	Josephs, O.
2071	Pte	Jennings, D.		4557	,,	Joyce, H. H.
1087	,,	Jennings, E. E.				(M.M.)
384A	,,	Jennings, W. J.		54	Dvr	Joyce, J.
4065	,,	Jepson, C. E.		*2957	Pte	Justice, A.
3578	,,	Jevons, H.		1758	,,	Justice, M. D.
2074	,,	Joass, C. P.				
2669	,,	Jobson, F. R.		3272	Dvr	Kay, H. L.
1089	,,	Johanson, E.		1444	Pte	Kane, W. S.

NOMINAL ROLL 379

*2673	Pte	Kean, W. E.	11	Pte	King, S. E.
*2078	„	Keeling, T. E.	1217	„	King, T.
*2964	„	Keen, R. H.	207	„	Kingsford, R. P.
4525	„	Keilor, J.	3582	„	Kingston, E. H.
695	„	Kellerman, H. R.	4132	„	Kingston, T. E.
3263	„	Kellett, W. E.	4266	„	Kinsella, J.
1242	„	Kelly, B.	26	Dvr	Kirk, R.
435	Cpl	Kelly, J. R. C.	4267	Pte	Kirkbride, K. W.
*915	Pte	Kelly, J. R.	1573	Cpl	Kirkby, A.
4558	„	Kelly, R.	696	Pte	Kirkpatrick, G.
3	Sgt	Kelly, S. H.	2376	„	Kitchen, J. F.
4793	Pte	Kelly, S. J.	1091	„	Klein, A. J.
5043	„	Kelly, T. A.	4561	„	Knight, A.
4560	„	Kelly, W.	2166	„	Knight, A. E.
1098	„	Kemp, D.			(M.M.)
1572	„	Kemp, P. S. K.	1762	„	Knight, D. C.
2356	„	Kemp, S.	1189	„	Knight, F. R.
4066	„	Kendall, G. H.	.1351	„	Knight, H. H.
*3830	„	Kendall, L. S.	*2672	„	Knight, L. S.
209	„	Kennedy, A.	*2962	„	Knight, W.
3383	„	Kenny, R. W.	208	„	Knight, W.
4069	„	Kenny, J. P.	1257	„	Knoblanche, V. D.
1763	„	Kenway, J.			
4417	„	Keough, J. J.	2081	„	Knox, J.
2377	„	Keogh, R.	1574	„	Krestensen, P. S.
917	„	Kepple, F. W.	1575	„	Krestensen, P. J.
4068	„	Kerin, L. B.	673	„	Kulmar, A. F.
1093	„	Kerin, J. C.	3586	„	Kvarvstrom, G. D.
4268	„	Kerin, W. F.			
3583	„	Kerr, J. P.			
3261	„	Kerr, W.	465	Cpl	Lahiff, H.
1091	„	Klein, A. J.			(M.M.)
3381	„	Kornfeld, O. L.	2378	Pte	Laidler, W.
206	„	Kiddle, C. J.	*2512	„	Laing, D.
2375	„	Kindlysides, J.	4380	„	Laing, H.
3581	„	King, A.	3266	„	Laing, J.
*2186A	„	King, C. D.	463	Sgt	Laing, J. W.
*1096	„	King, D.			(M.M.)
*1325	„	King, E.	*4531	Pte	Laity, E.
2374	„	King, E. A.	*4366	„	Lamb, H.
*208	Sgt	King, E. C.	3384	„	Lamb, J. E.
3382	Pte	King, E. J.	2379	„	Lamerton, B. J.
916	„	King, F. H.	919	„	Lambert, E. J.
1095	„	King, H. A.	1287	Sgt	Lambourne, W.

1765	Cpl	Lamplough, W. L.		4796	Pte	Lean, C. G.
3584	Pte	Lancaster, G. W.		4797	,,	Lean, W. C.
*2085	Cpl	Lancaster, V. L. (D.C.M.)		3260	,,	Leask, C. A.
				*1309	Cpl	Leask, E. G.
2083	Pte	Lane, A. L.		2969	Pte	Leary, E. J.
1163	,,	Lane, D. J.		699	Dvr	Leary, R. H.
4071	,,	Lane, G. H.		4045	Pte	Le Breton, L. W.
4070	,,	Lane, H.		1259	,,	Ledwidge, P. J.
2651	,,	Lane, H. J.		1873	,,	Lee, C. E.
*4519	,,	Lane, P. R.		*4535	,,	Lee, E. V.
2380	,,	Lane, R.		1258	,,	Lee, G. E.
4567	,,	Lane, W.		4444	,,	Lee, J. F.
*4563	,,	Lansdowne, L. R.		462	,,	Lee, W. A.
				3835	,,	Lees, L. O.
4269	,,	Lang, T. N.		*3269	,,	Lees, T. J.
1302	,,	Langbein, A. J.		3831	,,	Leeson, C.
798	Sgt	Langmaid, J. G.		4377	,,	Leeson, W. W.
2683	Pte	Langford, E. J.		2087	Cpl	Leggett, S.
3089	,,	Langley, S. A.		3833	Pte	Leggett, T. H. C.
1764	,,	Langtry, L. R.		700	Cpl	Leighton, C. H.
4652	,,	Lansdowne, J. P.		1766	Pte	Lemon, P.
3559	,,	Large, T. H.		1769	,,	Leslie, J. G.
2359	,,	Larkins, E.		1102	Sgt	Lethbridge, W.
1774	,,	Larney, H. J.		68	Pte	Lett, H. A.
1771	,,	Lassere, E. S.		754	,,	Letter, R. J.
705	,,	Lassere, J.		464	Dvr	Le Vell, R.
2084	,,	Latcham, W.		3264	Pte	Lever, D. J.
4270	,,	Latimer, B. K.		3265	,,	Lever, E. A. G.
*221	Dvr	Laurie, A. D. G.		3264	,,	Lever, L. J.
1305	Cpl	Lavender, C. G.		1766	,,	Levis, R.
456	Pte	Laver, E.		218	,,	Lewis, H. W.
217	,,	Law, M. B.		1163	,,	Lewis, J. K.
4568	,,	Lawhawk, C. J.		2790	,,	Lewis, O. O.
27	,,	Lawler, T.		*469	,,	Lewis, W.
2685	,,	Laws, E. E.		2968	,,	Lewis, W. A.
590	Cpl	Lawson, F.		2679	,,	Lewis, W. E.
1100	Pte	Lawson, P.		4273	,,	Lewitz, A. T.
3587	,,	Lawson, R. G.		*4272	,,	Lewitz, R. J.
2360	,,	Lawson, J.		3834	,,	Lidbury, J. F. S.
4564	,,	Lawton, H. P.		2674	,,	Limond, D.
*3803	,,	Layton, D. W.		*3078	,,	Lindsay, J. D. M.
*1104	,,	Leahy, R. J.		1874	,,	Ling, O.
2086	,,	Leake, W. J.		921	,,	Linklater, L. H.
				466	Sgt	Linsley, W. H.

NOMINAL ROLL 381

2088	Pte	Linter, T. A.
2089	Cpl	Lister, E. H. (M.M.)
809	Sgt	Lister, J.
1772	Pte	Littlejohns, H.
1255	„	Llloyd, A. O.
455	„	Lloyd, D. V.
2384	„	Lloyd, J. W.
*2676	„	Lloyd, L. C.
3832	„	Lloyd, R. F.
3588	„	Lloyd, T. R.
4800	Cpl	Lloyd, W.
3267	Pte	Lobley, J. B.
2386	„	Lobley, W.
1767	„	Locke, W.
4805	„	Locock, A. J.
2681	„	Locock, H.
4378	„	Lodding, W. G.
460	„	Logan, W. D.
4359	„	Logie, M. N.
2090	„	Logue, F. G.
2091	„	Logue, R. S.
2242	„	Looker, L. A.
1576	„	Lomax, S.
401	„	Lonsdale, C. M.
4802	„	Lonsdale, L. J.
2092	„	Long, J. C. J.
2383	„	Long, J. W.
2093	„	Long, P. A.
81	Cpl	Lording, R. E.
702	Pte	Loton, G. S.
*4798	„	Lotthamer, H. W.
525A	„	Loughry, J. V.
2687	„	Louis, H.
703	„	Love, F.
2675	„	Love, G.
*461	„	Love, W.
1247	„	Loveridge, A. E.
1099	„	Lovig, L.
1770	„	Lovitt, L. W. G.
*920	„	Low, A. A.
*451	Sgt	Lowbridge, G.
*2675	Pte	Love, G.
3586	„	Lowe, G. C.
3836	Pte	Love, J. W.
4379	„	Lowe, W.
3268	„	Lowry, E. J.
*467	„	Lucre, C. H.
1773	„	Ludwick, C. E.
922	„	Luff, A.
2929	„	Lugg, H.
704	„	Lutge, J.
5048	„	Lutham, L. O.
1577	„	Lycett, H.
2677	„	Lyddiard, W. W.
*2498	„	Lyle, F. A.
2682	„	Lynn, D.
2971	„	Lyons, G. M. L.
3271	„	Lyons, J. C.
3272	„	Lyons, L.
3270	„	Lyons, V.
1105	„	Lynch, D.
458	„	Lynch, P. K.
2678	„	Lysaght, F. E.
2387	„	Macdonald, J.
3823	„	Macdonald, S.
1176	Sgt	Macdonald, W. C.
2703	Pte	Mackay, S. J.
1347	„	Mackie, J. M.
29	Sgt	Mackay, K.
1578	Pte	Mackenzie, A.
2096	„	Mackenzie, J.
1599	„	Mackenzie, W. A.
1298	„	Mackie, J. M.
929	„	Mackie, M.
480	„	Maclean, D.
1118	„	Macleod, J.
4282	„	Maclennan, D. G.
4669	„	Macrae, G. E.
1175	„	Maculay, W. J.
1581	„	Maess, C.
3272	„	Magner, V.
*3273	Cpl	Magner, N.
3851	Pte	Maguire, B.

3599	Pte	Maguire, F.	2098	Pte	Martin, H.
69	„	Mahoney, J. W.	*2983	„	Martin, R. C.
2974	„	Major, G. T.	*1583	„	Martin, R. L.
*483	Sgt	Malcolm, E. S.	4386	„	Martin, P. J.
1205	Pte	Mallinson, W.	2695	„	Martin, W.
2388	„	Malcolm, T. A.	1314	„	Martindale, H. W.
492	„	Maloney, F.			
1785	„	Maloney, M. J.	4073	„	Maskell, R. H.
1881	„	Manefield, J.	3843	„	Massey, J. C.
1292	„	Manefield, J.	584	Sgt	Massey, T. M. (M.M.)
941	„	Mann, E. N.			
*2097	„	Mann, G. S.	2367	Pte	Matson, H. J.
939	„	Manning, E. C.	2475	„	Matson, W. J.
5052	„	Mansfield, W. H.	*1460	„	Matthews, A. F.
472	„	Manton, A. E.	2446	„	Matthews, D. R.
2366	„	Marchant, C. G.	481	Sgt	Mathews, E. H. (D.C.M.)
1260	„	Markey, A.			
474	„	Marks, C. T.	2101	Pte	Mather, R. (M.M.)
*4083	„	Marriott, T. C.			
2795	„	Marsh, C. W.	3846	„	Maudsley, S. C.
2691	„	March, C. L. L.	4894A	„	Maudsley, L. R.
*4276	„	Marsh, E. W.	1269	„	Maxwell, A. F.
1207	„	Marsh, S. B.	*3557	„	Maxwell, A. R.
3591	„	Marshall, A.	3592	„	Maxwell, B. S.
2987	„	Marshall, F. F.	5136	„	Maxworthy, W. E.
*4277	„	Marshall, W. G.			
2390	„	Mason, E.	*718	„	May, A. (M.M.)
3085	„	Marsham, T. F.	2591	„	May, C. J.
4074	„	Mathews, L. J.	1164	„	May, C. S.
722	„	Matthews, A. F.	2988	„	May, J. H.
481	Sgt	Mathews, E. H.	5057	„	Mayberry, F. H.
4075	Pte	Matthews, G. J.	*R.2102	Pte	Maynard, S.
3590	„	Matthews, C. J.	4808	Pte	Mazey, F. D.
796	„	Matthews, J.	*2392	„	Meadowcroft, F.
2980	„	Matthews, R.	*4382	„	Meaker, E. E.
474	„	Marks, C. T.	*2393	„	Medhurst, W. E.
1349	Cpl	Maroney, J. A.	3597	„	Meehan, R.
3855	Pte	Marsden, G. W.	3840	„	Meldrum, J. S.
2100	„	Martens, A. O.	2698	„	Melville, J.
5053	„	Martin, A.	2686	„	Melville, H. T.
3285	„	Martin, D.	5060	„	Mendham, J. J.
720	„	Martin, E.	724	„	Membrey, J. V.
940	„	Martin, J. F.	3594	„	Menzies, W.
1583	„	Martin, J. W.	*578	C.Q.M.S.	Menzies, E.

NOMINAL ROLL 383

649	Pte	Menzies, T.
237	„	Meredith, F. L.
3593	„	Mercer, R. T.
2702	„	Mercer, S. J.
3362	„	Merchant, W. T.
4642	„	Meredith, A. C.
1109	„	Merlin, H. R.
1239	„	Merrilees, J. C.
4385	„	Merriman, E.
4662A	„	Merton, E. G.
336	Sgt	Metcalfe, T. W.
1791	Pte	Mess, G. G.
1779	„	Mess, W. J. T.
4573	„	Messina, V. F.
3281	„	Michael, C.
5058	„	Michie, R. G. P.
2986	L/Cpl	Mike, A.
490	Pte	Miles, A. E.
489	„	Miles, H.
2696	„	Millage, P. J.
3385	„	Miller, A.
2103	„	Miller, A. S. L.
*709	„	Miller, J.
55	Dvr	Miller, H. H.
1436	Pte	Miller, W. A.
1585	„	Millgate, T. W.
495	„	Milgate, P. (M.M.)
3598	„	Milham, A. J.
1110	Cpl	Mills, J. I.
2689	Pte	Mills, L. G.
*3854	„	Mills, R.
3280	„	Milner, M.
31	„	Milton, R. C.
710	Sgt	Milwain, R. M.
715	Pte	Millwood, F. W.
897	„	Minnican, R. S.
1586	„	Minouge, M. V.
*1193	„	Minter, F. G.
810	Cpl	Mitchell, C.
3269	Pte	Mitchell, E. D.
942	„	Mitchell, E. J.
1587	„	Mitchell, J.
2692	Sgt	Mitchell, L. I.
707	Pte	Mitchell, R. C.
1781	„	Mitchell, S. C.
5731	„	Mitchell, W.
*4328	„	Moate, C. W.
1193	„	Moody, F. G.
4082	„	Moncrieff, E. W.
1107	„	Monkton, R.
4847	„	Moon, H.
4383	„	Moon, N. H.
4574	„	Montgomery, P.
2701	„	Morton, W. G.
*R.2102	Pte	Maynard, S.
*3852	„	Monro, W. F.
2978	„	Moor, J. J.
932	„	Moore, A. W.
1588	Cpl	Moore, C. J.
2982	Pte	Moore, C. J.
4077	„	Moore, H.
2492	Sgt	Moore, L. H. (M.M.)
4078	Pte	Moore, M. G.
*478	„	Moore, W.
2107	„	Moorhouse, C.
2977	„	Morden, F.
479	„	Morgan, W. H.
4079	„	Morgan, J. G. (M.M.)
2106	„	Morgan J. K.
2493	„	Morley, J. C.
2394	„	Moroney, M.
3274	„	Morris, A. J.
2108	C.Q.M.S.	Morris, B. L.
*2972	Pte	Morriss, F. F.
5062	„	Morris, F. J.
*3079	„	Morriss, G. L.
1178	Cpl	Morrissey, F. J.
3845	Pte	Morrison, C.
1587	„	Morrison, C.
5063	„	Morrison, J.
1191	Cpl	Morrison, K. J.
*324	„	Morrison, T. J.
3596	Pte	Moran, V. F.
2395	„	Moscrop, S.

717 Pte	Mortimer, H.	
3387 „	Moses, J. M.	
*3386 „	Moses, R. L.	
1791 Cpl	Moss, G. G.	
2397A Pte	Moss, L.	
1779 „	Moss, W. J. T.	
3284 „	Mostran, A. E.	
3595 „	Motbey, P. H.	
4145 „	Motbey, J. W. (M.M.)	
2690 „	Mottershead, A. S.	
1113 „	Moonsey, V. A.	
3388 „	Moyes, W. H.	
1112 Cpl	Muggeridge, E. W. H.	
236 Pte	Mulligan, K.	
2691 „	Mulcahy, J. C.	
2976 „	Mullen, E. J.	
2694 „	Mulroney, E. P.	
470 Sgt	Munday, W. F. (M.M.)	
*2973 Pte	Munro, N. E. S.	
2497 „	Murdock, A. T.	
233 Sgt	Murdock, S. R. (D.C.M.)	
2110 Pte	Murphy, A. J.	
234 Sgt	Murphy, A. H.	
1593 Pte	Murphy, D. J.	
1108 „	Murphy, E. G.	
2700 „	Murphy, F. H.	
2984 „	Murphy, F. L.	
2111 „	Murphy, J.	
*2693 „	Murphy, J. P. F.	
2699 „	Murphy, J. R.	
1299 „	Murphy, P. J.	
4274 „	Murphy, W. D.	
5482 „	Murphy, T.	
2112 „	Murrell, L. J.	
2535 „	Murrell, S.	
1159 „	Murn, J.	
*4569 „	Murray, A. G.	
3589 Cpl	Murray, A. H.	
3600 Pte	Murray, A. R.	
*1590 Cpl	Murray, C. W.	
238 Sgt	Murray, H. F.	
4081 Pte	Murray, J.	
1597 „	Murray, J. B.	
3839 „	Murray, P.	
*930 „	Murray, R. G.	
1591 „	Mutch, C. J.	
937 Cpl	Myles, J. H.	
3670 Pte	McAllister, A. W.	
475 „	McArdle, C. B.	
1594 Sgt	McBride, E. R.	
*4152 Pte	McBride, H.	
1119 „	McBride, W.	
4559 Cpl	McCallum, A. J.	
4390 „	McCann, T. J.	
2115 Pte	McCarthy, C. E.	
240 Sgt	McCartney, J. A.	
936 Pte	McClenaughan, J. W. K.	
494 Cpl	McClennan, J.	
477 Sgt	McCloskey, C. H. (D.C.M.)	
4086 Pte	McClure, M. A.	
2400 „	McCormack, V.	
580 Cpl	McCormick, J. H.	
*1595 Pte	McCoullough, H. G.	
4662 „	McCoullough, N. E.	
241 Sgt	McCoy, N. R.	
2990 Pte	McCraw, W. J.	
3275 „	McCredie, J. D.	
1805 Sgt	McCristal, F.	
4662 Pte	McCullough, H. G.	
2117 „	McDermott, W. A. L. (M.M.)	
926 „	McDiarmid, H.	
927 „	McDiarmid, R.	
1803 Sgt	Macdonald, A. M.	

NOMINAL ROLL 385

1176	Pte	McDonald, W. G.
1596	„	McDonald, A. R.
1804	Cpl	McDonald, D.
924	Pte	McDonald, E. J.
3283	„	McDonald, F.
5067	„	McDonald, F.
2095	„	McDonald, H. T.
*4813	„	McDonald, J. T.
486	„	McDonald, S. R.
4087	„	McDonnell, W. H.
3838	Cpl	McDowell, F. W.
4	Sgt Cook	McDuff, J.
1798	Cpl	McElroy, C. J.
3853	Pte	McEwan, L. H.
4815	„	**McFarlane, C.**
1261	„	McFarlane, M. S.
1579	„	McFarlane, W. M.
1412	„	McFayden, E.
4391	„	McFeeters, J. B.
721	„	McFarvey, S. E.
1348	„	McGee, F. H.
1222	Sgt	McGillicuddy, F. (M.M.)
4561	Cpl	McGillivray, H.
928	Pte	McGilvray, A. S.
1800	Cpl	McGinnity, M.
*496	Pte	McGivern, J. B.
1168	„	McGlone, J.
2707	„	McGovern, J. P.
*473	C.S.M.	McGowan, J. B. (D.C.M.)
2401	C.Q.M.S.	McGowen, F.
3487	Pte	McGrath, C.
488	Dvr	McGrath, L. A.
3849	Pte	McGreal, J.
2705	„	McGreal, J. R.
272	Cpl	McGregor, G. C.
931	Pte	McGregor, J. J.
2402	„	McGregor, R.
*711	Pte	McGregor, T.
4578	„	McGuire, W. V.
476	„	McHattie, W. J.
498	„	McIlroy, W.
716	„	McIntyre, H. E.
2709	„	McIntyre, J. J.
3838	„	McIntyre, V. R.
925	„	McKay, N. J.
1114	„	McKechnie, G.
4814	„	McKee, S. L.
2706	„	McKee, W.
2711	„	McKenzie, J. T.
3841	„	McKenzie, L. E.
892	„	McKenzie, M.
*1598	Cpl	McKenzie, N.
1116	Pte	McKenzie, T. W.
30	Cpl	McKeown, T.
4205	Pte	McKersie, N.
*938	„	McKillop, D. J.
2993	„	McKinnon, A. B.
1233	C.S.M.	McKinnon, E. G. (M.S.M.)
2952	Pte	McKinnon, D.
4278	Cpl	McKinnon, L.
487	Pte	McKinnon, L. H.
5196	Sgt	McKinnon, R.
485	Pte	McLachlan, W.
4582	„	McLachlan, W.
1115	Dvr	McLean, D.
723	Pte	McLean, E. F.
1801	„	McLean, H. A.
3389	„	McLean, J. M.
4572	„	McLean, P. F.
2405	„	McLeish, A.
4579	„	McLeish, H. L.
*934	Sgt	McLellan, D.
*2404	Pte	McLeod, A.
712	„	McLeod, D. B.
4313	„	McLeod, J.
945	„	McLeod, K. C.
3856	„	McLeod, W.
1799	„	McKay, D.
29	Dvr	McKay, K.
925	Pte	McKay, N. J.

AA

2120 Cpl McKenzie, C.
*3837 Pte McMahon, J. E.
2708 „ McMahon, J. H. (M.M.)
1414 „ McMicking, R. T.
2121 „ McMullen, F. G.
*4279 „ McNamara, J.
1262 „ McNamara, W. J.
4817 „ McNulty, C. A.
3856 „ McQuillan, J.
*1165 „ McRoberts, W. L.
3278 „ McSweeney, G. J.
4089 Cpl McVeity, D. B.
*4085 Pte McVeity, W.
946 „ McVey, R. H.
*4575 „ McWatt, J.
713 Cpl McWilliam, J.

*3601 Pte Naden, A. W.
729 „ Nagle, W. F.
949 „ Nankivell, P. J. (M.M.)
2406 „ Neal, L. C.
1353 „ Neaylon, J. P.
1807 „ Neill, H.
725 „ Nelmes, E.
250 Cpl Nelson, C. L.
727 Pte Nelson, F. A.
*728 „ Nelson, H. O.
1121 „ Nelson, H. H.
2994 „ Nelson, T. J.
501 „ Nesbitt, D.
2644 „ Nesbitt, V.
1315 „ Newitt, A. C.
4583 „ Newman, A. A.
4285 „ Newman, A. H.
1318 „ Newman, C. S.
*2714 „ Newson, J. F.
4646 „ Nicoll, A. C.
4284 „ Nicholas, L. A.

*1879 Pte Nichols, F. J.
2408 „ Nicholle, A. C.
2407 A/Cpl Nicholls, M.
3390 Pte Nicholson, H. L.
502 „ Nicholson, J. B.
1122 „ Nicholson, R.
1809 „ Nicholson, R. L.
5070 „ Nicholson, R. O.
500 „ Nickisson, F.
4088 „ Niemi, K.
948 L/Cpl Nightingall, S.
2122 Pte Nilsen, A.
3286 „ Noble, G. H.
2123 „ Noble, J.
4392 „ Noble, J. J.
950 „ Noden, A. E.
1223 Sgt Nolan, H. R.
*3602 Pte Noonan, J. W.
1808 Cpl Norris, C. J.
2124 Pte Norris, F.
1028 Cpl Norris, W. R.
4089 „ North, F. C. (M.M.)
2409 Pte Northey, S.
2857 „ Northrop, E. W.
10 Sgt Norman, W. H. (M.M.)
2410 Pte Nowland, D. M.
4823 „ Nugent, B. L.
726 „ Nyman, G.

2411 „ Oakes, W. H.
3858 „ Oates, J. T.
1810 „ Oakes, W. F.
3080 L/Cpl Obdroyd, H.
505 Pte O'Brien, E.
2715 „ O'Brien, G.
2713 „ O'Brien, H.
2412 „ O'Brien, J. J.
255 Dvr O'Callaghan, D.
2413 Pte O'Connell, J. F.
3392 „ O'Connell, W.
253 „ O'Connor, C. H.
730 „ O'Connor, J.

NOMINAL ROLL 387

3606	Pte	O'Connor, M.
4091	,,	O'Connor, M. J.
1811	,,	O'Connor, W.
4586	,,	O'Donnell, H. B.
4133	,,	O'Donnell, J. F.
4330	,,	O'Dwyer, D.
3351	,,	Ogden, H.
1246	Cpl	Ogle, G.
952	Pte	Ogle, T.
3393	,,	O'Halloran, B. H.
299	,,	O'Hara, H. H.
3080	,,	Oldroyd, H.
4826	,,	O'Keefe, W.
4588	,,	O'Leary, L. G.
4647	,,	Oldfield, E. J.
3391	,,	Oliver, A.
3289	,,	Oliver, W.
*252	,,	Olsen, H.
4587	,,	O'Neil, H.
1812	,,	O'Neill, J. P.
2716	,,	O'Neill, M.
1813	,,	O'Neill, W. H.
3288	,,	O'Reilly, P.
1336	,,	Ormerod, J. E.
880	Cpl	Orth, F. A.
3287	Pte	Osborne, E. W.
2717	Cpl	Osborne, N. C.
4090	Pte	O'Shea, J. B.
2125	,,	Osland, J.
*2414	,,	Osmond, R.
506	,,	Ostinga, D. J. McL.
4585	,,	Ostler, E.
953	,,	O'Sullivan, R.
3604	,,	O'Toole, L.
2416	,,	O'Toole, J. V.
3605	,,	Otton, E. T.
2127	,,	Oswald, T. H.
2418	,,	Outhwaite, G. A.
2417	,,	Outhwaite, W. R.
1289	,,	Owen, G. T.
1182	,,	Owen, W. J.
*1326	,,	Owen, W. W. S.

4092	Pte	Oyston, T.
1126	,,	Packer, F.
954	Sgt	Packham, C. W.
*3865	Pte	Packham, S. J.
2722	,,	Packwood, L. H.
963	,,	Pacoe, W. W.
5074	,,	Page, A.
2729	,,	Page, A. H.
3607	,,	Page, C. R.
*1277	C.S.M.	Paine, A. R.
*3206	Pte	Palfreyman, W. P.
726	,,	Palmer, A.
337	Sgt	Palmer, H.
521	Pte	Palmer, L.
*618	,,	Pall, F. W.
510	,,	Pardy, A.
1599	,,	Parfitt, A. H.
1131	,,	Parfray, A. T.
3862	,,	Park, A. B.
1823	,,	Parker, A. D.
*732	Cpl	Parker, A. E.
2420	Pte	Parker, C. P.
1815	,,	Parker, T. W.
2128	,,	Parker, W. B.
1130	,,	Parker, W. G.
*2419	,,	Parker, W. P.
2421	,,	Parkes, W. (M.M.)
2723	,,	Parkinson, F. G.
*2719	,,	Parkinson, J.
2422	,,	Parkinson, H.
2859	,,	Partridge, H. R.
*4589	,,	Passmore, G.
2131	,,	Patrick, A.
5075	Sgt	Paterson, G. W.
3611	Pte	Patterson, R. W.
733	,,	Pattison, R.
740	,,	Paul, R. R.
2130	,,	Pavey, T. S.
1818	,,	Pawley, A. H.
2132	,,	Paxley, R. G.
4147	,,	Paxton, G.

*4094	Pte	Payne, E. L.	2133	Pte	Pickering, K.
4658	,,	Payne, G.	3002	,,	Pickering, F. H.
3291	,,	Payne, R. S.			(M.M.)
515	,,	Payne, S.	511	Cpl	Pickersgill, C. E.
1327	Cpl	Payten, J. M.	512	Pte	Pickersgill, J. A.
266	Pte	Peachey, G. E.	2425	Cpl	Pidgeon, H.
2423	,,	Peacock, E. E.	4146	Pte	Pierce, H.
10	,,	Pead, W. H.	1817	Sgt	Piggott, A.
*4274	,,	Pearce, A. B.	3610	Pte	Pike, A.
2424	,,	Pearce, E.	4007	,,	Pilmer, R. G.
1186	,,	Pearse, F. V.	1822	Cpl	Pirie, A. J.
*1801	Cpl	Pearce, H. J.	2720	Pte	Pittaway, G. W.
*1600	Pte	Pearce, R. J.			(M.M.)
		(M.M.)	1816	,,	Phelan, P. J.
5077	,,	Pearce, T. E.	*2385	,,	Phillips, A. F.
3616	,,	Pearson, W. E.	2724	,,	Phillips, J. B.
*962	,,	Peberdy, F. T. S.	3294	,,	Phillips, J. V.
*2726	,,	Peck, R. P.	734	,,	Phillips, R.
*3860	,,	Pederson, C.	1825	,,	Phillips, W. J.
4314	,,	Peebles, J. H.	32	,,	Plater, R. J.
274	,,	Pedley, E. S.	1128	,,	Platts, R. G.
519	,,	Peel, T.	2134	,,	Player, W.
3003	,,	Pegrum, H.			(M.M.)
3296	,,	Peisley, R. D.	2135	,,	Pockett, E. W.
1514	,,	Pender, A. W.	3001	Cpl	Pollard, A.
3295	,,	Pendergast, J. V.	33	Pte	Pollock, R.
577	Sgt	Pennefather, H.	4268	,,	Pleass, F.
2404	Pte	Penny, W. H.	268	,,	Poole, E. W.
1125	,,	Peny, W. M.	2136	,,	Pooley, G. J.
265	Sgt	Penrose, J. E.	2137	,,	Pooley, W. A.
738	Pte	Percy, R. E.	3610	L/Cpl	Porter, A. R.
1123	Cpl	Perkins, A.	297	Pte	Porter, J. A.
3866	Pte	Perkins, A. J.	955	Pte	Porter, J. E.
*517	,,	Perkins, J. A. T.	3913	,,	Potter, C. W.
957	,,	Perkins, H. F.			(M.M.)
*739	,,	Perks, J.	*2426	,,	Porter, L.
3864	,,	Perks, J. J.	3086	,,	Porteus, H. C.
267	,,	Perry, J.	811	Sgt	Potter, G.
1125	,,	Perry, W. M.	2427	Pte	Powe, B. W.
961	,,	Peters, C. W. A.			(M.M.)
4648	,,	Peterson, J.	2727	,,	Powell, S. A.
3000	,,	Pettit, L.	520	,,	Powell, W.
4594	,,	Petty, A. T. A.	*1127	,,	Powell, W. T.
4095	,,	Pickard, W. H.	1132	,,	Power, R. L.

NOMINAL ROLL 389

*1601	Cpl	Powis, C. E.	4104	Pte	Ralph, C. E.
*4394	,,	Pratt, C. H. H.	3872	,,	Ramsay, A. K.
1819	Pte	Presland, J. J.	4676	,,	Ramsay, J. F.
2388	,,	Prest, E. A.	3395	,,	Ramsey, W. H.
513	Cpl	Price, D. J.	1136	,,	Ramus, F. J.
2428	Pte	Price, J. L.	3868	,,	Randall, C. F.
2998	,,	Price, N. C.	2142	,,	Randall, G.
3609	,,	Price, S. A.	3619	,,	Randolph, W. H.
*2430	,,	Price, W.	2734	,,	Rankin, D. F.
*3615	,,	Price, W. A.	*1603	,,	Rankin, D. P.
4649	,,	Price, W. J. H.			(M.M.)
2430	,,	Pringle, G. R.	4836	,,	Raschke, T. E.
2431	,,	Pritchard, A. E.	3628	,,	Rathbone, W. A.
2432	,,	Pritchard, A. G.	2141	,,	Rattary, D.
*2141	,,	Pritchard, H. E.	4840	,,	Rawcliffe, J. H.
516	,,	Pritchard, G. W.	4839	,,	Rawcliffe, H.
*518	,,	Pritchard, L. G.	*4723	,,	Rawcliff, A.
735	,,	Proud, H.	*2392	,,	Rawnsley, A. A.
		(M.M.)	3620	,,	Raybould, L. F.
*4134	,,	Proval, L.	3877	,,	Rayner, L. J.
4135	,,	Provan, R.			(M.M.)
1158	,,	Prudhomme, H. L.	741	,,	Raysmith, F. W.
			968	,,	Rea, R. C.
4827	,,	Pullen, H. J.	3621	,,	Read, F. E.
1129	,,	Pullar, F.	*4595	,,	Read, M. K.
2725	,,	Punch, P. F.	2737	,,	Reed, T.
*1142	,,	Pye, A.	528	,,	Read, R. E.
			3010	,,	Read, H. J.
			2144	,,	Reay, S. R.
4832	,,	Quigley, T. J.	1827	,,	Reenes, J. F. F.
1826	,,	Quinlan, F.	527	,,	Rees, E. S.
4418	,,	Quinlan, L. T.	2143	,,	Rees, F. D.
3401	,,	Quinn, P. F.	802	C.S.M.	Rees, W. E.
4650	,,	Quinn, F. H.	2736	Pte	Redman, F.
2731	,,	Quinn, G. A.	744	,,	Redmond, W. J.
2370	,,	Quinn, T.	2738	Cpl	Regan, J.(M.M.)
4148	,,	Quinn, W. J.	3622	Pte	Reid, A. W.
			2145	,,	Reid, J.
1602	Cpl	Race, E.	4597	,,	Reid, M.
63	,,	Radford, E. W.	3625	,,	Reilly, T.
4838	Pte	Radnedge, H. G.	1119	,,	Reilly, S. F.
3396	,,	Ragg, H. J.	211	,,	Rendoth, A.
3197	,,	Rainbow, E.	*2433	,,	Reeves, J.
3015	,,	Raindle, L.	1828	,,	Reeves, J. F. F.

1696	C.S.M.	Reuben, D. M. (D.C.M., M.M.)
2741	Pte	Reynolds, C. H.
2436	„	Rhodes, W. H.
1436	„	Rial, C. H.
3312	„	Rice, J. F.
964	„	Rich, J. R.
*1134	„	Rich, D. C.
277	„	Richards H. C.
3008	„	Richards, R. H.
1406	„	Richards, W.
1604	„	Richardson, A.
742	„	Richardson, A. N.
1029	Cpl	Richardson, E. H.
3629	Pte	Richardson, R. W. T.
555	Dvr	Richardson, T. H.
3871	Pte	Rider, E. H.
969	„	Ridley, A. L.
965	Sgt	Ridley, C. L.
1023	Cpl	Ridley, E. R.
5082	Pte	Riddle, W. R.
*3310	„	Ring, J. A.
967	Sgt	Ringrose, P. L.
2435	Pte	Ritchie, B.
1135	„	Ritchie, J. H.
4098	„	Ritchie, R. E.
276	„	Ritchie, W. H.
3306	„	Ritchie, W.
745	„	Rixon, E. A.
*3614	„	Rixon, T. S.
529	„	Roach, H.
*4102	„	Roams, J.
2437	„	Robards, H. T.
4289	„	Robb, C. G.
*278	Dvr	Robbins, G.
4288	Pte	Roberts, A.
4655	„	Roberts, E.
3005	„	Roberts, H.
2397	„	Roberts, J.
4843	Pte	Roberts, J.
4099	„	Roberts, J. A.
1827	„	Roberts, L. E.
2398	„	Roberts, L. J.
1830	„	Roberts, R. E.
2147	„	Roberts, S. P.
3870	„	Roberts, T.
3303	„	Roberts, W. E.
4137	Sgt	Robertson, E. C.
3014	Pte	Robertson, J.
2148	„	Robertson, H. J.
3301	„	Robins, C. J.
278	„	Robbins, G.
2062	„	Roche, J. P.
210	„	Roe, W. F.
3874	„	Robinson, A.
*3309	Cpl	Robinson, C. A.
1263	Sgt	Robinson, E. D.
2985	Pte	Robinson, F. G.
*147	„	Robinson, H. J.
*5797	„	Robinson, H. J.
1312	„	Robinson, H. I.
1241	„	Robinson, L. C.
4598	„	Robinson, V.
2150	L/Cpl	Robinson, S. J.
*746	Pte	Robson, C. E.
326	„	Rochford, J.
2438	„	Roderick, E. A.
1133	„	Rogers, H.
4844	„	Rolfe, R. W.
4399	„	Rose, G. V.
*2439	„	Rose, J. E.
3623	„	Rose, H. R.
1829	„	Rogers, H. H.
2440	„	Roser, A.
3653	„	Ross, F.
4599	„	Ross, H. K.
966	„	Ross, T. R.
*523	„	Ross, W. P.
4149	„	Rowan, C. A.
4269	„	Rowe, J. A.
524	„	Rowan, H.

NOMINAL ROLL 391

4097	Pte	Rowbotham, F. L.
3394	„	Rowland, J. T.
*40096	„	Rowley-Collier, F.
2442	Sgt	Rowley, F. H.
*4287	Pte	Rowley, H. L.
4397	„	Roulstone, R. S.
463	„	Roundtree, T.
4136	Sgt	Rowlings, A. E.
2444	Pte	Ruttley, F. H.
232	„	Runge, A.
5131	„	Rush, P. C.
4316	„	Russ, H. J.
3915	„	Russell, E. E.
2443	„	Russell, W. A.
*743	„	Ryan, D. B.
4834	„	Ryan, J.
4101	„	Ryan, F.
4400	„	Ryan, J.
3011	„	Ryan, J. J.
3875	„	Ryan, J. P.
3006	„	Ryan, L. J.
3618	„	Ryan, M.
2139	„	Ryan, P.
*1606	„	Ryan, P. E.
34	„	Ryan, W.
*4833	„	Ryan, W. S.
3081	„	Rylatt, R.
4604	„	Saddler, J.
*3890	„	Sales, W. H.
2445	„	Salmon, J. R.
*3666	„	Sanderson, B.
*542	„	Sandham, P.
3642	„	Sandow, R. F.
1832	„	Sandridge, A. L.
2640	Cpl	Sander, C. (M.M.)
4404	Pte	Sandus, P. H.
*4600	„	Sandry, F. J.
4298	C.Q.M.S.	Sands, G.
1317	Pte	Sarell, E. J.
546	Dvr	Sarlow, W. J.
3326	Pte	Satler, A. E. G.
2151	„	Saunders, A. E.
*2447	„	Saunders, J. P.
*3636	„	Savage, M. J.
1317	„	Savell, E. J.
1831	„	Sawyer, J. A.
2637	Pte	Sayers, B. G. (M.M.)
537	„	Scarlett, G.
*2165	C.S.M.	Schmitzer, T. J.
759	Pte	Scholes, F.
2152	„	Scotman, H.
440	„	Scott, A. E.
4140	„	Scott, A. E.
3326	„	Scott, A. E.
287	Cpl	Scott, A. W.
1141	Pte	Scott, D. M.
3321	„	Scott, H. E.
287	„	Scott, H. W.
2744	„	Scott, J. B.
1835	„	Scott, N. C.
288	„	Scott, T. G.
3317	„	Scott, W.
*286	„	Scott, W. F.
2499	„	Scully, M.
*302	„	Scragg, A. G.
*976	„	Seader, S. J.
2448	Cpl	Seaman, H. V.
2758	Pte	Seers, L. C.
2489	„	Selby, S. G. W.
2153	„	Self, J.
*4299	„	Severs, J.
4291	„	Sexton, C. F.
1140	„	Sexton, J.
3403	„	Shanhan, H. E.
543	Sgt	Sharman, C. F.
*1609	Pte	Sharp, C.
2154	„	Sharp, F. R.
2449	„	Sharp, H.
1166	„	Sharpe, H. H.
975	„	Sharpe, W.
2576	„	Sharpe, W. H.
2155	„	Shaw, H. A.

2450	Pte	Shaw, R. D. K.	980	Pte	Skippington, W.
2452	„	Shearman, L.	2455	„	Skillicorn, E.
82	„	Sheehan, J.	304	„	Skinner, A. J.
3879	„	Sheehy, F. M.	2456	„	Skinner, C. H.
2888	„	Sheehy, T.	2755	„	Skinner, H. V.
2780	„	Shephard, T.	2457	„	Skinner, W. J.
291	„	Shepherd, A.	2332	„	Slack, J. W. A.
3315	„	Shepherd, E. G.	1139	„	Slaten, A. M.
3020	„	Shepherd, H. G.	3032	„	Slater, E.
3018	C.S.M.	Shepherd, H. J.	530	„	Slater, W. W.
			1137	„	Slaughter, T.
1284	Sgt	Shepherd, J. G.	4659	„	Sleeman, S. T.
3316	Pte	Shepherd, M. M.	*3880	„	Sloan, E. T.
4109	„	Shepherd, W. E.	3023	„	Small, R. E.
2757	„	Sheppard, J. W.	2743	„	Smallcombe, B. C.
1707	„	Shill, A.			
1273	Sgt	Shipp, E. H.	1610	„	Smith, A.
*531	Pte	Shone, E.	3021	„	Smith, A. C.
2156	Cpl	Short, C. F.	35	„	Smith, A. E.
2747	Pte	Short, J. R. S.	1307	„	Smith, A. E.
1608	„	Sim, C.	*3886	„	Smith, A. J.
5446	„	Simmons, W. G.	*3255	„	Smith, A. J.
4292	„	Simmonds, F. E.	979	Cpl	Smith, A. L.
930	„	Simondson, F. N.	3030	„	Smith, A. V.
			978	Pte	Smith, B.
2157	„	Simpson, C. F.	1613	„	Smith, B.
544	„	Simpson, R.	4319	„	Smith, C.
4856	„	Simpson, R. E.	988	„	Smith, C. A.
4607	„	Simpson, S.	1834	„	Smith, C. A.
519	Cpl	Simpson, S. L.	3632	„	Smith, C. C.
980	Sgt	Simpson, V. V.	1212	„	Smith, C. C.
1121	Pte	Simpson, W. G.	*3892	„	Smith, C. H.
3036	„	Sims, W. A.	4107	„	Smith, C. J.
2158	„	Sinclair, D.	2159	Cpl	Smith, C. S. (M.M.)
4847	„	Sinclair, G. H.			
*4290	„	Sinclair, J. T.	981	Sgt	Smith, D. (M.M.)
83	„	Sjoberg, E. C.			
2164	„	Sjoblom, A. A.	*4294	Pte	Smith, D. J.
4852	„	Skaines, T.	5092	„	Smith, E. H.
3887	„	Skeats, A. G.	540	Dvr	Smith, E. W.
980	„	Skeffington, W.	2410	Pte	Smith, F. E. B.
2750	„	Skelton, A. R.	984	Sgt	Smith, G. W. (M.M.)
2454	„	Skene, C.			
1265	Cpl	Skene, J. E.	*1142	Pte	Smith, G. C.

NOMINAL ROLL 393

4603	Pte	Smith, G. S.
540	Dvr	Smith, G. W.
1611	Pte	Smith, H.
*541	,,	Smith, H. F.
538	,,	Smith, J. A. S.
2458	,,	Smith, J. A.
4854	,,	Smith, J.
*2752	,,	Smith, J. D.
983	,,	Smith, J. E.
3031	,,	Smith, J. E. G.
4106	,,	Smith, J. F.
*1306	,,	Smith, J. J.
535	,,	Smith, J. T.
36	,,	Smith, L. J.
4850	,,	Smith, O. J.
1612	,,	Smith, P.
2495	,,	Smith, R. (M.M.)
3318	,,	Smith, R.
586	Cpl	Smith, R. C.
3024	,,	Smith, R. H.
3639	Pte	Smith, R. T.
1837	Cpl	Smith, V.
4402	Pte	Smith, T. H.
982	,,	Smith, W. F.
539	Sgt	Smith, W. G. (M.M.)
56	Dvr	Smith, W. H.
*4601	Pte	Smith, W. J. (M.M.)
2161	,,	Smurthwaite, R. E.
37	,,	Smyth, A. A.
2411	,,	Smyth, W. J.
3636	,,	Smyth, T. S.
3025	,,	Smeddon, R.
547	R.Q.M.S.	Sneesby, W. J.
4611	Pte	Snow, W. J. R.
339	Cpl	Sorley, R.
4135	Pte	Souter, J. H.
2460	,,	South, C. E.
2166	,,	South, R. F.
3325	,,	Southam, H.
4295	Sgt	Southam, R.
3325	Cpl	Southam, A.
3319	Pte	Southworth, W. E.
2413	,,	Sparks, D.
5093	,,	Spain, E. J.
*4105	,,	Sparkes, J. E.
1204	,,	Sparrow, H.
3881	,,	Speed, H.
*4613	,,	Speed, H.
*972	,,	Speedie, T. A.
3884	,,	Speerin, H.
3041	,,	Speers, J. W.
*4614	Cpl	Spence, A. M.
3878	Pte	Spencer, J. F.
2414	,,	Spice, W.
2756	,,	Spithill, A. J.
*4846	,,	Springett, G.
4857	,,	Sproule, R. A.
*5118	,,	Staines, W.
*973	,,	Stamborough, E. A. L.
2115	,,	Staniford, C. P.
1839	,,	Stanley, E. C.
*1120	,,	Stanley, G. S.
2754	,,	Stanton, T. J.
974	Dvr	Stapleton, J. T.
1614	Cpl	Staples, H. E. G. (M.M.)
755	Pte	Steed, F.
*3634	,,	Steele, A. H.
3633	,,	Steele, D. N.
977	,,	Steele, G.
300	,,	Steer, J.
2461	,,	Steggles, J. R.
1838	,,	Stephen, V. H.
2751	,,	Stephens, A. H.
4297	,,	Stephens, G.
4608	,,	Stephens, H. P.
*750	,,	Stephens, L. A.
758	,,	Stephens, G. E.
3026	,,	Stevenson, A.
1179	,,	Stephenson, G. C.

1213	Sgt	Stevenson, H. H.	1836	Pte	Sutherland, N. A.
749	Pte	Stevenson, H. J.			
468	„	Stephenson, J. W.	1225	C.Q.M.S.	Sutherland, N. J.
1615	Cpl	Stevenson, K. A.	753	Pte	Sutherland, R. C.
*548	„	Stevenson, T.			
2751	Pte	Stevens, A. H.	334	C.S.M.	Sutherland, W. A.
3883	„	Stevens, H. C.			
4855	„	Stevens, R. C.	3640	Pte	Sutton, E. G.
57	„	Stewart, A. E.	4611	„	Sutton, P. W.
4609	„	Stewart, J. D.	3638	„	Sutton, T. B.
*536	„	Stewart, R. R.	3028	„	Sutton, W. H.
1228	Dvr	Stewart, W. F.	303	„	Sweeney, J. L.
756	Cpl	Stinson, H. G. L.	4610	„	Sweeney, W. F.
4654	Pte	Stirling, R. G.	4848	„	Sweetman, W.
2631	„	St. John, T.	2735	„	Swift, C. H.
4112	„	Stokes, F. D.	4111	„	Swift, W. H.
1616	„	Stokes, S.	2463	Cpl	Swinton, A.
3029	„	Stone, B.	971	Pte	Swinton, W. G.
2746	„	Stone, C. W.	985	„	Sykes, G. W.
4845	„	Stone, H. W.	2749	„	Symonds, J.
1167	„	Stone, J.			
5095	„	Stone, M. R. H.	2649	Cpl	Table, W.
1833	„	Storer, W. J.	3042	Pte	Tainsh, S.
1143	„	Storey, D. B.	992	„	Tamlyn, W.
1144	Cpl	Storey, J. B.	*549	„	Tarrant, J.
3641	Pte	Storey, T. A.	2167	„	Tarrant, S. G.
2162	„	Stow, A. H.	2761	„	Tattersall, H.
3630	„	Straiton, J.	2168	„	Tarry, G.
4110	„	Strang, D.	*3894	„	Tasker, A. V.
289	„	Strike, S. W.	1845	Sgt	Taylor, E. J.
764	„	Strong, J.	557	Pte	Taylor, C.
3322	„	Stuart, E.	*4860	Cpl	Taylor, E. V.
2163	„	Stuart, R. H.	1147	Pte	Taylor, F.
4139	Sgt	Stubbs, A. C.	3083	„	Taylor, F. C.
4605	„	Stuckey, L. A.	2491	„	Taylor, J.
1617	Pte	Styles, E. T.	6003	„	Taylor, H.
4851	„	Sullivan, A.	3897	„	Taylor, L. F.
3033	„	Sullivan, A. E.	773	„	Taylor, R.
752	„	Sullivan, C. W.	765	Cpl	Taylor, R. M.
4296	„	Sullivan, J.	*1846	Pte	Taylor, R. M.
3882	„	Sullivan, J.	58	Dvr	Taylor, S. J.
2753	„	Sullivan, T. J.	993	„	Taylor, S. P.
1618	„	Summers, R. B.	3045	Pte	Taylor, T.

NOMINAL ROLL 395

3643	Pte	Taylor, W. J.
771	,,	Taylor, W. T.
2422	,,	Teague, E.
*2464	,,	Teakel, C.
4858	,,	Tenglien, H.
766	,,	Terrill, A. O.
768	,,	Tevelein, C. A.
*1149	,,	Thaxter, A.
*1146	,,	Theisinger, N. L.
*2759	,,	Thelning, W. P.
4614	,,	Thickett, J.
2763	,,	Thirkell, A. T.
3043	Sgt	Thomas, B. B.
1847	Pte	Thomas, E. N.
4615	,,	Thomas, J.
2466	Sgt	Thomas, H. L.
		(M.M.)
2467	Cpl	Thomas, R. J.
		(M.M.)
2169	Pte	Thomas, J.
4115	,,	Thomas, R. H.
1286	,,	Thomas, R. L.
2468	,,	Thomas, T.
*2765	,,	Thomas, W. F.
*1621	,,	Thompson, A. J.
2170	,,	Thompson, L. C.
554	,,	Thompson, R. J.
2205	,,	Thompson, T.
*769	Cpl	Thomson, A.
2764	Pte	Thomson, J. L.
2170	,,	Thompson, L. C.
2760	,,	Thomson, R.
59	Dvr	Thomson, W.
2762	Pte	Thornthwaite, J.
1963	Cpl	Thurley, A. E.
		(M.M.)
*2171	Pte	Tickner, F.
4616	,,	Tickner, V. C.
2172	,,	Tidball, W. A.
4311	,,	Tierney, P. H.
4320	,,	Tierney, P. F.
5097	,,	Tilbury, A. C.
3646	,,	Timmins, N. L.
4144	,,	Timothy, S. J.

4405	Pte	Tipper, E. J.
*1623	Pte	Tisbury, C. F.
1622	Cpl	Tisbury, F. H.
*4617	,,	Tisdell, L. S.
4116	Pte	Titley, G. E.
2179	,,	Todd, G.
774	,,	Todd, J.
2177	,,	Todd, P.
3645	,,	Toope, F. A.
3895	,,	Tolhurst, A. T.
1150	,,	Tomlinson, T. E.
2129	,,	Tomlinson, B.
1267	,,	Torney, W. J.
3893	,,	Townsend, J.
4859	,,	Townsend, J.
1844	,,	Townsend, J.
3329	,,	Tough, J. F.
1350	,,	Tooze, J. P.
1257	,,	Touchey, J. B.
3330	,,	Tozer, R. E.
770	,,	Trainor, H.
2174	,,	Trappell, A. W.
84	,,	Tregale, M. R.
3048	,,	Treherne, G. R.
*4117	,,	Treleaven, L. T.
3084	,,	Trenholm, C. R.
2430	Cpl	Trevana, W. C.
3644	Pte	Trevillion, P. H.
3328	,,	Trevorrow, T.
2176	,,	Trice, F.
2179	,,	Trick, F. C. J.
2431	,,	Trickett, W.
184	,,	Triglone, T. R.
2470	,,	Trimmingham, R. C.
309	Dvr	Tripp, L.
310	Cpl	Tripp, W.
		(M.M.)
9	Pte	Trompp, C. H.
*977	,,	Tucker, C. W.
2792	Sgt	Turley, A.
		(M.M.)
991	Pte	Turnbull, J.
555	,,	Turnbull, J. A.

2471 Pte	Turnbull, R.	
39 „	Turner, A. L.	
5098 „	Turner, F. J.	
2178 „	Turner, G.	
60 Dvr	Turner, H. W.	
*767 Pte	Turner, J.	
5099 „	Turner, J.	
5100 „	Turner, R. L.	
5101 „	Turner, T. E.	
3088 Cpl	Turner, W. A.	
1127 Pte	Turner, W. H.	
311 „	Twyford, W. E.	
4618 „	Twomey, J.	
4300 „	Twomey, T.	
803 Sgt	Tysoe, E. J.	
312 Pte	Ullstrom, C. W.	
3906 „	Underwood, W. A.	
4119 „	Underwood, M. R.	
3331 „	Underwood, J. B.	
4118 „	Upton, H. C.	
312 „	Ullstrom, C. W.	
1210 „	Upton, W. C.	
1151 Cpl	Urquhart, J. A.	
558 Pte	Urwin, E. R.	
5257 „	Vale, G.	
*776 Cpl	Vale, T. G.	
996 Pte	Van Wouwe, C. L.	
493 „	Valentine, W.	
1848 „	Venus, C. A.	
3334 „	Vigar, A.	
313 „	Victor, W. T.	
2181 „	Vickery, R.	
3901 „	Vincent, C.	
3333 „	Vincent, C. R.	
*777 „	Vincent, L. S.	
1152 Sgt	Vincent, O.	
3902 Pte	Vincent, P. L.	
4863 „	Vindin, G.	

3649 Pte	Voysey, E.	
4169 „	Wade, H. V.	
1863 „	Wagstaff, W.	
4878 „	Wailes, F. C.	
3655 „	Wake, L. J.	
*4876 „	Wakeling, H.	
4875 „	Wakeling, G. F.	
8 „	Walker, A.	
792 „	Walker, A. C. (M.M.)	
4411 „	Walker, A. C.	
3047 „	Walker, D.	
88 C.Q.M.S.	Walker, E. F.	
2784 Pte	Walker, E. G.	
3650 „	Walker, G.	
4301 „	Walker, W. H.	
3905 „	Wall, A. H.	
3907 „	Wall, G.	
*783 „	Wall, J. D.	
1854 „	Wall, K. J.	
3903 „	Wallbank, C. S.	
3664 „	Wallace, A. L.	
2182 „	Wallace, H. L.	
1624 „	Wallace, T.	
4625 „	Walden, H. T.	
1853 „	Walsh, F.	
997 „	Walsh P. A.	
998 „	Walsh, R. C.	
2183 „	Walsh, V. J.	
1643 Cpl	Wallin, C. O.	
317 Dvr	Wallwork, T. W.	
3061 Pte	Walter, W. H.	
2473 „	Walwyn, W.	
2192 „	Warboys, A. L.	
*4407 „	Warby, H. A.	
*2184 „	Ward, C.	
1010 „	Ward, P. M.	
1153 „	Ward, R. D.	
1001 „	Ward, W. A. (M.M.)	
2436 „	Ware, C. R. J.	
1156 „	Warlond, C.	

NOMINAL ROLL 397

1882	Pte	Warrell, H.
4663	,,	Warman, R. H.
1851	Cpl	Warne, W. G.
3654	Pte	Warner, J. A.
3657	,,	Warton, J. B.
3065	,,	Warrender, W.
*1157	,,	Warrington, J. D.
5103	,,	Wassell, A. W.
4631	,,	Waters, A. J.
4873	,,	Waters, E. J.
3400	,,	Waters, W. R.
*564	,,	Watkins, J. H.
4305	,,	Watson, H. E.
3345	,,	Watson, J. S.
2779	,,	Watson, J.
4670	,,	Watson, J.
2474	Cpl	Watson, J.
*4407	,,	Watson, J. H.
4120	Pte	Watson, L. W.
2475	,,	Watson, N. L.
*5104	,,	Watson, R. E.
3660	,,	Watt, J.
3061	,,	Watter, W. H.
2476	,,	Watters, C. R.
4656	,,	Watters, F. J.
41	,,	Watters, V. E.
*582	Sgt	Watterson, R.
3340	,,	Watterston, L.
1850	Pte	Watts, A. B.
*3050	,,	Watts, A. G.
2777	,,	Watts, A. J.
*3051	,,	Watts, B.
*2477	Sgt	Watts, H. G.
2479	Pte	Watters, J. W.
1003	,,	Watts, J. L.
*3052	,,	Watts, W. L.
2478	Cpl	Watts, W. W. (M.M.)
2479	Pte	Wattus, J. W.
4877	,,	Waugh, R. W.
2783	,,	Wearne, M. B.
*2770	Sgt	Webb, A.
1282	,,	Webb, A. E.
*568	Sgt	Webb, W. H.
*2185	Cpl	Webster, A. H.
2781	Pte	Webster, D.
5105	,,	Weedon, A. F.
5106	,,	Weedon, W. E. J.
785	,,	Weedon, H. H.
2480	Cpl	Weiley, G. E. (M.M. & BAR)
2771	Pte	Welch, S.
*1311	,,	Welling, E. F.
1160	Sgt	Wellings, L. C. (M.S.M.)
3656	Pte	Wells, C. J.
1002	Cpl	Wells, S. B.
252A	Pte	Wells, W.
3663	,,	Wenham, G.
569	,,	Went, H. R.
1011	Cpl	Westaway, J. L.
3661	Pte	Wethered, G.
1283	Sgt	Westbrook, C. G.
4309	Pte	Westbury, R. T.
4121	,,	Weston, P.
*3064	,,	Weston, T.
778	,,	Westwood, H. J.
4669	,,	Wheeler, H. R.
4669	,,	Wheeler, H. R.
4307	,,	Whelan, B. J. D.
4308	,,	Whelan, J. P.
4869	,,	Whelan, W. B.
2186	,,	Whiley, E. A.
1625	,,	Whitaker, C.
5123	,,	Whitaker, E.
1859	,,	Whitchurch, W.
3341	,,	White, F. B.
787	,,	White, F. C.
3398	,,	White, G. E.
3399	,,	White, H. G.
1009	,,	White, H. W.
2481	,,	White, J. (M.S.M.)
1008	,,	White, J. J.
2440A	,,	White, N.
*1627	,,	White, R.

2187 Pte	White, R. C.	
2769 „	White, R. H.	
4122 „	White, R. J.	
3397 „	White, W. E.	
3910 „	White, S. W.	
1866 „	Whitehead, A.	
563 „	Whitehead, E.	
2774 „	Whiteman, L. H.	
3060 „	Whitfield, E.	
1012 „	Whitfield, G. S.	
4144 Pte	Whitmore, F.	
3338 „	Whittam, G. S.	
*782 „	Whitton, J. D.	
3649 „	Whitton, R. H.	
2773 „	Whyatt, A. (M.M. & BAR)	
3651 „	Whybro, H.	
3058 „	Whyte, J.	
779 Cpl	Wiggins, C. E.	
1006 Pte	William, R. P.	
1869 „	Wilson, F. C.	
2190 „	Wilson, J.	
570 C.Q.M.S.	Wilson, L.	
1855 Pte	Wilson, R.	
319 „	Wilson, T.	
61 „	Wilson, T. B.	
1860 „	Whittle, H. R.	
1268 „	Whittle, W. W.	
182 „	Whitton, J. D.	
1856 „	Whyte, H.	
779 Cpl	Wiggin, C. E.	
5107 Pte	Wilcock, A. L.	
2786 „	Wilcockson, A. H.	
1007 Cpl	Wilkinson, E.	
2768 Pte	Wilkinson, L. G.	
249A „	Wilkie, J. P.	
2767 „	Wilkins, F.	
*2188 „	Williams, A. E.	
5108 „	Williams, A. J.	
1871 „	Williams, E. G.	
1870 „	Williams, F.	
3662 L/Sgt	Williams, G.	
1354 Pte	Williams, J.	
4143 Pte	Williams, J. F.	
*3337 „	Williams, J. J.	
1862 „	Williams, J. P.	
4867 „	Williams, J. T.	
1005 „	Williams, H. R.	
1864 „	Williams, V. C.	
2796 „	Williamson, H. E. (M.M.)	
1168 „	Williamson, H.	
2766 „	Willing, W. R.	
*804 Sgt	Willis, E. E.	
2778 Pte	Willis, G. P. H.	
3665 „	Willison, F. C.	
4622 „	Wilson, A. C.	
999 Pte	Wilson, E. A.	
2476 „	Wilson, F. W.	
4620 „	Wilson, G.	
*4124 „	Wilson, G. W.	
4627 „	Wilson, H.	
*2190 „	Wilson, J.	
3352 „	Wilson, J. A.	
4123 „	Wilson, J. D.	
3547 „	Wilson, J. H.	
570 „	Wilson, L. J.	
4142 „	Wilson, M.	
2191 „	Wilson, R.	
4621 „	Wilson, T.	
3652 „	Wilson, W. K.	
3335 „	Winder, L. A.	
*3658 „	Windred, A. S.	
3352 „	Wing, C. R.	
559 „	Winstone, W. H.	
42 Cpl	Winn, F. C.	
43 Pte	Winn, N. J.	
2908 „	Windred, C. J.	
1865 „	Windsor, A. H.	
3342 Pte	Wing, C. R.	
2446 „	Winter, A.	
2189 „	Winterbine, G. H.	
*1004 „	Wishart, J. H.	
2482 „	Wisken, E. B.	
786 „	Wither, T. S.	
790 „	Withey, G.	

NOMINAL ROLL 399

1852	Pte	Witney, W. S.
2483	„	Wulfe, T.
*781	„	Wood, A.
2490	Cpl	Wood, J. (D.C.M.)
2782	Pte	Wood, W.
1155	„	Wood, W. E.
*2194	„	Woods, C. A.
4864	„	Woods, A.
3062	„	Woods, J.
560	„	Woods, J.
2194	„	Woods, C. A.
2193	Sgt	Woodbine, D. (M.M.)
3653	Pte	Woolard, A.
4868	„	Woolard, H.
2785	„	Woolcock, E. C.
*3906	Cpl	Wooldridge, H. V.
4303	Pte	Woolley, A. A.
*4322	„	Woolley, S. C.
*567	„	Woolston, W. J.
2780	„	Woolfgang, E. D.
*2448	„	Wotton, F. A.
2776	„	Wootton, F. G.
2775	L/Cpl	Wootton, H.
*2192	Sgt	Worboys, A. L.
7	Sgt	Wrapson, G. W.
70	Cpl	Wright, E. S.
3066	Pte	Wright, G. A.
1858	Sgt	Wright, G. W.
*4302	Pte	Wright, H.
1857	„	Wright, H. P. G.
3402	„	Wright, J.
1000	Cpl	Wright, P.
3048	Pte	Wyer, J.
1626	„	Wylie, J.
*789	Cpl	Wymark, R. D.
1154	Pte	Wynd, A. G.
565	Cpl	Wynn, D. M.
*2485	Pte	Wynn, J. C.
2486	„	Yeates, N. K. H.
*795	„	Yeo, C.
*3068	Cpl	Yeomans, R. T.
3911	Pte	York, A.
2199	„	Young, J. E. W.
794	„	Young, J. M.
3069	„	Young, H. (M.M.)
*321	„	Yardy, R. A.
2487A	„	Zimmerman, H. N. C.

Halstead Press Pty Limited,
9-19 Nickson Street, Sydney

www.ingramcontent.com/pod-product-compliance
Lightning Source LLC
Chambersburg PA
CBHW021825220426
43663CB00005B/135